Camille Denizot and Liana Tronci (Eds.)
Building Modality with Syntax

Trends in Linguistics
Studies and Monographs

Editors
Chiara Gianollo
Daniël Van Olmen

Editorial Board
Walter Bisang
Tine Breban
Volker Gast
Hans Henrich Hock
Karen Lahousse
Natalia Levshina
Caterina Mauri
Heiko Narrog
Salvador Pons
Niina Ning Zhang
Amir Zeldes

Editor responsible for this volume
Daniël Van Olmen

Volume 372

Building Modality with Syntax

Focus on Ancient Greek

Edited by
Camille Denizot and Liana Tronci

DE GRUYTER
MOUTON

ISBN 978-3-11-221407-7
e-ISBN (PDF) 978-3-11-077838-0
e-ISBN (EPUB) 978-3-11-077852-6
ISSN 1861-4302

Library of Congress Control Number: 2023938215

Bibliographic information published by the Deutsche Nationalbibliothek
The Deutsche Nationalbibliothek lists this publication in the Deutsche Nationalbibliografie;
detailed bibliographic data are available on the internet at http://dnb.dnb.de.

© 2025 Walter de Gruyter GmbH, Berlin/Boston
This volume is text- and page-identical with the hardback published in 2023.
Typesetting: Integra Software Services Pvt. Ltd. Printing and binding: CPI books
GmbH, Leck

www.degruyter.com

Editors' acknowledgments

We would like to thank all the contributors to the volume and the other participants in the workshop "Building modality with syntax. Focus on Ancient Greek", which was held online at the 54th Annual Meeting of the Societas Linguistica Europaea on 31 August – 1 September 2021. Special thanks go to Richard Faure for his friendly support during the different stages of our project.

We are also grateful to all the reviewers who kindly accepted to help us in preparing the volume; they have to remain anonymous but their work contributed to improving the quality of the volume.

Finally, our thanks go to the series editors and the editorial board, especially Daniël van Olmen, for welcoming our volume into the series *Trends in Linguistics. Studies and Monographs [TiLSM]* and for helping improve it, and to the editorial team of De Gruyter Mouton as well, in particular Barbara Karlson, for their support.

Camille Denizot & Liana Tronci

Contents

Editors' acknowledgments —— V

List of abbreviations —— IX

Camille Denizot & Liana Tronci
1   For a syntactic approach to modality and its application to Ancient Greek —— 1

Marina Benedetti & Chiara Gianollo
2   Modal uses of knowledge verbs in Ancient Greek —— 25

Martin Masliš
3   Information source and complementation in Classical Greek. The case of verbs of seeing and knowledge acquisition —— 51

Camille Denizot, Liana Tronci & Sophie Vassilaki
4   Syntactic patterns of modality in temporal clauses: *Hóte* vs. *hótan* in the diachrony of Ancient Greek —— 85

Giuseppina di Bartolo
5   Variation and change of counterfactual conditionals in Postclassical Greek: Evidence from private papyrus letters —— 121

Emilia Ruiz Yamuza
6   Conditional subordinate clauses and verbal moods. A case study —— 143

Rodrigo Verano & Alberto Pardal Padín
7   (Inter)subjectivity, modality, and syntax in Classical Greek: *Dokéō* and *phaínomai* in addressee-oriented assertions in the dialogues of Plato —— 167

Ezra la Roi
8   A pragmatic syntax of counterfactual mood attraction and mood (a)symmetry from Archaic to Classical Greek —— 193

Antonio R. Revuelta Puigdollers
9   Mood, modality and speech acts in clause combination.
     The case of conditionals —— 221

List of contributors —— 261

Index locorum —— 263

Index verborum —— 267

Index notionum —— 269

List of abbreviations

A. Glosses
Interlinear glosses follow the conventions of the Leipzig glossing rules (www.eva.mpg.de/lingua/resources/glossing-rules.php), to which we have added:

ACT	active
AOR	aorist
IMPF	imperfect
INTJ	interjection
MED	medium
MOD	modal particle
MP	medio-passive
OPT	optative
PTCL	particle
PPRF	pluperfect

B. Abbreviated references

LSJ	Liddell Henry, Scott Robert, Jones Henry, *Greek-English Lexicon*, Oxford: Clarendon Press, 1940.
TLG	*Thesaurus Linguae Graecae*® Digital Library. Ed. Maria C. Pantelia. University of California, Irvine. http://www.tlg.uci.edu

Abbreviations of Ancient Greek authors and their works follow the *Greek-English Lexicon* by Liddell, Scott and Jones (see Index locorum for full references).

C. Presentation of the Greek examples
For Greek texts, we provide a version in Greek alphabet (with line breaks in poetic texts indicated by the sign /), its transliteration (see below), glosses and English translation. In long examples, only the relevant parts are transliterated and glossed. The part of the original Greek and the English translation that is not detailed is indicated by square brackets.

D. Transliteration
The principle adopted here for transliteration is orthographical[1] (see Table 1).
  Ancient Greek accents are musical ones: acute accents denote a rise (and fall on the following syllable), grave accents denote the absence of a rise (thus are not noted in the transliteration), and circumflex accents denote a rise and fall intona-

---

[1] For the sake of cohesion, we chose an orthographical transliteration and not a phonetic one because of the diachronic diversity of the texts cited in the volume.

tion on the same (long) syllable. Since a vowel marked by a circumflex is always long, the length of the vowel is not indicated when marked by a circumflex. Breathings, i.e. diacritics indicating the presence or absence of initial [h], are transliterated by an initial h- when relevant.

Table 1: Principles for transliteration.

Greek letters		Transliteration	Pronunciation (V-IV C. BCE)
Α	α	a	[a]
Β	β / ϐ	b	[b]
Γ	γ	g	[g]
Δ	δ	d	[d]
Ε	ε	e	[e]
Ζ	ζ	z	[zd]
Η	η	ē	[ɛː]
Θ	θ	th	[tʰ]
Ι	ι	i	[i]
Κ	κ	k	[k]
Λ	λ	l	[l]
Μ	μ	m	[m]
Ν	ν	n	[n]
Ξ	ξ	x	[ks]
Ο	ο	o	[o]
Π	π	p	[p]
Ρ	ρ	r	[r]
Σ	σ / ς	s	[s]
Τ	τ	t	[t]
Υ	υ	u	[y]
Φ	φ	ph	[pʰ]
Χ	χ	kh	[kʰ]
Ψ	ψ	ps	[ps]
Ω	ω	ō	[oː]
Digraphs			
αι		ai	[ai̯]
αυ		au	[au̯]
ει		ei	[eː]
ευ		eu	[eu̯]
οι		oi	[oi̯]
ου		ou	[uː]
ᾳ		āi	[aːi̯]
ῃ		ēi	[ɛːi̯]
ῳ		ōi	[oːi̯]

Camille Denizot & Liana Tronci
1 For a syntactic approach to modality and its application to Ancient Greek

Abstract: This introductory chapter has two goals. On the one hand, it aims at providing a critical overview of the literature on modality and related issues, by discussing the different approaches and their problems and results. On the other hand, it gives some suggestions for a new approach to modality, which is syntactic and distributional in a broad sense, as it focuses on the different types of modal markers and, particularly, on their combinatory values. A presentation of the contributions of the volume is also provided.

Keywords: Modal markers, approaches to modality, syntax, data-driven approach, syntax-semantic-pragmatic interface

1 Introduction

The aim of this introductory chapter is to provide the reader with a usable introduction to modality, which serves not only as a general reference for the topics dealt with in the papers collected in the volume, but also as a critical survey of previous studies and the currently debated issues on the matter.

Despite the intensive research carried out in recent years, modality "remain[s] among the most intriguing and puzzling" issues in linguistics (Nuyts 2016: 2). Our proposal is to adopt a syntactic viewpoint, a data-driven perspective and a corpus-based approach. In particular, we argue that the different linguistic devices that a language uses to "build" modality (e.g. moods, modal verbs, modal adverbs, etc.) should not be considered separately from one another but in interaction. We also contend that the role of the syntactic structure, i.e. the different verb complementation strategies, the relation between main and dependent clauses, the types

---

Acknowledgments: This article is the result of joint work by the two authors. However, for academic purposes, Camille Denizot is responsible for Sections 3 and 4.1, Liana Tronci for Sections 2 and 4.2. Both authors are responsible of Section 1. The authors thank the contributors to the volume and Richard Faure for their insightful comments and remarks.

Camille Denizot, University of Paris Nanterre, e-mail: cdenizot@parisnanterre.fr
Liana Tronci, University for Foreigners of Siena, e-mail: tronci@unistrasi.it

of dependent clauses, etc. should be taken into account, as well as the compositionality of modal meanings.

The Chapter is organised as follows. Section 2 is devoted to an overview of previous studies on modality and discusses in particular the typological approach, the different types of modalities identified, as well as the different classifications proposed by scholars. Section 3 illustrates the basics of our approach to modality, which consists in (a) prioritising syntactic analysis, (b) investigating a single language, and (c) favouring corpus-based studies. Finally, in Section 4, we focus on Ancient Greek and, after describing previous research on modality, we present the studies collected in the volume.

2 Approaching modality

In the last forty years, the debate on modality has focused particularly on the following two aspects: (a) the nature of the relevant semantic categories of modality, their limits and interactions; (b) the relationship of modality to speech acts and the role of the pragmatically-oriented notion of "speaker attitude" in shaping modality.

However, the state of the art has not established a firm and uncontroversial ground for future research on either of these questions. As regards (a), we observe that the semantic notions linked to modality tend to proliferate, e.g. necessity vs. possibility, realis vs. irrealis, factuality vs. non-factuality, as do classifications, e.g. epistemic vs. root modality, event vs. propositional modality, volitive vs. non-volitive modality, besides the traditional three-term classification into deontic, epistemic and dynamic modality (see Section 2.2 below). As regards (b), the discussion of the interface between modality and pragmatics makes it clear that the notion of modality is pervasive and multifaceted and that its relations to the other grammatical categories are difficult to determine (see Section 2.3 below).

2.1 Broad vs. narrow definitions of modality

Starting from the seminal work of Palmer (1986), many studies have remarked on the difficulty of finding a unanimous definition of modality: "it may be impossible to come up with a succinct characterization of the notional domain of modality" (Bybee *et al.* 1994: 176). As an illustration of this difficulty, it suffices to compare the following three definitions of modality. According to Lyons (1977: 452), modality is the "opinion or attitude of the speaker" towards the contents of the clause; therefore, each utterance includes a form of modality. Conversely, according to Declerck

(2011: 43), "there is modality whenever there is reference to actualization of a situation in a world that is not represented as being the factual world". In the latter case, modality concerns only a subset of utterances, as factual sentences are not included. In a narrower and strictly semantic perspective, modality relates to the concepts of *possibility* and *necessity*, which function as variants in a paradigm that includes only two choices (van der Auwera and Plungian 1998: 80).

The debate on modality has also concerned its status as a grammatical category. While traditional accounts consider modality as being similar to other grammatical categories, such as tense, aspect, number, gender, etc. (Palmer 2001: 1), in some recent accounts it is considered to be a "supercategory [...] which is much more loosely structured – and in fact probably belongs at a higher level of abstraction – than categories such as time and (types of) aspect" (Nuyts 2016: 33).

In summary, modality is a pervasive and multifaceted linguistic category, which is relevant at different levels of linguistic analysis, i.e. syntax, semantics, and pragmatics (see the papers collected in Leiss and Abraham 2014 for an overview). The place of this "exceptionally complex functional category" (Abraham 2020: XXI) among the other grammatical categories is difficult to determine (cf. Nuyts 2016; Arregui *et al.* 2017). The debate on modality, particularly in typological studies, has covered the semantic and the pragmatic aspects of modality (cf. Portner 2009; Nuyts and van der Auwera 2016 for an overview), as discussed in Sections 2.2 and 2.3 below.

2.2 Structuring modality: Semantic categories

According to Nuyts (2006: 2), "there is no unanimity among scholars regarding the list of categories to be called *modal*, but in one traditional version, modality comprises three basic semantic dimensions: *dynamic*, *deontic* and *epistemic*". Deontic and epistemic modalities are the most uncontroversial categories. Scholars usually consider them scalar classes, related to different semantic notions, going, for instance, from moral desirability to obligation and permission, in the case of deontic modality. Dynamic modality, conversely, is the most controversial class, as not only is the label "dynamic" debated, e.g. by Goossens (1985), who prefers "facultative modality", and Hengeveld (1988), who names it "inherent modality", but also the internal classification into "participant-inherent", "participant-imposed" and "situational modality" is not universally accepted (see Nuyts 2016: 34–35 for a discussion).

Besides this usual classification of modality, other arrangements of the modal domain have been suggested. Bybee and colleagues (Bybee 1985, Bybee *et al.* 1994, Bybee and Fleischman 1995) propose another tripartite classification, which introduces the difference between speaker and agent, thus combining semantic and pragmatic features and integrating illocutionary forces within the field of modality. According to them, three classes should be recognised, i.e. epistemic modality, agent-oriented modality, and speaker-oriented modality. While agent-oriented modality expresses obligations, desires, abilities, permissions concerning the agent of the clause, speaker-oriented modality covers "markers of directives, such as imperatives, optatives or permissives, which represent speech acts through which a speaker attempts to move an addressee to action" (Bybee and Fleischman 1995: 6).

The difference between speaker and participant, be it the agent or another participant, is also relevant for the classification proposed by van der Auwera and Plungian (1998), who consider possibility and necessity as the two basic semantic concepts inherent to modality. Their classification includes four classes. The former two, i.e. participant-internal modality and participant-external modality, concern the participant involved in the state of affairs that is described in the clause, and relate to a possibility or necessity that is internal vs. external to him. Conversely, the latter two, i.e. deontic modality and epistemic modality, relate to the speaker. Deontic modality expresses "circumstances external to the participant as some person(s), often the speaker, and/or as some social or ethical norm(s) permitting or obliging the participant to engage in the state of affairs", while epistemic modality "refers to a judgment of the speaker" (van der Auwera and Plungian 1998: 80–81). Note that "deontic" and "epistemic" as they are used here, are not comparable to the use of Nuyts (2016) discussed above in Section 2.2.

Binary classifications of the domain of modality have also been proposed. In Palmer (2001), *event modality* is opposed to *propositional modality*, as the former covers deontic and dynamic modality, while the latter expresses epistemic modality and evidentiality. Talmy (1988) and Sweetser (1990) propose to classify modal meanings into *epistemic* vs. *root modality*, where the latter includes deontic modality and partially dynamic modality. Finally in Narrog (2005), the opposition is between *volitive* and *non-volitive modality*; the former involves an element of will or force towards the realization of the state of affairs (i.e., in other words, deontic modality and volition) while the latter covers dynamic and epistemic modality, as well as evidentiality.[1]

2.3 Structuring modality: Pragmatic categories

Linked to the pragmatically oriented notion of "speaker attitude" (cf. Palmer 2001; Nuyts 2005, among others), other pragmatic notions have become relevant for identifying modality, e.g. *subjectivity*, *performativity* and *evidentiality*. As Narrog

---

1 See Section 2.3 for evidentiality.

(2012b: 13–46) points out, *subjectivity* is a polysemous label in linguistics, which has been used to refer to many different phenomena.² In relation to modality, *subjectivity* is "the speaker's personal conjecture" as opposed to *objectivity*, i.e. "objectively accessible facts" (Lyons 1977: 797–805; cf. also Narrog 2012a, 2012b). The notion of subjectivity has increasingly taken hold in research on modality, not only from a synchronic viewpoint (see, among others, the papers collected in Baumgarten *et al.*, 2012), but also from a diachronic one (see Traugott 1989; Langacker 1990; Traugott and Dasher 2002; De Smet and Verstraete 2006a). In diachronic studies, the term of *subjectification*, i.e. the diachronic process according to which meanings "become increasingly based in the speaker's subjective belief state / attitude toward the proposition" (Traugott 1989: 35; cf. also Traugott 2010), has been coined to account for the processual counterpart of subjectivity.³

In some accounts of modality, subjectivity is somehow connected to *performativity* or *speaker involvement*, which is, according to Coates (1983), the involvement of the speaker in the logical inference and his / her commitment to the truth of a proposition as opposed to his / her logical statements. In her investigation of English modal verbs, Coates (1983) shows that subjectivity also concerns objective utterances and relates to both epistemic and root modality (cf. in particular the analysis of *should* and *ought*, where a merger between epistemic and root modality is observed).

The notion of *evidentiality* is also connected to subjectivity, as both give information on the speaker's source of knowledge. According to Nuyts (2001: 34), evidentiality refers to whether the speaker "suggest[s] that (s)he alone knows the evidence and draws a conclusion from it" or the speaker "indicate[s] that the evidence is known to (or accessible by) a larger group of people who share the conclusion based on it", thus leading to "shared responsibility" ("subjective" vs. "intersubjective" types; see also Narrog 2012b: 28). Squartini (2016: 58) stresses the relation of evidentiality to the "'epistemological' process [...] through which a given piece of information has been acquired". As is well-known, investigation on evidentiality started regarding phenomena in non-European languages (cf. Aikhenvald 2004 for an overview) and later expanded to European languages (see, among others, the recent book edited by Wiemer and Marín Arrese 2022). According to the source of knowledge, one can distinguish *experiential, inferential* and *hearsay/reportative* evidentiality (Nuyts 2006: 10). Some scholars, e.g. Bybee (1985) and Palmer (1986), include evidentiality in the category of epistemic modality, as it relates to knowl-

---

2 *Subjectivity* was first introduced into French linguistics by scholars such as Bréal (1897); Bally (1965 [1932]) and Benveniste (1966 [1958]) and later adopted in pragmatic and cognitive approaches, cf. Narrog (2012b: 16–21). See also Jespersen (1924: 313–321). As for the relationship between subjectivity and deixis, cf. Lyons (1982).
3 For an application to Ancient Greek, see Allan (2013).

edge (see also Wiemer 2018). The closeness of evidentiality and epistemic modality is also argued for by Boye (2012), who, however, suggests including the two categories in the super-category of epistemicity. Other scholars combine epistemicity and evidentiality in the super-categories of *epistemological modality* (Hengeveld 1988) and *propositional modality* (Palmer 2001).

2.4 Addendum: On the margins of modality

This overabundance of notions, categories and sub-categories evidences how difficult it is to determine what modality is and how it works in language. The tendency to differentiate modal meanings *ad infinitum* is also criticised by Narrog (2012b: 8), who reminds us to "keep in mind that semantic distinctions that do not correspond to formal distinctions in language are of questionable value". The problem does not concern only terminology, but also the number and the type of categories and sub-categories included within the field of modality. Besides the major notions and the categories that we have just discussed, some scholars have associated to modality other notions and categories, which are on the margins of modality in current accounts (see the papers collected in Nuyts and van der Auwera 2016 for a discussion).

The first notion is *mood*, which is ambiguous, as it properly refers to the morphological expression of modality in verbal systems but is sometimes confused with modality. The opposition between indicative mood and other moods, e.g. subjunctive, conditional, optative, etc., is usually considered to express the opposition between *realis* and *irrealis*, but in many languages past tenses of the indicative can also denote *irrealis*. The notion of mood is also related to *clausal moods*, i.e. the basic utterance types in a language, namely declarative, interrogative, and imperative.

The second aspect to be considered concerns two further types of modality, namely *alethic* modality and *boulomaic* modality, which are not recognised by all scholars.

Alethic modality arises from modal logic (von Wright 1951) and "concerns the necessary or contingent truth of propositions" (Nuyts 2016: 38). It is opposed to epistemic modality, in terms of "mode of truth" (alethic modality) vs. "mode of knowing" (epistemic modality). This distinction is considered to be similar to objective vs. subjective epistemic modality in Lyons (1977). Some scholars reject the distinction between epistemic and alethic modality, as in English there is no distinction between "what is logically true and what the speaker believes, as a matter of fact, to be true" (Palmer 2001: 11). More recently Gosselin (2010: 311–325) has argued for the relevance of alethic modality, as when uttering 'it is raining' or 'the table is square', the speaker presents their own sentence as true regardless of what they believe. Following this approach to alethic modality, the judgment of the speaker is suspended.

Boulomaic modality "concerns an indication of the degree of the speaker's (or someone else's) liking or disliking (affectively) of the state of affairs" (Nuyts 2016: 39). It is connected to the notion of *volition*, which primarily refers to desires. Volition is associated to deontic modality in some studies (e.g. Palmer 1986), and to dynamic modality in others (Palmer 2001). In the latter study, the relevant notion for defining deontic modality is *intention* instead of volition, besides obligation and permission (Palmer 1986); note that the notion of intention is not taken into account in other studies.

The last notion to be accounted for is *non-factuality* as opposed to *factuality*. *Non-factuality* relates to non-realised or non-actualised states of affairs (Kiefer 1987: 90, 1997: 243; Narrog 2005, 2012b: 6; Declerck 2011: 27) and is opposed to realised or actualised states of affairs. The opposition between *factuality* and *non-factuality* overlaps the *realis* vs. *irrealis* opposition. One of the most investigated domains of non-factuality is *counterfactuality*, where modal markers, often combined with tense-aspectual markers, for instance past-tense markers and negations, characterize some types of sentences, namely *if*-sentences (cf., among others, Wierzbicka 1997; Declerck and Reed 2001; Edgington 2021).

Allan (2013) provides an application to Ancient Greek of how the different notions can be combined together into a scale of *modal strength*. In his account of the semantic domain of modality, Allan proposes four degrees of modal strength ranging from the maximum degree of modal strength (*realis*) to the minimum degree of modal strength (*counterfactuality*). *Realis* "relates to actual events, i.e. events that are presented as having actually occurred in the past or as actually occurring in the present", while *counterfactuality* "pertains to actions which the speaker knows to be not true, i.e. events have not been / are not being realized" (Allan 2013: 4–5). The steps in-between are *necessity* and *possibility*, both of them involving deontic and epistemic counterparts. *Deontic necessity* implies that an agent performs an action because of a strong external condition, while in *epistemic necessity* the speaker considers the realization of the event to be necessary or at least probable. Finally, within *possibility*, *deontic possibility*, when an agent is given permission to perform an action, is distinguished from *epistemic possibility*, when the speaker believes that the proposition is possibly true.

2.5 Summary

Two facts emerge from this brief review of the literature. First, it is very difficult to define modality and, especially, its level of relevance. Second, within the functional approach, we observe that semantic notions and labels, but also categories and classifications tend to proliferate excessively. In our opinion, the following questions remain unanswered within the functional-typological approach. First, does modality pertain to the level of the clause or the sentence? What is the interaction between the different relevant notions, e.g. the speaker and the agent? Second, from a methodological point of view, we wonder to what extent it is fruitful to classify modal meanings crosslinguistically. In our opinion, it would be better to investigate modality within a single language and, then, adopt a comparative approach that takes into account not only modal meanings but also modal markers and combinations of them. To this end, a more suitable perspective would be to explore the possibility of establishing, for each language, a list of modal markers and to investigate their interaction in order to understand how modal nuances arise.

3 Our perspective: How to build modality with syntax

Given this background and the abundance of labels and notions, we need a simple working definition of modality that meets our requirements, i.e. a definition that allows us to describe the complexity of modal phenomena in a single language, Ancient Greek. With this approach, we expect a better understanding of modality itself.

3.1 What is a modal marker?

It is well known that modal markers can be of various kinds. This view contrasts with traditional grammatical accounts, in which modality is mostly associated with verbal moods (a) and/or modal verbs (b).

(a) When modality is associated with *verbal moods*, it is considered a verbal category, on a par with tense and aspect (and the widely used label TAM(E), i.e. Tense-Aspect-Mood-(Evidentiality) reflects this view). The reason for the association has deep roots in the history of linguistics, since it is only from the 1970s that *modality* appeared alongside *moods* in English-speaking linguistics (see van der Auwera and Zamorano Aguilar 2016).

Grammars of Ancient Greek are representative of this tradition. For example, in a recent reference grammar (van Emde Boas *et al.* 2019: 438–446), the authors do not mention modality and list the functions of verbal moods according to their use in main and dependent clauses, also using general descriptive labels (e.g. reality, desirability, etc.). This type of approach is understandable: the number of verbal moods and the complexity of their semantic components in Ancient Greek call for an explanation, and modality is thus mainly associated with verbal moods.[4] However, restricting modality to verbal moods tends to exclude other devices from the field of investigation (see § 3.3 for a tentative inventory in Ancient Greek).

(b) The association of modality with *modal verbs* is a well-represented approach in studies on English and Germanic languages: in English, the definition of modality overlaps with that of modal verbs. Among others, we can mention Leech's (2006: 64) glossary, where the entry "modality" refers to "modal (auxiliary verb)" defined as "a member of a small class of verbs that have meanings relating to modality, that is to such concepts as possibility or permission (*can, may*), obligation, necessity or likelihood (*must, should*), prediction, intention or hypothesis (*will, would*)". This approach is understandable since English does not have verbal moods, and modal verbs appear to supply them (cf. Huddleston 1976 for an overview on English modal verbs). It is thus modal verbs that call for an explanation in English: they are a special category of verbs, which are polyfunctional and also display formal peculiarities (e.g. they share the so-called NICE-properties of auxiliaries – pertaining to negation, inversion, code and emphasis – as labelled by Huddleston and Pullum 2002: 93). While modal verbs and modality happen to overlap in English grammars, this approach may prove problematic in other languages because modal verbs are not to be found in all languages.[5]

In both cases (a) and (b), modality is restricted to a few grammatical forms, either verbal moods or modal verbs; moreover, the question of how these forms interact with other elements in the clause (or in the sentence) is left open. This may pose a problem since many more types of devices have been acknowledged as modal forms.[6] For German, Kratzer (2012 [1981]) already mentioned sentence adverbs (*möglicherweise* 'possibly'), impersonal constructions (*es ist möglich dass* 'it is possible that') or suffixes *-lich* and *-bar* on adjectives (*zahlbar* 'payable', *zugänglich* 'accessible').

The types of modal markers are language-specific and a complete list of possible markers is probably not available yet (e.g. it has been argued that word order

---

4 Though dominant, this approach is not general, e.g. in the Spanish-speaking tradition. See Crespo *et al.* (2003: 282–283), who make use of the distinction between epistemic vs. non-epistemic modality. In a recently published grammar, Revuelta Puigdollers (2021: 639–640) provides a definition of modality and applies the distinction between epistemic and deontic to different types of sentences; a list of modal markers different from verbal moods is also given (Revuelta Puigdollers 2021: 643–647).
5 Cf. Hansen and de Haan (2009: 512): "Whereas modality as a functional domain can safely be assumed to be a universal concept, modals as specific morphosyntactic means of expression of modal notions are to be treated as a typologically relevant, but not as a universal category".
6 E.g. in Huddleston and Pullum (2002), the approach to modality is focused on modal auxiliaries, but 'the linguistic expression of modality' encompasses other means that are duly mentioned (Huddleston and Pullum 2002: 173–175).

could be a modal marker in Danish, see Christensen and Heltoft 2010). As Arregui *et al.* (2017: 18) remark, "modal meanings could be available for all syntactic categories and at all the different levels of syntactic structure". In fact, when studying the modal system of a single language, an *a priori* categorization presents the risk of leaving aside a number of relevant devices. The idea that the notion of modal marker is elusive is shared by scholars of different theoretical approaches, from Kratzer (2012: 31), who argues that "there is no syntactic category corresponding to the notional category of modality", to Gosselin (2010: 50), who is more sceptical ("[i]t is even doubtful that a class of modal markers can be identified").

Given this indeterminacy, we need a definition of modality that is able to tackle the variety of modal devices.

3.2 A definition of modality that paves the way for a syntactic approach

For that purpose, we use as a working definition Martin (2005: 15):

> Modality is the set of operations which, on the basis of very variable linguistic elements that are semantically interpreted, determine the commitment to the proposition, by suspending or modifying the inherent operator of truth. (our translation)[7]

In this account, modality is defined in relationship to the commitment to the truth of the proposition – which is a broad definition that encompasses other notions than possibility and necessity.[8] The relevant aspect of this approach, however, is that modality is not located in a small number of "modal" markers, but is the result of a calculation, a set of operations. Modality is due to the combined effect of several elements. The calculation is made from diverse linguistic elements, which vary according to the language under study. As Martin (2005: 15) states, "the question now is much simpler: does this linguistic element have a modal impact or not, i.e. does it have a repercussion on the commitment to the utterance?"[9]

---

[7] "La modalité est l'ensemble des opérations qui, à partir d'éléments linguistiques très variables sémantiquement interprétés, déterminent la prise en charge de la proposition, en suspendant ou en modifiant l'opérateur inhérent de vérité" (Martin 2005: 15).
[8] Richard Faure (p.c.) draws our attention to the fact that commitment is a valuable parameter to account for epistemic modality, but is less relevant in the case of deontic modality (the deontic source is not necessarily related to the speaker).
[9] "La question désormais est beaucoup plus simplement celle-ci: tel élément linguistique a-t-il ou non une incidence modale, c'est-à-dire a-t-il ou non une répercussion sur la prise en charge de l'énoncé?" (Martin 2005: 15).

Even though in Martin's (2005) definition the "set of operations" concerns the cognitive level, we believe that this combinatorial approach to modality is also relevant for our syntactic approach. We define syntax in a very broad way as the convergence of two operations, concerning (a) the paradigmatic choices, where the focus is on the differences of forms (varying from morphemes to utterances) correlated with the differences of meanings, and (b) the syntagmatic combinations, where the focus is on the relevance of the combined elements and the meanings they acquire by the combination itself. We aim at describing modality in the interaction of different linguistic elements contributing to the modal meaning, taking into account the distribution, the hierarchy and the linear order of these elements.

Our goal is to describe how modal meanings are "built" by the interaction of different linguistic elements, taking into account their distribution and hierarchy in the clause or sentence. We propose a data-driven approach, which starts from some relevant (language-specific) elements (e.g. modal verbs, moods, modal particles, but also indefinites, negative markers, etc.) and investigates how relevant their syntactic behaviour is in building modal meanings. This approach, which is syntactic and distributional in a broad sense, moves the focus from the modal categories to the linguistic markers that contribute to modality and may help us better understand what modality is.

3.3 Why Ancient Greek?

Ancient Greek is an interesting test bench for investigating modality because of its wealth of modal markers and their possible interaction in the same clause. To begin with, Ancient Greek has a rich system of verbal moods (indicative, subjunctive and optative) and a modal particle *án* (ἄν) (also *ke* (κε) in some dialects and Archaic Greek) which may combine with the moods in a sophisticated way, as illustrated in (1)–(3), which presents only a sample:

(1) a. ἦλθες
    êlthes
    come.2SG.IND.AOR
    'you came' (*factual*)

  b. ἦλθες ἄν
    êlthes án
    come.2SG.IND.AOR MOD
    'you would (have) come' (*irrealis*)

(2) a. (μὴ) ἔλθῃς
    (mē) élthēis
    NEG come.2SG.SBJV.AOR
    '(don't) come' (*directive*)

  b. ἐ-ὰν ἔλθῃς
    (e-an) élthēis
    if-MOD come.2SG.SBJV.AOR
    '(if) you come' (*eventualis*, only in particular subordinate clauses)

(3) a. ἔλθοις   b. ἔλθοις   ἄν
       élthois   élthois   án
       come.2SG.OPT.AOR   come.2SG.OPT.AOR MOD
       'may you come' (*wish*)   'you could / can come' (*possibility*)

The set under (a) displays examples with indicative (1a), subjunctive (2a) and optative (3a); the corresponding set under (b) repeats the same verbal moods with the addition of a modal particle. The sample gives a first idea of the complexity of the modal system. Scholars have dedicated studies to both moods (recently, Rijksbaron 2006; Willmott 2007, but there is a long tradition dating back to Goodwin 1896) and the modal particle (Basset 1988; Gerö 2000; Beck *et al.* 2012). The existence of two distinct negatives in combination with the verbal moods is also a question at stake (Moorhouse 1959; Gerö 1997, and more recently Chatzopoulou 2018, who analysed the difference between them in terms of sensitivity to (non)veridicality).

Modality is not restricted to the morphology of the verb, but is also visible in lexical verbs with modal meanings (Basset 1979 on *méllō* / μέλλω 'to be likely', Ruiz Yamuza 2008a on three verbs expressing obligation *khrḗ* / χρή 'to be necessary', *deî* / δεῖ 'to be needed', *opheílō* / ὀφείλω 'to owe, to be obliged to'; see also Allan 2013 on the last one). We use the label "lexical verbs with modal meanings" and not "modal verbs" since the question of their status as modal verbs has been debated, and other verbs with modal meanings have been proposed (*ekhō* / ἔχω 'to have', *dúnamai* / δύναμαι 'to be able', *kinduneúō* / κινδυνεύω 'to risk', cf. Ruiz Yamuza 1994, 1997, 2008b).

Some fifty years ago in an exploratory paper, Seiler (1971) argued that modality was to be sought outside the categories of mood, and reproached the current state of research for neglecting other factors. This reproach does not hold anymore and linguists studying modality in Ancient Greek are aware of the non-verbal modal categories. Among them adverbs and particles have been particularly studied for their modal value, in interaction with verbal moods, e.g. *ísōs* / ἴσως, *tákha* / τάχα 'perhaps', and *skhedón* / σχέδον 'almost' (Ruiz Yamuza 2001; cf. also Conti 2019), *tukhón* / τυχόν 'by chance' (Denizot and Vassilaki 2017), and the epistemic particles *ê* / ἦ and *ára* / ἄρα (la Roi 2019), and που / *pou* (Koier 2013).[10]

However, the list of "modal-oriented" grammatical devices is longer and may include other devices such as e.g. indefinites, which may interact with other modal

---

[10] Revuelta Puigdollers (2021: 647) mentions other adverbs that remain to be studied as modal markers: adverbs indicating a degree of knowledge (such as *dḗpou* / δήπου 'probably', *anamphisbētḗ:tōs* / ἀναμφισβητήτως 'undoubtedly', *asphalôs* / ἀσφαλῶς 'surely'), the origin of the knowledge of the propositional content (e.g. *dêthen* / δῆθεν 'supposedly', *homologouménōs* / ὁμολογουμένως 'as everybody admits'), or expressing deontic modality (among others *orthôs* / ὀρθῶς 'rightly', *dikaíōs* / δικαίως 'justly').

markers. Besides the combinations of modal elements, we should also consider the types of (main and dependent) clauses, the types of illocutionary acts, etc. Two research directions have still to be explored. On the one hand, we need to determine which linguistic devices behave as modal markers outside verbal morphology and modal particles. On the other hand, we need to investigate how all these forms (and categories) interact and influence each other and which syntactic operations are at work in building modal meanings.

4 The syntactic dimension of modality in Ancient Greek

4.1 Previous studies

Since different modal markers can appear in the same clause, the nature of their interaction has to be addressed.

The question was identified as early as the 1970s. Halliday (1970) recognised the possible interplay between verbal and non-verbal modal markers (e.g. a modal verb and an adverb), concluding that "there is thus no single place in the clause where modality is located" (Halliday 1970: 331). Modal markers can be "modally harmonic" or "modally non-harmonic" following Lyons (1977: 801) and this phenomenon has been investigated in some restricted areas (e.g. Hoye 1997 for modal verb and adverb collocations in English).

The co-utterance of several modal markers in the same clause has been investigated from different theoretical perspectives:

(a) In a modular perspective, inspired by generative theory, the question is tackled in terms of interfaces. The exploration of semantic-syntax interfaces (other interfaces have also been explored, cf. Maienborn *et al.* 2019) is present from the earliest works on modality, such as Kratzer (2012). For instance, Hacquard (2011) argues that root modality and epistemic modality correspond to two different syntactic positions and that their semantic difference is based on their syntactic difference; Arregui *et al.* (2017) aimed at exploring which kinds of modal meanings are available at different levels of syntactic structure. This perspective is not developed for Ancient Greek, to the best of our knowledge.

(b) In a functionalist perspective, the question is tackled in terms of layers (see Aijmer 2016 for a more detailed and nuanced account). In the model developed by Hengeveld (1988) from the seminal work by Bolkestein (1980), inherent modalities

(= level 1 modality) such as ability or volition are internal to the state of affairs; objective modalities (level 2 modality) are concerned with the speaker's evaluation of the actuality of a state of affairs against his knowledge of possible situations; epistemological modalities (level 3 modalities) pertain to the propositional content and are part of the information the speaker wants to convey to the hearer. This layered representation is explicitly referred to in Ancient Greek studies e.g. by Ruiz Yamuza (2014) and is the dominant approach for this language, also in a diachronic perspective.[11]

(c) In a cognitivist perspective, the question is tackled in terms of constructions, i.e. regular combinations of words associated with meanings that are shared by speaker and addressee (for the speaker and the addressee) meanings. In this framework, the "basic building blocks" (Koier 2013: 8) of a clause or sentence are the constructions, and not the single words. The constructionist approach is particularly useful for explaining combinations of words in which the whole meaning cannot be compositionally analysed starting from the single components. It goes without saying that these combinations are also characterized by syntactic, lexical and pragmatic features that are compositional and do not pertain to the lexical items in themselves; they are learned and stored separately by speakers, i.e. as constructions. We refer to Boogaart and Fortuin (2016) for a general presentation and to Cappelle and Depraetere (2016), among others, for an application. Several studies have used this approach explicitly for Ancient Greek modal markers, e.g. Koier (2013) on the particle που / *pou*, Drummen (2013) on the use of optative mood with the modal particle *án* / ἄν (2013), and Danesi *et al.* (2018) on non-canonically case-marked subjects in relation to verbs with modal meanings.

(d) In a distributionist and data-driven approach, we limit ourselves to mentioning the following studies.

First, Denizot and Vassilaki (2016) investigated the syntactic and semantic properties of the subjunctive + *án* / ἄν in relative clauses, by comparing it to Modern Greek non-past perfective. The authors show that there are relevant syntactic and semantic similarities in the distribution of these modal markers in the two languages, which point to the persistence of the modal category of *eventualis*, despite the differences concerning the two verbal systems.

Second, in a study devoted to result clauses, Revuelta Puigdollers (2017) moved the focus from the use of verbal moods (which is the traditional approach for this structure in Ancient Greek) to the mutual relationships between different factors,

---

[11] See recently la Roi (2022a, 2022b).

i.e. connectors between main and dependent clauses, intensifiers and correlative expressions as well as verbal moods and sentence types.

Third, Bartolotta and Kölligan (2020) investigated the interaction between attitudinal particles and adverbs, e.g. ἄρα / *ára*, γε / *ge*, μάλα / *mála*, and a specific subset of archaic verbal forms, i.e. injunctives, in counterfactual constructions in Homeric Greek. According to the authors, the particles and adverbs played an important role as expressions of epistemic values before the innovation in the verbal system that led to the emergence of the indicative mood.[12]

Whatever theoretical frame is adopted, the syntactic component of modality deserves further exploration. By 'syntactic component of modality', we mean two possible directions. On the one hand, the way different devices jointly contribute to creating a specific modal meaning can thus be captured at the clause level. On the other hand, the modal meaning can influence the meaning of its components (subclauses, reference of the indefinites, scope of the negation, among others).

4.2 Overview of the chapters in the volume

The aim of this volume is to present corpus-based studies devoted to several syntactic aspects of modality in Ancient Greek, within different theoretical frameworks and approaches. The eight papers in the volume shed new light on modal categories such as epistemicity, possibility, counterfactuality, evidentiality, subjectivity, and show how these modal meanings arise from the combination of different linguistic devices in specific syntactic contexts (e.g. combinations of modal elements, interaction of main and dependent clauses, types of illocutionary acts, etc.).

The volume addresses the following three major issues:
(a) The role of subordination strategies in creating modal meanings;
(b) The combinatory value of different modal devices in specific subordinate clauses;
(c) The interaction among clauses in building modality.

The volume opens with two papers devoted to the first thematic issue, namely the role of subordination, particularly clausal complementation, in building modal meanings. The first paper (Chapter 2 "Modal uses of knowledge verbs in Ancient Greek") is co-authored by **Marina Benedetti and Chiara Gianollo** and investigates the different complementation patterns of the verbs of knowledge ἐπίσταμαι

---

[12] See also la Roi (2019) for the compatibility of the potential optative with the particles *ê* / ἦ and *ára* / ἄρα.

(epístamai), οἶδα (oîda) and γιγνώσκω (gignṓskō), which express both epistemic knowledge ('know that') and performative knowledge ('know how to'). The goal of the study is to investigate whether the different modal meanings depend on the different syntactic constructions, particularly in the domain of non-finite (infinitive and participle) complementation, and, in that case, whether the semantic difference between epistemic and dynamic modality can be analysed as a grammaticalization process leading from lexical to functional, i.e. modal, verbs. By investigating a large corpus, composed of Archaic and Classical Greek works, the authors conclude that the dynamic modal meaning emerges when the verb is complemented by an infinitive, which is a defective sentential domain, as it does not allow tense inflection or agreement features. Therefore, the combination of the knowledge verb and its infinitival complement expresses a single event and the construction is mono-clausal. However, there is no grammaticalization, according to the authors, as the verb of knowledge retains its argument structure, unlike modal verbs such as δύναμαι (dúnamai) 'can', which, conversely, behaves like an auxiliary verb, as it has no autonomous argument structure.

In the second paper (Chapter 3 "Information source and complementation in Classical Greek: The case of verbs of seeing and knowledge acquisition"), **Martin Masliš** investigates the three different complementation strategies that occur with verbs of seeing and knowledge, i.e. the participial construction, and the finite complement clauses introduced by ὅτι (hóti) and ὡς (hōs). The goal of the research is to investigate whether and how these complementation patterns differ from one another with respect to the notion of information source. The analysis takes into account the verbs ὁράω (horáō) 'I see' and its suppletive aorist εἶδον (eîdon) 'I saw', γιγνώσκω (gignṓskō), ἐπίσταμαι epístamai and οἶδα (oîda) 'I know', and μανθάνω (manthánō) 'I learn' in the corpus of the ten Attic orators. The results of the analysis show that there is a difference between the participial strategy and the finite complementation strategies. While the former conveys evidential meanings involving direct perception and circumstantial inference, the latter relate propositional contents that the participants of the communication either already know (hóti) or do not readily accept as a common ground of the communication (hōs).

The two studies in the second thematic section adopt a diachronic approach and focus on how modal meanings arise from the combination of different modal devices in specific types of subordinate clauses. In the first paper dealing with the issue (Chapter 4 "Syntactic patterns of modality in temporal clauses: *hóte* vs. *hótan* in the diachrony of Ancient Greek"), **Camille Denizot, Liana Tronci and Sophie Vassilaki** investigate how the modal pattern that expresses eventuality (subjunctive mood combined with the modal particle ἄν (án)) interacts syntactically and semantically with the subordinator ὅτε (hóte) 'when'. The study adopts a contrastive approach and is based on a large corpus, composed of texts of Archaic, Classical and Postclassical Greek. The analysis of the distribution of the clauses with ὅτε (hóte) vs. ὅταν (hótan = hóte + án) shows that the syntactic and semantic features that oppose the two types of clauses changed over the centuries, despite the apparent continuity of the modal devices that occur in the combination.

In the second paper of the section (Chapter 5 "Variation and change of counterfactual conditionals in Postclassical Greek. Evidence from private papyrus letters"), **Giuseppina Di Bartolo** proposes an analysis of counterfactual conditionals in the corpus of private letters from Greek documentary papyri of the Roman and Byzantine periods (1st–7th c. CE). The paper investigates how the devices devoted to expressing counterfactual conditionals changed in Postclassical Greek, focusing particularly on the verbal form of apodosis (the imperfect). It studies how the complex subordinator εἰ μὴ ὅτι (ei mē hóti) lit. 'if not that', which rarely occurred in Classical Greek literary texts (without conveying counterfactuality), emerged in the Septuagint and spread in low-register varieties of Postclassical Greek. The author analyses the collocation *ei mē hóti* as an elliptical construction for 'if it (were) not that', including a complement clause governed by *ei mē*. From the point of view of information structure, the author argues that the clause governed by *ei mē hóti* conveys new information, which usually denies the recipient's expectation. This is additionally marked by clause-initial καί (kaí) 'and' in some cases. Different features of low register texts are highlighted in the paper, for instance the apparently chaotic use of verbal moods and tenses.

The papers collected in the third thematic section aim at investigating in which ways clause combination contributes to building modality. The first two papers of the section deal with constructions in which modal meanings emerge in dialogic contexts, i.e. are linked to the relation between speaker and addressee. In these papers, therefore, the syntactic analysis also touches on relevant pragmatic issues, e.g. politeness, subjectivity, etc.

The paper by **Emilia Ruiz Yamuza** (Chapter 6 "Conditional subordinate clauses and verbal moods: A case study") explores how parenthetic clauses meaning 'if you want' interact with the matrix clause from the points of view of verbal moods and sentence types in a corpus of dialogic texts (Homeric poems, Plato and Attic theatre). The author identifies two constructions, namely (1) *eán* (= *ei* + modal particle *án*) plus subjunctive, and (2) *ei* plus indicative, which co-occur with different verbal moods in the main clause, i.e. type (1) with the imperative or the subjunctive and type (2) with the indicative. Within the framework of Construction Grammar, which the author adopts, the two sequences of 'if you want' are analysed as two different constructions as they not only display differences in the formal devices, but also have different form-function relationships. In fact, the first type of 'if you want' construction conveys polite orders, while the second type conveys examples or reformulations. From the point of view of modality, the first type expresses modal contents in itself, while this is not the case for the second type.

In the second paper of the section (Chapter 7 "(Inter)subjectivity, modality, and syntax in Classical Greek: *Dokéō* and *phaínomai* in addressee-oriented assertions in the dialogues of Plato"), **Rodrigo Verano and Alberto Pardal Padín** investigate the relationship between modality and (inter)subjectivity in clauses formed by the verbs δοκέω (*dokéō*) 'seem' and φαίνομαι (*phaínomai*) 'appear' that occur in Plato's dialogues. Despite the semantic resemblance, the two verbs have a different syntactic behaviour, also when they are combined with the 1st person dative experiencer μοι (*moi*) 'to me'. While *dokéō* generalises the construction *dokeî moi* 'it seems to me' that constitutes a single unanalysable unit, the sequence *phaínomai moi* occurs in two different constructions from the point of view of modality. One of them expresses epistemic modality, as the factuality of the clause governed by *phaínomai* relies on the speaker's knowledge, while the other expresses evidential modality, without any commitment of the speaker on the factuality of the proposition. The degree of subjectivity is also different in the two constructions, the first one being more subjective than the second one.

The last two papers of the section explore the relation between modality and clause combination by dealing with counterfactual conditionals, i.e. complex constructions in which the main and the subordinate clause have such a close semantic and syntactic relation that the main clause (apodosis) cannot exist independently from its subordinate (protasis).

The paper by **Ezra la Roi** (Chapter 8 "A pragmatic syntax of counterfactual mood attraction and mood (a)symmetry from Archaic to Classical Greek") proposes a new analysis of mood attraction in counterfactual sentences that consist of a matrix and a subordinate clause. He argues that counterfactual mood attraction is a pragmatically conditioned phenomenon, as it depends on whether the matrix clause can transfer the counterfactual implicature to the subordinate clause. For the transfer to occur, the events of the two clauses and their polarity must be closely related in terms of time and causality, as they have to be sequential and causally dependent on each other. This type of mood attraction is also different from non-counterfactual mood attraction, as in the latter both semantic and pragmatic factors are at work, i.e. the mood meaning in context and the meaning of the matrix clause, while in counterfactual mood attraction only pragmatic factors are relevant.

Finally, **Antonio R. Revuelta Puigdollers**' paper (Chapter 9 "Mood, modality and speech act in clause combination: Formal and pragmatic features") deals with conditional clauses and discusses, first, how the features related to mood, modality and speech act in conditional clauses as a whole differ from those of their constituent clauses (main and subordinate) kept separately and, second, whether there are differences between the indirect speech acts conveyed by the conditionals and the corresponding direct speech acts. Through a corpus-based research on Classical Greek works, the author argues that some conditionals are very specialised and idiomatic speech acts, which correspond to indirect oaths and directives (e.g. 'I'll kill you, if you don't go out'). The latter are stronger than the corresponding direct speech act (e.g. 'Go out!'), as they add an argument (e.g. 'I'll kill you') to support the validity of the oath or the directive. The interpretation of the conditional as an indirect oath or directive is the result of different features that concern (a) the propositional content, which is provided by the subordinate clause, (b) the mood, tense and sentence type, which do not depend on the main clause, (c) the evaluation of the state of affairs of the main clause and the agency of both the main and the subordinate clauses.

References

Abraham, Werner. 2020. *Modality in syntax, semantics and pragmatics*. Cambridge: Cambridge University Press.
Aijmer, Karin. 2016. Mood and modality in functional linguistic approaches. In Jan Nuyts & Johan van der Auwera (eds.), *The Oxford handbook of modality and mood*, 495–513. Oxford: Oxford University Press.
Aikhenvald, Alexandra. 2004. *Evidentiality*. Oxford: Oxford University Press.
Allan, Rutger J. 2013. Exploring modality's semantic space: Grammaticalisation, subjectification and the case of ὀφείλω [*opheílō*]. *Glotta* 89. 1–46.
Arregui, Ana, María Luisa Rivero & Andrés Salanova (eds.). 2017. *Modality across syntactic categories*. Oxford: Oxford University Press.
van der Auwera, Johan & Vladimir Plungian. 1998. Modality's semantic map. *Linguistic Typology* 2. 79–124.
van der Auwera, Johan & Alfonso Zamorano Aguilar. 2016. The history of modality and mood. In Jan Nuyts & Johan van der Auwera (eds.), *The Oxford handbook of modality and mood*, 9–41. Oxford: Oxford University Press.
Bally, Charles. 1965 [1932]. *Linguistique générale et linguistique française*. Bern: Francke.
Bartolotta, Annamaria & Daniel Kölligan. 2020. Modality and injunctive in Homeric Greek: The role of epistemic particles and adverbs in counterfactual constructions. In Martti Leiwo, Marja Vierros & Sonja Dahlgren (eds.), *Papers on Ancient Greek Linguistics. Proceedings of the ninth international colloquium on Ancient Greek linguistics (ICAGL 9)*, 417–445. Helsinki: Societas Scientiarum Fennica.
Basset, Louis. 1979. *Les emplois périphrastiques du verbe grec ΜΕΛΛΕΙΝ [MELLEIN]. Étude de linguistique grecque et essai de linguistique générale*. Lyon: Maison de l'Orient.
Basset, Louis. 1988. Valeurs et emplois de la particule dite modale en grec ancien. In Albert Rijksbaron, Henk A. J. Mulder & Gerry C. Wakker (eds.), *In the footsteps of Raphael Kühner*, 27–37. Amsterdam: J. C. Gieben.
Baumgarten, Nicole, Inke Du Bois & Juliane House. 2012. *Subjectivity in language and in discourse*. Bingley: Emerald Group Publishing.
Beck, Jana E., Sophia A. Malamud & Iryna Osadcha. 2012. A semantics for the particle ἄν [*án*] in and outside conditionals in Classical Greek. *Journal of Greek Linguistics* 12(1). 51–83.

Benveniste, Émile. 1966 [1958]. De la subjectivité dans le langage. In *Problèmes de linguistique générale, 1*, 258–266. Paris: Gallimard.
Bolkestein, A. Machtelt. 1980. *Problems in the description of modal verbs: An investigation of Latin*. Assen: Van Gorcum.
Boogaart, Ronny & Egbert Fortuin. 2016. Modality and mood in cognitive linguistics and construction grammar. In Jan Nuyts & Johan van der Auwera (eds.), *The Oxford handbook of modality and mood*, 514–548. Oxford: Oxford University Press.
Boye, Kasper. 2012. *Epistemic meaning. A crosslinguistic and functional-cognitive study*. Berlin & New York: de Gruyter Mouton.
Bréal, Michel. 1897. *Essai de sémantique: Science des significations*. Paris: Hachette.
Bybee, Joan L. 1985. *Morphology: A study of the relation between meaning and form*. Amsterdam: John Benjamins.
Bybee, Joan L. & Suzanne Fleischman. 1995. Modality in grammar and discourse: An introductory essay. In Joan L. Bybee & Suzanne Fleischman (eds.), *Modality in grammar and discourse*, 1–14. Amsterdam: John Benjamins.
Bybee, Joan L., Revere D. Perkins & William Pagliuca. 1994. *The evolution of grammar: Tense, aspect and modality in the languages of the world*. Chicago: The University of Chicago Press.
Cappelle, Bert & Ilse Depraetere. 2016. Short-circuited interpretations of modal verb constructions. *Constructions and Frames* 8. 7–39.
Chatzopoulou, Katerina. 2018. *Negation and nonveridicality in the history of Greek*. Oxford: Oxford University Press.
Christensen, Tanya Karoli & Lars Heltoft. 2010. Mood in Danish. In Björn Rothstein & Rolf Thieroff (eds.), *Mood in the languages of Europe*, 85–102. Amsterdam: John Benjamins.
Coates, Jennifer. 1983. *The semantics of the modal auxiliaries*. London: Croom Helm.
Conti, Luz. 2019. De la duda a la certeza: Sobre el uso de ἴσως [ísōs] en el teatro griego. *Incontri Linguistici* 42. 111–136.
Crespo, Emilio, Luz Conti & Helena Maquieira. 2003. *Sintaxis del griego clásico*. Madrid: Gredos.
Danesi, Serena, Cynthia A. Johnson & Jóhanna Barðdal. 2018. Where does the modality of Ancient Greek modal verbs come from? The relation between modality and oblique case marking. *Journal of Greek Linguistics* 18(1). 45–92.
Declerck, Renaat. 2011. The definition of modality. In Adeline Patard & Franck Brisard (eds.), *Cognitive approaches to tense, aspect, and epistemic modality*, 21–44. Amsterdam & Philadelphia: John Benjamins.
Declerck, Renaat & Susan Reed. 2001. *Conditionals*. Berlin & New York: Mouton de Gruyter.
Denizot, Camille & Sophie Vassilaki. 2016. La notion d'éventuel comme catégorie linguistique: Deux formes modales du grec ancien et du grec moderne. *Bulletin de la Société de Linguistique de Paris* 111(1). 277–316.
Denizot, Camille & Sophie Vassilaki. 2017. La fabrique de l'éventuel en grec: Les fortunes de τυχόν [tukhón]. In Theodoros Markopoulos, Rutger J. Allan & Frédéric Lambert (eds.), *The Greek future and its history*, 253–283. Louvain-la-Neuve: Peeters.
De Smet, Hendrik & Jean-Christophe Verstraete. 2006. Coming to terms with subjectivity. *Cognitive Linguistics* 17(1). 365–392.
Drummen, Annemieke. 2013. A constructionist approach to the potential optative in classical Greek drama. *Glotta* 89. 68–108.
Edgington, Dorothy. 2021. Counterfactual conditionals. In Otávio Bueno & Scott A. Shalkowski (eds.), *The Routledge handbook of modality*, 30–39. Abingdon, Oxon & New York: Routledge.

van Emde Boas, Evert, Albert Rijksbaron, Luuk Huitink & Mathieu de Bakker. 2019. *The Cambridge grammar of Classical Greek*. Cambridge: Cambridge University Press.
Gerö, Eva-Carin. 1997. *Negatives and noun phrases in Classical Greek: An investigation based on the corpus Platonicum*. Bern: Peter Lang.
Gerö, Eva-Carin. 2000. The usage of ἄν [*án*] and κε [*ke*] in Ancient Greek: Towards a unified description. *Glotta* 76. 177–191.
Goodwin, William W. 1896. *Syntax of the moods and tenses of the Greek verbs*. Boston: Ginn & Company.
Goossens, Louis. 1985. Modality and the modals: A problem for functional grammar. In A. Machtelt Bolkestein, Casper de Groot & J. Lachlan Mackenzie (eds.), *Predicates and terms in functional grammar*, 203–217. Dordrecht: Foris.
Gosselin, Laurent. 2010. *Les modalités en français. La validation des représentations*. Amsterdam & New York: Rodopi.
Hacquard, Valentine. 2011. Modality. In Klaus von Heusinger, Claudia Maienborn & Paul Portner (eds.), *Semantics: An international handbook of natural language meaning*, vol. 2, 1484–1515. Berlin: Mouton de Gruyter.
Halliday, Michael A. K. 1970. Functional diversity in language as seen from a consideration of modality and mood in English. *Foundations of Language* 6. 322–361.
Hansen, Björn & Ferdinand de Haan. 2009. Modal constructions in the language of Europe. In Björn Hansen & Ferdinand de Haan (eds.), *Modals in the languages of Europe. A reference work*, 511–559. Berlin & New York: Mouton de Gruyter.
Hengeveld, Kees. 1988. Illocution, mood and modality in a functional grammar of Spanish. *Journal of Semantics* 6. 227–269.
Hoye, Leo. 1997. *Adverbs and modality in English*. London: Longman.
Huddleston, Rodney. 1976. Some theoretical issues in the description of the English verb. *Lingua* 40 (4). 331–383.
Huddleston, Rodney & Geoffrey K. Pullum. 2002. *The Cambridge grammar of the English language*. Cambridge: Cambridge University Press.
Jespersen, Otto. 1924. *The philosophy of grammar*. London: George Allen & Unwin Ldt.
Kiefer, Ferenc. 1987. On defining modality. *Folia Linguistica* 21. 67–94.
Kiefer, Ferenc. 1997. Modality and pragmatics. *Folia Linguistica* 31. 241–253.
Koier, Elizabeth. 2013. *Interpreting particles in dead and living languages. A construction grammar approach to the semantics of Dutch* ergens *and Ancient Greek* που [*pou*]. Utrecht: LOT.
Kratzer, Angelika. 2012 [1981]. The notional category of modality. In *Modals and conditionals*, 27–69. Oxford: Oxford University Press.
Langacker, Ronald W. 1990. *Concept, image, and symbol: The cognitive basis of grammar*. Berlin & New York: Mouton de Gruyter.
Leech, Geoffrey. 2006. *A glossary of English grammar*. Edinburgh: Edinburgh University Press.
Leiss, Elisabeth & Werner Abraham (eds.). 2014. *Modes of modality. Modality, typology, and universal grammar*. Amsterdam & Philadelphia: John Benjamins.
Lyons, John. 1977. *Semantics*. Cambridge: Cambridge University Press.
Lyons, John. 1982. Deixis and subjectivity: *loquor, ergo sum*? In Robert J. Jarvella & Wolfgang Klein (eds.), *Speech, place, and action*, 101–124. New York: John Wiley & Sons.
Maienborn, Claudia, Klaus von Heusinger & Paul Portner. 2019. *Semantics. Interfaces*. Berlin & Boston: De Gruyter.
Martin, Robert. 2005. Définir la modalité. *Revue de linguistique romane* 69. 7–18.
Moorhouse, Alfred C. 1959. *Studies in the Greek negatives*. Cardiff: University of Wales Press.

Narrog, Heiko. 2005. Modality, mood, and change of modal meanings: A new perspective. *Cognitive Linguistics* 16(4). 677–731.
Narrog, Heiko. 2012a. Modality and speech-act orientation. In Johan van der Auwera & Jan Nuyts (eds.), *Grammaticalization and (inter)subjectification*, 21–36. Brussels: Royal Academy of Sciences.
Narrog, Heiko. 2012b. *Modality, subjectivity, and semantic change: A cross-linguistic perspective*. Oxford: Oxford University Press.
Nuyts, Jan. 2001. *Epistemic modality, language and conceptualization: A cognitive-pragmatic perspective*. Amsterdam: John Benjamins.
Nuyts, Jan. 2005. The modal confusion: On terminology and the concepts behind it. In Alex Klinge (ed.), *Modality: Studies in form and function*, 5–38. London: Equinox.
Nuyts, Jan. 2006. Modality: Overview and linguistic issues. In William Frawley (ed.), *The expression of modality*, 1–26. Berlin: Mouton de Gruyter.
Nuyts, Jan. 2016. Analyses of the modal meanings. In Jan Nuyts & Johan van der Auwera (eds.), *The Oxford handbook of modality and mood*, 31–49. Oxford: Oxford University Press.
Nuyts, Jan & Johan van der Auwera (eds.). 2016. *The Oxford handbook of modality and mood*. Oxford: Oxford University Press.
Palmer, Frank R. 1986. *Mood and modality*, 1st edn. Cambridge: Cambridge University Press.
Palmer, Frank R. 2001. *Mood and modality*, 2nd edn. Cambridge: Cambridge University Press.
Portner, Paul. 2009. *Modality*. Oxford: Oxford University Press.
Revuelta Puigdollers, Antonio R. 2017. Result clauses in Ancient Greek: Negation, mood and sentence level. In Felicia Logozzo & Paolo Poccetti (eds.), *Ancient Greek linguistics: New approaches, insights, perspectives*, 609–624. Berlin & Boston: De Gruyter.
Revuelta Puigdollers, Antonio R. 2021. El verbo III. Modo y modalidad. In Maria Dolores Jiménez López (ed.), *Sintaxis del griego antiguo*, 637–678. Madrid: Editorial CSIC.
Rijksbaron, Albert. 2006. *The syntax and semantics of the verb in Classical Greek. An introduction*. Chicago & London: The University of Chicago Press.
la Roi, Ezra. 2019. Epistemic modality, particles and the potential optative in Classical Greek. *Journal of Greek Linguistics* 19(1). 58–89.
la Roi, Ezra. 2022a. Interlocked life cycles of counterfactual mood forms from Archaic to Classical Greek: Aspect, actionality and changing temporal reference. *Indogermanische Forschungen* 127. 235–282.
la Roi, Ezra. 2022b. Down the paths to the past habitual: Its historical connections with counterfactual pasts, future in the pasts, iteratives and lexical sources in Ancient Greek. *Folia Linguistica Historica*. https://doi.org/10.1515/flin-2022-2042 (last accessed March 2023).
Ruiz Yamuza, Emilia. 1994. Verbos modales en griego antiguo I: ἔχω [*ékhō*] + infinitivo en Platón. *Emerita* 62. 1–22.
Ruiz Yamuza, Emilia. 1997. Verbos modales en griego clásico: δύναμαι [*dúnamai*]. In Francisco R. Adrados & Alfonso Martínez Díez (eds.), *IX congreso español de estudios clásicos (Madrid, 27 al 30 de septiembre de 1995)*, vol. 2 (Lingüística Griega), 227–232. Madrid: Sociedad Española de Estudios Clásicos y Ediciones Clásicas.
Ruiz Yamuza, Emilia. 2001. Desplazamientos semánticos en adverbios de modalidad en griego antiguo. *Habis* 32. 659–675.
Ruiz Yamuza, Emilia. 2008a. *Tres verbos que significan 'deber' en griego antiguo*. Zaragoza: Libros Pórtico.
Ruiz Yamuza, Emilia. 2008b. Análisis del comportamiento del verbo κινδυνεύω [*kinduneúō*]. *Habis* 39. 377–396.

Ruiz Yamuza, Emilia. 2014. Mood and modality. In Georgios Giannakis (ed.), *Encyclopaedia of Ancient Greek language and linguistics*, vol. 2, 452–459. Leiden & Boston: Brill.
Seiler, Hansjakob. 1971. Abstract structures for moods in Greek. *Language* 47(1). 79–89.
Squartini, Mario. 2016. Interactions between modality and other semantic categories. In Jan Nuyts & Johan van der Auwera (eds.), *The Oxford handbook of modality and mood*, 50–67. Oxford: Oxford University Press.
Sweetser, Eve. 1990. *From etymology to pragmatics*. Cambridge: Cambridge University Press.
Talmy, Leonard. 1988. Force dynamics in language and cognition. *Cognitive Science* 12. 49–100.
Traugott, Elizabeth C. 1989. On the rise of epistemic meaning in English: An example of subjectification in semantic change. *Language* 65. 31–55.
Traugott, Elizabeth C. 2010. Revisiting subjectification and intersubjectification. In Kristin Davidse, Lieven Vandelanotte & Hubert Cuyckens (eds.), *Subjectification, intersubjectification and grammaticalization*, 29–70. Berlin: Mouton de Gruyter.
Traugott, Elizabeth C. & Richard B. Dasher. 2002. *Regularity in semantic change*. Cambridge: Cambridge University.
Wiemer, Björn. 2018. Evidentials and epistemic modality. In Alexandra Y. Aikhenvald (ed.), *The Oxford handbook of evidentiality*, 85–108. Oxford: Oxford University Press.
Wiemer, Björn & Juana I. Marín Arrese. 2022. *Evidential marking in European languages. Towards a unitary comparative account*. Berlin & Boston: De Gruyter.
Wierzbicka, Anna. 1997. Conditionals and counterfactuals: Conceptual primitives and linguistic universals. In Angeliki Athanasiadou & René Dirven (eds.), *On conditionals again*, 15–59. Amsterdam & Philadelphia: Benjamins.
Willmott, Jo. 2007. *The moods of Homeric Greek*. Cambridge: Cambridge University Press.
von Wright, Georg H. 1951. *An essay in modal logic*. Amsterdam: North-Holland Publishing Company.

Marina Benedetti & Chiara Gianollo
2 Modal uses of knowledge verbs in Ancient Greek

Abstract: In Ancient Greek – as in several other languages – knowledge verbs may express, besides epistemic knowledge ('know that'), also performative knowledge ('know how to'), thus getting close to the domain of dynamic modality. This study focuses on the semantic and syntactic behaviour of the Ancient Greek knowledge verbs *epístamai, oîda, gignṓskō*, in order to detect the conditions enabling their modal uses (in particular with non-finite complementation patterns) and to explore the hypothesis of an ongoing grammaticalization process. With respect to the first issue, it is argued that the dynamic modal reading appears when the knowledge verb is complemented by a tense-defective infinitival complement, characterized by obligatory subject coreference (control). With respect to the second issue, the coexistence of the epistemic and the modal dynamic value is understood as a stable feature of the language, rather than as a result of achieved grammaticalization. This clearly emerges from the contrast with a functional (raising) modal verb such as *dúnamai* 'can'.

Keywords: Modal verbs, epistemic verbs, non-finite complements, control, raising

1 Introduction: 'know that' and 'know how'

Several languages provide evidence for an interaction between knowledge verbs and the domain of modality. Primarily, a knowledge verb in its fundamental meaning ("know that") conveys an epistemic component (it denotes "a state of knowledge or a process of acquisition of knowledge about a propositional content on the part of an experiencer", Cristofaro 2003: 106). Moreover, in some languages, "know" appears to express a kind of root dynamic modality ("know how", a meaning classed by Cristofaro 2003: 101 under the category of modal predicates), cf. (1a–b):

Acknowledgments: Even though this paper is the outcome of joint work by the authors, for academic purposes the final editing is to be attributed to Marina Benedetti for Sections 1, 2, 3.1, to Chiara Gianollo for Sections 3.2, 4. Both authors are responsible for Section 5.

Marina Benedetti, Università per Stranieri di Siena, e-mail: benedetti@unistrasi.it
Chiara Gianollo, Università di Bologna, e-mail: chiara.gianollo@unibo.it

https://doi.org/10.1515/9783110778380-002

(1) a. *Mary knows **that** she plays the piano extremely well.*
    b. *Mary knows **how** to play the piano extremely well.*

This duality of behaviour is observed, for instance, with Latin *scire*, Italian *sapere*, Modern Greek *kséro*, and appears to be a cross-linguistically widespread phenomenon: the Database of Cross-Linguistic Colexifications (Rzymski, Tresoldi et al. 2019) lists colexifications of the meanings "know" and "be able" in various language families (besides Indo-European, also Chukotko-Kamchatkan, Nakh-Daghestanian, Nivkh, Sino-Tibetan, Tungusic, Turkic, Uralic).

Also in Ancient Greek, knowledge verbs, besides conveying an epistemic attitude, can receive a dynamic modal reading.[1] In other words, they can act either as expressions of epistemic knowledge (knowledge of propositions) or of performative knowledge (knowledge as ability) (see Tsohatzidis 2012; Torrego 2019 on the linguistic correlates of this conceptual distinction).

Interestingly, the different interpretations are consistently associated with different structural properties. For instance, English *know* needs to be complemented by a *how to*-clause in order to convey a dynamic reading (cf. (1b)). The fact that the dynamic modal reading on the one hand and the epistemic reading on the other hand are associated with different types of complementation seems to hold more generally. Roussou (2010) discusses the fact that in Modern Greek *kséro* 'know' is complemented by an *oti*-clause when it is used as an epistemic attitude report, while it is complemented by a *na*-clause in the dynamic modal reading, cf. (2a–b):

(2) Modern Greek (adapted from Roussou 2010: 582–583)
    a. *Ksero   oti   o   Janis   elise   to   provlima.*
       know.1SG   that   ART.SG   Janis   solved.3SG   ART.SG   problem
       'I know that John solved the problem.'
    b. *Ksero   na   aghapao.*
       know.1SG   how   love.1SG
       'I know (how) to love.' (lit. '[how] I love')

In some languages the dynamic modal use of knowledge verbs displays syntactic properties of modal auxiliaries, specifically the possibility of selecting a same-subject infinitival complement that is transparent to certain syntactic operations, such as e.g. clitic climbing (on this, cf. Section 3.2). These properties are taken to indi-

---

1 As observed by la Roi (2020) in a paper focussed on the verb *heurískō* 'find' "there is both Ancient Greek evidence (ἐπίσταμαι [*epístamai*] and οἶδα [*oîda*] as 'know' and 'be able to') and cross-linguistic evidence that knowledge verbs can evolve into verbs of ability" (la Roi 2020: 199).

cate monoclausality ('restructuring' in the generative literature), thus leading to an interpretation of the knowledge verb as an auxiliary-like element.

Historically, this situation can indeed cause reanalysis of the verb's morpho-syntactic and semantic properties: English *can*, for instance, originates from a verb meaning 'know' (*cunnan* 'have knowledge of', 'have the mental or intellectual capability to', 'know how to', Lightfoot 1979: 100; Goossens 1992), cf. (3a–b).

(3) Old English (from Lightfoot 1979: 98–99)
    a. Bede, *Ecclesiastical History* II.13
       hwæt þær foregange, oððe hwæt þær eftfylge, we
       what there precede.3SG or what there come.after.3SG we
       ne **cunnun**.
       not know.1PL
       'What came before, or what comes after, we do not know.'
    b. Bede, *Ecclesiastical History* IV.24
       ne **con** ic noht singan.
       not can.1SG I not sing.INF
       'I cannot sing.'

The same root (IE *ĝneh₃- 'know') is in both German *kennen* 'know' (originally a causative derivative) and *können* 'can', the latter a result of the same process of reanalysis seen for English.

The path from knowledge verbs to the expression of dynamic modality is well-attested cross-linguistically (Bybee, Perkins and Pagliuca 1994: 187–194; van der Auwera and Plungian 1998: 88–93; Heine and Kuteva 2002: 186; Traugott 2011). Van der Auwera and Plungian (1998: 91) explicitly designate "know" as a *premodal* meaning and identify the first step of its semantic development in the expression of learnt participant-internal possibility; subsequently, an extension of meaning leads to the expression of a more general participant-internal possibility, which can be *learnt / intellectual* or *inherent / physical* (van der Auwera and Plungian 1998: 82).

Dynamic modal meanings express a type of participant-oriented modality (Hengeveld 2004, and references cited there), that is, a generic ability (intrinsic or episodic ability granted by the circumstances), with no implication of actuality (Aijmer 2004). In the literature it is often debated whether dynamic modality is a properly modal meaning (cf. Gisborne 2007; Portner 2009: 197–220 for an overview of the semantic arguments; Roberts and Roussou 2003: 47 for the syntactic ones; on Ancient Greek see Allan 2013). Independently of this debate, from a historical point of view the connection of dynamic meanings with the modality domain is witnessed by the fact that they are often found as the first step of grammaticalization clines involving the development of more straightforward modal meanings, such as participant-external possibility, deontic modality and epistemic modality.

As for knowledge verbs specifically, their somehow intermediate semantic status as premodals is mirrored by their morphosyntactic properties, since across languages they can be located at different degrees in the continuum from lexical to functional (auxiliary-like) predicates when they express dynamic modality. Also, they can be more or less conventionalised means to express dynamic modality in a given language: for instance, English *know* can express performative knowledge (knowledge as ability), but it is not its default expression; instead, *can*, which as mentioned is etymologically related to *know*, is a *bona fide* modal verb and represents the default expression for dynamic modality in the language (*Mary can play the piano*).

In our study we focus on the dynamic modal readings of knowledge verbs in Ancient Greek, with the aim of reaching an improved understanding of their conditions of use and of their diachronic status. The questions we address are the following:

(i)   What are the semantic and syntactic conditions that enable modal uses of knowledge verbs in Ancient Greek?
(ii) Why do precisely these conditions lead to the emergence of the modal reading?
(iii) Do the modal uses emerge diachronically as a step on a grammaticalization path leading from a lexical verb to a functional (auxiliary-like, modal) verb? Or are they rather a stable feature of the language, to be explained by the co-existence of certain structural prerequisites?

We will deal with question (i) in Section 2, with question (ii) in Section 3, and with question (iii) in Section 4. Section 5 briefly concludes the study, summarising its main findings. In our analysis, we make use of categories defined within the generative theoretical framework, such as the notions of control, raising, and restructuring; however, these categories are employed here for descriptive purposes in such a way that they are compatible with the theoretical assumptions of most other syntactic frameworks (e.g. the treatment of raising within the framework of Cognitive Grammar, or the layered model of the clause in Functional Grammar).

2 The Ancient Greek Data

The Ancient Greek phenomena under discussion can be observed in the behaviour of verbs such as *epístamai, oîda,* and *gignṓskō*.² These verbs occur with a range of finite and non-finite complements, which we describe in what follows in order to detect the structural conditions under which the dynamic modal reading appears.

2.1 Finite complements

Finite complements (introduced by the conjunctions *hóti* or *hōs*),³ are uniformly associated with an epistemic reading ('know that'). This is illustrated in the passages below, with *epístamai*. The complement and the matrix clause share the same subject in (4a), whereas they have different subjects in (4b).

(4) a. ἐπίστασθε ὅτι ἀπολέεσθε κάκιστα. (Hdt. 3.71.13)
      epístasthe   hóti apoléesthe kákista
      know.2PL.IMP that die.2PL.FUT miserably
      'You must all know that you will perish miserably.'
  b. ἐπιστάμενος ὅτι τῷ δικαίῳ τὸ ἄδικον πολέμιόν ἐστι. (Hdt. 1.96.8)
      epistámenos hóti tôi   dikaíōi to   ádikon
      know.PTCP.NOM that ART.DAT just.DAT ART.NOM unjust.NOM
      polémión esti
      hostile.NOM be.3SG.PRS
      'Knowing that injustice is hostile to justice.'

The same behaviour can be observed with *oîda* and *gignṓskō*.

When complemented by finite clauses, knowledge verbs maintain their fundamental non-modal meaning. Therefore, in the following, we shall not dwell upon finite complementation, but will be focused on non-finite complementation patterns, and their relationship with modal (ability) vs. non-modal (epistemic) reading.

---

2 Data are obtained through the electronic resource TLG from a wide corpus of Archaic and Classical Greek (including the works of Homer, Hesiod, Hymns, Aeschylus, Sophocles, Euripides, Sappho, Theognis, Aesop, Thucydides, and Herodotus). Translations are adapted from those of the Loeb Classical Library.
3 On the contrast between the two complementizers (which does not concern the modal / epistemic contrast of interest here) cf. Cristofaro (1998); Faure (2014); Bentein (2015).

2.2 Non-finite complements

With non-finite complements, the contrast between modal (ability) and non-modal (epistemic) use is essentially associated to the contrast between infinitive and participle.

This is illustrated in (5) and (6) by means of examples with *epístamai*.

(5) πᾶσα γὰρ ἀγαθὴ γυνὴ [...] σωφρονεῖν ἐπίσταται. (E. *Fr.* 909.3 Nauck)
    pâsa   gar   agathē   gunē   sōphroneîn   epístatai
    all.NOM in.fact   good.NOM wife.NOM be.wise.INF know.3SG.PRS
    'Every good wife knows how to be wise.'

(6) a. πρὸς πόλιν δ' ἐπίσταμαι / σθένουσαν ἥκων. (S. *OC.* 733–734)
       pros pólin   d'   epístamai   sthénousan   hḗkōn
       to   city.ACC PTCL know.1SG.PRS   powerful.ACC come.PTCP.NOM
       'I know that I have come to a city that has great power.'
    b. τὸν σὸν δὲ παῖδα σωφρονοῦντ' ἐπίσταμαι. (E. *Fr.* 1067.1 Nauck)
       ton   son   de   paîda   sōphronoûnt'   epístamai
       ART.ACC   your.ACC PTCL son.ACC   be.wise.PTCP.ACC know.1SG.PRS
       'I know that your son is wise.'

In (5) *epístamai* has the dynamic modal meaning 'be able to' and the complement is a same-subject infinitival clause. By contrast, in (6) *epístamai* has its full lexical meaning 'possess information', 'know that' and the complement clause has a participle: the complement and the matrix clause share the same subject in (6a) and have different subjects in (6b).

Similar patterns can be observed with *oîda* (a perfect form with stative meaning). It has a dynamic modal meaning 'be able to' in (7), with a same-subject infinitive complement, whereas it expresses epistemic knowledge ('know that') in (8a–b), respectively with and without subject coreference between the complement and the matrix clause.

(7) οἶδ' ἐπὶ δεξιά, οἶδ' ἐπ' ἀριστερὰ νωμῆσαι βῶν. (*Il.* 7.238)
    oîd'   epi dexiá oîd'   ep' aristera nōmêsai   bôn
    know.1SG.PRF to right know.1SG.PRF   to left   direct.INF shield.ACC
    'I know how to wield to right, and how to wield to left my shield.'

(8) a. οὐ γὰρ οἶδα δεσπότας κεκτημένος. (E. *Hec.* 397)
 ou gar oîda despótas kektēménos
 NEG in.fact know.1SG.PRF masters.ACC get.PTCP.NOM
 'In fact I am not aware that I have masters.'
 b. τοὺς φιλτάτους γὰρ οἶδα νῷν ὄντας πικρούς. (A. *Ch.* 234)
 tous philtátous gar oîda nôin
 ART.ACC closest.ACC in.fact know.1SG.PRF us.DAT.DU
 óntas pikroús
 be.PTCP.ACC hostile.ACC
 'In fact I know that our closest kin are bitterly hostile to us both.'

Further evidence of this pattern is offered by *gignóskō*, as shown by the contrast between the infinitive complement in (9) (with an ability reading) and the participial complement in (10a–b) (with an epistemic reading):

(9) γνῷ τρέφειν τὴν γλῶσσαν ἡσυχωτέραν. (S. *Ant.* 1089)
 gnôi tréphein tēn glôssan hēsukhōtéran
 know.3SG.SBJV keep.INF ART.ACC tongue.ACC quieter.ACC
 'Let him learn how to keep his tongue quieter.'

(10) a. ἔγνωκα γὰρ δὴ φωτὸς ἠπατημένη. (S. *Aj.* 807)
 égnōka gar dē phōtos ēpateménē
 know.1SG.PRF in.fact PTCL man.GEN deceive.PTCP.PASS.NOM
 'I know that I have been deceived by the man.'
 b. ἔγνων γάρ μιν [...] οἰωνὸν ἐόντα. (*Od.* 15.532)
 égnōn gár min oiōnon eónta
 know.1SG.AOR in.fact him.ACC bird.of.omen.ACC be.PTCP.ACC
 'For I knew that he was a bird of omen.'

It must be added that the modal use of *gignóskō* is very rare. In our corpus, including more than 1000 occurrences of this verb, the modal dynamic reading is found only in example (9).[4] Its uniqueness is in itself a matter of interest. It shows that we are dealing with a productive pattern: a knowledge verb may occasionally be used in the modal meaning 'be able to'. Remarkably, we have here the same root (*$\hat{g}neh_3$-) as in English *know, can,* etc.

---

4 Here, the aorist form *gnôi* suggests an ingressive reading, hence 'become able to', 'learn (how) to'; on the ingressive value of aorist forms cf. Napoli (2014).

A further option, which is extremely rare, is the *Accusative and Infinitive* construction, that is, an infinitive complement clause with an expressed subject that takes accusative case. In our corpus, we only find two examples, both with *epístamai* (S. *Ant.* 1092–1094; Hdt. 3.139.16 = ex. (11)) and both with a subject that is not co-referent with the subject of the matrix clause. In this construction, the knowledge verb has its full lexical meaning.

(11) ὁ μὲν δὴ Συλοσῶν ἠπίστατο τοῦτό οἱ ἀπολωλέναι δι' εὐηθίην. (Hdt. 3.139.16)
  ho men dē Sulosôn ēpístato   toûtó
  ART.NOM PTCL PTCL Syloson.NOM know.3SG.IMPF DEM.ACC
  hoi   apolōlénai   di'   euēthíēn
  him.DAT lose.INF.PASS.PRF because.of good.heartedness.ACC
  'Syloson knew that this had been lost to him because of his good nature.'

Given its rarity, we disregard this construction in what follows, noting however that there is an important difference between fuller infinitive clauses with an expressed subject and bare infinitive complements with no expressed subject and obligatory coreference with the subject of the matrix clause.

2.3 Summary of distribution

As emerges from the passages above, there is a correlation between the form of the complement and the semantic value of the main verb.[5] In particular,
a. the *dynamic modal* reading emerges when the complement clause is a same-subject infinitival clause (where the subject is never expressed), that is, what we call a 'bare infinitive';[6]

---

[5] In general, the association between differences in meaning and differences in complementation patterns is quite common in Ancient Greek, and has been repeatedly observed in the literature. For a general overview cf. Cristofaro (2008, 2012); as the author observes, "some predicates can take more than one complement clause type, with a change in the meaning of the sentence" (Cristofaro 2008: 572). This interrelation does not necessarily imply that the meaning of the matrix verb is *determined* by the form of the complement (cf. la Roi 2020).
[6] For a similar behaviour of knowledge verbs in Latin, cf. Torrego (2019). As suggested by an anonymous reviewer, this phenomenon, in Greek, may be put in relation with the association between infinitives and non-factivity (cf. Huitink 2009). However, the applicability the notion of (non)factivity to bare infinitives (as opposed to fuller infinitive clauses, to which Huitink 2009 refers) can be questioned, as argued by Benedetti and Gianollo (2022), since they do not express a full proposition.

b. the *non-modal knowledge* meaning emerges with the other kinds of complementation, namely participle complement clauses and finite complement clauses (both with no constraint on subject reference).

A schematic representation of the main contrasts opposing modal and non-modal readings is offered in Table 1:

Table 1: Contrast between the modal and the non-modal reading.

	Knowledge verb	
	Modal ("be able to")	Non-modal ("know that")
Complement clause	Infinitive	Participle / Finite complement
Embedded subject	+ Coref. with matrix subj.	± Coref. with matrix subj.
	NOT expressed	± expressed

In the non-modal reading, the lack of any constraint on subject coreference is associated with the fact that the matrix verb and the complement clause represent two distinct events[7] ('I have come to a city that has great power, *and* I know it', ex. (6a); 'your son is wise, *and* I know it', ex. (6b)), with independent temporal reference. By contrast, in the modal reading the matrix verb and the embedded infinitive represent a single event, and the embedded infinitive does not have independent temporal reference (cf. Section 3.2).

With respect to so-called "non-finite" complementation specifically, we observe a fundamental difference between participle and infinitive complements of knowledge verbs. Bare infinitives, in these structures, constitute a defective sentential domain (Pires 2006), in the sense that they do not contain autonomous specifications of certain features (primarily, tense and agreement), hence their subject establishes an obligatory referential dependency with the subject of the matrix verb.[8] Participles, instead, constitute an autonomous sentential domain, in the sense that, thanks to autonomous tense and agreement specifications, they are able to license their own subject, which remains therefore referentially independent from the subject of the matrix verb (cf. Bary and Haug 2011; Goldstein 2016: chapter 7; Benedetti and Gianollo 2020).[9]

---

[7] On the interrelation between argument coreference and event integration cf. Givón (2001: 40 and *passim*), Cristofaro (2003: 117–122).
[8] They fall into the class of "dynamic" infinitives; cf., e.g., Rijksbaron (2006: 96–98).
[9] The Ancient Greek data raise interesting issues (which we shall not dwell upon here) into the debated notion of finiteness / non-finiteness and its interpretation on morphological or syntac-

3 The dynamic modal construction: Syntactic analysis

In this Section we further explore the nature of the construction which enables the dynamic modal reading. In Section 2 we concluded that, for all the knowledge verbs examined, this construction involves a same-subject infinitival complement, and we preliminarily observed that bare infinitives of this kind can be considered a defective sentential domain. In this Section, we substantiate this claim by examining, on the one hand, the properties of the matrix verb (Section 3.1) and, on the other hand, the properties of the dependent infinitive (Section 3.2). This way, we propose an account for why the dynamic modal reading emerges precisely under these structural conditions.

In what follows, we will focus on the verb *epístamai* for exemplification.

3.1 Argument structure (knowledge verb)

In the pattern *knowledge verb + infinitive* (henceforth *dynamic "know"*), the knowledge verb fully retains its argument structure. Namely, it retains the ability of assigning a semantic role to both the internal (Section 3.1.1) and the external argument (Section 3.1.2).

3.1.1 The semantic role of the internal argument

The ability of *dynamic "know"* to assign a semantic role to the internal argument results from the parallelism between the infinitive and nominal complements. More precisely, the distribution of the infinitive complement shows remarkable affinities with nominal ones, both paradigmatically and syntagmatically.

Paradigmatically, the infinitive can alternate with a noun phrase, as shown in the Homeric passages in (12): depending on the participle of *oîda* (*eidótes / eidóte*), the genitive noun phrase *mákhēs (pásēs)* 'of (all) fight' alternates with the corradical infinitive *mákhesthai* '(to) fight'.

---

tic terms. Important assessments, addressing finiteness with reference both to Greek data and to general aspects, can be found in Joseph (1983). For the recent theoretical debate on finiteness cf. Nikolaeva (2007); Melum Eide (2016); Chamoreau and Estrada-Fernández (2016).

(12) a. ἐὺ εἰδότες ἶφι **μάχεσθαι** (*Il.* 2.720)
   eu   eidótes   îphi   mákhesthai
   well know.PTCP.NOM.PL forces.INSTR fight.INF
   'Well skilled *to fight* mightily'
b. **μάχης** εὖ εἰδότε πάσης (*Il.* 5.11)
   mákhēs   eû   eidóte   pásēs
   fight.GEN well know.PTCP.NOM.DU all.GEN
   'Both well skilled *in all fight*'

Syntagmatically, infinitive and noun phrase may also be coordinated, as shown in (13): here, depending on *epístamai*, the noun phrase *pollous katharmoús* 'many atonements' is conjoined with the infinitives *légein* '(to) speak' and *sigân* '(to) keep silent':

(13) ἐγὼ [...] ἐπίσταμαι / **πολλοὺς καθαρμούς**, καὶ **λέγειν** ὅπου δίκη / **σιγᾶν** θ' ὁμοίως. (A. *Eu.* 276–278)
   egō   epístamai   pollous   katharmoús   kai   légein
   I.NOM   know.1SG.PRS   many.ACC   atonements.ACC   and   speak.INF
   hópou   díkē   sigân=th'   homoíōs
   when   right.NOM   be.silent.INF = and likewise
   'I know many atonements, and to speak when it is proper and be silent in turn.'

Interestingly, as shown by (12)–(13), the modal dynamic reading is not exclusive of the infinitive complementation; rather, it represents a potentiality of the governing verb, compatible with both infinitive and noun phrase complements. Depending on *eidóte*, the noun phrase *mákhēs*, similarly to the infinitive *mákhesthai*, refers to an ability (that of performing fights); the same holds for the noun phrase *pollous katharmoús*, coordinated with the infinitive *légein* in (13) and referring to the ability of performing many atonements.

The commonality that noun phrase complements share in this construction is that their semantics allows an ability reading connected to performative knowledge. Note that the ability reading is not restricted to *action* nouns in a narrow sense (as in the case of *mákhēs* 'fight' in (12b), which we chose because it allows an immediate comparison with the inf. *mákhesthai* in (12a)). It also occurs with nouns which would be labelled as *concrete*, such as *aikhmḗ* 'spear' or *tóxon* 'bow'. Depending on *oîda*, these nouns may behave like action nouns ('the use of the spear', 'the use of the bow'): cf. *aikhmês eu eidṓs* 'well skilled in [the use of] spear' (*Il.* 15.525), *tóksōn eu eidṓs* 'well skilled in [the use of] bows' (*Il.* 2.718).[10]

There is an interesting asymmetry between infinitives and noun phrase complements: the latter are not associated exclusively with performative knowledge; e.g., in Pl. *Phd.* 61b, the object noun phrase *múthous tous Aisṓpou* 'the fables of Aesop', depending on *epístamai* refers to acquaintance knowledge ("knowledge of specific experiences involving persons, entities and events", Torrego 2019: 21) and thus does not produce a modal reading.

The affinity between the infinitive and NP complementation is further confirmed by the fact that the infinitive itself may be substantivised, being preceded by the definite article:[11]

(14) ἄναξ Ἄπολλον, οἶσθα μὲν τὸ μὴ ἀδικεῖν. (A. *Eu.* 86)
    ánax   Ápollon   oîstha   men to   mē   adikeîn
    lord.VOC Apollo.VOC   know.2SG.PRF   PTCL ART.ACC NEG do.wrong.INF
    'Lord Apollo, you know how to avoid doing wrong.' (lit. 'the not-doing wrong')

3.1.2 The semantic role of the external argument

Dynamic "know" retains the ability of assigning a semantic role to the external argument as well: namely, it imposes a [+animate] restriction on its subject, which is co-referent with the understood subject of the infinitive.

In view of the ability of the knowledge verb to assign a semantic role to the external argument, we shall assume that, when the complement is a bare infinitive, a mechanism of *control* accounts for the same-subject constraint (as seen in Section 2.3, a feature of dynamic as opposed to epistemic "know").[12] Cf. (15=5) where the control relationship between the subject of *epístatai*, i.e. *guné*, and the PRO subject of the infinitive *sōphroneîn* is highlighted:

(15) πᾶσα γὰρ ἀγαθὴ γυνὴ [...] σωφρονεῖν ἐπίσταται. (E. *Fr.* 909.3 Nauck) (= ex.(5))
    pâsa   gar   agathē   gunē$_i$ (PRO$_i$) sōphroneîn   epístatai
    all.NOM in.fact   good.NOM   wife.NOM   be.wise.INF   know.3SG.PRS
    'Every good wife knows how to be wise.'

---

10 For a thorough investigation of nominal complements with knowledge verbs in Latin, cf. Torrego (2019).
11 For an overview of the articular infinitive in Ancient Greek, cf. Fykias (2014).
12 On PRO and control infinitives in Ancient Greek cf., e.g., Joseph (2002); Sevdali (2013). On some debated issues on PRO in Modern Greek cf. Philippaki-Warburton and Catsimali (1999), with references.

For the control relation to obtain, of course, the subject of the embedded predicate must be compatible with the semantic prerequisite that knowledge verbs impose on their subject, namely, it must be [+animate].

3.2 Defective sentential domain (infinitive complement)

In the pattern *knowledge verb + infinitive*, the infinitive complement shows various hallmarks of a defective sentential domain (that is, of being a domain lacking certain features). Defectivity can, in turn, be argued to be responsible for the transparency of the embedded domain with respect to certain operations.

In this construction, the infinitive is defective for tense: in its inflection, we find only aspectual stems (present / aorist), and not forms necessarily carrying temporal values (such as future infinitives).[13]

In our corpus, the present strongly prevails quantitatively over the aorist: depending on *epístamai*, we have 87 present infinitives (from 62 different verbs) and 9 aorist infinitives (from 7 different verbs). Moreover, we found no instances of the same verb lexeme occurring in both present and aorist infinitive: this points to a sort of lexical distribution (rather than to a grammatical opposition).

As is generally assumed, lack of independent temporal reference is a mark of integration between the embedded infinitive and the main verb, which together represent a single event.[14]

A test that can be adopted to determine the defective nature of the embedded domain is the availability of an operation that points to the domain's transparent nature, namely clitic climbing. Clitic climbing takes place when a clitic argument

---

13 Future infinitives instead occur, expressing temporal values, in subordinate clauses depending, e.g., on verbs of thinking: cf. *oíomai* in *Il.* 3.341 (*kikhḗsesthai dé s' oíō* 'and I think I shall overtake you') and *Il.* 1.204 (*to de kai teléesthai oíō* 'I think this will come to pass') – respectively with and without subject coreference between the matrix verb and the infinitive complement. On the lack of temporal distinctions between present and aorist dynamic infinitives, cf. Rijksbaron (2006: 98, 102–103). By contrast, tense is encoded in the complementation construction of knowledge verbs with participles (which, as observed in Section 2.2, leads to an epistemic value for the knowledge verb). For example the present participle *óntes* and the future participle *kinduneúsontes* depending on the participle *gnóntes* 'knowing' are opposed as present vs. future in Th. 3.28: *gnóntes [...] oút' apokōlúein dunatoi óntes, eí t' apomonōthḗsontai tês sumbáseōs, kinduneúsontes* 'realizing that *they are not able* to prevent this and that *they will be in peril* if excluded from the capitulation'.

14 On the interrelation between *event integration* at the semantic level and *clause integration* at the syntactic level cf. Givón (2001: 40; on modality verbs, p. 55); Cristofaro (2003: 111–122); cf. also Noonan ([1985] 2007) on the correlation between dependent time reference and the reduced form of complements, and p. 68 for a specific observation on Ancient Greek infinitives.

of the embedded infinitive is realised in a position connected to the main verb, cf. Italian *lo* 'it' in (16):

(16) Italian
    a. *Francesco **sa** suonare bene il pianoforte.*
       'Francesco knows how to play the piano well.' (= can play the piano well)
    b. *Francesco **sa** suonar**lo** bene.*
    c. *Francesco **lo sa** suonare bene.*
       'Francesco knows how to play it well.'

In (16b) the pronominal object argument of the infinitive is realised next to the infinitive *suonare* 'play', whereas in (16c) it is realised next to the main verb *sa* 'knows' (i.e. within the main clause). Note that this is only possible when the main verb is complemented by a bare infinitive and has the dynamic modal reading. If the infinitive is preceded by the complementiser *di* and the main verb receives the "know that" interpretation, clitic climbing is impossible, as shown in (17):

(17) Italian
    a. *Francesco **sa di** suonar**lo** bene.*
    b. **Francesco **lo sa di** suonare bene.*
       'Francesco knows that he plays it well.'

Clitic climbing is considered to be a sign of the fact that the main verb and the infinitive represent a single syntactic domain, thus allowing for displacement of the clitic argument. This phenomenon, known in the generative syntactic literature as restructuring, is interpreted as a sign of monoclausality (see the discussion in Cinque 2004).

    Clitic climbing has been acknowledged to be a diagnostics for monoclausality also in Ancient Greek, showing that some infinitival complements form a single syntactic domain with their selecting verb.[15] However, in our corpus we find only two cases of clitic climbing with knowledge verbs in a dynamic modal reading, both from Homer and both with *epístamai*: *Il.* 16.141–142 (= 19.388–389), shown in (18), and *Il.* 21.320–321:

---

[15] Cf. Goldstein (2016: chapter 8) on infinitive complements and references cited there (especially p. 261 fn. 2); furthermore Janse (2008), with discussion.

(18) τὸ μὲν οὐ δύνατ' ἄλλος Ἀχαιῶν / πάλλειν, ἀλλά **μιν** οἶος ἐπίστατο πῆλαι Ἀχιλλεύς. (*Il.* 16.141–142 = 19.388–389)

to	men	ou	dúnat'	állos	Akhaiôn	pállein
DEM.ACC	PTCL	NEG	can.3SG.IMPF	other.NOM	Achaeans.GEN	wield.INF

allá **min** *oîos* *epístato* *pêlai* *Akhilleús*
but it.ACC alone.NOM know.3SG.IMPF wield.INF Achilles.NOM

'This (= the spear) no other of the Achaeans could wield, but Achilles alone knew how to wield it.'

In (18), the clitic pronoun *min* 'it' (the spear) is selected as an argument by the infinitive *pêlai* 'wield'; however, it is realised as an element of the matrix clause, in clause-second position (the so-called Wackernagel position). Goldstein (2016) interprets Wackernagel's Law as an interface phenomenon involving both prosodic and syntactic factors. According to Goldstein (2016: 293), the same generalizations on clitic distribution that he formulates for Herodotus apply to Homer as well, *modulo* differences in frequency that he attributes to a difference in literary genre (but not meter *per se*). Namely, pronominal clitics are clausal clitics: they occur in second position (that is, hosted by the first prosodic word) within a specific syntactic domain, represented by the clause (that is, a CP in formal syntactic terms). Hence, cases like (18), where a pronominal clitic occurs in the matrix clause despite being selected semantically by the infinitive, would show that the infinitive is not a full clause, and the main verb and the infinitive represent a single syntactic domain.

However, given the fact that we could retrieve only two instances in our corpus, the argument based on clitic climbing as a diagnostics of structural defectivity remains inconclusive for Ancient Greek.[16]

To conclude this Section, the strong semantic dependency between the matrix and the embedded predicate, which consists in the mechanism of subject control and in the creation of a unitary tense domain, points towards an analysis of dynamic modal uses of knowledge verbs in terms of monoclausality. What enables the dynamic modal reading of knowledge verbs is, thus, the presence of a single event, which is obtained either by means of infinitival complementation or, as we saw in Section 3.1.1, by means of appropriate noun phrase complementation.

---

16 An anonymous reviewer observes that, based on a preliminary query by means of Dendrosearch (see Keersmaekers *et al.* 2019), clitic climbing appears to be available with Ancient Greek verbs that exhibit an auxiliary-like behavior, such as e.g. *ethélō* 'be willing', *boúlomai* 'will', *méllō* 'be likely'. We are very grateful to the reviewer for useful discussion on this issue.

4 Have Ancient Greek knowledge verbs developed into modal verbs?

4.1 The lexical > functional cline

The syntactic analysis proposed for dynamic "know" in Section 3 coincides with the account provided by Wurmbrand (2004) for so-called lexical restructuring verbs.

Wurmbrand (2004) distinguishes lexical restructuring verbs from functional restructuring verbs on the basis of cross-linguistically observed properties. Functional restructuring verbs (e.g. German *scheinen* 'seem') fall into the class of auxiliaries: they do not possess an argument structure; the arguments are provided by the lexical complement predicate. Functional restructuring verbs are raising verbs (Wurmbrand 1999), in the sense that they do not assign a thematic role to the subject with which they agree in person and number; the subject receives a thematic role from the lexical complement predicate. Lexical restructuring verbs (e.g. German *versuchen* 'try'), instead, are full lexical verbs that retain their argument structure, hence assign a thematic role to their subject and their object. The co-reference with the subject of the infinitival complement is achieved through a mechanism of control.

We can understand the distinction between functional and lexical restructuring verbs as a way to formalise the different degrees that are cross-linguistically observed in the continuum from lexical to functional (auxiliary-like) predicates. Also for Ancient Greek we observe these different degrees in the case of premodal and modal meanings. This raises the diachronic question introduced in Section 1: is dynamic "know" moving along this continuum, that is, is its modal meaning emerging in a process of grammaticalization from a lexical to a functional verb? In other words: has dynamic "know" developed into a modal verb in Ancient Greek?

Grammaticalization clines with modals have been studied especially for the history of English (cf., among others, Traugott 1972; Lightfoot 1979; Bybee, Perkins and Pagliuca 1994; van der Auwera and Plungian 1998; Traugott and Dasher 2002; Roberts and Roussou 2003) and have been connected to semantic, syntactic and morphological changes. However, despite several recurring characteristics, modal verbs form a syntactically heterogeneous class, often also within the same language, thus the answer to the questions above is not straightforward.

For Ancient Greek, we lack clear syntactic diagnostics for modal verbs.[17] Based on cross-linguistic evidence, we take *bona fide* modal verbs to be auxiliary-like ele-

---

[17] But see de la Villa Polo (1989), who proposes some useful syntactic diagnostics to detect the auxiliary status of a class of verbs in Ancient Greek, comprising modal verbs.

ments of the functional lexicon appearing in monoclausal raising structures (that is, functional restructuring verbs in Wurmbrand's 2004 classification). In order to evaluate the status of Ancient Greek dynamic "know" on the lexical > functional grammaticalization cline, in Section 4.2 we compare it with the typical unmarked verb expressing dynamic modality in Ancient Greek, the verb *dúnamai* 'can', which is almost uncontroversially considered a modal verb (cf. Ruiz Yamuza 1997; Kölligan 2021; but *dúnamai*, as well as *epístamai* and *oîda*, is classed among "premodal" predicates by Allan 2013).[18]

4.2 An Ancient Greek modal verb: *dúnamai* 'can'

The behaviour of *dúnamai* shows affinities with that of knowledge verbs in the expression of dynamic modality. Also *dúnamai*, in fact, takes a same-subject infinitival complement, which is not inflected for tense (only present and aorist infinitives occur, without temporal distinction), does not allow an overt subject and allows clitic climbing; cf. (19):

(19) ἡ γῆ ἥδε οὐκ ἡμετέρη ἐστὶ οὐδέ **μιν** δυνησόμεθα ὑποχειρίην ποιήσασθαι. (Hdt. 6.107.17)
hē gê hḗde ouk hēmetérē esti oudé
ART.NOM land.NOM this.NOM NEG our.NOM be.3SG.PRS and.not
***min** dunēsómetha hupokheiríēn poiḗsasthai*
it.ACC can.1PL.FUT subjugated.ACC make.INF
'This land is none of ours, nor shall we be able to subdue it.'

In (19), the clitic pronoun *min* 'it' (the land) is selected as an argument by the infinitive *poiḗsasthai*; however, it is realised as an element of the matrix clause, in clause-second position, showing that main verb and infinitival complement represent a single syntactic domain.

By the way, the affinity between *dúnamai* and *epístamai* is already suggested by ancient commentators to Homer: in discussing (20), Aristonikos (Friedländer 1853, *ad loc.*) observes that *epistḗsontai* is used "instead of" *dunḗsontai*.

---

18 Allan's classification is based on semantic criteria: "premodal" predicates "assign an objective physical or mental property to a participant or his immediate situation" (Allan 2013: 32), whereas "modal" predicates are centered on the speaker's involvement in the conceptualization of the state of affairs.

(20) οὐδέ οἱ ὀστέ' ἐπιστήσονται Ἀχαιοὶ / ἀλλέξαι. (*Il.* 21.320–321)
    oudé   hoi   osté'   epistḗsontai   Akhaioí   alléxai
    and.not   him.DAT   bones.ACC know.3PL.FUT   Achaeans.NOM collect.INF
    'nor will the Achaeans know how to collect his bones.'

Anyway, the relationship between *dúnamai* and *epístamai* does not imply semantic equivalence. Let us compare the following Homeric passages, with the infinitive *mákhesthai* depending on *epístamai* and *dúnamai* respectively.

(21) νῶϊ δὲ καί κ' ἀγαθοῖσιν ἐπισταίμεσθα μάχεσθαι. (*Il.* 13.238)
    nôi   de   kaí k'   agathoîsin   epistaímestha   mákhesthai
    we.NOM.DU PTCL also MOD   brave.DAT   know.1PL.OPT   fight.INF
    'But we two would know well how to do battle even with the brave.'

(22) οὐ γὰρ ἀνὴρ πρόπαν ἦμαρ ἐς ἠέλιον καταδύντα / ἄκμηνος σίτοιο δυνήσεται ἄντα μάχεσθαι. (*Il.* 19.162–163)
    ou   gar   anḗr   própan   êmar   es   ēélion   katadúnta
    NEG   in.fact   man.NOM   all.ACC   day.ACC   to   sun.ACC   go.down.PTCP.ACC
    ákmēnos   sítoio   dunḗsetai   ánta   mákhesthai
    fasting.NOM   food.GEN   can.3SG.FUT   against   fight.INF
    'For there is no man who will be able the whole day long until sunset to fight against the foe, fasting the while from food.'

Epistaímestha mákhesthai in (21) refers to an ability specifically related to some intellectual skills (i.e. it falls into the domain of "learnt / intellectual participant-internal possibility", a specific subtype of the general "participant-internal possibility"; van der Auwera and Plungian 1998), whereas *ou dunḗsetai mákhesthai* in (22) has no such implication. What is negated in (22) is not someone's military know-how, but someone's possibility of fighting (in the specific case, undermined by fasting).[19] *Dúnamai* denotes a generic ability, thus representing the unmarked member in the *dúnamai* ~ *epístamai* opposition.[20]

This recalls the contrast observed, e.g., between French *savoir* and *pouvoir* and commented by van der Auwera and Plungian (1998: 82) to show the difference

---

19 This contrast is independent from the presence of the negation in (22). If we add a negation in (21), it is the know-how, not its actualization which would be negated. On the frequency of negated *dúnamai* in Homer, cf. Kölligan (2021).

20 *Dúnamai* is not restricted to the encoding of inherent / physical ability; cf., e.g. *trissas d' ou dúnatai pepitheîn phrénas oud' apatêsai* (*h.Ven.* 7–8) 'But there are three [goddesses] whose minds she cannot persuade or outwit', where the assumption of inherent / physical ability seems unlikely.

between *learnt / intellectual* or *inherent / physical* participant-internal possibility (cf. Section 1):

(23) *Ceux qui ne **savent** ou ne **peuvent** lire [...]* (Grevisse 1980: 800)
 'Those who do not know how to read (those that have not learnt it) and those who cannot read (e.g., the blind).'

The semantic component "learnt / intellectual ability" which characterises the modal uses of knowledge verbs is clearly related to the semantic restrictions on the subject's animacy observed above (cf. Section 3.1.2).

In this context, it is interesting to observe that knowledge verbs may lose this requirement during grammaticalization: for instance, in Italian it is possible to find dynamic "know" with an inanimate subject, as in (24).

(24) *Quella era proprio una giornata favolosa, come **sa** essere favolosa solo una giornata primaverile.*
 'That was really a beautiful day, as only a spring day can (lit. knows) be.'
 (CORIS1980_2000_SubCorpus:NARRAT)

However, no comparable cases occur in our Ancient Greek corpus, pointing to the fact that in Ancient Greek dynamic "know" is not as advanced on the grammaticalization cline as in Italian.

Pursuing the comparison between *dúnamai* and dynamic "know" further, we will claim that, besides not being semantically equivalent, the two verbs are not syntactically equivalent either.

As observed in Section 3.1, knowledge verbs in their modal uses have an argument structure, assigning a semantic role to the clause arguments. This property is not shared by *dúnamai*: on the one hand, it does not take object noun phrase complements as an alternative to the infinitive (differently from *epístamai*, cf. Section 3.1.1);[21] on the other hand, it does not impose semantic restrictions on the clausal subject (differently from *epístamai*, cf. Section 3.1.2).

---

21 An anonymous reviewer rightly points out that object noun phrases with *dúnamai* are indeed possible when they are quantificational (e.g. *Od.* 4.237: *Zeus [...] dúnatai gar hápanta* 'Zeus is indeed capable of everything'). In these cases, it is plausible to assume that these objects are not assigned a semantic role, but serve to measure out the event; hence, as adverbial measure phrases, they do not represent evidence with respect to argument structure. Interestingly, Lightfoot (1979: 101) notes that *can* was the last modal in English to lose the possibility of taking direct objects.

As can be easily shown, with *dúnamai* semantic restrictions on the clausal subject depend on the embedded infinitive. So, when the embedded infinitive is the verb 'see', as in (25), the clausal subject must necessarily be animate:

(25) δοιὼ δ' οὐ δύναμαι ἰδέειν κοσμήτορε λαῶν. (*Il.* 3.236)
 doiō   d'   ou   dúnamai   idéein   kosmḗtore   laôn
 two.ACC PTCL NEG can.1SG.PRS see.INF marshalers.ACC people.GEN
 'But I cannot see two marshalers of armies.'

By contrast, with a verb such as 'bear' (which admits both animate and inanimate subjects), the *dúnamai* construction preserves both possibilities: cf. (26), with an animate subject ('fools') and (27), with an inanimate subject ('ship'):

(26) τὰ μὲν ὦν / οὐ δύνανται νήπιοι κόσμῳ φέρειν. (Pi. *P.* 3.81–82)
 ta   men ôn   ou dúnantai   nḗpioi   kósmōi   phérein
 these.ACC PTCL thus NEG can.3PL.PRS fools.NOM grace.DAT bear.INF
 'Now fools cannot bear them (= evils) gracefully.'

(27) οὐδὲ φέρειν δύναταί μιν νηῦς εὐεργής. (*h. Bacch.* 18)
 oude   phérein dúnataí   min   nēûs   euergḗs
 and.not bear.INF can.3SG.PRS him.ACC ship.NOM sturdy.NOM
 'And our sturdy ship cannot support him.'

Given the absence of thematic restrictions imposed by *dúnamai*, the same-subject constraint with *dúnamai* is best explained through raising (and not control, as in the case of *epístamai*). The subject is selected and receives a thematic role from the embedded infinitive, and agrees in person and number with the modal verb (cf. Section 4.1).

4.3 Summary of comparison

The comparison between *dúnamai* and dynamic "know" leads to the following conclusions.

First, Ancient Greek *dúnamai* can be considered a dynamic modal auxiliary on the basis of semantic and syntactic tests; the relationship with the embedded infinitive can be analysed as a raising construction, in virtue of the absence of argument structure for the main verb. Ancient Greek *dúnamai* falls therefore in the class of functional restructuring verbs.

Secondly, in their ability reading, Ancient Greek knowledge verbs (dynamic "know") conform only in part to the modal pattern: they do not acquire the status of auxiliaries, since they retain their argument structure, as shown by semantic constraints imposed on their subject and by the possibility of taking NP objects. They fall into the class of lexical restructuring verbs, which take part in control constructions with their embedded infinitive.

In this respect, the answer to the question whether dynamic "know" has developed into a modal verb is negative: it has some hallmarks of auxiliary-like verbs, but it is not fully grammaticalised as a modal auxiliary.

5 Conclusions

In this Section we go back to the research questions formulated in Section 1 and we summarise the answers provided by our corpus study:

(i) What are the semantic and syntactic conditions that enable modal uses of knowledge verbs in Ancient Greek?

With respect to this question, we concluded that the dynamic modal reading appears when the knowledge verb is complemented by a tense-defective infinitival complement. In this structure, there is obligatory subject coreference, which we analysed as due to a mechanism of control. We furthermore characterised infinitives in these structures as a defective sentential domain, hence, as a particularly reduced predicative structure, which does not contain autonomous specification of tense and agreement features. This allowed us to address question (ii):

(ii) Why do precisely these conditions lead to the emergence of the modal reading?

Since in Ancient Greek the infinitive complementation of knowledge verbs with a dynamic modal reading is a defective sentential domain, semantically it does not constitute an autonomous predicational domain. This led us to analyse the construction as monoclausal and to conclude that the dynamic modal reading of knowledge verbs emerges when a single event is expressed by the combination of the main and the embedded predicate. This happens with defective infinitives, but also finds interesting correlates in nominal complementation. The structural defectiveness of the complement of knowledge verbs seems to be correlated with dynamic modal readings in a broader cross-linguistic perspective (see e.g. Cinque 2004 for Italian *sapere*; Roussou 2010 for Modern Greek *kséro*). These observations led us to question (iii):

(iii) Do the modal uses emerge diachronically as a step on a diachronic grammaticalization path from a lexical verb to a functional (auxiliary-like) verb? Or are they rather a stable feature of the language, to be explained by the co-existence of certain structural prerequisites?

We concluded that knowledge verbs in a dynamic modal reading retain their argument structure in Ancient Greek, hence they are still lexical verbs. In this, they are different from a modal verb like *dúnamai* 'can', which behaves like an auxiliary, with no autonomous argument structure. The main difference we detected is the presence of control with knowledge verbs, as opposed to raising with functional modal verbs.

On the basis of this conclusion, we believe that there is no ongoing grammaticalization in the case of Ancient Greek knowledge verbs. The verbs are not developing a fully functional variant in the sense of Roberts and Roussou (2003); van Gelderen (2004); Wurmbrand (2004). Our corpus study, comprising Archaic and Classical Greek texts, shows that dynamic readings of knowledge verbs are a diachronically invariant feature of the language in the period we surveyed. The knowledge and the ability value coexist (with different complementation patterns), differently from what is observed in e.g. the diachrony of English with *cunnan > can*. Similarly, instead, to the synchrony of English (*know that* vs. *know how*), in Ancient Greek the knowledge and the dynamic modal value are distinguished by the complementation pattern.

Interestingly, this coexistence, associated with different complementation patterns, persists, through lexical discontinuity, into Modern Greek, with *kséro* 'know that / know how' (on this cf. especially Roussou 2010). Thus, the phenomenon here investigated appears to be a long-term trend in the history of Greek, which survives the loss of the infinitive (Joseph 1983).

References

Aijmer, Karen. 2004. The semantic path from modality to aspect: *Be able to* in a cross-linguistic perspective. In Hans Lindquist & Christian Mair (eds.), *Corpus approaches to grammaticalization in English*, 57–78. Amsterdam: Benjamins.

Allan, Rutger J. 2013. Exploring modality's semantic space. Grammaticalization, subjectification and the case of ὀφείλω [*opheílō*]. *Glotta* 89. 1–46.

van der Auwera, Johan & Vladimir A. Plungian. 1998. Modality's semantic map. *Linguistic Typology* 2. 79–124.

Bary, Corien & Dag T. T. Haug. 2011. Temporal anaphora across and inside sentences: The function of participles. *Semantics and Pragmatics* 4. 1–56.

Benedetti, Marina & Chiara Gianollo. 2020. Criteria for subjecthood and non-canonical subjects in Classical Greek. In Bridget Drinka (ed.), *Historical Linguistics 2017: Selected papers from the 23rd International Conference on Historical Linguistics*, 30–48. Amsterdam: Benjamins.

Benedetti, Marina & Chiara Gianollo. 2022. The role of factivity in Ancient Greek complementation patterns. Presentation at ICAGL – International colloquium of Ancient Greek linguistics, Universidad Autónoma de Madrid, June 17, 2022.

Bentein, Klaas. 2015. Minor complementation patterns in Post-classical Greek (I–VI AD): A sociohistorical analysis of a corpus of documentary papyri. *Symbolae Osloenses* 89(1). 104–147.

Bybee, Joan, Revere Perkins & William Pagliuca. 1994. *The evolution of grammar: Tense, aspect and modality in the languages of the world*. Chicago: University of Chicago Press.

Chamoreau, Claudine & Zarina Estrada-Fernández. 2016. Finiteness and nominalization. An overview. In Claudine Chamoreau & Zarina Estrada-Fernández (eds.), *Finiteness and nominalization*, 1–10. Amsterdam: Benjamins.

Cinque, Guglielmo. 2004. 'Restructuring' and functional structure. In Adriana Belletti (ed.), *Structures and beyond: The cartography of syntactic structures*, vol. 3, 132–191. Oxford: Oxford University Press.

Cristofaro, Sonia. 1998. Grammaticalization and clause linkage strategies: A typological approach with particular reference to Ancient Greek. In Anna Giacalone Ramat & Paul Hopper (eds.), *The limits of grammaticalization*, 59–88. Amsterdam: Benjamins.

Cristofaro, Sonia. 2003. *Subordination*. Oxford: Oxford University Press.

Cristofaro, Sonia. 2008. A constructionist approach to complementation: Evidence from Ancient Greek. *Linguistics* 46. 571–606.

Cristofaro, Sonia. 2012. Participial and infinitival complement sentences in Ancient Greek. In Volker Gast & Holger Diessel (eds.), *Clause linkage in cross-linguistic perspective*, 335–362. Berlin & Boston: De Gruyter Mouton.

Faure, Richard. 2014. Argument clause. In Georgios K. Giannakis (ed.), *Encyclopedia of Ancient Greek language and linguistics online*. Vol. I, 172–178. Leiden & Boston: Brill. [First published online 2013: http://dx.doi.org/10.1163/2214-448X_eagll_COM_00000035].

Friedländer, Ludwig (ed.). 1853. *Aristonici Περὶ σημείων Ἰλιάδος reliquiae emendatiores* [New edition of the surviving parts of Aristonicos' *On the critical signs of* the Iliad]. Göttingen: Dieterich.

Fykias, Ioannis. 2014. Infinitives (Syntax). In Georgios K. Giannakis (ed.), *Encyclopedia of Ancient Greek language and linguistics online*. Vol. II, 229–236. Leiden & Boston: Brill. [First published online 2013: http://dx.doi.org/10.1163/2214-448X_eagll_COM_00000189].

van Gelderen, Elly. 2004. *Grammaticalization as economy*. Amsterdam: Benjamins.

Gisborne, Nikolas. 2007. Dynamic modality. *SKASE Journal of Theoretical Linguistics* 4(2). 44–61.

Givón, Talmy. 2001. *Syntax: An introduction*. Vol II. Amsterdam: Benjamins.

Goldstein, David. 2016. *Classical Greek syntax. Wackernagel's law in Herodotus*. Leiden: Brill.

Goossens, Louis. 1992. CUNNAN, CONNE(N), CAN: The development of a radial category. In Günter Kellermann & Michael D. Morrissey (eds.), *Diachrony within synchrony: Language history and cognition*, 377–384. Frankfurt: Lang.

Grevisse, Maurice. 1980. *Le bon usage. Grammaire française avec des remarques sur la langue française d'aujourd'hui*. 11e édition revue. Paris: Duculot.

Heine, Bernd & Tania Kuteva. 2002. *World lexicon of grammaticalization*. Cambridge: Cambridge University Press.

Hengeveld, Kees. 2004. *Illocution, mood and modality*. In Geert E. Booij, Christian Lehmann, Joachim Mugdan & Stavros Skopeteas (eds.), *Morphologie / Morphology. Ein internationales Handbuch zur*

Flexion und Wortbildung / An international handbook on inflection and word-formation. Vol. 17.2, 1190–1201. Berlin & Boston: De Gruyter Mouton.

Huitink, Luuk. 2009. Pragmatic presupposition and complementation in Classical Greek. In Stéphanie Bakker & Gerry Wakker (eds.), *Discourse cohesion in Ancient Greek*, 21–40. Leiden & Boston: Brill.

Janse, Mark. 2008. Clitic doubling from Ancient to Asia Minor Greek. In Dalina Kallulli & Liliane Tasmowski (eds.), *Clitic doubling in the Balkan languages*, 165–202. Amsterdam: Benjamins.

Joseph, Brian D. 1983. *The synchrony and diachrony of the Balkan infinitive: A study in areal, general, and historical linguistics*. Cambridge: Cambridge University Press.

Joseph, Brian D. 2002. On some control structures in Hellenistic Greek: A comparison with Classical and Modern Greek. *Linguistic Discovery* 1. 1–16.

Keersmaekers, Alek, Wouter Mercelis, Colin Swaelens & Toon Van Hal. 2019. Creating, enriching and valorizing treebanks of Ancient Greek. In *Proceedings of the 18th international workshop on treebanks and linguistic theories (TLT, SyntaxFest 2019)*, 109–117. Paris: Association for Computational Linguistics (ACL).

Kölligan, Daniel. 2021. Getting there? Greek δύναμαι [*dúnamai*] 'be able'. In Georgios K. Giannakis, Luz Conti, Jesús de la Villa & Raquel Fornieles (eds.), *Synchrony and diachrony of Ancient Greek*, 151–161. Berlin & Boston: De Gruyter Mouton.

Lightfoot, David. 1979. *Principles of diachronic syntax*. Cambridge: Cambridge University Press.

Melum Eide, Kristin (ed.). 2016. *Finiteness matters. On finiteness-related phenomena in natural languages*. Amsterdam: Benjamins.

Napoli, Maria. 2014. Aorist. In Georgios K. Giannakis (ed.), *Encyclopedia of Ancient Greek language and linguistics*. Vol. I, 136–137. Leiden & Boston: Brill. [First published online 2013: http://dx.doi.org/10.1163/2214-448X_eagll_SIM_00000415]

Nikolaeva, Irina (ed.). 2007. *Finiteness. Theoretical and empirical foundations*. Oxford: Oxford University Press.

Noonan, Michael. 2007 [1985]. Complementation. In Timothy Shopen (ed.), *Language typology and syntactic description*, Vol II, 52–150. 2nd edn. Cambridge: Cambridge University Press.

Philippaki-Warburton, Irene & Georgia Catsimali. 1999. On control in Greek. In Artemis Alexiadou, Geoffrey Horrocks & Melita Stavrou (eds.), *Studies in Greek syntax*, 153–168. Dordrecht: Kluwer.

Pires, Acrisio. 2006. *The minimalist syntax of defective domains: Gerunds and infinitives*. Amsterdam: Benjamins.

Portner, Paul. 2009. *Modality*. Oxford: Oxford University Press.

Rijksbaron, Albert. 2006. *The syntax and semantics of the verb in Classical Greek*. 3rd edn. Amsterdam: Gieben.

Roberts, Ian & Anna Roussou. 2003. *Syntactic change: A minimalist approach to grammaticalization*. Cambridge: Cambridge University Press.

la Roi, Ezra. 2020. The development of εὑρίσκω [*heurískō*] 'find' as evidence towards a diachronic solution of the matching-problem in Ancient Greek complementation. *Philologia Classica* 15(2). 191–207.

Roussou, Anna. 2010. Selecting complementizers. *Lingua* 120. 582–603.

Ruiz Yamuza, Emilia. 1997. Verbos modales en griego antiguo: δύναμαι [*dúnamai*]. In Francisco Rodríguez Adrados & Alfonso Martínez Díez (eds.), *Actas del IX congreso español de estudios clásicos, Madrid, 27 al 30 de septiembre de 1995*. Vol. II, 227–232. Madrid: Ediciones Clásicas.

Rzymski, Christoph, Tiago Tresoldi et al. 2019. The database of cross-linguistic colexifications, reproducible analysis of cross-linguistic polysemies. https://clics.clld.org

Sevdali, Christina. 2013. Ancient Greek infinitives and phases. *Syntax* 16(4). 324–361.

Torrego, Esperanza. 2019. The expression of knowledge in Latin: *Cognosco, nosco, scio, nescio* and *ignoro*. In Lidewij van Gils, Caroline Kroon & Rodie Risselada (eds.), *Lemmata linguistica latina. Vol. II. Clause and discourse*, 20–47. Berlin & Boston: De Gruyter Mouton.
Traugott, Elizabeth Closs. 1972. *A history of English syntax*. New York: Holt, Rinehart, and Winston.
Traugott, Elizabeth Closs. 2011. Modality from a historical perspective. *Language and Linguistics Compass* 5(6). 381–396.
Traugott, Elizabeth Closs & Richard B. Dasher. 2002. *Regularity in semantic change*. Cambridge: Cambridge University Press.
Tsohatzidis, Savas L. 2012. How to forget that "Know" is factive. *Acta Analytica* 27(4). 449–459.
de la Villa Polo, Jesús. 1989. La identificación de la auxiliaridad verbal en Griego. *Cuadernos de Filología Clásica* 22. 195–208.
Wurmbrand, Susi. 1999. Modal verbs must be raising verbs. In *Proceedings of the 18th West Coast conference on formal linguistics* (WCCFL 18), 599–612. Somerville, MA: Cascadilla Press.
Wurmbrand, Susi. 2004. Two types of restructuring – Lexical vs. functional. *Lingua* 114. 991–1014.

Martin Masliš
3 Information source and complementation in Classical Greek. The case of verbs of seeing and knowledge acquisition

Abstract: Verbs of visual perception and knowledge display a similar pattern of complementation in Classical Greek. Constructions governed by verbs of seeing may involve participial complements (usually in the accusative, henceforth AccPtcp), which prototypically refer to directly perceived states of affairs, and finite complements introduced by *hóti* 'that' or *hōs* 'that', which express knowledge acquisition. This pattern is mirrored by knowledge verbs, which allow AccPtcp as a minor complementation strategy alongside subordinate clauses with *hóti* or *hōs*. As a result, all three complement types may occur with predicates of knowledge, though the exact principles that govern their distribution are far from clear.

This paper aims to elucidate the synchronic functional differences between AccPtcp, *hóti* and *hōs* with verbs of seeing and knowing in classical Attic prose (the late 5th and 4th century BCE) by applying the notion of information source. It will be argued that AccPtcp with predicates of knowledge may serve as an evidential strategy to convey the values of visual source and circumstantial inference from the vantage point of the subject of the main clause. Both evidential values involve direct perception that underlies knowledge acquisition. The complementizer *hóti* often indicates propositional content that is underpinned by generally accessible evidence and is easily assimilated or already known by the participants of the communication. Finally, *hōs*, grammaticalized from the corresponding adverbial meaning 'how', may mark propositions that some interlocutors do not readily accept in the common ground of the communication. These uses of *hóti* and *hōs* match the distinction between intersubjective and subjective statements, which are conceptualized as evidentially contrasting. The hypotheses are tested on a corpus of forensic and political speeches by the ten Attic orators.

Keywords: Evidential strategies, complementation, inference, information source, intersubjectivity

---

Acknowledgements: This work has been supported by the Charles University Research Centre program No. 204053 (UNCE/HUM/016) and by the SVV 4 project at the Faculty of Arts, Charles University.

Martin Masliš, Charles University, Prague, e-mail: Martin.Maslis@ff.cuni.cz

https://doi.org/10.1515/9783110778380-003

1 Introduction

The aim of this paper is to analyze a group of selected Ancient Greek verbs of visual perception, knowledge acquisition, and the constructions in which they appear. These two classes of verbs, jointly with verbs covering other sensory modalities, are usually treated together under the label *uerba sentiendi* in traditional grammars – i.e. verbs denoting sensory and intellectual perception (e.g. Kühner and Gerth 1904: 50–51). Both classes display a similar complementation pattern in Classical Greek in that they admit both participial complements and subordinate clauses introduced by either *hóti* 'that' or *hōs* 'that'. This study focuses on the semantic differences between the constructions that involve the combinations of the verbs in question with any of the three complements. Accusative with infinitive (AccInf), which is marginal, is excluded for the reasons discussed below.

The exact principles that govern the distribution of complementation strategies in Greek are unclear; the outstanding issues are summarized in the following section. To address the distributional crux, I follow the line of research that purports that some syntactic patterns can be better understood by including the notion of information source in the overall picture.[1] Semantic distinctions that pertain to this domain may be grammaticalized, in which case we treat their exponents as evidentials and refer to the category as evidentiality (Aikhenvald 2004). Possible choices include *sensory source* (*visual* or *auditory*), *inference* (*circumstantial* or *generic*, also called *assumption*), *quotative* and *hear-say*. Even though most languages lack grammaticalized evidentiality, speakers may press other grammatical or syntactic structures into service to express source of information. This gives rise to evidential strategies. Employing this framework in Ancient Greek linguistics is not entirely new. Neuberger-Donath (1982) applies evidential distinctions to solve the crux of the distribution of *hóti* and *hōs*, but her paper at the time could not benefit from the more fine-grained typological accounts of evidentiality, which came only later. Van Rooy (2016) tests Neuberger-Donath's proposal on a corpus of selected works by Plato and concludes that evidential distinctions, alongside pragmatics and epistemic modality, play an important role in determining which conjunction is used. This paper subscribes to the methodological underpinning of these earlier contributions while taking advantage of the recent advances in the sub-field of evidentiality. In this way, a more coherent and typologically corrobo-

---

[1] I follow Aikhenvald (2020) who reserves the term "evidentials" for grammaticalized means while referring to the conceptual domain as "information source". I use the adjective "evidential" in the sense "pertaining to information source", but this convention should not suggest that I posit evidentiality as a grammatical category for Classical Greek.

rated account of the role of information source in Classical Greek complementation may emerge.

Regarding the domain in question, constructions governed by verbs of seeing and knowing are a suitable subject of research for the following reasons. Firstly, the lexical semantics of the verb often ensure that the sense of the construction belongs to the domain of information source (Aikhenvald and Storch 2013; Whitt 2010). Given the choice of the studied verbs, the focus naturally lies on the evidential values of visual source and inference. Secondly, the relative variety of the allowed complementation patterns opens the way to a fine-grained semantic analysis of evidential values in Classical Greek and the links between them. The hypothesis is that the relations between the constructions that share a common constituent – be it the type of matrix predicate or the complement – may be explained by comparing their distribution in Greek with the structure of the semantic domain as it is manifested cross-linguistically. One of the proposals put forward in this paper is that the component of immediate perception, which ties visual source and various types of inference together, predicts the use of the participle in the accusative (AccPtcp) with verbs of seeing and knowledge in Greek. Another evidential dimension applied to the data here is the notion of (inter)subjectivity (Nuyts 2001). It describes the degree to which the evidence that something is the case is shared among the participants of communication. Low intersubjectivity could be one of the factors that contributes to the use of *hōs* in some contexts.

The verbs selected for this study are *horáō* 'see' and its suppletive aorist *eîdon* 'see.AOR', which represent verbs of visual perception, and *gignōskō* 'come to know', *epístamai* 'know', *manthánō* 'learn', and *oîda* 'know',[2] representing verbs of knowledge. Complements with declarative infinitives, being as rare as they are, are not included because they cause the main verb to function as a predicate of propositional attitude (see Noonan 2007: 124–126 for this predicate type; cf. Benedetti and Gianollo, this volume). Consequently, the studied verbs will interest us only to the extent that they function as predicates of immediate perception or knowledge acquisition. Constructions with the matrix predicate in the passive voice (e.g. VERB$_{PASS}$ + participle in the nominative) have been excluded. Rare constructions with participle in the nominative, used when the subjects of the main clause and the participle are co-referential (Rijksbaron 2006 [1984]: 119) are not relevant for this study and have been likewise excluded. Subordinate clauses with *hōs* have been taken into

---

[2] The verb *oîda* 'know' is an inherited perfect containing the root *weyd- 'catch sight of'. The etymological connection to *eîdon* 'see.AOR' almost certainly does not carry over into the synchrony of Ancient Greek. The meaning 'know' (< 'having seen') is a Proto-Indo-European innovation as attested by the cognates in Indo-Aryan, Germanic, Slavic, and Celtic (Kümmel and Rix 2001: 665–667).

consideration only if the context in which they appear does not readily admit the interpretation 'how', which is the original meaning of *hōs*.

The hypotheses are tested on the corpus of the ten Attic orators (the late 5th and 4th century BCE), which comprises forensic and political speeches. The research corpus was selected as a subset of the TLG corpus and queried through the application Diogenes (version 4). The counts of analyzed occurrences are listed in Table 1. In the case of the frequent constructions *horáō* + AccPtcp, *eîdon* + AccPtcp, *gignṓskō* + AccPtcp, *gignṓskō* + *hóti*, *oîda* + AccPtcp, and *oîda* + *hóti*, a representative sample of the occurrences was selected and analyzed.

Table 1: Counts of analyzed occurrences in the research corpus.

	AccPtcp	hóti	hōs	TOTAL
horáō	120	29	4	153
eîdon	45	23	1	69
gignṓskō	20	45	17	82
manthánō	1	26	7	34
epístamai	20	56	2	78
oîda	73	120	14	207
TOTAL	279	299	45	623

This paper is structured as follows. In Section 2, an overview of existing literature and theories is presented. Section 3 discusses constructions that express immediate visual perception. Section 4 provides a detailed analysis of the evidential values expressed by predicates of knowledge complemented by participial phrases. Section 5 explores finite complements. The findings are summarized and conclusions are drawn in Section 6.

2 Existing theories about complementation in Classical Greek

The verbs in question admit four patterns of complementation in Classical Greek. Infinitival complements, realized as nominative or accusative with infinitive (AccInf), convey propositions with no existential presupposition (De Boel 1980: 293; Cristofaro 1996: 119, 2008: 578). Thus, verbs of knowledge and more rarely verbs of seeing with AccInf resemble verbs of opinion, which routinely take this complement (e.g. *nomízō* 'think', *hēgéomai* 'consider'). The information in the complement clause is presented by the speaker as an opinion of the subject of the matrix verb, which may or may not be true. Although the now-standard way of describing such constructions involves the relatively recent notion of non-factivity (Huitink 2009: 22–28 with references), the basic difference between the meaning of cognitive verbs with AccInf and the constructions with AccPtcp, *hóti*, or *hōs* is captured in older standard grammars as well (e.g. Kühner and Gerth 1904: 68–72; Schwyzer and Debrunner 1950: 395–396). Since infinitival complements code propositional attitude and not access to propositional content, they will not be given further consideration.

Differences between the other three complement types are less clear-cut. There is an agreement that clauses with *hōs* after verbs of saying in Attic may convey reservations on the part of the reporting speaker (Kühner and Gerth 1904: 356; Humbert 1960: 184–185; van Emde Boas *et al.* 2019: 504–505). Nothing of the sort is claimed about other types of governing verbs. This produces asymmetry, as *hōs* imposes a special modal meaning when used with one type of matrix predicate but not with others. A solution is proposed by Cristofaro (1996: 70–75), who argues that the opposition between factual *hóti* and non-factual *hōs* emerged because *hōs* signals presupposed content with low informative value. In factual contexts, clauses with *hóti* are said to prototypically carry the characteristics [+focus], [-topic], [-known], while *hōs* conveys [-focus], [+topic], [+known]. Thus, in the domain of pragmatics, propositions introduced by *hōs* are not asserted and do not advance the flow of communication, while the opposite holds true for *hóti*. The original contrast is supposedly mirrored by the modally distinctive meanings, as low information value can be connected with non-factuality and low speaker commitment. However, Cristofaro (1996) admits that the pragmatic distinction is not clear-cut and many contexts allow both conjunctions (cf. also Huitink 2009: 33, fn. 25). Moreover, the proposed semantic extension that requires *hōs* as a marker of presupposed and hence true content to signal non-factual and false propositions is problematic.

Neuberger-Donath (1982) attacks the problem of *hóti* and *hōs* by employing the notion of information source. She argues that in Homer, Herodotus, and the tragedies, the statements in the clauses with *hōs* represent the conclusions available exclusively to the subject of the matrix verb. Clauses with *hóti*, on the other hand, signify that the embedded proposition is based on the evidence that is also available to other interlocutors. Neuberger-Donath describes the opposition between *hóti* and *hōs* in terms of "objective" versus "subjective" statements. However, she neither provides much theoretical footing nor offers a cross-linguistic corroboration for her hypothesis, save for a remark about Turkish and the languages of the Balkan *Sprachbund* that possess evidentials. Her theory is taken up and expanded in Section 5 of this paper.

The original purpose of participial complements was to refer to directly perceived events in the construction governed by verbs of seeing. The complement is most often headed by a nominal in accusative or nominative. The latter is reserved for when the subject of the main verb and the participle is the same. When the complement appears with verbs of knowledge, its contrastive value is hard to pinpoint. The picture is further complicated by the fact that verbs of seeing may be used in a cognitive sense, which is the only possible interpretation when they are complemented by *hóti* or *hōs* (Cristofaro 1996: 118). However, as Basset (1999) rightly points out, the cognitive reading of verbs of seeing is not limited to finite complements – it also arises with AccPtcp. Thus, the problem of determining the principles behind the distribution of the three complement types concerns predicates of knowledge in general regardless of their lexical verbal class.

Huitink (2009) zooms in on the opposition between AccPtcp and *hóti* when they complement *oîda* 'know', *epístamai* 'know', and *gignóskō* 'come to know' in Classical Greek prose. To tease out the principles that regulate the choice of complementation, Huitink employs the notion of presupposition, which is twofold (Lambrecht 1994: 60–65). First, semantic presupposition, which concerns (semi-)factive contexts that contain new and asserted information, is said to be entailed by clauses with *hóti*. Second, pragmatic presupposition is signaled by AccPtcp and means that the information is the underlying theme of the narrative and can be retrieved from the preceding context. This solution takes AccPtcp to be a presupposition marker akin to *hōs* in Cristofaro's interpretation. Even though this analysis accounts for many of the occurrences of AccPtcp, there are contexts in which a participial complement conveys a foregrounded proposition. Resorting to a solution that allows a degree of license comparable to that which underpins Cristofaro's analysis would be possible but not entirely satisfactory. Finally, Faure (2017: 562) argues that AccPtcp with predicates of knowledge signifies that the speaker or subject "[has] access to an event that grounds the truth of the proposition *p*, and [believes] *p*". This essentially agrees with the hypothesis put forward in Section 4, which shows that assigning such a meaning to a syntactic pattern is not problematic.

The aforementioned issues are hard to overcome if we are to follow a predominantly pragmatic account of complementation. In what follows, I attempt to demonstrate that when information source is factored in, the distributional patterns become partially clearer. The first step in the analysis is to examine the expressions that convey immediate visual perception. After describing their syntactic and semantic properties in Section 3.1, I will argue in Section 3.2 that seeing and acquiring knowledge ought to be analyzed as distinct operations.

3 Participial complements and immediate visual perception

3.1 Syntactic and semantic properties

Coding of immediate perception in Classical Greek conforms to the typological tendency that participial complements are especially common in this context (Noonan 2007: 142; Cristofaro 2003: 105). The most common configuration consists of a nominal phrase in the accusative with a noun or pronoun that heads a participle (AccPtcp)[3] and serves as the direct object of a perception verb in the active voice:

(1) ὁ μὲν γὰρ **οὐδένα** ὁρῶν **διατρέχοντα**, πῶς ἂν ἐφυλάξατο μηδένα βαλεῖν; (Antiph. 3.4)
ho   men gar **oudéna**   horôn
DEM.NOM.SG PTCL PTCL no.one.ACC.SG seeing.NOM.SG
diatrékhonta,   pôs   an   ephuláxato
run.across.PTCP.PRS.ACC.SG how.Q   MOD keep.guard.3SG.IND.AOR
mēdéna   baleîn?
no.one.ACC.SG   hit.INF.AOR
'[My son] saw **no one running across**, so how could he have taken precautions against striking anyone?' (Translation K. J. Maidment)

In Functional (Discourse) Grammar and its layered model of clause structure, predicates of immediate perception take complements that denote states of affairs, as opposed to propositional contents (Dik and Hengeveld 1991; see Hengeveld and Mackenzie 2008: 128–281 on the model in general; cf. also a critical assessment in Boye 2010a: 394–401). In addition, some further semantic restrictions apply. The situation time of the main clause must be simultaneous with the situation time of the complement, which also cannot be modified by any temporal satellites. Furthermore, the state of affairs has to be perceivable and the verbal form in the complement cannot be negated. Another property of immediate perception is that it does not presuppose the truth of the complement, which results in non-factive reading (Dik and Hengeveld 1991: 240–242).

The requirement of simultaneity narrows the choice of participle. If the matrix predicate refers to the present time, the aspect of the participle can either be imperfective (the present stem) or resultative (the perfect stem). The perfective aspect

---

3 Predicates of seeing require a direct object in accusative. Verbs of hearing, e.g. *akoúō* 'I hear', may also take objects in genitive, which indicates that the stimulus is physically perceived.

(the aorist stem) is admissible only if the main clause refers to the past. In this case the perfective aspect does not code the action as anterior to that of the main clause but rather temporally bounded within the situation time of the matrix predicate[4] (van Emde Boas et al. 2019: 619). A complement with a perfect participle can convey immediate perception only if it describes a visible target state. It is important to note that the development of the Greek perfect in the post-Homeric period often renders it unsuitable to appear in the context of immediate perception. By the middle of the 5th century BCE, the morphology of the perfect stem encompassed both resultative and anterior perfects.[5] True resultatives entail a target state of the subject as a result of a preceding action, whereas anterior perfects project the relevance of a past event at the topic time. In contrast to target states, some of which are visible, relevance is not something that can be perceived through the senses. Consequently, immediate perception and anterior perfects are incompatible. Their co-occurrence with verbs of seeing ought to be interpreted as expressing acquisition of knowledge, which presupposes propositional reading of the complement:

(2) νυνὶ δ' ὁρᾶτε μὲν δήπου τὰ πλεῖστα **τοὺς προδότας ἀπολωλεκότας**. (D. 9.49)
    nuni   d'   horâte   men   dḗpou   ta
    now   PTCL   see.2PL.IND.PRS PTCL surely ART.ACC.PL
    pleîsta   **tous**   **prodótas**
    the.greatest.number.ACC.PL   ART.ACC.PL   traitor.ACC.PL
    apolōlekótas
    destroy.PTCP.PRF.ACC.PL
    'But now you must surely see that **traitors have caused** most **disasters**.'
    (Translation J. H. Vince)

Even the perfects that denote resultant states need not convey immediate perception when they complement verbs of seeing. If the emphasis lies on the visible resultant state and the anterior event that caused it remains backgrounded, the construction conveys visual perception. However, if it is the preceding action and its current relevance that are stressed, the complement is propositional, and we are dealing with the acquisition of knowledge.

---

4 For instance, Aeschin. 2.151.
5 The literature on the semantics of the Ancient Greek perfect and how it changed throughout the history of the language is vast. The account here and the use of terminology follow Bentein (2014). Haug (2008) and Allan (2016: 100–113) offer scenarios for how such a change from the resultative to the anterior perfect could have occurred. A comprehensive survey of the literature can be found in Crellin (2016: 11–16).

(3) ἑώρων γὰρ **τὴν** μὲν **πόλιν** τῶν Θηβαίων οἰκτρῶς **ἠφανισμένην** ἐξ ἀνθρώπων
[...] **τὰ** δὲ **σώματα** τῶν ἐνοικούντων **ἐξηνδραποδισμένα**. (Hyp. 6.col.7)
heórōn   gar   tēn   men   pólin   tôn
see.3PL.IND.IMPF PTCL ART.ACC.SG   PTCL city.ACC.SG   ART.GEN.PL
Thēbaíōn   oiktrôs   ēphanisménēn   ex
Theban.GEN.PL tragically destroy.PTCP.PRF.PASS.ACC.SG   from
anthrṓpōn   ta   de   sṓmata   tôn
human.GEN.PL ART.ACC.PL PTCL   body.ACC.PL   ART.GEN.PL
enoikoúntōn   exēndrapodisména
inhabitant.GEN.PL   enslave.PTCP.PRF.PASS.ACC.PL

'[The Athenian troops] saw **the city** of Thebes tragically **annihilated** from the face of the earth and **the persons** of its inhabitants **in slavery**.' (Translation J. O. Burtt)

In (3), the perfect participles *ēphanisménēn* 'destroyed' *or* 'that (it) had been destroyed' and *exēndrapodisména* 'enslaved' *or* 'that (they) had been enslaved' convey either visible states, i.e. states of affairs, or facts, i.e. propositions. This anticipates the point, elaborated in Section 3.2, that the boundary between sensory perception and the acquisition of knowledge is not clear when it comes to participial complements with verbs of seeing in Classical Greek.

3.2 Immediate visual perception and information source

At first glance, it seems straightforward that Classical Greek constructions denoting immediate visual perception in its prototypical form could be matched with the evidential value of visual source – i.e. the subject of the matrix verb knows that something is the case through having seen an event. However, the fact that the Greek constructions contain complements that are not propositional poses a problem. As we have seen in Section 3.1, complements conveying immediate perception denote states of affairs and not propositions, as it is only the former that can be perceived through the senses. Boye (2010b) persuasively argues that evidential meanings are associated with propositional contents as opposed to states of affairs. On the conceptual level, as Boye claims, the notion of information source cannot concern states of affairs couched *in* the real world; rather, it applies to objects of cognition, i.e. propositions, which are *about* the real world.

The fact that propositions are often supported by what is physically perceived should not suggest that the contents of sensory perception are somehow equivalent to the contents of cognition. On the plane of coded semantic meaning, constructions of immediate perception exclusively denote what is or has been in the senses (Dretske 1969: 20, 29; Schüle 2000: 1–8). From this follows that they lack the key part of the utterances that are marked for the evidential value of visual source. Namely, they do not convey any information that would be supported by visual perception, but instead they denote acts of visual perception itself. Another obstacle that prevents these constructions from being classified as semantically evidential is that the subject of the matrix verb need not believe that what s/he sees is the case (Dretske 1969: 29; Dik and Hengeveld 1991: 241):

(4) a. *Peter saw Thomas reading a book, but he thought Thomas was just asleep in the chair.* [immediate perception]
b. **Peter saw that Thomas was reading a book, but he thought Thomas was just asleep in the chair.* [knowledge acquisition]

Despite the lack of overt evidential semantics in these constructions, analyses of English and German data reveal that an evidential reading may arise as a conversational implicature.[6] In addition to describing an act of visual perception, an utterance or its context may pragmatically imply the acquisition of knowledge on the part of the subject of the matrix verb. On its face value, the pragmatically informed analysis may be applied to cases like the following:

(5) ὁρῶντες γὰρ **τὸν Εὐκτήμονα** κομιδῇ **ἀπειρηκότα** ὑπὸ γήρως καὶ οὐδ' <ἐκ> τῆς κλίνης ἀνίστασθαι **δυνάμενον**, [ἐσκόπουν ὅπως καὶ τελευτήσαντος ἐκείνου δι' αὐτῶν ἔσοιτο ἡ οὐσία]. (Is. 6.35)

horôntes	gar	**ton**	**Euktémona**	komidêi
seeing.NOM.PL	PTCL	ART.ACC.SG	Euctemon.ACC	completely

apeirēkóta	hupo	gḗrōs	kai	oud'	ek
fail.PTCP.PRF.ACC.SG	by	old.age.GEN.SG	and	not.even	from

tês	klínēs	anístasthai	**dunámenon**
ART.GEN.SG	bed.GEN.SG	raise.up.INF.PRS	can.PTCP.PRS.ACC.SG

'Seeing that **Euctemon was completely incapacitated** by old age and **could not** even leave his bed, [they began to look about for a means whereby all his property should be under their control after his death].' (Translation E. S. Forster)

---

6 See Dretske (1969: 166–167) and Boye (2018: 271); cf. also Whitt (2018: 140–143) for a slightly different analysis, and Boye and Harder (2009: 27–30) for a discussion of pragmatically conditioned evidential strategies. The matter is further complicated by the prevalent metaphor UNDERSTANDING is SEEING, which merges the two domains with potentially no traces of physical perception in the target meaning (cf. Sweetser 1990: 33). Such a complete transfer would apply to the constructions with unambiguously propositional complements like *horáō* + *hóti*. By contrast, I assume that the original meaning of the matrix verb remains relatively accessible to the participants of the communication if it is compatible with the syntactic type of the complement, e.g. *horáō* + AccPtcp.

In (5), the schemers who tried to obtain Euctemon's property witnessed firsthand his poor physical condition. Their subsequent plans imply that they knew that Euctemon was incapacitated. The pragmatic analysis amounts to drawing a distinction between expressed and implied propositions, the latter of which arise through implicature (Boye 2010b: 296). Accordingly, the complement *ton Euktḗmona apeirēkóta* 'Euctemon being incapacitated' expresses a perceived state of affairs, but at the same time it implies a covert proposition 'that Euctemon is incapacitated', which is supported by visual perception. While this analysis seems appropriate for English, which employs different complementation strategies to capture immediate sensory perception and acquisition of knowledge, it is less suitable for Greek. Since participial complements in Classical Greek are propositional when they appear with actual verbs of knowledge, a more straightforward solution is possible. Rather than claiming that an expressed state of affairs pragmatically implies or coerces a proposition, a more fitting description is that the context determines whether the complement is a proposition or not. The context of (5) requires that the schemers realized that something was the case, hence the complement *ton Euktḗmona apeirēkóta* is to be interpreted as a semantically coded (as opposed to implied) proposition dependent on a verb of seeing that serves as a predicate of knowledge.

It thus follows that the construction of AccPtcp with verbs of seeing is ambiguous in Classical Greek. Even if an occurrence fulfils all the requirements of immediate visual perception, the governing verb may be interpreted as a predicate of knowledge and its participial complement as denoting a proposition. What is more interesting is that in cases like (5), the propositional content (e.g. 'that Euctemon is incapacitated') represents a belief about a directly perceived state of affairs. In other words, the evidential value can be equated with visual source. This illustrates why it is not adequate to treat the opposition between cognition and perception as an either-or situation (cf. Basset 1999; Cristofaro 1996: 118). While it holds that seeing does not imply knowing and that knowing cannot be reduced to seeing, both domains may combine in the evidential value of visual source. I will return to this point in Section 4.

Expressions of pure immediate perception with no cognitive overtones are hard to identify. The reason is that human experiencers rarely see something without acquiring any knowledge about the world, especially when the situation is deemed worthy of a linguistic representation. Contexts that come close to this prototype emphasize visual imagery, either real or imagined, in which knowledge acquisition plays only a marginal role, if at all:

(6) [ἀλλὰ ταῖς γε διανοίαις ἀποβλέψατ' αὐτῶν εἰς τὰς συμφοράς], καὶ νομίσαθ' ὁρᾶν **ἁλισκομένην τὴν πόλιν**, τειχῶν κατασκαφάς, ἐμπρήσεις οἰκιῶν, **ἀγομένας γυναῖκας** καὶ παῖδας εἰς δουλείαν, πρεσβύτας ἀνθρώπους, **πρεσβύτιδας γυναῖκας** ὀψὲ **μεταμανθάνοντας** τὴν ἐλευθερίαν, **κλαίοντας, ἱκετεύοντας** ὑμᾶς. (Aeschin. 3.157)

kai nomísath' horân **haliskoménēn** tēn
and think.2PL.IMP.AOR see.INF.PRS capture.PTCP.PRS.PASS.ACC.SG ART.ACC.SG
pólin, teikhôn kataskaphás, empréseis oikiôn,
city.ACC.SG wall.GEN.PL destruction.ACC.PL burning.ACC.PL house.GEN.PL
agoménas **gunaîkas** kai paîdas eis
lead.PTCP.PRS.PASS.ACC.PL woman.ACC.PL and child.ACC.PL to
douleían, presbútas anthrṓpous, **presbútidas gunaîkas**
slavery.ACC.SG old.ACC.PL human.ACC.PL old.ACC.PL woman.ACC.PL
opse **metamanthánontas** tēn eleutherían,
late unlearn.PTCP.PRS.ACC.PL ART.ACC.SG freedom.ACC.SG
klaíontas, **hiketeúontas** humâs
weep.PTCP.PRS.ACC.PL beseech.PTCP.PRS.ACC.PL you.ACC.PL

'[Behold their disaster in your imagination;] imagine that you see **their city taken**, the razing of their walls, the burning of their homes; **their women** and children **led** into captivity; their old men, **their aged matrons**, late in life **learning to forget** what freedom means; **weeping, supplicating** you.' (Translation C. D. Adams)

In what follows, different evidential meanings associated with the expressions of knowledge acquisition are treated in detail. After examining the general properties of the expressions in Section 4.1 and noting their compatibility with evidential semantics in Section 4.2, Section 4.3 deals with the evidential value of visual source. Sections 4.4 and 4.5 are devoted to inference based on visual and other data. Some interim conclusions are drawn in Section 4.6.

4 Predicates of knowledge with participial complements

4.1 Syntactic and semantic properties

As we have seen in the previous section, verbs of seeing in Greek can also function as predicates of knowledge. This semantic extension is a cross-linguistic tendency (Sweetser 1990: 32–34; Dik and Hengeveld 1991: 238; Schüle 2000: 28–33). For the equivalents of *see*, Viberg (1984: 157–158) identifies the target senses of 'understand' and 'know', which also applies to *horáō* 'see' and *eîdon* 'see.AOR'. This shift to a different predicate class is often formally marked by a change in complement type. Different marking is motivated by the fact that predicates of knowledge are complemented by propositions, as opposed to states of affairs (Dik and Hengeveld 1991: 238). Cross-linguistically, complements that convey propositions tend to include predicates that resemble independent verbal forms (Noonan 2007: 130). This is borne out by the fact that predicates of knowledge in Greek, regardless of their lexical source, prototypically take subordinate clauses introduced by either *hóti* or *hōs*. However, the same predicates can also take AccPtcp, which spread from the constructions of immediate perception (Cristofaro 2012: 344; la Roi 2020).

According to the analysis of Dik and Hengeveld (1991), propositional complements with predicates of knowledge are not subject to the semantic restrictions that apply to the expressions of immediate perception. The situation time of the main verb and the complement need not be simultaneous, and the verbal form in the complement can be negated:[7]

(7) [οἱ δὲ φίλοι Ἀστυφίλου καὶ οἱ συστρατιῶται,] ὁρῶντες τὸν πατέρα τὸν ἐμὸν ἀρρωστοῦντα, **ἐμὲ δὲ οὐκ ἐπιδημοῦντα**, [αὐτοὶ καὶ προὔθεντο καὶ τἆλλα πάντα τὰ νομιζόμενα ἐποίησαν]. (Is. 9.4)
horôntes   ton   patéra   ton   emon
seeing.NOM.PL   ART.ACC.SG   father.ACC.SG ART.ACC.SG   my.ACC.SG
*arrōstoûnta   **eme**   **de**   **ouk**   **epidēmoûnta***
be.sick.PTCP.PRS.ACC.SG   I.ACC.SG   PTCL   NEG   be.at.home.PTCP.PRS.ACC.SG
'[Astyphilus's friends and fellow soldiers,] seeing that my father was ill and **I was not at home**, [themselves laid out the remains and performed all the other customary rites].' (Translation E. S. Forster)

Naturally, the state of affairs referred to by the proposition does not have to be visible. Concerning such participial complements in Greek, van Emde Boas *et al.* (2019: 617–618) state that the participle can have any stem and that its aspectual value carries a relative-tense implication. This predicts, for example, that aorist participles may refer to anterior events. However, this is rare in the case of verbs of seeing with a cognitive meaning in the studied sample of the corpus, as there is only one clear instance of an aorist participle with anterior reference after *horáō* (see example (16) below). Other occurrences of an aorist participle after *eîdon* are moti-

---

7 Other Greek examples of a negated participle with *horáō* and *eîdon* are Isoc. 4.48–49 and 10.18.

vated by the aspectual value of the stem and convey temporally bounded events or the starting point of a state:[8]

(8) ἤδη γάρ ποτε εἶδον **μισηθέντας τοὺς** τὰ τῶν πλησίον αἰσχρὰ λίαν σαφῶς **λέγοντας**. (Aeschin. 3.174)

édē	gár	pote	eîdon	**misēthéntas**
already	PTCL	at.some.time	see.1SG.IND.AOR	hate.PTCP.AOR.PASS.ACC.PL

tous	ta	tôn	plēsíon	aiskhrà	lían
ART.ACC.PL	ART.ACC.PL	ART.GEN.PL	near.ADV	shameful.ACC.PL	very

saphôs	**légontas**
openly	say.PTCP.PRS.ACC.PL

'Before now I have seen that **those who recount** too openly the shameful acts of those who are close to them **end up being hated**.'

To some degree, temporal depth can be expressed by the complements with a perfect participle.[9] As we have seen in Section 3, the perfect stem in Classical Greek can have the value of the anterior perfect or resultative, both of which entail a preceding event. Naturally, this way of referring to past actions is never divorced from the semantic component of simultaneity, since the perfect participle also conveys a resultant state or current relevance. As for the participial complements with *horáō* and *eîdon* that refer to posterior events, there are only two examples in the sample – D. 18.63 and the following one from Andocides:

(9) οὐδ᾽ ὡς ἄνευ ἀγῶνος ἑώρα **ἐσόμενα τὰ πράγματα**. (And. 1.122)

oud'	hōs	áneu	agônos	heóra
not.even	this.way	without	struggle.GEN.SG	see.3SG.IND.IMPF

esómena	ta	**prágmata**
be.PTCP.FUT.ACC.PL	ART.ACC.PL	matter.ACC.PL

'He saw that not even this way **the matter would turn out well** without a struggle.'

Besides these less frequent configurations, the participles in question most often appear in the present stem and convey simultaneity (cf. Duhoux 2000: 171).

---

[8] Aorist participles denoting simultaneous bounded events are also in Isoc. 14.41, 19.44, 19.46, D. 19.138, and Is. 11.37.
[9] For instance, Aeschin. 2.97, D. 9.22, and example (2) above.

Actual verbs of knowledge like *oîda* 'know', *gignṓskō* 'come to know', and *epístamai* 'know' differ from this pattern. Their complements do not disqualify aorist[10] or future participles[11] with a relative-tense implication:

(10) ἠπίστατο μὲν γὰρ **πολλοὺς** καὶ τῶν Ἑλλήνων καὶ τῶν βαρβάρων ἐκ ταπεινῶν καὶ φαύλων πραγμάτων μεγάλας δυναστείας **κατεργασαμένους**. (Isoc. 9.59)
*ēpístato   men   gar **pollous**   kai tôn*
know.3SG.IND.IMPF PTCL PTCL many.ACC.PL and ART.GEN.PL
Hellḗnōn   kai tôn   barbárōn   ek   tapeinôn
Greek.GEN.PL and ART.GEN.PL barbarian.GEN.PL from low.GEN.PL
kai phaúlōn   pragmátōn   megálas
and slight.GEN.PL matter.GEN.PL great.ACC.PL
*dunasteías   **katergasaménous***
dynasty.ACC.PL overthrow.PTCP.AOR.ACC.PL
'He knew that **many** Greeks and barbarians, starting from low and insignificant beginnings, **had overthrown** great dynasties.' (Translation G. Norlin)

Furthermore, present participles can stand in lieu of the imperfect in the corresponding direct speech and refer to a past event:[12]

(11) μαρτυροῦσι μὴ εἰδέναι **Ἀστύφιλον** ταῦτα **διατιθέμενον**. (Is. 9.10)
*marturoûsi   mē   eidénai   **Astúphilon***
testify.3PL.IND.PRS NEG know.INF.PRF Astyphilus.ACC
*taûta   **diatithémenon***
this.ACC.PL dispose.PTCP.PRS.ACC.SG
'They testify that they are not aware that **Astyphilus made such a will**.'

The likely explanation as to why the construction of verbs of seeing used cognitively + AccPtcp often retains the property of simultaneous reference is its affinity to the source construction that denotes immediate sensory perception. This original use, as we have seen in Section 3, is compatible with the present and perfect stem participles, which convey simultaneity, and the aorist participles that refer to

---

10 Other examples with *epístamai* in [Lys.] 6.49, Lys. 34.4, 15.122; with *oîda* in Isoc. 17.40, D. 18.85, Is. 6.64.
11 With *gignṓskō* in [D.] 33.16; with *epístamai* in Isoc. 6.62, D. 29.11; with *oîda* in D. 7.33, Aeschin. 3.99, Antiph. 1.13.
12 Other examples with *epístamai* in Lys. 7.7, 19.35, and 34.4; with *oîda* in Is. 6.64.

simultaneous temporally bounded events. On the other hand, no such limitations apply to the construction of actual verbs of knowledge + AccPtcp.

In the case of the construction of verbs of seeing + AccPtcp in which the complement does not carry any formal signs of propositional content, it is sometimes difficult to distinguish the expressions of knowledge acquisition from those that denote immediate visual perception. The most useful criterion appears to be the nature of the event referred to in the complement. If it cannot be perceived through the senses, the construction signifies the acquisition of knowledge. This, however, does not exhaust all the possible configurations in which the complement denotes a proposition. Disambiguation is sometimes possible only by gauging whether the subject of the matrix verb realizes that something is the case or not.

4.2 Predicates of knowledge + AccPtcp and information source

Constructions governed by predicates of knowledge, including verbs of seeing used in a cognitive sense, may convey evidential meanings (Whitt 2010; Boye 2018: 271). One of the enabling factors is that these predicates take complements that denote propositions. If we accept the broad definition according to which evidentials and evidential strategies are linguistic means that express the source of information in the utterance, propositional complements fulfil the information requirement. Unlike complements denoting mere states of affairs, a propositional complement refers to a piece of knowledge *about* a state of affairs. This overcomes the hurdle that rules out evidential entailment in the case of pure immediate perception.

4.3 Visual source

Determining the exact type of information source for a proposition is less straightforward. A suitable starting point for the enquiry is the construction of verbs of seeing used cognitively + AccPtcp. As we have seen in example (5), the conclusion that something is the case may be cast as a proposition that refers to a directly perceived state of affairs (cf. Faure 2017). Dretske (1969: 78–93) labels this configuration as primary epistemic seeing. This use of the construction can be disambiguated from its non-propositional counterpart in two ways. Firstly, the presence of formal signs of propositional content like negated verbal forms, as in (12), or temporal satellites points towards knowledge acquisition as opposed to immediate perception. Secondly, as some instances of knowledge acquisition or recollection do not formally differ from the contexts that denote immediate perception, the surrounding context may provide hints as to whether the subject of the main predicate acquires any knowledge. If s/he does, one possible evidential value is visual source, which is to be equated with primary epistemic seeing.

(12) [τοὺς μὲν οὖν ἄλλους ὁρμῆσαι πρὸς φυγὴν τὴν αὐτῶν σωτηρίαν ζητοῦντας,] ἕνα δέ τινα τῶν νεωτέρων, ὁρῶντα **τὸν πατέρα πρεσβύτερον ὄντα καὶ οὐχὶ δυνάμενον** ἀποχωρεῖν ἀλλὰ ἐγκαταλαμβανόμενον, ἀράμενον φέρειν. (Lycurg. 1.95)

héna   dé   tina   tôn   neōtérōn,
one.ACC.SG PTCL someone.ACC.SG ART.GEN.PL younger.GEN.PL
horônta   ton   patéra   presbúteron   ónta
seeing.ACC.SG ART.ACC.SG father.ACC.SG older.ACC.SG be.PTCP.PRS.ACC.SG
kai   oukhi   dunámenon   *apokhōreîn   alla*
and   NEG   can.PTCP.PRS.ACC.SG leave.INF.PRS but
egkatalambanómenon,   arámenon   phérein
catch.in.PTCP.PRS.ACC.SG lift.PTCP.AOR.ACC.SG carry.INF.PRS

'[Most men took to flight,] but one of the youths, seeing that **his father was quite old and could not escape** and that he was being overtaken [by the fire], lifted him up and carried him.' (Translation J. O. Burtt)

As for the part *ton patéra presbúteron ónta* lit. 'his father being quite old' in (12), it can be analyzed as referring to a proposition, perceived state of affairs or a perceived individual (*ton patéra*) + an adjunct participle with an adjective (*presbúteron ónta*). Dik and Hengeveld (1991: 250–254) treat equivalents of *presbúteron ónta* as predicative adjuncts and argue that they (a) temporally localize a state of affairs (in our case 'father is old') relative to the state of affairs expressed by the core predication ('a young man saw') and (b) serve as attributes to their head noun. Thus, expressions like this do imply perception of an individual, but the individual is conceptualized as involved in a state of affairs (cf. Rijksbaron 2006 [1984]: 118–119, fn. 2). Moreover, the context in (12) suggests that the complement also refers to a realization, which makes it a proposition (cf. Duhoux 2000: 298–305 for a similar interpretation based on different arguments). Similarly, the participle *egkatalambanómenon* 'being caught in' ultimately refers to a perceived state of affairs, but a propositional reading is unproblematic and fits the context at hand.

(13) εἶδον μὲν ἐγὼ καὶ οἱ συμπρέσβεις ἅπαντες **ὁμηρεύοντα τὸν υἱὸν** τὸν Κερσοβλέπτου παρὰ Φιλίππῳ. [καὶ ἔτι καὶ νῦν τοῦθ' οὕτως ἔχει]. (Aeschin. 2.81)

eîdon	men	egō	kai	hoi	sumprésbeis
see.1SG.IND.AOR	PTCL	I.NOM	and	ART.NOM.PL	fellow.ambassador.NOM.PL

hápantes	homēreúonta		ton	huion
all.NOM.PL	be.captive.PTCP.PRS.ACC.SG		ART.ACC.SG	son.ACC.SG

ton	Kersobléptou	para	Philíppōi
ART.ACC.SG	Cersobleptes.GEN	by	Philip.DAT

'I, as well as all my colleagues in the embassy, saw **that the son** of Cersobleptes **was a hostage** at Philip's court; [and this is still the case].' (Translation C. D. Adams)

In (13), the remark added after the utterance that describes what the ambassadors saw hints that the participial complement of *eîdon* also denotes a proposition. In both (12) and (13), the subject of the matrix verb acquires a piece of knowledge by directly observing a state of affairs.

Verbs of knowledge complemented by AccPtcp may be used in similar contexts, even though their lexical meaning does not stem from the domain of sensory perception.

(14) ἐπίστασθε δέ, ὦ βουλή, ὅσοι μάλιστα τῶν τοιούτων ἐπιμελεῖσθε, **πολλὰ** ἐν ἐκείνῳ τῷ χρόνῳ **δασέα ὄντα** ἰδίαις καὶ μορίαις ἐλάαις, [ὧν νῦν τὰ πολλὰ ἐκκέκοπται]. (Lys. 7.7)

epístasthe	dé,	ô	boulḗ,	hósoi	málista
know.2PL.IND.PRS	PTCL	INTJ	council.VOC.SG	REL.NOM.PL	especially

tôn	toioútōn	epimeleîsthe,	**polla**
ART.GEN.PL	such.things.GEN.PL	take.care.of.2PL.IND.PRS	many.N.ACC.PL

en	ekeínōi	tôi	khrónōi	**daséa**
in	that.DAT.SG	ART.DAT.SG	time.DAT.SG	thickly.wooded.N.ACC.PL

ónta	idíais	kai
be.PTCP.PRS.ACC.PL	private.DAT.PL	and

moríais	eláais
of.burial.DAT.PL	olive.tree.DAT.PL

'You are aware, gentleman – especially those of you who have the supervision of such matters – that **many plots** at that time **were thick** with private and sacred olive-trees [which have now for the most part been uprooted].' (Translation W. R. M. Lamb)

(15) [Τελέδημος Κλέωνος, Ὑπερείδης Καλλαίσχρου, Νικόμαχος Διοφάντου] μαρτυροῦσι [...] εἰδέναι **Αἰσχίνην** Ἀτρομήτου **Κοθωκίδην συνερχόμενον** νυκτὸς εἰς τὴν Θράσωνος οἰκίαν καὶ **κοινολογούμενον** Ἀναξίνῳ. (D. 18.137)
marturoûsi   eidénai   **Aiskhínēn**   Atromḗtou
testify.3PL.IND.PRS know.INF.PRF Aeschines.ACC Atrometus.GEN
Kothōkídēn   **sunerkhómenon**   nuktós   eis   tḗn
of.Cothocidae.ACC   come.PTCP.PRS.ACC.SG   night.GEN.SG   to   ART.ACC.SG
Thrásōnos   oikían   kaì   **koinologoúmenon**   Anaxínōi
Thraso.GEN house.ACC.SG and communicate.PTCP.PRS.ACC.SG Anaxinus.DAT
'[Teledemus, son of Cleon, Hypereides, son of Callaeschrus, Nicomachus, son of Diophantus,] testify that to their knowledge **Aeschines**, son of Atrometus, **of Cothocidae, comes** by night to the house of Thraso and **holds communication** with Anaxinus.' (Translation C. A. Vince and J. H. Vince)

In (14), the speaker reminds the councilmen of a fact they likely know from personal experience. The deposition of the witnesses in (15) most probably entails that they saw what Aeschines did.

4.4 Circumstantial inference based on visual perception

Not all occurrences of the construction entail knowledge about an event perceived firsthand. The experiencer may physically see an event, realize that what s/he sees is the case, and infer that something else must be true. The state of affairs referred to in the deduced proposition does not have to be visible or directly accessible to the experiencer. Dretske (1969: 153) calls this type of knowledge acquisition "secondary epistemic seeing". The evidential value that applies here is circumstantial inference based on visual input (Anderson 1986: 274–275).

(16) ὁρῶντες **αὐτοὺς** οὐ μόνον τοῖς σώμασιν ἡμῶν ἀλλὰ καὶ τοῖς ἀναθήμασι **πολεμήσαντας.** (Isoc. 4.156)
horôntes   **autoús**   ou   mónon   toîs   sṓmasin
seeing.NOM.PL they.M.ACC.PL NEG only ART.DAT.PL body.DAT.PL
hēmôn   alla   kaì   toîs   anathḗmasi   **polemḗsantas**
we.GEN   but   also ART.DAT.PL offering.DAT.PL wage.war.PTCP.AOR.ACC.PL
'[Future generations shall comprehend the impiety of the Persians,] seeing that **they waged that war** not against our persons only, but even against our votive offerings to the gods.' (Translation G. Norlin)

In (16), the subject of the participle *horôntes* 'seeing' could not see the Persians damaging the sanctuaries firsthand. It is rather through seeing the ruins themselves that future generations may infer that the war was waged in a particular way. Further examples of circumstantial inference can be quoted:

(17) τούτῳ μὲν οὖν ἑώρα **ἕνα** μόνον **υὸν ὄντα**. (Is. 2.10)
 toútōi   men oûn heóra   héna   mónon
 this.DAT.SG PTCL PTCL see.3SG.IND.IMPF one.M.ACC.SG only
 huon   ónta
 son.ACC.SG be.PTCP.PRS.ACC.SG
 'He saw that this one [i.e. my opponent] had only one son.' (Translation E. S. Forster)

(18) ἑτέραν γὰρ ἐγὼ γέγραφα μαρτυρίαν τοῖς εἰδόσι **Τίμαρχον τουτονὶ καταλιπόντα** τὴν πατρῴαν οἰκίαν καὶ **διαιτώμενον** παρὰ Μισγόλα. (Aeschin. 1.47)
 hetéran   gar   egō   gégrapha   marturían
 other.ACC.SG PTCL I.NOM write.1SG.IND.PRF affidavit.ACC.SG
 *toîs   eidósi   **Tímarkhon   toutoni***
 ART.DAT.PL know.PTCP.PRF.DAT.PL Timarchus.ACC this.ACC
 katalipónta   *tēn   patrṓian   oikían   kai*
 leave.PTCP.AOR.ACC.SG ART.ACC.SG of.father.ACC.SG house.ACC.SG and
 diaitṓmenon   *para Misgóla*
 live.PTCP.PRS.ACC.SG by   Misgolas.GEN
 'For I have prepared another affidavit for those who know that **this man Timarchus left** his father's house and **lived** with Misgolas.' (Translation C. D. Adams)

It would be a stretch to claim that the states of affairs denoted by the complements in these examples can be visually perceived. In each case, the subject of the matrix verb could not have arrived at the realization that something is the case solely through immediate perception. In (17), observing the litigant in various life situations leads to the conclusion that he cannot have more than one son. The witnesses in (18) similarly infer something about the living arrangement of Timarchus based on observing his whereabouts. In all these examples, some mental effort on the part of the experiencer is required that allows him or her to deduce some unobvious truth based on what is visually perceived.

It could be argued that cases like (17) and (18) in fact refer to states of affairs that are directly witnessed and thus represent visual source. It is true that grammatical inferentials in the languages of the world are often used when the speaker observes some traces after the event itself (De Haan 2001: 195). Such occurrences are clearly non-firsthand because the anteriority of the event entails that it could not be witnessed. However, simultaneous inferences are also attested (Aikhenvald 2004: 102). The objection chiefly bears on the question of what can be seen in a primary epistemic way and where the line is between visual source (i.e. firsthand) and circumstantial inference (i.e. non-firsthand) based on visual perception. Both evidential values involve some cognitive effort to get from the content of perception to a piece of information. The approach adopted here allots a wider range of possible meanings to circumstantial inference and reserves visual source for the cases when the output of the visual apparatus closely resembles the belief content and not much deducing is needed. In other words, visual source describes what a naïve observer with limited encyclopedic knowledge might learn about the world by simply observing his or her environment, while circumstantial inference requires more effort to acquire a piece of knowledge.

4.5 Circumstantial inference based on direct perception

Some occurrences of the construction refer to knowledge acquisition that is not supported by purely visual perception. The subject of the matrix verb may draw upon all types of sensory evidence to acquire a piece of knowledge. For instance, one can visually observe human behavior and its effect on the physical world while also following what the people in question are saying. This broad evidential basis means that the state of affairs spelled out in the complement may be cognitively complex and point to abstract referents.

(19) ὁρῶ δέ, ὦ ἄνδρες, τὴν πλείστην διατριβὴν τῶν λόγων **ποιούμενον** περὶ τὴν τοῦ παιδὸς οὐσίαν καὶ περὶ τὴν ἐμήν. (Is. 11.37)
horô   dé,   ô   ándres,   tēn   pleístēn
see.1SG.IND.PRS PTCL INTJ man.VOC.PL ART.ACC.SG most.ACC.SG
*diatribēn   tôn   lógōn   **poioúmenon**   peri*
speech.ACC.SG ART.GEN.PL word.GEN.PL make.PTCP.PRS.ACC.SG about
tēn   toû   paidos   ousían   kai   peri
ART.ACC.SG ART.GEN.SG child.GEN.SG property.ACC.SG and about
tēn   emḗn
ART.ACC.SG my.ACC.SG
'I notice, gentlemen, that [my opponent] embarks on (lit. **makes**) a lengthy discussion of my fortune and of that of the child.' (Translation E. S. Forster)

(20) εἴτε βοηθησάντων μόνον ὑμῶν εἰς Ὄλυνθον, ἀκινδύνως ὁρῶν **ἔχοντα τὰ οἴκοι**, [προσκαθεδεῖται καὶ προσεδρεύσει τοῖς πράγμασι, περιέσται τῷ χρόνῳ τῶν πολιορκουμένων]. (D. 1.18)

eíte	boēthēsántōn		mónon	humôn	eis	Ólunthon,
or	help.PTCP.AOR.GEN.PL		only	you.GEN.PL	to	Olynthus.ACC
akindúnōs	horôn			**ékhonta**	**ta**	**oíkoi**
safely	see.PTCP.PRS.NOM.SG			have.PTCP.PRS.ACC.PL	ART.ACC.PL	at.home

'Or if you confine yourselves to helping Olynthus, [Philip] will know that **his base is** secure (lit. the things at home have it safely) [and will give close and undivided attention to his operations, until at last he overcomes the resistance of the besieged].' (Translation J. H. Vince)

(21) ἐπιστάμεθα **Μειδίαν πείθοντα** τόν τε Στράτωνα τὸν διαιτητὴν καὶ ἡμᾶς, [ὄντας ἐκείνοις τοῖς χρόνοις ἄρχοντας, ὅπως τὴν δίαιταν αὐτῷ ἀποδιαιτήσομεν], καὶ **διδόντα** δραχμὰς πεντήκοντα. (D. 21.93)

epistámetha	**Meidían**	**peíthonta**		tón=te
know.1PL.IND.PRS	Meidias.ACC	persuade.PTCP.PRS.ACC.SG		ART.ACC.SG=and
Strátōna	ton	diaitētēn	kai	hēmâs
Strato.ACC	ART.ACC.SG	arbitrator.ACC.SG	and	we.ACC
kai	**didónta**	drakhmas	pentḗkonta	
and	give.PTCP.PRS.ACC.SG	drachm.ACC.PL	fifty	

'We know that **Meidias tried to induce** Strato, the arbitrator, and us, [who were at that time archons, to reverse the judgement against him,] and **he offered** us fifty drachmas.' (Translation A. T. Murray)

In (19), the speaker refers to the content of the speech made by the other litigant. Naturally, he cannot physically see what the speech is about, as this can be learnt only by listening to what the opponent has to say. Example (20) illustrates the point that evidence is not limited to the outputs of the visual apparatus but also includes the overall perception of one's environment. I propose that the AccPtcp here is motivated by the fact that Philip collects the evidence himself and independently deduces that something is the case. Note that the evidential value would not be hear-say even if some partial evidence stemmed from messenger reports. The difference is that hear-say concerns reported propositions, whereas inference may involve reported evidence, which is in turn used to independently deduce a conclusion. The AccPtcp in (21) is more prototypical because the witnesses rely on sensory data that exceed the purely visual.

4.6 Interim conclusions

How can we make sense of these three types of knowledge acquisition and the fact that they are coded by the same Greek construction? The key point is that visual source and circumstantial inference are structurally similar. De Haan (2001) argues that all evidential values can be described by a combination of two features, [+/-direct] and [+/-firsthand]. The feature [+firsthand] refers to witnessed events and [+direct] points to personal access to evidence. According to De Haan, circumstantial inference is the only value marked by the non-aligned features [+direct] and [-firsthand] – i.e. the speaker does not witness the event s/he is referring to [-firsthand], but s/he has direct access to the evidence [+direct]. In evidential systems of different languages, inference can formally pattern with either visual source (both [+direct]) or hear-say (both [-firsthand]). Although De Haan postulates that [+direct] excludes reported evidence, I claim that the feature ought to be understood according to the way in which the evidence is used. If the subject relies on the evidence to independently arrive at a realization, the feature [+direct] is warranted. This modification still produces the original distribution of visual ([+direct]), circumstantial inference ([+direct]), and hear-say ([-direct]), since the last value entails that the proposition and not just the underlying evidence is reported.

The Classical Greek construction of predicates of knowledge with AccPtcp follows the feature [+direct]. The construction signifies that the subject of the main verb independently realizes that something is the case based on the available evidence. The pattern of polysemy we have examined branches out from the non-evidential use of the construction of verbs of seeing + AccPtcp, which denotes immediate visual perception. The semantic component of direct perception is retained when the construction denotes knowledge acquisition. As we progress from visual source to circumstantial inference based on direct perception of any kind, the perceptual basis broadens. As the evidence becomes more complex and possibly spreads over space and time, the process of inferring becomes less trivial.

This analysis also explains why AccPtcp can sometimes lead to the implication of presupposed content (Huitink 2009). The construction is motivated by direct access to the evidence and independent inferring, which may be limited to the subject of the matrix verb. This orientation towards the subject sometimes involves propositions that are already known to other interlocutors or, alternatively, refer to personal knowledge about hypothetical events (cf. Faure 2017).[13] Thus, participial

---

[13] The fact that participial complements cannot be equated with factual statements or real events is also pointed out by la Roi (2020: 201–204), who adduces examples of *heurískō* 'find' + AccPtcp that

complements do not entail asserted propositions, but rather propositions justified by the personal experience and deduction of the subject. This means that the construction may occasionally imply strong assertion, as in the witness reports quoted in this section, but it is not a coded semantic property. Furthermore, the component of subjective reasoning explains why general truths are only very rarely expressed by AccPtcp with predicates of knowledge.[14] Rather than with AccPtcp, culturally shared knowledge and hence the domain of intersubjectivity in general seem to be associated with finite complements, to which we now turn.

5 Finite complements with *hóti* and *hōs*

While there is a scholarly consensus that clauses with *hōs* after verbs of speaking tend to convey low speaker commitment in Attic, the same is not claimed about other predicate types. We have seen in Section 2 that to account for the overall distribution, explanations couched purely in pragmatics are not sufficient. However, it is possible to re-frame the difference between the two conjunctions in terms of information source, so that no asymmetry across predicate types arises. I propose that shared access to evidence and shared conclusions are predominantly associated with *hóti*, while non-adverbial *hōs* marks propositions whose truth is not accepted in the common ground of the communication at the time of utterance. I agree with Cristofaro (1996: 75) that complements with *hōs* are semantically non-assertive, which ultimately follows from the etymological meaning 'how / by means of' of the conjunction. Such subordinate clauses, however, do not always convey presupposition. Clauses introduced by adverbial connectors may merely imply that the underlying proposition is true (e.g. 'I know how you did it' → 'You did it'), but they do not entail it (e.g. 'I know how loyal you are' → 'You are not loyal at all'), since the referred-to manner or intensity may be such that the state of affairs does not occur at all. This lack of asserted propositional content also marks complements introduced by non-adverbial *hōs*, and it may manifest itself in the realm of information source.

---

convey propositional attitude, the meaning usually reserved for AccInf. This likewise indicates that the motivating factors behind AccPtcp are not just pragmatic presupposition or factivity.

14 A curious exception are the clauses in which the subject is a god, hero, or lawgiver (e.g. Isoc. 10.17, D. 36.27). If the analysis presented here is correct, the privileged epistemic position of superhuman beings implied by AccPtcp may be comparable to the special status of Amazonian shamans, which are entitled to use visual evidentials when ordinary humans cannot (Aikhenvald and Storch 2013: 32–33).

The new proposal accounts for low primary speaker commitment with verbs like *légō* 'speak' + *hōs*. The statement in the subordinate clause, which is usually reported, is not justified by generally accessible evidence and is not to be accepted by the participants of the communication. Regarding predicates of knowledge, the lack of acceptance at the time of utterance is most often descriptive rather than prescriptive, as it may concern only the audience, while the speaker does not express any misgivings about the embedded proposition. Almost all the contexts in which non-adverbial *hōs* appears in the studied corpus entail that the audience has not yet accepted that something is the case. This interpretation follows from the morphosyntax of the main clause, which may display one of the following features:

a) Negated matrix predicate;[15] matrix predicate with negative semantic load: e.g. D. 23.123 (*eîdon*); Isoc. 8.32, 14.25 (*oîda*)
b) Matrix predicate in the future tense: e.g. Isoc. 17.40, D. 1.14 (*gignóskō*); And. 2.22, Is. 10.3, [D.] 40.52 (*oîda*)
c) Matrix predicate as a dynamic infinitive: e.g. Isoc. 21.8, D. *Ex.* 1.2 (*gignóskō*); Isoc. 18.4, D. 27.55, [D.] 59.14, Is. 3.67 (*manthánō*);
d) Matrix predicate in a purpose clause: D. 55.8, [D.] 40.5, 46.18 (*oîda*)
e) Matrix predicate in a non-indicative mood: Isoc. 18.4 (*manthánō*); Isoc. 5.32, Isoc. *L.* 2.15, D. 34.47 (*gignóskō*).

The following examples illustrate points a), b), and c) respectively.

(22) καὶ μὴν **οὐδ' ἐκεῖνό** γ' **ὁρῶ, ὡς** τῇ μὲν πόλει ἀσφαλὲς τὸ τὰ αὐτῆς πράττειν, σοὶ δὲ κίνδυνος, [εἰ μηδὲν τῶν ἄλλων πλέον περιεργάσει]. ([D.] 10.72)
kai mēn **oud' ekeînó** g' **horô,** **hōs**
and PTCL not.even that.ACC.SG PTCL see.1SG.IND.PRS COMPL
têi men pólei asphales to ta
ART.DAT.SG PTCL city.DAT.SG safe.NOM.SG ART.NOM.SG ART.ACC.PL
hautês práttein, soi de kíndunos
herself.GEN.SG do.INF.PRS you.DAT.SG PTCL danger.NOM.SG
'And there is **another thing I do not see – that** it is safe for the state to mind its own business, but dangerous for you [if you do not go beyond your fellow-citizens in meddling with affairs].' (Translation J. H. Vince)

---

15 The tendency of *hōs* to occur with negated matrix verbs is also mentioned by Kühner and Gerth (1904: 356), who adduce an example with *ereî* '[nobody] will say' (X. *An.* 1.3.5).

(23) ὡς δὲ ἀληθῆ **λέγω**, ἐκ τῶν ψηφισμάτων **γνώσεσθε** ἃ ἐψηφίσατο ἡ βουλὴ περὶ αὐτῆς. (Is. 6.50)
hōs de alēthê **légō**, ek tôn
COMPL PTCL true.ACC.PL speak.1SG.IND.PRS from ART.GEN.PL
psēphismátōn **gnṓsesthe** ha
decree.GEN.PL come.to.know.2PL.IND.FUT which.ACC.PL
epsēphísato hē boulḗ peri autês
vote.3SG.IND.AOR ART.NOM.SG council.NOM.SG about she.GEN
'**That I am speaking** the truth [i.e. that the woman in not a free-born] **you will learn** from the decrees which the Council passed concerning her.' (Translation E. S. Forster)

(24) δεῖ δέ [...] **μαθεῖν** ὑμᾶς **ὡς** οὐδὲ καθ' ἕνα νόμον Ἀρίσταρχος εἰς τοὺς φράτορας τοὺς ἐκείνου εἰσῆκται. (Is. 10.8)
deî dé **matheîn** humâs **hōs**
is.necessary.3SG.IND.PRS PTCL learn.INF.AOR you.ACC.PL COMPL
oude kath' héna nómon Arístarkhos eis tous
NEG according one.ACC.SG law.ACC.SG Aristarchus.NOM to ART.ACC.PL
phrátoras tous ekeínou eisêktai
clansman.ACC.PL ART.ACC.PL that.GEN.SG introduce.3SG.IND.PRF
'It is necessary for you to **learn that** no law whatever authorized the introduction of Aristarchus into the ward of the other one [i.e. Aristarchus the elder].' (Translation E. S. Forster)

I have found only three contexts with non-adverbial *hōs* that involve the audience's positively knowing something, i.e. D. 4.13, 16.9, and Is. 3.19. Other five instances of factual *hōs* after a present indicative verb refer to the knowledge of a third party or of the speaker, which is not necessarily accepted by the audience: D. 60.30, Is. 7.34, Isoc. 14.34, [D.] 11.3, 11.7. There are at least 35 instances, of 45 in total, that conform to the hypothesis presented here.[16]

By using *hōs* instead of *hóti* with predicates of knowledge, speakers attenuate the proposition without necessarily implying low commitment to its truth. The perspective taken is that of the audience, which may view the facts as not yet established. Presented conclusions are therefore not shared between the participants of the communication at the time of utterance and the addressee may register the proposition as a conjecture. Nuyts (2001: 33–39) argues that such semantics occu-

---

[16] Determining the count exactly is problematic because of the ambiguity between adverbial and non-adverbial *hōs*.

pies one pole of the opposition between subjective and intersubjective statements, which are evidential in nature. In the case of subjective utterances, "the speaker suggests that s/he alone knows the evidence and draws a conclusion from it" (Nuyts 2001: 34). Nuyts' analysis resembles the theory of Neuberger-Donath (1982), who claims that clauses introduced by *hōs* signal that the subject of the main clause has exclusive access to the evidence. However, given the behavior of such complements in Greek, a slight revision is needed. Rather than pinning the value "subjective" to the actual speaker or the subject of the main clause, it is better to define it negatively as a simple lack of intersubjectivity. In this way, it may apply to the speaker who has dominant access to the evidence that something is the case (e.g. (23)), but it may also pertain to a claim of a third party that is neither the speaker nor the addressee. In both cases, the proposition is not (yet) accepted by (some of) the interlocutors, because its truth value is not immediately obvious.

The discourse pragmatic value of *hōs*, which signals backgrounded and non-essential content, should be considered distinct from the evidential value, which may but need not trigger the implicature of low speaker commitment. Both meanings should be understood as different offshoots of the original non-assertive value of *hōs*, so that we avoid positing the problematic development:

(25) presupposed true content (~ low informative value)? > low speaker commitment (~ false content)

Instead, I propose the following scenario:

(26) non-assertive *hōs* ('how') >   (a) presupposed true content
                                     (b) evidence and conclusions not available to all interlocutors (+ low speaker commitment)

Propositions under (a) are not asserted because this has already been done in the previous discourse, whereas the lack of assertion under (b) follows from insufficient justification available to the addressee and / or speaker. This evidential strategy could have evolved from the etymological meaning 'how' because some nontrivial facts can be accepted only if we first learn *how* something could have happened instead of being simply told *that* it happened. The presented analysis essentially agrees with Van Rooy (2016), who proposes that the opposition between *hóti* and *hōs* ought to be understood as an interface phenomenon covering epistemic modality (i.e. speaker commitment), information structure, and information source. The scenario sketched here illustrates how such an interface could have emerged on the side of *hōs*.

Clauses with *hóti* are not in complementary relation with clauses introduced by *hōs*, because they also occur in the contexts associated with the latter. However, *hóti* is also used when the embedded proposition is generally accepted by the participants of the communication. This acceptance may concern generic knowledge or specific information that has already been assimilated.

(27) οἶμαι δὴ **πάντας εἰδέναι ὅτι** μάλιστα συκοφαντεῖν ἐπιχειροῦσιν οἱ λέγειν μὲν δεινοί, ἔχοντες δὲ μηδέν. (Isoc. 21.5)
*oîmai   dē   **pántas   eidénai   hóti**   málista*
think.1SG.IND.PRS PTCL all.ACC.PL know.INF.PRF COMPL especially
sukophanteîn   epikheiroûsin   hoi   légein
accuse.falsely.INF.PRS try.3PL.IND.PRS ART.NOM.PL speak.INF.PRS
men deinoí,   ékhontes   de   mēdén
PTCL skilful.NOM.PL   having.NOM.PL   PTCL nothing.ACC.SG
'I think that **you all know that** malicious prosecution is most generally attempted by those who are clever speakers but possess nothing.' (Translation G. Norlin)

(28) ἀλλ' **ἀκριβῶς ἐπίστασθε ὅτι** χρημάτων ἕνεκα καὶ χάριτος πολλοὶ ἐπείσθησαν τῶν μαρτύρων ἢ ἀμνημονεῖν ἢ μὴ ἐλθεῖν ἢ ἑτέραν πρόφασιν εὑρεῖν. (Lycurg. 1.20)
*all' **akribôs   epístasthe   hóti**   khrēmátōn   héneka*
but   exactly   know.2PL.IND.PRS   COMPL   money.GEN.PL   because.of
kai   kháritos   polloí   epeísthēsan
and   favor.GEN.SG   many.NOM.PL   persuade.3PL.IND.PASS.AOR
tôn   martúrōn   ē   amnēmoneîn   ē   mē
ART.GEN.PL   witness.GEN.PL   either   forget.INF.PRS   or   NEG
eltheîn   ē   hetéran   próphasin   heureîn
come.INF.AOR   or   other.ACC.SG   excuse.ACC.SG   find.INF.AOR
'You **know too well that** desire for bribes and favors induces many witnesses to forget what they know, to fail to appear, or to contrive some other excuse.' (Translation J. O. Burtt)

(29) **ὅτι** μὲν γὰρ αἰσχρὰ καὶ δεινὰ καὶ οὐ προῖκα τὰ πεπραγμένα, **πάντες ὑμεῖς ἑοράκατε.** (D. 19.157)
***hóti** men   gar   aiskhrà   kai   deina   kai*
COMPL   PTCL PTCL disgraceful.NOM.PL   and   terrible.NOM.PL and
*ou   proîka   ta   pepragména,   **pántes***
NEG   for.free ART.NOM.PL   do.PTCP.PRF.NOM.PL   all.NOM.PL

humeîs   heorákate
you.NOM.PL see.2PL.IND.PRF
'**That** the deeds done were disgraceful, monstrous, and venal, **all of you have already discovered.**' (Translation C. A. Vince and J. H. Vince)

The association of *hóti* with encyclopedic knowledge illustrates the point that pragmatic factors are not the only regulating mechanism at play. Given that generic information is often presupposed and predictable, the pragmatic account of complementation predicts that such statements should be introduced by *hōs*. This, however, is not the case. An explanation based on evidential distinctions better accounts for the distribution. According to such an explanation, clauses with *hóti* may signal that access to evidence and conclusions is generally available to the interlocutors and that the proposition can be integrated into the flow of the communication (similarly Neuberger-Donath 1982).

The proposed semantic distinction can be also described in terms of "engagement" that bears on the relative accessibility of an entity, state of affairs or proposition to the speaker and addressee (Evans, Bergqvist and San Roque 2018; Bergqvist and Kittilä 2019 and references therein; cf. also Hyslop 2014).[17] Thus, languages like Kogi (Arwako-Chibchan) possess a dedicated set of markers that capture symmetry or asymmetry of knowledge between speech participants. While some "engagement" systems emphasize the status of the proposition itself, "engagement" paradigms in languages like Foe (Kutubuan) and Wola (Engan), both spoken in New Guinea, pertain to the mutual (in)accessibility of the source of information (Evans, Bergqvist and San Roque 2018: 151–153 with references). In the case of *hóti* and *hōs*, it is hard to determine whether we are dealing with (a)symmetries pertaining exclusively to the information, its source or both. Given the lack of grammaticalization of this domain in Greek, positing arrangements with different scope in individual contexts does not seem to pose any problems.

The fact that *hóti* can also be used when the speaker merely urges the audience to acknowledge a proposition suggests that evidential meanings are just one facet of the complex semantics of the two conjunctions. Asserting that something is the case, which is the basic meaning of the completive *hóti*, is certainly not limited to the cases when the interlocutors already share their conclusions. The essential evidential difference between the two conjunctions is that when the speaker uses *hōs*, s/he acknowledges that the proposition may not be readily assimilated by the addressee. On the other hand, *hóti* discounts the possibility that some interlocutors might find the proposition unjustified, and it marks the statement as uncontrover-

---

[17] I thank an anonymous reviewer for pointing this out to me.

sial. The choice is "a matter of how the speaker presents it rather than of how it 'really is'" (Nuyts 2001: 34–35). This account is in accord with the fact that *hóti* from the 4th century BCE onwards gradually assumes the position of a general subordinator, which represents the unmarked choice (Cristofaro 1998: 275–276). Thus, the development eliminates the marked strategy that tracks the expectations of the audience.

Given the three complementation strategies with predicates of knowledge and the evidential meanings they convey, is it possible to further systematize the cluster of visual source and circumstantial inference (both AccPtcp), generic and accepted propositions (*hóti*), and subjective statements (*hōs*)? Squartini (2008) proposes that there are three sub-types of inference, which form a gradient:

(30) circumstantial inferences — generic inferences — conjectures

Circumstantial inferences are defined in the same way as in this study. Generic inferences involve reasoning based on previously assimilated or general world knowledge.[18] Finally, conjectures are marked by a lack of evidence based on either sensory input or general knowledge. The vantage point of each sub-type is the speaker. This gradient may be mapped onto the evidential systems that grammatically distinguish some or all three options. Moreover, Squartini shows that the same framework also explains the distribution of evidential strategies in French and Italian, in which modal auxiliaries, the future tense, and some evidential adverbs do not span the entire gradient but cover only one or two adjacent segments.

The cross-linguistic validity of the gradient seems to be confirmed by the Greek data if we specify that the vantage point need not coincide with the speaker. Circumstantial inferences are expressed by predicates of knowledge + AccPtcp; the vantage point is the subject of the matrix verb. The two other options in Greek include the perspective of the speaker and addressee and refer to the general stance towards the proposition based on the available evidence. Squartini's generic inferences can be equated with generic and accepted propositions introduced by *hóti*. Conjectures, on the other hand, entail that generally accessible evidence is lacking, which translates to an asymmetrical status of the proposition between the participants. This part of the gradient is represented by *hōs* in Greek.

In addition to the languages with grammaticalized "engagement" systems already mentioned, some more examples of encoded (inter)subjectivity are adduced by Nuyts (2001: 36). Turkish (Aksu-Koç and Slobin 1986), Lhasa Tibetan

---

[18] Aikhenvald (2004: 174–176) calls this evidential value assumption, though she acknowledges that it is a kind of inference.

(DeLancey 1986), and Chinese Pidgin Russian (Nichols 1986) possess evidential markers that distinguish statements that cannot be easily assimilated from those that can. Sherpa codes propositions underpinned by direct experiential evidence differently than those that are generally known (Woodbury 1986). Finally, Hengeveld and Olbertz (2012) demonstrate that the perspective of the addressee who is confronted with new information can be expressed through grammatical means in many languages of the world.

6 Conclusions

This study illustrates that the notion of information source can be applied to Classical Greek to help to account for some difficult distributional patterns, which cannot be sufficiently explained by pragmatics alone. Evidential meanings of the constructions that consist of predicates of knowledge with a propositional complement may be encoded or arise as more or less entrenched implicatures. In the case of AccPtcp, the component of direct perception underlying knowledge acquisition stems from the original *locus* of the complement, which is to express immediate sensory perception. Accordingly, the Greek construction may express the evidential values of visual source and circumstantial inference. Finite complements introduced by *hóti* or *hōs* differ in that the former signals asserted proposition, while the latter does not. This contrast may be exploited by speakers when they use *hōs* to flag some propositions as not yet accepted by themselves or the addressee, which helps manage the flow of argumentation.

The proposed analysis is reconcilable with the cross-linguistic findings, according to which similar contrasts and semantic groupings can be found in the languages of the world with and without grammaticalized evidentiality. Regarding AccPtcp, the connection between visual source and circumstantial inference that we find in Greek is explained and cross-linguistically corroborated by the analysis of De Haan (2001). The overall range of evidential meanings that are associated with the studied constructions has a close parallel in the inferential gradient introduced by Squartini (2008). Of course, it is not claimed that the account of complementation in Classical Greek presented here supersedes or contradicts the established theories. It merely seeks to supplement them so that more light can be thrown on the obscure principles that govern the choice of the individual complementation strategies.

Greek texts

Brémond, Émile & Georges Mathieu. 1963–1967 [1929–1938]. *Isocrate. Discours*, vol. 1–2. Paris: Les Belles Lettres.
Butcher, Samuel H. 1966 [1903–1907]. *Demosthenis orationes*, vol. 1–2.1. Oxford: Clarendon Press.
Carey, Christopher. 2007. *Lysiae orationes cum fragmentis*. Oxford: Oxford University Press.
Conomis, Nicos C. 1970. *Lycurgi oratio in Leocratem*. Leipzig: Teubner.
Dalmeyda, Georges. 1966 [1930]. *Andocide. Discours*. Paris: Les Belles Lettres.
Gernet, Louis. 1965 [1923]. *Antiphon. Discours*. Paris: Les Belles Lettres.
Jensen, Christian. 1963 [1917]. *Hyperidis orationes sex*. Leipzig: Teubner.
Martin, Victor & Guy de Budé. 1962 [1927–1928]. *Eschine. Discours*, vol. 1–2. Paris: Les Belles Lettres.
Roussel, Pierre. 1960. *Isée. Discours*. Paris: Les Belles Lettres.

References

Aikhenvald, Alexandra Y. 2004. *Evidentiality*. Oxford: Oxford University Press.
Aikhenvald, Alexandra Y. 2020. Evidentiality and information source. In Chungmin Lee & Jinho Park (eds.), *Evidentials and modals*, 19–40. Leiden & Boston: Brill.
Aikhenvald, Alexandra Y. & Anne Storch. 2013. Linguistic expression of perception and cognition: A typological glimpse. In Alexandra Y. Aikhenvald & Anne Storch (eds.), *Perception and cognition in language and culture*, 1–45. Leiden & Boston: Brill.
Aksu-Koç, Ayhan & Dan I. Slobin. 1986. A psychological account of the development and use of evidentials in Turkish. In Wallace Chafe & Johanna Nichols (eds.), *Evidentiality: The linguistic coding of epistemology*, 159–167. Norwood, NJ: Ablex.
Allan, Rutger J. 2016. Tense and aspect in Greek: Two historical developments; Augment and perfect. In Steven E. Runge & Christopher J. Fresch (eds.), *The Greek verb revisited*, 81–121. Bellingham, WA.: Lexham Press.
Anderson, Lloyd B. 1986. Evidentials, paths of change, and mental maps: Typologically regular asymmetries. In Wallace Chafe & Johanna Nichols (eds.), *Evidentiality: The linguistic coding of epistemology*, 273–312. Norwood, NJ: Ablex.
Basset, Louis. 1999. Des participiales parmi les complétives. In Bernard Jacquinod (ed.), *Les complétives en grec ancien. Actes du colloque international de Saint-Étienne (3–5 septembre 1998)*, 33–44. Saint-Étienne: Publications de l'Université de Saint-Étienne.
Benedetti, Marina & Chiara Gianollo. 2023. Modal uses of knowledge verbs in Ancient Greek. (this volume).
Bentein, Klaas. 2014. Perfect. In Georgios Giannakis, Vit Bubenik, Emilio Crespo, Chris Golston, Alexandra Lianeri, Silvia Luraghi & Stephanos Matthaios (eds.), *Encyclopedia of Ancient Greek language and linguistics*, vol. 3, 46–49. Leiden & Boston: Brill.
Bergqvist, Henrik & Seppo Kittilä. 2019. Epistemic perspectives: Evidentiality, egophoricity, and engagement. In Henrik Bergqvist & Seppo Kittilä (eds.), *Evidentiality, egophoricity and engagement*, 1–21. Berlin: Language Science Press.
Boye, Kasper. 2010a. Reference and clausal perception-verb complements. *Linguistics* 48(2). 391–430.

Boye, Kasper. 2010b. Evidence for what? Evidentiality and scope. *STUF Language Typology and Universals* 63(4). 290–307.
Boye, Kasper. 2018. Evidentiality: The notion and the term. In Alexandra Y. Aikhenvald (ed.), *The Oxford handbook of evidentiality*, 261–272. Oxford: Oxford University Press.
Boye, Kasper & Peter Harder. 2009. Evidentiality: Linguistic categories and grammaticalization. *Functions of Language* 16(1). 9–43.
Crellin, Robert S. D. 2016. *The syntax and semantics of the perfect active in literary Koine Greek*. Chichester: Wiley-Blackwell.
Cristofaro, Sonia. 1996. *Aspetti sintattici e semantici delle frasi completive in greco antico*. Firenze: La Nuova Italia.
Cristofaro, Sonia. 1998. Grammaticalization and clause linkage strategies: A typological approach with particular reference to Ancient Greek. In Anna Giacalone Ramat & Paul J. Hopper (eds.), *The limits of grammaticalization*, 59–88. Amsterdam & Philadelphia: John Benjamins.
Cristofaro, Sonia. 2003. *Subordination*. Oxford: Oxford University Press.
Cristofaro, Sonia. 2008. A constructionist approach to complementation: Evidence from Ancient Greek. *Linguistics* 46(3). 571–606.
Cristofaro, Sonia. 2012. Participial and infinitival complement sentences in Ancient Greek. In Volker Gast & Holger Diessel (eds.), *Clause linkage in cross-linguistic perspective*, 335–362. Berlin & New York: De Gruyter Mouton.
De Boel, Gunnar. 1980. Towards a theory of the meaning of complementizers in Classical Attic. *Lingua* 52(3). 285–304.
De Haan, Ferdinand. 2001. The place of inference within the evidential system. *International Journal of American Linguistics* 67(2). 193–219.
DeLancey, Scott. 1986. Evidentiality and volitionality in Tibetan. In Wallace Chafe & Johanna Nichols (eds.), *Evidentiality: The linguistic coding of epistemology*, 203–213. Norwood, NJ: Ablex.
Dik, Simon C. & Kees Hengeveld. 1991. The hierarchical structure of the clause and the typology of perception-verb complements. *Linguistics* 29(2). 231–259.
Dretske, Fred I. 1969. *Seeing and knowing*. London: Routledge and Kegan Paul.
Duhoux, Yves. 2000. *Le verbe grec ancien: Éléments de morphologie et de syntaxe historiques*. Louvain-la-Neuve: Peeters.
van Emde Boas, Evert, Albert Rijksbaron, Luuk Huitink & Mathieu de Bakker. 2019. *Cambridge grammar of Classical Greek*. Cambridge: Cambridge University Press.
Evans, Nicholas, Henrik Bergqvist & Lila San Roque. 2018. The grammar of engagement II: Typology and diachrony. *Language and Cognition* 10(1). 141–170.
Faure, Richard. 2017. Argument participial clauses viewed as abstract objects in Classical Greek. In Felicia Logozzo & Paolo Poccetti (eds.), *Ancient Greek linguistics. New approaches, insights, perspectives*, 551–564. Berlin & Boston: Walter de Gruyter.
Haug, Dag T. 2008. From resultatives to anteriors in Ancient Greek: On the role of paradigmaticity in semantic change. In Thorhallur Eythórsson (ed.), *Grammatical change and linguistic theory*, 285–305. Amsterdam & Philadelphia: John Benjamins.
Hengeveld, Kees & Lachlan Mackenzie. 2008. *Functional discourse grammar: A typologically-based theory of language structure*. Oxford: Oxford University Press.
Hengeveld, Kees & Hella Olbertz. 2012. Didn't you know? Mirativity does exist! *Linguistic Typology* 16(3). 487–503.
Huitink, Luuk. 2009. Pragmatic presupposition and complementation in Classical Greek. In Stéphanie Bakker & Gerry Wakker (eds.), *Discourse cohesion in Ancient Greek*, 21–40. Leiden & Boston: Brill.
Humbert, Jean. 1960. *Syntaxe grecque*. Paris: Klincksieck.

Hyslop, Gwendolyn. 2014. The grammar of knowledge in Kurtöp: Evidentiality, mirativity, and expectation of knowledge. In Alexandra Y. Aikhenvald & Robert M. W. Dixon (eds.), *The grammar of knowledge: A cross-linguistic typology*, 108–131. Oxford: Oxford University Press.

Kühner, Raphael & Bernhard Gerth. 1904. *Ausführliche Grammatik der griechischen Sprache. Satzlehre: Zweiter Band*. Hannover & Leipzig: Hahnsche Buchhandlung.

Kümmel, Martin & Helmut Rix. 2001. *LIV: Lexikon der indogermanischen Verben*. Wiesbaden: Reichert.

Lambrecht, Knud. 1994. *Information structure and sentence form: Topic, focus, and the mental representations of discourse referents*. Cambridge: Cambridge University Press.

Neuberger-Donath, Ruth. 1982. Der Gebrauch von ὅτι [*hóti*] und ὡς [*hōs*] in Subjekt- und Objekt-Sätzen. *Rheinisches Museum für Philologie* 125(3/4). 252–274.

Nichols, Johanna. 1986. The bottom line: Chinese Pidgin Russian. In Wallace Chafe & Johanna Nichols (eds.), *Evidentiality: The linguistic coding of epistemology*, 239–257. Norwood, NJ: Ablex.

Noonan, Michael. 2007. Complementation. In Timothy Shopen (ed.), *Language typology and syntactic description*, 52–150. Cambridge: Cambridge University Press.

Nuyts, Jan. 2001. *Epistemic modality, language, and conceptualization. A cognitive-pragmatic perspective*. Amsterdam & Philadelphia: John Benjamins.

Rijksbaron, Albert. 2006 [1984]. *The syntax and semantics of the verb in Classical Greek. An introduction*. 3rd edn. Chicago & London: The University of Chicago Press.

la Roi, Ezra. 2020. The development of εὑρίσκω [*heurískō*] 'find' as evidence towards a diachronic solution of the matching-problem in Ancient Greek complementation. *Philologia Classica* 15(2). 191–207.

Schüle, Sandra. 2000. *Perception verb complements in Akatek, a Mayan language*. Tübingen: Tübingen University dissertation.

Schwyzer, Eduard & Albert Debrunner. 1950. *Griechische Grammatik. Zweiter Band: Syntax und syntaktische Stilistik*. München: Verlag C.H. Beck.

Squartini, Mario. 2008. Lexical vs. grammatical evidentiality in French and Italian. *Linguistics* 46(5). 917–947.

Sweetser, Eve. 1990. *From etymology to pragmatics: Metaphorical and cultural aspects of semantic structure*. Cambridge: Cambridge University Press.

Van Rooy, Raf. 2016. The relevance of evidentiality for Ancient Greek: Some explorative steps through Plato. *Journal of Greek Linguistics* 16(1). 3–46.

Viberg, Åke. 1984. The verbs of perception: A typological study. In Brian Butterworth, Bernard Comrie & Östen Dahl (eds.), *Explanations for language universals*, 123–162. Berlin: Mouton de Gruyter.

Whitt, Richard J. 2010. *Evidentiality and perception verbs in English and German*. Bern: Peter Lang.

Whitt, Richard J. 2018. Evidentiality and propositional scope in Early Modern German. *Journal of Historical Pragmatics* 19(1). 122–149.

Woodbury, Anthony C. 1986. Interactions of tense and evidentiality: A study of Sherpa and English. In Wallace Chafe & Johanna Nichols (eds.), *Evidentiality: The linguistic coding of epistemology*, 188–202. Norwood, NJ: Ablex.

Camille Denizot, Liana Tronci & Sophie Vassilaki
4 Syntactic patterns of modality in temporal clauses: *Hóte* vs. *hótan* in the diachrony of Ancient Greek

Abstract: This paper focuses on the eventuality pattern *án* + subjunctive and investigates how it interacts with the subordinator *hóte* syntactically and semantically. The data are taken from three corpora, which are representative of three stages of Ancient Greek, namely Homeric poems (for Archaic Greek), a selection of Classical prose works (for Classical Greek), and the New Testament, compared to the Septuagint (for Koine Greek). In the distributional approach adopted here, temporal clauses with *án* + subjunctive (i.e. *hótan* clauses) are compared with the temporal clauses without modal particle, i.e. *hóte* clauses. Analysis of the data shows that despite the continuity of the eventuality meaning, the syntactic and semantic features that oppose *hótan*- vs. *hóte*-clauses changed during the three stages of Greek.

Keywords: Modal particle, temporal clauses, subjunctive, eventuality, Ancient Greek diachrony

1 Introduction

Modality can be expressed by moods or more generally modal markers, but also by a combination of modal markers in a syntactic pattern. To explore the role of syntax in the expression of modality, Ancient Greek temporal clauses are a promising field, because they offer the possibility of combining a modal particle with a modal form in a subordinate clause and can be compared to alternative patterns.

The modal particle is a complex modal marker in Ancient Greek, since it combines with modal forms following a heterogeneous distribution. The modal par-

---

Acknowledgements: This article is the result of joint work by the three authors. However, for academic purposes, Camille Denizot is responsible for Sections 2 and 4, Liana Tronci for Sections 1 and 3, and Sophie Vassilaki for Sections 5 and 6.

Camille Denizot, University of Paris Nanterre, e-mail: cdenizot@parisnanterre.fr
Liana Tronci, University for Foreigners of Siena, e-mail: tronci@unistrasi.it
Sophie Vassilaki, University of Languages and Civilizations – Inalco Paris, e-mail: sophie.vassilaki@inalco.fr

https://doi.org/10.1515/9783110778380-004

ticle *án* (ἄν)¹ is not compatible with all moods and tenses, e.g. it cannot be used with imperatives or present indicatives; in main clauses, the modal particle can be combined with the past indicative or with the optative, but not with the subjunctive. Conversely, it combines with the subjunctive only in a subset of subordinate clauses. When the modal particle is used in subordinate clauses, it can appear with certain subordinators but not all: e.g. in purpose clauses *án* can appear when the subordinator is *hína* (ἵνα) but not when it is *hōs* (ὡς). These characteristics show that the contribution of the modal particle to modality is not simple and should be understood in combination with other markers (verbal moods, types of clauses, etc.). As an attempt to do so, our study focuses on the combination of the subjunctive mood and the modal particle since their combination is the only one that is restricted to subordinate clauses.

The subordinate clauses where the combination of the modal particle with the subjunctive can appear belong only to three types: hypothetical clauses (*eán* / ἐάν + subjunctive), temporal clauses (*hótan* / ὅταν, for example), and relative clauses (e.g. *hos án* / ὅς ἄν). We have argued that this restricted combination, which is remarkably stable through diachrony, is not due to chance (Denizot and Vassilaki 2016). Among the three subordinate clauses, we focus here on temporal clauses because they are considered somehow independent from the main clause, as far as modality is concerned. Since temporal clauses have a framing role, their modality is less entailed by the modality of the main clause. On the other hand, hypothetical clauses are often caught in a protasis / apodosis relationship, which partly shapes the understanding of modality in each part; relative clauses have a referential relationship to some element in the main clause.

Among the different temporal clauses, we chose to focus on those introduced by the subordinator *hóte* (ὅτε), which can be combined with the modal particle (*hót-an* = *hóte* + modal particle *án*) or occur without the modal particle. It is worth pointing out that the modal particle is tightly combined with the subordinator, with a univerbated *hótan*, which is not the case for all temporal subordinators.² Our study deals with *hóte* for the following reasons:

---

1 In Archaic Greek also *ke* (κε), cf. Section 3. Note that the semantic and syntactic status of the two particles *án* and *ke* is not clear: they are usually labelled as "particles" in dictionaries and grammars (e.g. from Kühner and Gerth 1898 to Rijksbaron 2006 and van Emde Boas *et al.* 2019) but appear to be necessary in some clauses. We use this traditional label to begin with.
2 Also *epeidán* (ἐπειδάν 'when, as') and *hopótan* (ὁπόταν 'when') display the same univerbation, unlike *héōs* (ἕως, 'until'), *prín* (πρίν 'before'), *hēníka* (ἡνίκα, 'when') where the modal particle can be separated from the subordinator. Cf. Kühner and Gerth (1898: §398).

(a) it is the closest equivalent to 'when' (a simpler temporal relationship than 'before' or 'until');
(b) it is well attested under its two forms *hóte* and *hótan*, an interesting situation that allows for contrasts;
(c) it is well attested at different stages of Ancient Greek (from Archaic Greek to Koine Greek).

The following pair shows the contrast of the two types of temporal clauses (with and without modal particle), still valid in New Testament Greek.³

(1) ὅταν δὲ ἔλθῃ ὁ υἱὸς τοῦ ἀνθρώπου ἐν τῇ δόξῃ αὐτοῦ [καὶ πάντες οἱ ἄγγελοι μετ' αὐτοῦ], τότε καθίσει ἐπὶ θρόνου δόξης αὐτοῦ. (*Ev.Matt.* 25.31)
hót-an   de   élthēi   ho   huios   toû   anthrṓpou
when-MOD PTCL come.3SG.SBJV.AOR ART.NOM son.NOM ART.GEN man.GEN
en   têi   dóxēi   autoû,   tóte   kathísei   epi   thrónou
in ART.DAT glory.DAT he.GEN then sit.3SG.IND.FUT upon throne.GEN
dóxēs   autoû
glory.GEN he.GEN
'But when the Son of Man comes in his glory, [and all the angels with him], then he will sit upon his glorious throne.'

(2) καὶ ὅτε ἦλθον ἐπὶ τὸν τόπον τὸν καλούμενον κρανίον, ἐκεῖ ἐσταύρωσαν αὐτὸν καὶ τοὺς κακούργους [ὃν μὲν ἐκ δεξιῶν ὃν δὲ ἐξ ἀριστερῶν.] (*Ev.Luc.* 23.33)
kai   hóte   élthon   epi   ton   tópon   ton
and when come.3PL.IND.AOR to ART.ACC place.ACC ART.ACC
kaloúmenon   kraníon,   ekeî   estaúrōsan   auton   kai
called.ACC calvary.ACC there crucify.3PL.IND.AOR he.ACC and
tous   kakoúrgous
ART.ACC criminals.ACC
'And when they had come to the place called Calvary, there they crucified Him, and the criminals [one on the right hand and the other on the left].'

Within the typological framework, it is usual to distinguish between "balanced" and "deranked" *when*-clauses, according to the verb forms that occur in the

---

3 Unless otherwise stated, English translations are taken from the following editions: *Iliad* (Murray 1924), *Odyssey* (Murray 1919), both available on https://www.perseus.tufts.edu/hopper/, Lysias (Lamb 1930), Demosthenes (Vince and Vince 1926, Vince 1930), *New Testament* (Rainbow Missions, Inc. World English Bible; revision of the American Standard Version of 1901, available on http://ebible.org/bible/web), *Septuagint* (https://www.sacred-texts.com/bib/sep/index.htm).

temporal clause. In balanced *when*-clauses, the verb form "is one that can occur in an independent declarative clause, e.g. an indicative verb form", whereas in deranked *when*-clauses the verb form "is one that cannot be used in independent declarative clauses" (Cristofaro 2013). It goes without saying that the distinction between balanced and deranked *when*-clauses overlaps with the issue of modality and its interaction with the conceptualization of temporal events. Ancient Greek appears to have a special behaviour with respect to the typology of *when*-clauses, as it not only displays a "deranked" verb form (i.e. the subjunctive + the modal particle) in some types of *when*-clauses, as opposed to "balanced" *when*-clauses with the verb in the indicative, but also shows diachronic changes in the distribution of the two types of *when*-clauses. As we will show, Ancient Greek displays different strategies to mark deranked *when*-clauses in the three stages of its history analysed here. Investigating how these strategies arise and are distributed in synchrony and diachrony can bring new insights not only for Ancient Greek linguistics but also for general and typological linguistics.

2 The two methodological principles of the study

2.1 A syntactic account of modality: How modal meanings arise within complex clauses

The aim of this study is to investigate how the modal particle *án* interacts with a specific mood (the subjunctive) and with a specific subordinator (*hóte*) – and, therefore, within a specific type of complex clause – to build a propositional content referentially. Before presenting our approach to modality, we discuss briefly how the "ingredients" of the modal pattern investigated here, namely the modal particle *án* and the subjunctive, have been accounted for in the literature.

As far as the modal particle *án* is concerned, two attempts have been made recently to give a unified account of the different uses of the particle, which combines, as is well known, with different verbal moods (subjunctive, optative, and past indicative) and, when combined with the subjunctive, occurs in different types of clause (temporal, conditional, and relative clauses). According to Gerö (2000: 183), *án* "is located in clauses which are within the scope of typical intensional (or "world-creating") predicates"; these predicates "set up so-called intensional contexts, which crucially involve reference not to the actual, "real" world, but to alternative (or possible) worlds". Although intensionality appears to be a relevant parameter, the way *án* combines with the subjunctive (vs. other moods) remains unexplored in Gerö's study. A similar criticism can be made of Beck *et al.* (2012), who account for the particle *án* as a universal quantifier over actual or possible situations; in combination with the subjunctive, quantification is over multiple situations per world. In summary, neither of the two studies investigates how the "multiple situations" or "possible worlds" created by the particle are syntactically built and become meaningful within a specific type of complex clause.

As far as the subjunctive is concerned, it is well known that it is a non-assertive mood, which is characterised as a purely representational form, without any temporal anchoring: the speaker utters the propositional content without expressing any opinion on whether the propositional content is the case or not. Given this characterisation, it seems difficult to understand how the subjunctive could occur in temporal clauses, which are supposed to have, conversely, temporal anchoring.

A different way to approach the topic is to consider the combination of the subjunctive + *án* as a compositional pattern conveying modal meanings. Two different meanings are usually recognised by grammars, i.e. the prospective meaning, for "single actions *in the future*", and the generic / iterative meaning, for "non-past *habitual / repeated action*" (van Emde Boas *et al.* 2019: 642–643, emphasis in the original; see also Revuelta Puigdollers 2020: 668–670). Here we argue for a unified account of the combination of the subjunctive + *án*, as already suggested by Basset (1988) and Denizot and Vassilaki (2016). The subjunctive + *án* is a modal pattern which codes an eventuality meaning;[4] this meaning is not determined outside the syntactic constructions in which it occurs, since it is not only constructed by combining the meaning of the subjunctive and that of the modal particle, but depends also on the different syntactic structures, i.e. subordinate clauses.

As Basset (1988) argues, the particle *án* links the representational content expressed by the subjunctive to a situation built by the speaker's point of view; this point of view is shaped by implicit representations about previous states of affairs, which are mentioned in the context or remain implicit. However, the combination of a purely representational content (subjunctive) with a relational element (*án*) builds a linguistic pattern that cannot be referential by itself. It becomes fully referential only through its syntactic relation to contextual elements that occur in the main clause and that allow the modal pattern formed by the subjunctive + *án* to occur.

This characterisation explains why the modal pattern (subjunctive + *án*), called here eventuality pattern, occurs only in dependent syntactic structures (temporal, conditional, and relative clauses) and frequently co-occurs with indefinite markers.

---

4 This terminology is in line with that of the French (*éventuel*) and German (*Eventualis*) grammatical traditions. We are not using the term in the sense of Bach (1986), where the term is plural, i.e. "eventualities", and functions as a hyperonym for *states*, *processes* and *events*.

One of the main textual functions of the eventuality pattern is to scan possible situations. In the case of temporal clauses, this means that the propositional content does not refer to a moment in time but to a situation built up by the speaker among a set of alternative possible situations. Thus the way the subjunctive and *án* interact in temporal clauses is contextually grounded and depends on the point of view of the speaker.

2.2 A diachronic account of modal markers: Three stages of Ancient Greek in comparison

The second relevant aspect of this study is to combine a synchronic investigation with a diachronic perspective. The reason for combining the two approaches is that there are strong differences in the field of modality, when comparing corpora of different centuries.

These strong differences are visible, for example, in the use of the modal particle. From a quantitative point of view, the use of modal particles peaks at the Classical period and subsequently decreases, as shown in Figure 1. The figure displays over- and under-representation of the two modal particles *án* and *ke(n)* when used alone, based on a calculation of z-scores;[5] this kind of representation is preferable to a raw number of utterances, because of the large difference in the size of corpora from century to century. A z-score is considered meaningful when below -2 for an under-representation and above +2 for an over-representation.[6] The high values of the z-scores displayed in Figure 1 show that the difference from century to century cannot be due to chance.

The difference in the number of attestations shown by Figure 1 explains why we collected data from relevant texts of the three stages of Ancient Greek, namely Archaic Greek (before the 5th century BCE), Classical Greek (5th–4th centuries BCE)

---

5 For the calculation of the z-score we used data from the TLG and restricted the calculation to a time span from the 8th century BCE to the 2nd century CE (the figure displayed by TLG is calculated on a longer time-span). We included the modal particles *án* (attested throughout the whole period) and *ke(n)* (attested only in Archaic Greek and rarely afterwards in an imitation of Archaic Greek or in quotations). An anonymous reviewer remarked that in Classical Greek ἐάν (if-MOD) is often written ἄν (like the modal particle), which is not visible when retrieving figures by the TLG (the lemma ἐάν actually includes the results of the lemma ἄν in the database). A tentative calculation including ἐάν as well did not change the general picture (e.g. the z-score is +10 in the 8th century BCE, +75 in the 5th century BCE, +67 in the 4th century BCE and -12 in the 2nd century CE).
6 When the data are regularly distributed only 5% of the data are over these two values (and only 0.3% for a z-score below -3 or above +3).

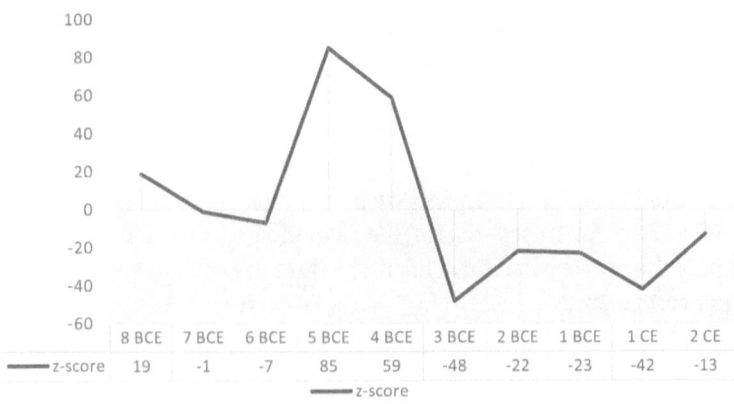

Figure 1: Over- and under-representation of the modal particle.

and Koine Greek (from the 3rd century BCE), in order to create three corpora, each of which was analysed synchronically. The three corpora are composed as follows:
(a) Archaic Greek: Homeric poems (traditionally 8th c. BCE, with traces of earlier Greek);
(b) Classical Greek: a prose corpus made of three different genres, i.e. oratory (all the speeches by Lysias without fragments, and a selection of deliberative speeches by Demosthenes),[7] philosophy (Plato's *Republic*), and historiography (Thucydides), all of them ranging from the end of the 5th c. BCE to mid-4th c. BCE;
(c) Koine Greek: the New Testament (NT) (1st–2nd c. CE), to which we have added the Septuagint (LXX) (3rd BCE) as a comparison corpus.[8]

The synchronic data thus obtained were compared in order to provide a diachronic account and to highlight similarities and differences.

This approach is different from that of previous studies devoted to *án*, which have discussed data from only one stage of Ancient Greek, e.g. Homeric Greek for Basset (1988) and Gerö (2000), and Classical Greek for Beck *et al.* (2012). In our

---

[7] I.e. speeches 1–24, including all political speeches (1–17) and a selection of law-court speeches (18–24).
[8] The Septuagint is the translation of the Old Testament of the Bible, from Hebrew to Greek. Conversely, the books of the New Testament, i.e. the four Gospels, the Acts of the Apostles, the Epistles and the Apocalypse were written in Greek, but the authors were mostly Jews. The language of the Septuagint and the New Testament presents many common features and is traditionally called Biblical Greek.

opinion, a broader investigation is necessary. Since Ancient Greek is not a unitary and homogeneous language over the many centuries of its history and documentation, the comparison of the different stages of the language provides us with new insights into the syntactic and semantic properties of the modal particle.

More concretely, we collected all occurrences of the eventuality pattern in *hóte*-clauses and we investigated their distribution against the *hóte*-clauses that do not host the eventuality pattern. In Table 1 we provide the quantitative data as they are distributed in our three corpora. For the sake of simplicity, the term '*hótan*' includes not only the univerbated form *hót'án* but also the variant *hóte ke(n)*, both attested in Homeric poems.

Table 1: Quantitative data of the three corpora.

	Archaic Greek (Homeric poems)	Classical Greek (sample of corpus prose)	Koine Greek (NT + LXX)
hótan	53	333	333
hóte	452	245	275
TOTAL	505	578	608

The spread of *hótan* as compared to *hóte* is visible in Table 1, but a qualitative analysis is necessary to understand the evolution.

3 Homeric Greek as a sample of Archaic Greek

As far as Homeric Greek is concerned, we took into account the two modal particles *án* and *ke(n)* in combination with the subjunctive. For the purposes of this study, the two particles are functionally equivalent, although there has been a long-standing debate on this issue, which we will not go into.[9]

According to the distributional approach adopted here, we collected all the occurrences of temporal clauses introduced by *hóte* (with and without a modal particle) in the editions of *Iliad* and *Odyssey* available on the TLG, giving a number of

---

9 It has also recently been stated that "[w]hether there is any distributional difference in the modal particles *ke(n)* and *án* in Homer remains to be investigated" (Goldstein 2016: 50, fn. 3). We refer to Homeric grammars (particularly Monro 1891: 333; Chantraine 1953: 345), and to the studies of Wackernagel (2009 [1920]: 284–287); Howorth (1955); Ruijgh (1992); Wathelet (1997). For a concise discussion of the different origin and dialectal distribution of Ionic *án* and Aeolic *ke(n)*, cf. Reece (2009: 73–78) and references therein.

505 occurrences.[10] Among them, the distribution of verbal moods and the modal particles *án* and *ke(n)* is as follows.

Table 2: Distribution of moods and the modal particles in *hóte*-clauses in Homeric Greek.

hóte-clauses	Subjunctive	Indicative	Optative	No verb[11]	Total
without modal particle	64	324	50	14	452
with *án*	27	1			28
with *ke(n)*	23	1	1		25
Total	114	326	51	14	505

Table 2 confirms two facts that are well known to grammarians, but have not been duly investigated so far. On the one hand, Homeric Greek already provides evidence of the close relationship between the modal particles at stake here and the subjunctive in *hóte*-clauses. On the other hand, this relationship is not so exclusive as to prevent the subjunctive from occurring alone in *hóte*-clauses, as is the case, conversely, in Classical and Koine Greek. If we look at the distribution of the subjunctive, we can observe that the subjunctive alone is found in more than half of the occurrences (64x out of 114x), while in the remaining part (50x), it is combined with *án* or *ke(n)*. The close relationship of these modal particles with the subjunctive is evident in our corpus: in only three instances (*Il.* 9.525, 12.41, *Od.* 24.88), the particles are combined with another verbal form than the subjunctive.[12]

With respect to later stages of Greek, the situation of Homeric Greek presents some differences as regards the eventuality pattern investigated here. Even though the sequence of the subordinator and the modal particle turns out to be fixed

---

10 The editions are that of Allen (1931) for the Iliad (*Homeri Ilias*, edidit Thomas W. Allen, Oxford, Clarendon Press) and Mühll (1962) for the Odyssey (*Homerus. Odyssea*, recognovit Peter von der Mühll, Munich and Leipzig, Saur).
11 The *hóte*-clauses without verb have the following distribution. In six instances (*Il.* 14.319, 14.321, 14.323, 14.326, 16.227, 16.406) the verb is elliptical and may be recovered from the previous clause. In the remaining eight instances (*Il.* 2.394, 12.132, 13.335, 13.571, 15.362, 18.219, *Od.* 5.281, 19.494) the clause is a locative / existential one (or a copulative one in some cases, e.g. *Il.* 18.219) and the verb 'to be' is omitted. Note that most occurrences are similes.
12 They are combined with the indicative in *Il.* 12.41 (*án*) and *Od.* 24.88 (*ken*) and with the optative in *Il.* 9.525 (*ken*). The first two passages are debated among philologists and the modal particles are deleted in some modern editions, e.g. Leaf (1895) replaces the verse-initial sequence *hōs d' hót' án* in *Il.* 12.41 by *hōs d' hóte* (*Homeri Ilias*, edited by Walter Leaf, New York, Macmillan & Co.), while Nauck (1877–1879) suggests *eûte d(é)* (*Homeri Ilias, cum potiore lectionis varietate*, edidit Augustus Nauck, Berlin, Weidmann).

already in Homeric Greek, as no other element usually occurs between them,[13] the subjunctive alone is capable of expressing the modal functions that, in later stages of Greek, only *án* + the subjunctive expresses (cf. Monro 1891: 263; Chantraine 1953: 256).[14] This means that there is a sort of free alternation between *hóte* + subjunctive and *hótan* + subjunctive in Homeric Greek, which is not the case in later stages of Greek. Homeric Greek data, thus, allow us to investigate not only the syntactic features that determine the opposition between *hótan*- and *hóte*-clauses, but also the conditions that give rise to the eventuality pattern (*án* or *ke(n)* + subjunctive) and that differentiate it from the subjunctive alone.

In the following two sections, we examine, first, the contrast between the eventuality pattern and the indicative in *hóte*-clauses (Section 3.1) and, then, the syntactic conditions under which the particles *án* and *ke(n)* occur with the subjunctive in *hóte*-clauses and how this combination emerges and is opposed to simple subjunctives (Section 3.2).

3.1 Subjunctive vs. indicative in *hóte*-clauses

As Table 2 above shows, *hóte*-clauses with the indicative are more frequent than *hóte*-clauses with the subjunctive in our corpus; the ratio is approximately 3 to 1. This is highly significant, especially when compared with later stages of Greek, where *hótan* + subjunctive occurs more than *hóte* + indicative (in Classical and Koine Greek) or even more than *hótan* + indicative (in Koine Greek). We will come back to this issue in Section 6; for the time being, let us examine the distribution of modal markers in *hóte*-clauses in Homeric Greek.

The first relevant aspect of *hóte*-clauses with the subjunctive is that they do not point to any reference in time, but build a prospective situation by conveying an eventuality meaning. This is particularly evident in the following two instances, in which the *hóte*-clauses with the subjunctive, combined with *án* in (3) and with *ke(n)* in (4), specify the noun phrase *émati tôi* 'in the day that'.

---

[13] With the exception of the passage *Od.* 11.218, which is unique in the corpus, not only because the subordinator and the modal particle are not contiguous, but also because the modal particle is *ke* and not *ken*, unlike all the other occurrences in the corpus.
[14] According to Willmott (2007: 8), the use of verbal moods in Homeric Greek is "less mechanical than in Attic". This is basically true, if we consider the interaction of the subjunctive with the modal particle, which is not fixed as in Classical Greek and can manifest modal differences.

(3) ἤματι τῷ ὅτ' ἄν οἱ μὲν ἐπὶ πρύμνῃσι **μάχωνται** / [στείνει ἐν αἰνοτάτῳ περὶ Πατρόκλοιο θανόντος]. (*Il.* 8.475–476)
ḗmati   tôi   hót'   an   hoi   men   epi   prúmnēisi
day.DAT DEM.DAT when MOD ART.NOM PTCL at sterns.DAT
mákhōntai
fight.3PL.SBJV.PRS
'On the day when at the sterns of the ships they shall be fighting [in grimmest stress about Patroclus fallen].'

(4) ἤματι τῷ ὅτε **κέν** σε Πάρις καὶ Φοῖβος Ἀπόλλων / [ἐσθλὸν ἐόντ'] **ὀλέσωσιν** ἐνὶ Σκαιῇσι πύλῃσιν. (*Il.* 22.359–360)
ḗmati   tôi   hóte   kén   se   Páris   kai   Phoîbos
day.DAT DEM.DAT when MOD you.ACC Paris.NOM and Phoebus.NOM
*Apóllōn   **olésōsin**   eni   Skaiêisi   púlēisin*
Apollo.NOM slay.3PL.SBJV.AOR in Scaean.DAT gate.DAT
'On the day when Paris and Phoebus Apollo shall slay thee, [valorous though thou art,] at the Scaean gate.'

The noun phrase *ḗmati tôi* does not point to a day located along a definite timeline, whether in the past or in the present. It is possibly located in the future, but the reference to time is not relevant here, as the focus is on the event denoted by the dependent clause. It is not important "when" the event will occur, but that, according to the speaker, it is possible that it occurs.

This is particularly evident when we compare this type of clause with those in which the same noun phrase *ḗmati tôi* is complemented by a "true" temporal clause with *hóte* + indicative.

(5) ἤματι τῷ ὅτε μιν κορυθαίολος **ἠγάγεθ'** Ἕκτωρ / ἐκ δόμου Ἠετίωνος, [ἐπεὶ πόρε μυρία ἕδνα]. (*Il.* 22.471–472)
ḗmati   tôi   hóte   min   koruthaíolos
day.DAT DEM.DAT when her.ACC of.flashing.helm.NOM
ēgágeth'   *Héktōr   ek   dómou   Ēetíōnos*
take.as.wife.3SG.IND.AOR Hector.NOM from house.GEN Eetion.GEN
'On the day when Hector of the flashing helm led her as his bride forth from the house of Eetion, [after he had brought bride-gifts past counting].'

In this case, the day that is referred to by *ḗmati tôi* is located in the past and has a referential meaning. The temporal clause that complements the noun functions as a modifier: it modifies the noun phrase in relation to the event that occurred. This means that the day mentioned in (5) exists regardless of the event that qualifies it. This is not the case when the temporal clause displays the subjunctive, as in (3)–(4) above. Here, the event described by the *hóte*-clause builds the referential content of the noun phrase *ḗmati tôi*, which could not occur in isolation. In this case, then, the temporal clause cannot be replaced by another kind of modifier; it is necessary for the sentence to be well-formed, since it points to the event that, according to the speaker, builds the setting for the main event he is predicting to occur.

Another type of syntactic combination for temporal clauses with *hóte* + indicative is illustrated in the following example (cf. also *Il.* 16.385, 21.5).

(6) [τῶν δ', ὥς τε νιφάδες χιόνος πίπτωσι θαμειαὶ] / **ἤματι χειμερίῳ, ὅτε τ' ὤρετο** μητίετα Ζεὺς / νιφέμεν [ἀνθρώποισι πιφαυσκόμενος τὰ ἃ κῆλα]. (*Il.* 12.278–280)
ḗmati   kheimeríōi   hóte   t'   ṓreto   mētíeta
day.DAT   wintry.DAT   when   PTCL start.3SG.IND.AOR counsellor.NOM
Zeus   niphémen
Zeus.NOM   snow.INF
'[And as flakes of snow fall thick] on a winter's day, when Zeus, the counsellor, bestirred him to snow, [shewing forth to men these arrows of his].'

Here, the temporal clause is not a complement of a noun phrase, as was the case with the noun phrase *ḗmati tôi* in (3)–(5); rather, it is an additional complement, which is not mandatory for the syntax of the sentence or for its semantic content. It develops the referential meaning of the noun phrase *ḗmati kheimeríōi* 'wintry day', by adding a sort of gloss to it. Note that the indicative in the *hóte*-clause in (6) relates to the repetition of the event of snowing on winter days and the aorist does not point to the past and has an aspectual meaning.

Summarising, time-reference is the crucial difference between *hóte*-clauses with the indicative and *hóte*-clauses with the subjunctive. The complementation patterns of the noun phrase *ḗmati tôi*, turn out to be an interesting minimal pair, which shows that the difference between the two types does not concern only the referential vs. non-referential meaning of the noun, but also the syntactic function of the temporal clause. Temporal clauses with the indicative play an attributive function with respect to the noun phrase. They provide additional information, which specifies the deictic reference to past time, literally 'in that day, when it happened [...]'. Conversely, when the noun phrase *ḗmati tôi* governs *hóte*-clauses with the subjunctive, it has no referential meaning and, therefore, no deictic time reference. It refers to an event, which will occur, according to the speaker, as a possible setting for another event that the speaker says will happen. We will come back to this issue in Section 3.3.

3.2 Syntactic and semantic features of *hóte*-clauses with the eventuality pattern

As already stated, *hóte* may combine with the subjunctive without the modal particle in Homeric Greek, unlike later stages of the language. Homeric Greek provides, therefore, the best conditions for investigating how the eventuality pattern arose and what the function of modal particles in combination with the subjunctive is.

According to Monro (1891: 263–264), "[t]he pure Subj. indicates that the speaker is supposing a case which may occur repeatedly, or at any time" and the modal particle *án* or *ke(n)* "connects a supposition with a particular event or state of things". The relation of temporal clauses with the subjunctive to the iterative-distributive meaning is also pointed out by Ruijgh (1992: 80–81), who also stresses the "futural" reference of this type of clause. In his opinion, it is not clear why *án* and *ke(n)* combine with the subjunctive in temporal clauses, since their meaning, i.e. 'then = at that moment in the future', is already denoted by the subjunctive alone. It can be observed, however, that *án* and *ke(n)* spread in many types of dependent clauses in Homeric Greek and their combination with several subordinators, *hóte* included, became increasingly fixed from Homer onwards. In line with Monro's opinion, Chantraine (1953: 255–257) explains the modal particles as markers of a "particular case" as opposed to the simple subjunctive, which was used, according to him, to convey "éventualité" (eventuality) and "généralité" (generality). The relationship with a "futural" state of affairs is also argued for by Howorth (1955: 74), who explicitly rejects the analysis of modal particles as markers of "a particular case" and stresses the "strong tendency to put ἄν or κε if the reference is to the future, regardless of whether they are concerned with a particular case or not" (Howorth 1955: 76–77).

Let us turn to the data. In our corpus, there are 64 occurrences of *hóte* + subjunctive without modal particles and 50 occurrences of *hóte* + subjunctive with *án* or *ke(n)*. The two classes of clauses show different morpho-syntactic and syntactic features that concern, generally speaking, the relationship with the speech situation, which is marked in clauses with the modal particles and unmarked in clauses without a modal particle. This observation is in line with the analysis that Basset (1988: 37) suggested for the particle *án*, which correlates, according to him, to the "speaker's actuality", functioning as a *shifter* (in the sense of Jakobson 1957).

The first feature concerns the category of person, in particular the agreement in person of the subjunctive and the occurrence or not of other elements (pronouns, possessives) that refer to the two persons (the first and the second one) of the speech situation. In temporal clauses without modal particles, the subjunctive usually appears in the third person, with only one exception (*Od.* 10.486). Conversely, in temporal clauses with modal particles, the subjunctive also occurs in the first and second person (10 occurrences out of 50).[15] Besides, even when the subjunctive is in the third person, other elements that relate to the first and second person can occur, e.g. pronouns and possessives in object positions (9 occurrences).[16] This means that there is some relation to the first or second person in almost half of the occurrences of *hóte*-clauses with a modal particle. Examples (7) and (8) show the two types:

(7) ἀλλ' **ὅτε κεν** δὴ νηυσὶν ἔπι γλαφυρῇσι **γένωμαι**. (*Il.* 8.180)
all' **hóte ken** dē nēusin epi glaphurêisi **génōmai**
but when MOD PTCL ships.DAT on hollow.DAT be.1SG.SBJV.AOR
'But when I be at length come amid the hollow ships.'

(8) [...] **ὅτ' ἄν μ'** ἐρέθῃσιν ὀνειδείοις ἐπέεσσιν. (*Il.* 1.519)
hót' án m' eréthēisin oneideíois epéessin
when MOD I.ACC anger.3SG.SBJV.PRS taunting.DAT words.DAT
'When she shall anger me with taunting words.'

The second feature concerns the type of sentence in which the temporal clause occurs. While *hóte*-clauses with the simple subjunctive usually depend on declarative sentences, *hóte*-clauses with the modal particle may occur in imperative sentences. This means that *hóte*-clauses with the simple subjunctive depend on sentences in which the verb is usually in the indicative and in the third person, while the verb that governs *hóte*-clauses with the modal particle may be an imperative or hortatory subjunctive and in the second person. The second type has also another distributional constraint, as it usually occurs in direct speech, while the first one may occur in both direct and indirect speech. In the following two examples, the temporal clauses are both in direct speech but their semantic contents are very different.

(9) Ἰδομενεῦ περὶ μέν σε **τίω** Δαναῶν ταχυπώλων / ἠμὲν ἐνὶ πτολέμῳ ἠδ' ἀλλοίῳ ἐπὶ ἔργῳ / ἠδ' ἐν δαίθ', **ὅτε** πέρ τε γερούσιον αἴθοπα οἶνον / Ἀργείων οἱ ἄριστοι ἐνὶ κρητῆρι **κέρωνται**. (*Il.* 4.257–260)
Idomeneû peri mén se **tíō** *Danaôn*
Idomeneus.VOC beyond PTCL you.ACC honour.1SG.IND.PRS Danaans.GEN
takhupólōn ēmen eni ptolémōi ēd' alloíōi epi
with.swift.steeds.GEN both in war.DAT and other.DAT in

---

15 *Il.* 1.567, 6.225, 7.335, 8.180, 8.420, 9.138, 9.280, 20.335, *Od.* 4.477, 8.242.
16 *Il.* 1.519, 4.53, 8.373, 22.359, *Od.* 2.99, 4.420, 13.180, 16.287, 19.6.

érgōi	ēd'	en	daíth'	**hóte**	pér	te	geroúsion
task.DAT	and	in	feast.DAT	when	PTCL	PTCL	of.the.elders.ACC

aíthopa	oînon	Argeíōn	hoi	áristoi			eni
flaming.ACC	wine.ACC	Argives.GEN	ART.NOM	chieftains.NOM			in

krētêri	kérōntai
bowl.DAT	mingle.3PL.SBJV.AOR

'Idomeneus, beyond all the Danaans with swift steeds do I show honour to thee both in war and in tasks of other sort, and at the feast, when the chieftains of the Argives let mingle in the bowl the flaming wine of the elders.'

(10) ἀλλ' ἀκέουσα **κάθησο**, ἐμῷ δ' **ἐπιπείθεο** μύθῳ, / μή νύ τοι οὐ **χραίσμωσιν** ὅσοι θεοί εἰσ' ἐν Ὀλύμπῳ / ἆσσον ἰόνθ', **ὅτε κέν** τοι ἀάπτους χεῖρας ἐφείω. (*Il.* 1.565–567)[17]

all'	akéousa	**kátheso**		emôi	d'	**epipeítheo**	múthōi
but	silent.NOM	sit.down.2SG.IMP.PRS		my.DAT	PTCL	obey.2SG.IMP.PRS	word.DAT

mḗ	nú	toi	ou	**khraísmōsin**	hósoi		theoí
NEG	PTCL	you.DAT	NEG	avail.3PL.SBJV.PRS	how.many.NOM		gods.NOM

eis'		en	Olúmpōi	âsson	iónth'		**hóte**	**kén**
be.3PL.IND.PRS		in	Olympus.DAT	nearer	go.PTCP.DAT		when	MOD

toi	aáptous	kheîras	**epheíō**
you.DAT	irresistible.ACC	hands.ACC	put.forth.1SG.SBJV.AOR

'Sit down in silence, and obey my word, lest all the gods that are in Olympus avail you not against my drawing near, when I put forth upon you my irresistible hands.'

These examples show another important difference concerning the syntactic anchoring of *hóte*-clauses. While *hóte*-clauses with a modal particle usually depend on the verb phrase of the main clause, as is the case in (10), *hóte*-clauses without a modal particle can depend on another constituent of the main clause, e.g. the prepositional phrase *en daíth(i)* in (9), with respect to which the temporal clause provides an explanation: 'in the feast, that is when […]'. We found five occurrences of this type in our corpus (*Il.* 4.259, 2.782, 5.500, 14.522, 16.365), which are all marked by the combination of the subordinator *hóte* with the particle τε 'and, that is'.

The last feature of *hóte*-clauses concerns the types of event that are expressed by *hóte*-clauses with and without modal particles. While the former denote events that are marked deictically by reference to the speech situation, the latter point

---

[17] As for the unusual occurrence of the two negators *mḗ* and *ou* in the same clause, see Chantraine (1953: 336–337).

to recurrent events, such as atmospheric phenomena (11), gnomic statements (12) and similes (13):

(11) [τὸν δ' οὔτ' ἄρ τε γέφυραι ἐεργμέναι ἰσχανόωσιν, / οὔτ' ἄρα ἕρκεα ἴσχει ἀλωάων ἐριθηλέων / ἐλθόντ' ἐξαπίνης] **ὅτ' ἐπιβρίσῃ** Διὸς ὄμβρος. (*Il.* 5.89–91)
hót' epibrísēi *Dios ómbros*
when fall.heavily.3SG.SBJV.AOR Zeus.GEN rain.NOM
'[This the close-fenced embankments hold not back, neither do the walls of the fruitful vineyards stay its sudden coming] when the rain of Zeus drives it on.'

(12) κρείσσων γὰρ βασιλεὺς **ὅτε χώσεται** ἀνδρὶ χέρηϊ. (*Il.* 1.80)
kreíssōn gar basileus **hóte khṓsetai** *andri*
mightier.NOM PTCL king.NOM when be.angry.3SG.SBJV.AOR man.DAT
khérēi
inferior.DAT
'For mightier is a king, when he is angry at a lesser man.'

(13) **ὡς δ' ὅτε** τίς τε κύων συὸς ἀγρίου ἠὲ λέοντος / **ἅπτηται** [κατόπισθε ποσὶν ταχέεσσι διώκων / ἰσχία τε γλουτούς τε, ἑλισσόμενόν τε δοκεύει,] / ὣς Ἕκτωρ ὤπαζε κάρη κομόωντας Ἀχαιούς. (*Il.* 8.338–341)
hōs d' hóte *tís te kúōn suos agríou*
as PTCL when some.NOM PTCL hound.NOM boar.GEN wild.GEN
ēe léontos **háptētai** *hōs Héktōr ṓpaze*
or lion.GEN grasp.3SG.SBJV.PRS so Hector.NOM follow.3SG.IND.IMPF
kárē komóōntas Akhaioús
heads.ACC with.long.hair.ACC Achaeans.ACC
'And even as a hound pursues [with swift feet] after a wild boar or a lion, [and snatches at him from behind either at flank or buttock, and watches for him as he wheels;] even so Hector pressed upon the long-haired Achaeans.'

Similes are frequently attested in our corpus and are a very interesting construction. Here, *hóte*-clauses build a setting that does not relate to any main event. We could say that, in this type of construction, *hóte*-clauses build the setting for a generic verb of "happening, taking place": 'as (it happens) when [...]'. In our corpus, *hót' án*-clauses, but not *hóte ken*-clauses, also occur in similes, with no apparent difference in distribution and semantic content with respect to *hóte*-clauses without a modal particle.

3.3 Summary

To summarise, in Homeric Greek the relationship between modal particles and verbal moods in temporal clauses is less rigid and fixed than in later stages of Greek. Verbal moods still had the capability to convey the opposition between factuality and eventuality meanings in *hóte*-clauses. The particles *án* and *ke(n)* play the role of connecting the eventuality meaning to the speech situation, i.e. the subjective point of view of the speaker with respect to the events.

Homeric Greek allows us to observe a stage of the language in which the eventuality pattern arose and started to spread. We have remarked that there is a complementary distribution between *hóte*-clauses with and without particles. The latter are characterised by verbs in the third person and no deictic reference to the speech situation, and denote recurrent and generic events. Conversely, *hóte*-clauses with modal particles are marked for the reference to the speech situation and denote specific and non-recurrent events.

This result is particularly interesting as it correlates with another feature that matches the opposition between reference vs. non-reference to the speech situation in Homeric Greek, i.e. the distribution of the augment in past tenses. Based on the study of Basset (1989), Willi (2018: 373) argues that "augmented past tenses are a prerogative of *discours* (so that an augmented aorist broadly corresponds to a French *passé composé*), whereas unaugmented past tenses characterise *histoire* (so that an unaugmented aorist matches a French *passé simple*)". In both phenomena, i.e. the occurrence of the modal particle in *hóte*-clauses and the presence of the augmented past tenses, the marked term of the opposition is that in which "there is an 'actual' (or 'speaker-referenced') perspective" (Willi 2018: 374; cf. also Bakker 2001: 14–15).

4 Classical Greek

In Classical Greek, the syntax of *án* in temporal clauses has become fixed and stable,[18] and the combination *hótan* + subjunctive is linked to an eventuality reading with different nuances. In order to study the differences between *hóte*- and *hótan*-clauses we focused on a sample of prose texts, pertaining to different textual genres, as shown in Table 3.

---

[18] More with *hóte* than with other subordinators.

Table 3: Corpus for Classical Greek.

Genre	Author	hótan	hóte	Total
Oratory	Lysias (without fragments)	33	51	84
	Demosthenes (speeches 1–24)	124	114	238
Philosophy	Plato (*Republic*)	146	18	164
Historiography	Thucydides	30	62	92
Total		333	245	578

4.1 Combinatory characteristics

In Classical Greek, the relation between *hótan* and the subjunctive (as compared to *hóte* with various moods) has become fixed. The pattern has several syntactic characteristics:[19]

(a) The modal particle is always combined with the subordinator *hóte* when the eventuality pattern is used (thus *hótan*); by contrast when the modal particle is used in a temporal clause outside the eventuality pattern (e.g. for an irrealis with the indicative, for a potential meaning with the optative mood),[20] the modal particle is placed later in the subordinate clause. The subordinator *hótan* is, thus, used only with a subjunctive mood.[21]

(b) *Hóte*-clauses are sensitive to the embedding context contrary to *hótan*-clauses. Moods typical of indirect speech can appear in a *hóte*-clause, which is not attested in our corpus for *hótan*-clauses.[22]

This fixed syntax is linked to a specialisation of the two subordinators.

---

[19] Other parameters were examined (e.g. position of the subordinate clause in relation to the embedding clause, distance of the verb from the subordinator, aspect of the subordinate verb) without revealing any clear differences. *Hóte*-clauses are, however, slightly more frequent in the 1st and 2nd person (27%) than *hótan*-clauses (17%).

[20] Cf. Lys. 19.13 for an irrealis and Pl. *R.* 415b1 for a potential.

[21] With only one exception in a debated passage, due to textual problems (Pl. *R.* 412d5, optative in the temporal clause, embedded in a clause in the optative).

[22] *Hóte*-clause with an infinitive: Th. 2.102.5; with an oblique optative: Lys. 20.27, Pl. *R.* 616a6.

4.1.1 *Hóte*-clauses as true temporal clauses

As a time-anchored subordinator, *hóte* may be used correlatively with *tóte* 'then' or to amplify temporal phrases expressing a date (e.g. 'at that time', 'after that', 'the previous day', etc.).[23] It is possible for a *hóte*-clause to amplify only a temporal adverb, without framing the main clause as in (14):

(14) πολλοὺς γὰρ ὑμῶν ὁρῶ δικάζοντας τῶν **τότε** παρόντων, **ὅτε** Λυσίθεος Θεόμνηστον εἰσήγγελλε [τὰ ὅπλα ἀποβεβληκότα οὐκ ἐξὸν αὐτῷ δημηγορεῖν]. (Lys. 10.1)

pollous	*gar*	*humôn*	*horô*	*dikázontas*	*tôn*	**tóte**
many.ACC	PTCL	you.GEN	see.1SG.IND.PRS	be.judge.ACC	ART.GEN	then

paróntōn	**hóte**	*Lusítheos*	*Theómnēston*	*eisḗggelle*
present.GEN	when	Lysitheos.NOM	Theomnestos.ACC	accuse.3SG.IND.IMPF

'For I see many of you in this place of judgement who were present at the time when Lysitheus was prosecuting Theomnestus [for speaking before the people, since he had lost the right to do so by having cast away his armour].'

Let us mention also a specific structure *éstin hóte* / ἔστιν ὅτε (lit. 'there.is when'), which is used in the meaning 'there is a time when'; the pattern can also be used as an adverbial ('sometimes') without a subordinating function.[24]

4.1.2 *Hótan*-clauses as clauses framing situations

By contrast, *hótan* is used for framing situations, and tends to occur in non-specific contexts. Indefinites often appear in *hótan*-clauses (75 examples, sometimes with several indefinites in an utterance vs. 6 examples of indefinites in *hóte*-clauses). Like *hóte*-clauses, *hótan*-clauses can expand a phrase of the main clause, but the phrase is not necessarily temporal as in (15) where the noun phrase has a qualifying function:

---

[23] E.g. 'at that time' (Lys. 18.26, D. 6.20, Th. 3.56.4), 'after that' (Lys. 20.22, D. 19.18), 'the previous day' (D. 21.119). The sequence *nûn hóte* 'now that' (lit. 'now when') is frequent enough to be mentioned in some grammars (Kühner and Gerth 1898: §565).
[24] 13 utterances of the structure in our corpus, out of which 4 used adverbially (Th. 5.102.1, 6.38.3, 7.21.3, Pl. *R.* 439c3).

(15) τοὺς γὰρ τοιούτους λόγους, **ὅταν** ἀπαγγελλόντων **ἀκούῃ**, [ὅτι κακῶς ἤκουεν, ὑμεῖς δ' ἀπεδέχεσθε, μεταβάλλειν αὐτοῦ τὴν γνώμην.] (D. 7.21)
tous   gar   toioútous   lógous   **hót-an**
ART.ACC   PTCL   such.ACC   words.ACC when-MOD
apaggellóntōn   **akoúēi**
referring.PTCP.GEN   hear.3SG.SBJV.PRS
'for tales of that sort, when he hears others saying [that he was referred to badly and that you accepted it, make him change his mind.]'

Hótan-clauses can also be used for scanning possible situations without referring to any particular moment of time. In (16) *hótan* occurs without a main verb as an equivalent of 'either [...] or', for typical situations and attitudes.

(16) [πολλὰ γὰρ ἂν ποιήσειεν ὁ τύπτων, ὦ ἄνδρες Ἀθηναῖοι, ὧν ὁ παθὼν ἔνι' οὐδ' ἂν ἀπαγγεῖλαι δύναιθ' ἑτέρῳ, τῷ σχήματι, τῷ βλέμματι, τῇ φωνῇ,] **ὅταν** ὡς ὑβρίζων, **ὅταν** ὡς ἐχθρὸς ὑπάρχων, **ὅταν** κονδύλοις, **ὅταν** ἐπὶ κόρρης. (D. 21.72)
hót-an   hōs   hubrízōn   **hót-an**   hōs   ekhthros
when-MOD   as   outrage.PTCP.NOM   when-MOD   as   enemy.NOM
hupárkhōn   **hót-an**   kondúlois   **hót-an**   epi   kórrēs
be.PTCP.NOM   when-MOD   fist.DAT   when-MOD   on   temple.GEN
[For the striker may do many things, Athenians, some of which the victim could not even name to another person – by gesture, by look, by tone;] when he strikes in wantonness or out of enmity; with the fists or on the temple.' (our translation)

4.2 The semantic characteristics of *hótan*-clauses

This general characterisation does have contextual nuances. Traditionally two main meanings of subjunctive + *án* are acknowledged, i.e. generic-iterative uses and prospective ones. They are sometimes presented as two distinct meanings.[25] However, it is well-known that the two meanings sometimes overlap as in (17):

---

[25] From Kühner and Gerth (1898: §567) to more recent accounts, e.g. van Emde Boas *et al.* (2019: 537–541); Revuelta Puigdollers (2020: 668–670).

(17) ὅταν τις τοιαῦτα λέγῃ περὶ θεῶν, χαλεπανοῦμέν τε καὶ χορὸν οὐ δώσομεν.
(Pl. *R.* 383c1)
hót-an   tis   toiaûta   légēi   peri
when-MOD someone.NOM such.things.ACC speak.3SG.SBJV.PRS about
theôn,   khalepanoûmén   te kai khoron   ou   dṓsomen
gods.GEN be.angry.1PL.IND.FUT and   chorus.ACC NEG give.1PL.IND.FUT
'When someone speaks about the gods in that way, we shall be angry and refuse him a chorus.' (our translation)

In (17) the speaker refers to a future state of affairs (thus a possible prospective reading); but the discussion is about how to handle poets referring to gods in a future constitution, which means that the future regulation is not linked to any specific utterance (thus a possible generic-iterative reading).

The idea that the two uses are two particular cases of a more general meaning has also been defended in the case of hypothetical clauses where the combination subjunctive + *án* also occurs (Wakker 1994; Rijksbaron 2006: 69–70). According to Wakker (1994: 174), the core meaning may be stated as follows: "there is – on account of the situation or of the general circumstances – reasonable chance that the condition will be realized". Wakker's point is that the interpretation of the hypothetical clause depends on the verbal form in the main clause: there is a generic-iterative reading when the main clause is generic itself, mainly in the present indicative; there is a prospective reading when the state of affairs in the main clause refers to the future (future tenses, but also directive acts and deontic expressions). The same type of explanation is found in Rijksbaron (2006: 80–82) for temporal clauses. The merit of an explanation such as Wakker's is to emphasise that the modal meaning of a clause is not only built by the mood in the clause under study but in the interaction between the main and the subordinate clauses. However, the criteria put forward are not always clear in temporal clauses, such as in (18), where the embedding clause in the infinitive aorist does not give any clue.[26]

---

[26] One could wonder whether the lexical meaning of the verb in the embedding clause is actually a clue ('to prepare oneself' supposes an intention for a state of affairs in the future). However the temporal clause can refer to the past (Lys. 31.32) with this kind of verb, and possibly also to the present.

(18) [προεῖπον ὡς ἐδύναντο ἀδηλότατα ἔκπλουν ἐκ τοῦ στρατοπέδου πᾶσι, καὶ] παρασκευάσασθαι **ὅταν** τις **σημήνῃ**. (Th. 7.50.3)
paraskeuásasthai ***hót-an*** *tis* **semḗnēi**
prepare.INF.AOR when-MOD someone.NOM signal.3SG.SBJV.AOR
'[As secretly as they could they gave orders to all to leave the camp by sea and] to prepare themselves at a given signal.' (lit. 'when someone gives a signal') (our translation)

We would like to argue that the different meanings of *hótan*-clauses in Classical Greek are not adequately described by a temporal mapping (generic-iterative effects when linked to present state of affairs) or by considerations on the likelihood of the propositional content.

First, the generic-iterative use does not always depend on the present reference of the state of affairs in the main clause. All kinds of tenses are possible for generic readings, if generality or iterativity is expressed in the main clause or by the context:[27]

(19) καὶ **ὅταν παύσηται** ἄρα, [εἶπον], χαίρων τις, ἡ τῆς ἡδονῆς ἡσυχία λυπηρὸν ἔσται. (Pl. *R.*583e1)
kai ***hót-an paúsētai*** *ára khaírōn tis*
and when-MOD cease.3SG.SBJV.AOR thus be.pleased.PTCP.NOM INDF.NOM
hē tês hēdonês hēsukhía lupēron éstai
the.NOM the.GEN pleasure.GEN quietness.NOM painful.N be.3SG.IND.FUT
'And so [I said] **when someone stops** being pleased, the cessation of pleasure will be painful.' (our translation)

In (19), even though the main clause is in the future, the reading of the temporal clause is generic and does not refer to a specific moment of the future. The propositional content of the *hótan*-clause sets up a scenario, built on an implicit representation deduced from the context.

Second, in the prospective meaning, even though the temporal clause refers to a unique state of affairs situated in the future, the future event is more or less hypothetical. In most of the examples of prospective meaning, it is possible to reformulate *hótan* by 'if and when':

---

27 For a clear generic use with past tense in the main clause, see Lys. 12.41.

(20) [(...) οἳ τῷ μὲν λόγῳ τῷ δήμῳ πολεμοῦσι, τῷ δὲ ἔργῳ τῶν ὑμετέρων ἐπιθυμοῦσιν·] ἅπερ κτήσονται, **ὅταν** ὑμᾶς ἐρήμους συμμάχων **λάβωσιν**. (Lys. 34.5)
*háper   ktḗsontai   **hót-an**   humâs   erḗmous*
REL.N.PL.ACC acquire.3PL.FUT when-MOD   you.ACC   deprived.ACC
*summákhōn   **lábōsin***
allies.GEN   take.3PL.SBJV.AOR
'[(...) who in speech make war on the people, but in fact are aiming at your property;] and this they will acquire **when they find** you destitute of allies.'

In this case, the meaning is not generic: the event described is unique, it may occur in the future, but it is not bound to happen. The speaker warns his audience: it is dangerous to have no allies. If ever, in the future, the Athenians are without allies, then the others will be able to accomplish their evil actions. It is clear that the speaker hopes that the situation will not to happen. It is a mere possibility, but the day this possibility becomes true, then it will entail a sure consequence (hence the future in the main clause). Interestingly enough, *hótan* clauses are used by Demosthenes (13 times) to refer to the expected speech of the other party ('my opponent will say such and such, according to what I have heard", cf. D. 21.24). Because of this 'if and when' meaning, some of these utterances are more causal than temporal, in rhetorical questions as in (21) as well as in other types of utterances.

(21) πῶς οὖν ἀπολεῖται, **ὅταν** τοὺς παρ' ἐκείνου δωροδοκοῦντας σὺ **σῴζῃς**; (D. 19.292)
*pôs   oûn   apoleîtai,   **hót-an**   tous   par'*
how   thus   be.destroyed.3SG.FUT when-MOD   the.ACC.PL   from
*ekeínou   dōrodokoûntas   su   **sṓizēis**?*
DEM.GEN   accept.bribe.PTCP.ACC.PL you.NOM   save.2SG.SBJV.PRS
'How can Philip be destroyed, **if you keep safe** the men corrupted by him?' (our translation)

As a contrast *hóte*-clauses are fully temporal. For example *hóte*-clauses + present (26 utterances) do not have a generic-iterative reading but are grounded in the speaker's present.[28] *Hóte*-clauses + imperfect (148 utterances) do not express rep-

---

28 E.g. Lys. 26.5.

etition.²⁹ A revealing contrast is given by *hóte*-clauses + future. The pattern is rare but not unattested (4 utterances in our corpus).³⁰

(22) [μὴ οὖν ἐξελέγξηθ᾽ ὡς κακῶς ἔχει τὰ Ἑλληνικά], συγκαλοῦντες **ὅτ᾽** οὐ πείσονται, καὶ πολεμοῦντες **ὅτ᾽** οὐ δυνήσεσθε. (D. 14.38)

sugkaloûntes	**hót'**	ou	peísontai	kai
summon.PTCP.NOM.PL	when	NEG	obey.3PL.FUT	and
polemoûntes	**hót'**	ou	dunḗsesthe	
make.war.PTCP.NOM.PL	when	NEG	be.able.2PL.FUT	

'[Do not reveal, then, how bad is the situation of the Greeks] by calling to council when they will not obey, and by declaring a war when you cannot afford it.' (lit. 'when you will not afford it') (our translation)

By contrast, with *hótan* + subjunctive clauses, the propositional content in (22) is presented as certain (it is sure that they won't obey): it is an assertive temporal clause, where the propositional content is anchored in time.³¹

To sum up, in the prospective meaning, the event is expected, foreseen by the speaker, and presented as such, with a degree of uncertainty; in the generic meaning, the event may happen at any time, but it is not necessarily unique nor specific. In both cases the propositional content is set up as a fictive scenario, grounded on actual situations: it does not represent a date but a fictive situation. This explains why there may be some overlap between the two traditionally-acknowledged meanings.³² In Classical Greek, the eventuality pattern which has become a fixed one in this type of temporal clauses permits a wider variety of nuances, as compared to Archaic Greek. These nuances, however, pertain to the semantics of the eventuality pattern: the speaker sets up a fictive scenario, which is not assertive, nor temporally anchored, and represents a possible world.

---

29 Cf. van Emde Boas *et al.* (2019: 538): "the imperfect, by presenting the action of the subordinate clause as incomplete, suggests that the action of the subordinate clause is going on at the same as that of the matrix clause". See. e.g. Lys. 12.25.
30 D. 14.38 (2x), 19.262, 20.28.
31 In grammars, it is sometimes said that "temporal clauses referring to the future always have ἄν [*án*] + subjunctive (prospective)" (van Emde Boas *et al.* 2019: 539). Even though utterances are scarce, they show clearly that modality is always involved in *hótan*-clauses, even when referring to the future.
32 In a recent account of temporal clauses, de la Villa Polo (2020) omits the traditional division between generic-iterative and prospective meaning. In this account, *hótan*-clauses can refer to virtual situations, which are simply possible or foreseeable (de la Villa Polo 2020: 880). Our conclusions also favor a unified meaning.

5 Koine Greek

In the New Testament, *hótan* and *hóte* still display the configurations attested in Classical Greek (Burton 1898; Blass and Debrunner 1961; Moulton 1976). *Hótan* occurs with the subjunctive, except for a few cases, mainly with the perfective/ aoristic stem, as shown in Table 4, whilst *hóte* occurs exclusively with the indicative (one contested exception), mainly with the aorist tense in formulaic time-anchored expressions and standard narrative schemas, some of which were already attested in the Septuagint.

Table 4: Distribution of *hóte* and *hótan* in the NT.

	Indicative				Subjunctive		Total
	Present	Aorist	Imperfect	Future	Present	Aorist	
hóte-clauses	3	76	16	6	–	–	101[33]
hótan-clauses	–	2	1	3 (?)	15	102	123

5.1 The main features of *hótan* in the NT

According to New Testament grammarians (Robertson 1919; Decker 2001), *hótan* refers to a conditional, possible, and, in many instances, iterative event.

In the New Testament corpus, *hótan* is still used for framing situations conveying an indefinite projecting value,[34] illustrating thus a diachronic continuity of meaning and form in the expression of eventuality:

(23) καὶ νῦν εἴρηκα ὑμῖν πρὶν γενέσθαι ἵνα **ὅταν γένηται** πιστεύσητε. (*Ev.Jo.* 14.29)
kai nûn eíreka humîn prin genésthai
and now tell.1SG.IND.PRF you.2PL.DAT before become.INF.AOR
hína **hót-an génētai** pisteúsēte
so.that when-MOD become.3SG.SBJV.AOR believe.2PL.SBJV.AOR
'And now I have told you before it comes, that when it does come to pass, you may believe.'

---

[33] We do not take into account here one passage (*Ev.Luc.* 13.35), where *hóte* occurs as a conjectural addition to the text.
[34] As Porter (1994: 240) puts it, indicative and subjunctive moods differ "in attitude between the writer asserting and merely projecting".

(24) μακάριοί ἐστε **ὅταν μισήσωσιν** ὑμᾶς οἱ ἄνθρωποι, καὶ **ὅταν ἀφορίσωσιν** ὑμᾶς [καὶ ὀνειδίσωσιν καὶ ἐκβάλωσιν τὸ ὄνομα ὑμῶν ὡς πονηρὸν ἕνεκα τοῦ υἱοῦ τοῦ ἀνθρώπου]. (*Ev.Luc.* 6.22)

makárioí	este	**hót-an**	misḗsōsin	humâs
blessed.NOM	be.2PL.IND.PRS	when-MOD	hate.3PL.SBJV.AOR	you.PL.ACC
hoi	ánthrōpoi	kai	**hót-an**	aphorísōsin	humâs
ART.NOM	men.NOM	and	when-MOD	separate.3PL.SBJV.AOR	you.PL.ACC

'Blessed are you when men shall hate you, and when they shall separate you from them [and reproach you, and throw out your name as evil, for the Son of Man's sake].'

The projective value of *hótan* appears clearly in contexts where a future situation, highly predictable and bound to happen ('when you are old'), is presented as opposed point by point to past, time-anchored events, introduced by *hóte* ('when you were young'):

(25) [ἀμὴν ἀμὴν λέγω σοι,] **ὅτε** ἦς νεώτερος, [ἐζώννυες σεαυτὸν καὶ περιεπάτεις ὅπου ἤθελες·] **ὅταν δὲ γηράσῃς**, [ἐκτενεῖς τὰς χεῖράς σου, καὶ ἄλλος σε ζώσει καὶ οἴσει ὅπου οὐ θέλεις]. (*Ev.Jo.* 21.18)

hóte	ês	neóteros [...]
when	be.2SG.IND.IMPF	younger.NOM
hót-an	de	gerásēis [...]
when-MOD	PTCL	get.old.2SG.SBJV.AOR

'[Most assuredly I tell you,] when you were young, [you dressed yourself, and walked where you wanted to.] But when you are old, [you will stretch out your hands, and another will dress you, and carry you where you don't want to go].'

As attested in synoptic examples, e.g. (26) and (27), *hótan* may be used, following the pattern of conditionals, in certain 'if and when' bipartite structures, in a similar way to *e-án* (ἐ-άν) 'if-MOD', which is by far, as expected, the prevailing encoding for this particular function (335 occ. vs. 123 occ. of *hótan*). The framing property of the *hótan* clause in (26) confers a sequential, resultative value to the main clause to which it is linked by the coordinator *kai* (καί), whereas this is not the case with merely conditional *eán*-clauses, e.g. (27), which is directly linked to the main clause apodosis:

(26) [ὁ λύχνος τοῦ σώματός ἐστιν ὁ ὀφθαλμός σου.] **ὅταν** ὁ ὀφθαλμός σου ἁπλοῦς ᾖ καὶ ὅλον τὸ σῶμά σου φωτεινόν ἐστιν, **ἐπὰν**[35] δὲ πονηρὸς ᾖ, [καὶ τὸ σῶμά σου σκοτεινόν]. (*Ev.Luc.* 11.34)

hót-an   ho   ophtalmós   sou   haploûs
when-MOD   ART.NOM   eye.NOM   you.GEN   good.NOM
êi   kai   hólon   to   sôma
be.3SG.SBJV.PRS and   whole.NOM ART.NOM body.NOM
sou   phōteinón   estin,   **ep-an**   de
you.GEN   shining.NOM be.3SG.IND.PRS when-MOD PTCL
ponēros   **êi**
evil.NOM   be.3SG.SBJV.PRS

'[The lamp of the body is the eye.] Therefore when your eye is good, your whole body is also full of light; but when it is evil, [your body also is full of darkness].'

(27) [ὁ λύχνος τοῦ σώματός ἐστιν ὁ ὀφθαλμός.] **ἐὰν** οὖν ᾖ ὁ ὀφθαλμός σου ἁπλοῦς [ὅλον τὸ σῶμά σου φωτεινὸν ἔσται.] **ἐὰν** δὲ ὁ ὀφθαλμός σου πονηρὸς ᾖ, [ὅλον τὸ σῶμά σου σκοτεινὸν ἔσται]. (*Ev.Matt.* 6.22)

e-an   oûn   **êi**   ho   ophtalmós sou   haploûs
if-MOD   PTCL   be.3SG.SBJV.PRS ART.NOM eye.NOM   you.GEN   good.NOM
e-án   de   ho   ophtalmós sou   ponēros   **êi**
if-MOD   PTCL   ART.NOM eye.NOM   you.GEN   evil.NOM   be.3SG.SBJV.PRS

'[The lamp of the body is the eye.] If therefore your eye is sound, [your whole body will be full of light]. But if your eye is evil, [your whole body will be full of darkness].'

Furthermore Koine Greek exhibits a new combinatory possibility which was not attested earlier, i.e. the use of *hótan* with the indicative mood (Blass and Debrunner

---

35 There are only three occurrences of *ep-án* (when.MOD) in the New Testament (*Ev.Luc.* 11.22, 11.34, *Ev.Matt.* 2.8). Two of them, co-occurring with *hótan*, are attested in the Gospel of Luke and seem to reflect the particular style of the author. In ex. (26), in which two properties, "good" vs. "evil", are set in opposition, *epán* (*de*) is used in parallel with *hótan*, as a quasi-synonym. The *hótan* clause refers to a normally expected, typical course of events scenario, while the use of *epán* seems to suggest a more alarming scenario (a more strongly stated condition) which is perhaps the most likely to happen. See the following instance: **hótan ho iskhuros kathōplisménos phulássēi tēn heautoû aulén, en eirénēi estin tà hupárkhonta autoû; epan de iskhuróteros autoû epelthōn nikésēi autón, tēn panoplían autoû aírei eph' hêi epepoíthei, kai ta skûla autoû diadídōsin** (*Ev.Luc.* 11.21–22), 'When (*hót-an*) the strong man, fully armed, guards his own dwelling, his goods are safe. But when (*ep-an*) someone stronger attacks him and overcomes him, he takes from him his whole armor in which he trusted, and divides his spoils'.

1961: 193). This combination, often inserted in formulaic constructions, is already attested in the Septuagint (ex. 28),[36] in 10 occurrences out of 210:

(28) καὶ ἐγίνετο **ὅταν ἐπῆρεν** Μωυσῆς τὰς χεῖρας, [κατίσχυεν Ἰσραήλ·] **ὅταν** δὲ **καθῆκεν** [τὰς χεῖρας, κατίσχυεν Ἀμαλήκ]. (*Ex.* 17.11)
kai   egíneto   **hót-an**   **epêiren**   Mōusês   tas
and   become.3SG.IND.IMPF   when-MOD   lift.3SG.IND.AOR Moses.NOM ART.ACC
kheîras, [...]   hót-an   de   kathêken
hands.ACC   when-MOD   PTCL   let down.3SG.IND.AOR
'And it came to pass, that as long as Moses held up his hand, [Israel prevailed;] and when he let down his hand, [Amalek prevailed].'

In the New Testament, there are 6 occurrences of the '*hótan* + indicative' construction, but most of them are considered marginal readings;[37] there is only one unanimously accepted occurrence:

(29) [καὶ τὰ πνεύματα τὰ ἀκάθαρτα,] **ὅταν** αὐτὸν **ἐθεώρουν** [προσέπιπτον αὐτῷ καὶ ἔκραζον λέγοντες ὅτι Σὺ εἶ ὁ υἱὸς τοῦ θεοῦ]. (*Ev.Marc.* 3.11)
hót-an   auton   **etheóroun**
when-MOD   him.ACC   see.3PL.IND.IMPF
'[The unclean spirits,] whenever they saw him, [fell down before him, and cried, "You are the Son of God!"]' (lit. 'when they saw')

The salient feature of *hótan* in the New Testament is that it becomes an aspect-conditioned subordinator. This kind of development seems connected to the general rise of aorist / perfective stems in Judeo-Christian Greek. As shown by Evans (2001: 124) on the Pentateuch data "there are 1,388 examples of the aorist subjunctive in the whole Pentateuch, and only 215 examples of the present." The limited attestation of the imperfect in the Greek Pentateuch "does reflect a general trend. The imperfect declines in frequency relative to the aorist indicative during the Postclassical period" (Evans 2001: 202). Statistics for extra-Biblical Greek "appear to demonstrate a decline in the frequency of the imperfect relative to the aorist indicative

---

36 Evans (2001: 199) considers this construction as a Hebraism. He quotes the following example: *kai **hótan katébē** (IND.AOR) ē drósos epi tēn parembolēn nuktós, **katébainen** (IND.IMPF) to manna ep' autês* (*Nu.* 11.9) 'And when the dew fell upon the camp by night, the manna was falling upon it', arguing that "[t]he aorist κατέβη translates an infinitive construct, the imperfect κατέβαινεν a Hebrew imperfect".
37 See *Apoc.* 4.9 (future), 8.1 (aorist), *Ev.Marc.* 11.25 (present), 11.19 (aorist), *Ev.Luc.* 13.28 (future).

during the Postclassical period, especially in the vernacular language" (Evans 2001: 218–219).

Indeed, as Table 4 above shows, the aorist / perfective stem of the subjunctive becomes clearly dominant by this period (102 occ. vs. 15 present) unlike the distribution in our Classical Greek corpus, where it is the present stem that prevails (212 occ. vs. 96 occ. of the aorist).

Another factor that may contribute to the high score of this new *hótan* combinatory in the New Testament is the Gospel text genre and its special narrative structure. *Hótan* is used in parabolic narratives, i.e. storytelling with unspecified spatial and temporal location and with a performative meaning, pronouncement-like stories, aphorisms, macarisms (as noted above, e.g. ex. (24)), whereas *hóte* is never attested in such contexts:

(30) [ἀπὸ δὲ τῆς συκῆς μάθετε τὴν παραβολήν] **ὅταν** ἤδη ὁ κλάδος αὐτῆς γένηται ἁπαλὸς [καὶ τὰ φύλλα ἐκφύῃ γινώσκετε ὅτι ἐγγὺς τὸ θέρος] οὕτως καὶ ὑμεῖς **ὅταν** ἴδητε [...] (*Ev.Matt.* 24.32)
hót-an   ḗdē   ho   kládos   autês
when-MOD   already   ART.NOM   branch.NOM   her.GEN
génētai   hapalos [...] hoútōs   kai   humeîs
become.3SG.SBJV.AOR   tender.NOM   so   PTCL   ART.NOM
hót-an   ídēte
when-MOD   see.2PL.SBJV.AOR
'[From the fig tree learn its lesson:] as soon as its branch becomes tender [and puts out its leaves, you know that summer is near.] So also you, when you see [all these things].'

5.2 The evolution of *hóte* as a time-anchored event marker

In continuity with its use in the Classical period, *hóte* occurs only with the indicative (aorist, imperfect and future), and denotes time-anchored events or actions with mainly past time reference (92 occ. out of 102). Most of them (76 occ.) are in the aorist. Both in the Septuagint and the New Testament, verbs occurring in *hóte*-clauses are mostly verbs of movement, verbs of perception (hearing and seeing), telic and achievement predicates (e.g. *hóte sunetélesan* 'when they had finished + N', *hóte eplḗsthēsan hēmérai* 'when the days were fulfilled', *hóte ḗngisan* 'when they drew near to + N', etc.). It often occurs in formulaic and conventional expressions, e.g. *kai egéneto hóte etélesen ho Iēsoûs* 'and it happened, when Jesus had finished [saying these things]', which is well attested also in the Septuagint (in some cases, they show overt intertextuality). In all cases, they refer to time-space location:

(31) ὅτε δὲ ἡμέρα ἐγένετο [τὴν γῆν οὐκ ἐπεγίνωσκον]. (*Act.Ap.* 27.39)
    hóte de **hēméra egéneto**
    when PTCL day.NOM become.3SG.IND.AOR
    'When it was day, [they did not recognize the land].'

(32) ἀλλὰ ἔρχεται ὥρα **καὶ νῦν ἐστιν ὅτε** οἱ ἀληθινοὶ προσκυνηταὶ προσκυνήσουσιν. (*Ev.Jo.* 4.23)
    alla   érkhetai   hṓra   **kai   nûn   estin**
    but   come.3SG.IND.PRS hour.NOM and   now   be.3SG.IND.PRS
    hóte hoi   alēthinoi   proskunētai   proskunḗsousin
    when   ART.NOM true.NOM   worshipers.NOM worship.3PL.FUT
    'But the hour is coming, and now is, when the true worshipers will worship [the Father in spirit and truth].'

Apart from these well-attested uses, *hóte* can be found in constructions displaying sequences of aorists and expressing relative time reference. They situate the event of the main clause in posteriority with respect to the action expressed in the *hóte*-clause. We give in (33) and (35) two examples from the Septuagint and the New Testament respectively.

(33) καὶ **ὅτε** συνετέλεσαν τὸ φαγεῖν καὶ πιεῖν, ἠθέλησαν κοιμηθῆναι [καὶ ἀπήγαγον τὸν νεανίσκον καὶ εἰσήγαγον αὐτὸν εἰς τὸ ταμίειον]. (*To.* 8.1, Codex Sinaiticus)
    kai   **hóte** sunetélesan   to   phageîn   kai
    and   when   finish.3PL.IND.AOR ART.ACC   eat.INF.AOR and
    pieîn,   ethélēsan   koimēthēnai
    drink.INF.AOR   want.3PL.IND.AOR   sleep.INF.AOR
    'When they had finished eating and drinking, they wanted to go to sleep; [so they led the young man out and led him into the room].'

In the Latin translation of the Vulgate *hóte* rendered by *postquam* 'after that' is a clear indication of the temporal meaning of the subordinator pointing to posteriority.[38] The following passage of Tobit (Codex Vaticanus) corresponds to this interpretation:

---

38 There are two distinct Greek traditions of manuscripts for the book of Tobit, the family of the short version, which consists of two manuscripts, the *Codex Vaticanus* and the *Codex Alexandrinus*, and the family of the long version, which consists of the *Codex Sinaiticus* (Littman 2008).

(34) a. **ὅτε** δὲ συνετέλεσαν δειπνοῦντες, εἰσήγαγον Τωβιαν πρὸς αὐτήν. (*To.* 8.1 Codex Vaticanus & Codex Alexandrinus)
hóte   de   sunetélesan   deipnoûntes
when PTCL finish.3PL.IND.AOR dine.PTCP.NOM.PRS
eisḗgagon   Tōbian   pros   autḗn
lead.3PL.IND.AOR Tobit.ACC to   her.ACC
'When they had finished eating they led the young man to her.'
b. **postquam** *vero cœnaverunt, introduxerunt juvenem ad eam.* (Vulg., *To.* 8.1)
'After that they had dined, they led the young man to her.' (literal translation)

(35) [οἱ οὖν στρατιῶται] **ὅτε** ἐσταύρωσαν τὸν Ἰησοῦν ἔλαβον τὰ ἱμάτια αὐτοῦ [καὶ ἐποίησαν τέσσαρα μέρη]. (*Ev.Jo.* 19.23)
hóte   estaúrōsan   ton   Iēsoûn   élabon
when crucify.3PL.IND.AOR ART.ACC Jesus.ACC take.3PL.IND.AOR
ta   himátia   autoû
ART.ACC garments.ACC his.GEN
'[Then the soldiers], when they had crucified Jesus, took his garments [and made four parts].'

These examples suggest a weakening of the *hóte* core value as a time-anchored subordinator, a phenomenon that must be considered in correlation with the evolution of the syntax of *hótan*, now attested, even if only marginally in the New Testament, with time-reference forms.

5.3 A hypothesis about the diachronic development

The New Testament data show that *hótan* + aorist stem may be considered as a 'future' (with an eventuality meaning) counterpart of *hóte* + aorist (indicative), the two forms being related on an aspectual basis, i.e. their common aspect stem and aoristic (indefinite) aspectual value (see Table 5).

This distribution of *hóte* and *hótan* is regular in the New Testament corpus, and it is supported by the fact that by this period *hótan* is completely univerbated – which means that *án* has lost in *hótan* most of its categorial status and features as a modal particle. This distribution offers a new morphological pattern for syntactic and modal change, leading thus to the diachronic emergence of a new temporal conjunction with extended use (both in tense and mood), comparable to the Modern Greek *ótan*, which will progressively supersede *óte* in Hellenistic Greek and subsequent periods.

Table 5: Diachronic account of *hótan*-clauses in Postclassical Greek.

Classical Greek	
ὅτ-αν ἔλθῃ [*hót-an élthēi*] when-MOD come.3SG.SBJV.AOR 'when he comes' (prospective value)	ὅτε ἦλθεν [*hóte êlthen*] when come.3SG.IND.AOR 'when he came' (time anchored past value)
Postclassical Greek	
ὅταν ἦλθεν [*hótan êlthen*] when.MOD come.3SG.IND.AOR 'when he came' ("aoristic past" value)	

6 Conclusion

We have argued that modality is not only expressed by modal markers but also by syntactic patterns. Our study shows that taking into account syntactic patterns helps us understand the modal markers themselves. A modal marker such as the modal particle *án* cannot be understood in isolation; we have studied (a) its occurrence in a specific kind of construction and (b) its appearance in specific texts, with (c) the further insight of diachrony.

(a) We have studied *án* in temporal clauses introduced by the subordinator *hóte* 'when', which permits a contrastive study with *hóte*-clauses without *án*, in combination with the presence or the absence of the subjunctive.

(b) The corpus-based approach has provided data that are better understood as considered in relation to textual genres. When they occur in a simile in Homeric Greek, in oratory in Classical Greek, or in blessings in the New Testament, the syntactic patterns develop different semantic nuances.

(c) Our diachronic approach, studying three stages of Ancient Greek, has allowed us to systematically compare how the subjunctive + *án* combination functions as a syntactic pattern; at each of the studied stages of the language, the syntactic pattern takes a different shape.

This approach has allowed us to offer a new description of the modal particle *án* and to reconsider its categorial status and its function in a specific kind of combination (*hótan* + subjunctive). Our study sheds new light on the following two aspects.

(i) The syntagmatic and paradigmatic properties of *án* are relevant for defining its role as a modal particle. Besides its interaction with the subjunctive mood and the subordinator, we also observed that the appearance of *án* in Homeric Greek correlates with a difference in person markers: at this stage, where the subordinator can combine with the subjunctive without the modal particle, *án* appears particularly when the verb is inflected in the first and second person, that is in clauses that are marked for reference to the speech situation. This makes a difference with respect to *hóte* clauses with the subjunctive alone. Besides person, another grammatical category that interacts with the modal particle is the category of aspect, especially in later stages of Ancient Greek. We have remarked that, in New Testament Greek, *hótan-* and *hóte*-clauses tend to occur with aoristic verbal stems of the subjunctive and indicative, respectively, and that *hótan*-clauses can also occur with indicative aorists, which is impossible in previous stages of Greek.

(ii) These syntagmatic properties change through the three stages of Ancient Greek, although the eventuality value is preserved as a semantic category.

In the temporal clauses we have studied, the eventuality value is the same through the different stages of Ancient Greek: the speaker sets up a fictive scenario, which is neither assertive nor temporally anchored and represents a possible world.

The value is expressed by a syntactic pattern and the weight of its components in the construction of the eventuality meaning changes through the three stages under study. In Homeric Greek, *hóte* clauses combine with a wide variety of verbal moods, and the eventuality value is highly dependent on the subjunctive. In Classical Greek, the combination of *hóte*-clauses with the subjunctive and a modal particle is fixed and stable which allows a wider range of nuances. In New Testament Greek, *hótan*-clauses tend to be associated with the aorist subjunctive, thus restricting the syntactic pattern. This specialisation in aspect and tense allows the indicative to occur with *hótan*, provided that indicatives are in the aorist stem, and is linked to the reconfiguration of verbal moods in Postclassical Greek.

This evolution has an influence on the properties of the subordinator *hóte* itself. In Homeric Greek, the eventuality value is built through the combination of the subordinator and the subjunctive, with or without the modal particle; the coalescence of the subordinator and the modal particle, both in form and in function, gives rise to two distinct subordinators, *hóte* and *hótan*: as a result *hóte* (without the modal particle) becomes a time-anchored event marker able to express posteriority.

References

Bach, Emmon. 1986. The algebra of events. *Linguistics and Philosophy* 9. 5–16.
Basset, Louis. 1988. Valeurs et emplois de la particule dite modale en grec ancien. In Albert Rijksbaron (ed.), *In the footsteps of Raphael Kühner*, 27–37. Amsterdam: Brill.
Basset, Louis. 1989 [2004]. L'augment et la distinction discours/récit dans *l'Iliade* et *l'Odyssée*. In Michel Casevitz (ed.), *Études homériques*, 9–16. Lyon: Maison de l'Orient et de la Méditerranée [republished in Louis Basset, *L'imaginer et le dire. Scripta Minora*, 101–108. Lyon: Maison de l'Orient et de la Méditerranée].
Bakker, Egbert J. 2001. Similes, augment, and the language of immediacy. In Janet Watson (ed.), *Speaking volumes: Orality and literacy in the Greek and Roman world*, 1–23. Leiden: Brill.
Beck, Jana E., Sophia A. Malamud & Iryna Osadcha. 2012. A semantics for the particle ἄν [án] in and outside conditionals in Classical Greek. *Journal of Greek Linguistics* 12. 51–83.
Blass, Friedrich & Albert Debrunner. 1961. *A Greek grammar of the New Testament and other early Christian literature*. Translated and edited by Robert W. Funk. Chicago, Illinois: The University of Chicago Press.
Burton, Ernest de Witt. 1898. *Syntax of the moods and tenses in New Testament Greek*. 3rd edn. Edinburgh: T. & T. Clark.
Chantraine, Pierre. 1953. *Grammaire homérique. Tome II: Syntaxe*. Paris: Klincksieck.
Cristofaro, Sonia. 2013. 'When' clauses. In Matthew S. Dryer & Martin Haspelmath (eds.), *The world atlas of language structures online*. Leipzig: Max Planck Institute for Evolutionary Anthropology. http://wals.info/chapter/126 (last accessed July 2022)
Decker, Rodney J. 2001. *Temporal deixis of the Greek verb in the Gospel of Mark with reference to verbal aspect*. Bern: Peter Lang.
Denizot, Camille & Sophie Vassilaki. 2016. La notion d'éventuel comme catégorie linguistique: Deux formes modales du grec ancien et du grec moderne. *Bulletin de la Société de Linguistique de Paris* 111(1). 277–316.
van Emde Boas, Evert, Albert Rijksbaron, Luuk Huitink & Mathieu de Bakker. 2019. *Cambridge grammar of Classical Greek*. Cambridge & New York: Cambridge University Press.
Evans, Trevor Vivian. 2001. *Verbal syntax in the Greek Pentateuch: Natural Greek usage and Hebrew interference*. Oxford: Oxford University Press.
Gerö, Eva-Carin. 2000. The usage of ἄν [án] and κε [ke] in Ancient Greek: Towards a unified description. *Glotta* 76. 177–191.
Goldstein, David. 2016. *Classical Greek syntax. Wackernagel's law in Herodotus*. Leiden & Boston: Brill.
Howorth, Roland H. 1955. The origin of the use of ἄν [án] and κεν [ken] in indefinite clauses. *The Classical Quarterly* 5. 72–93.
Jakobson, Roman. 1957. *Shifters, verbal categories, and the Russian verb*. Massachusetts: Harvard University Press.
Kühner, Raphael & Bernhard Gerth. 1898. *Ausführliche Grammatik der griechischen Sprache. Zweiter Teil: Satzlehre*. Hannover & Leipzig: Hannsche Buchhandlung.
Littman, Robert, J. 2008. *Tobias. The book of Tobit in Codex Sinaiticus*. Leiden & Boston: Brill.
Monro, David B. 1891. *A grammar of the Homeric dialect*. Oxford: Clarendon.
Moulton, James H. 1976. *A grammar of New Testament Greek*. 3rd edn. Edinburgh: T. & T. Clark.
Porter, Stanley. 1994. *Idioms of the Greek New Testament*. 2nd edn. Sheffield: Academic Press.
Reece, Steve. 2009. *Homer's winged words: The evolution of early Greek epic diction in the light of oral theory*. Leiden: Brill.

Revuelta Puigdollers, Antonio R. 2020. El verbo (III). Modo y modalidad. In Mª Dolores Jiménez López (ed.), *Sintaxis del griego antiguo*, 637–678. Madrid: Consejo Superior de Investigaciones Científicas.
Rijksbaron, Albert. 2006 [1984]. *The syntax and semantics of the verb in Classical Greek. An introduction*. 3rd edn. Chicago: The University of Chicago Press.
Robertson, Archibald. T. 1919. *A grammar of the Greek New Testament, in the light of historical research*. 3rd edn. London: Hodder & Stoughton.
Ruijgh, Cornelis J. 1992. L'emploi le plus ancien et les emplois plus récents de la particule κε/ἄν. In Françoise Létoublon (ed.), *La langue et les textes en grec ancien*, 75–84. Amsterdam: Gieben.
de la Villa Polo, Jesús 2020. Las oraciones subordinadas temporales y causales. In Mª Dolores Jiménez López (ed.), *Sintaxis del griego antiguo*, 876–889. Madrid: Consejo Superior de Investigaciones Científicas.
Wackernagel, Jacob. 2009 [1920]. *Lectures on Syntax, with special reference to Greek, Latin, and Germanic*. Introduction, translation, notes and bibliography David R. Langslow. Oxford: Oxford University Press [*Vorlesungen über Syntax. Mit besonderer Berücksichtigung von Griechisch, Lateinisch und Deutsch*. Volume 1. Basel: Birkhäuser & Cie].
Wakker, Gerry. 1994. *Conditions and conditionals. An investigation of Ancient Greek*. Amsterdam: Gieben.
Wathelet, Paul. 1997. Les particules *ke(n)* et *an* dans les formules de l'épopée homérique. In Albert Rijksbaron (ed.), *New approaches to Greek particles*, 247–268. Amsterdam: Gieben.
Willi, Andreas. 2018. *Origins of the Greek verb*. Cambridge: Cambridge University Press.
Willmott, Jo. 2007. *The moods of Homeric Greek*. Cambridge: Cambridge University Press.

Giuseppina di Bartolo
5 Variation and change of counterfactual conditionals in Postclassical Greek: Evidence from private papyrus letters

Abstract: This paper deals with counterfactual conditional clauses in Ancient Greek, focusing on evidence from private letters from Greek documentary papyri of the Roman and Byzantine periods (1st–7th century CE). It investigates variation and change in the constructions of counterfactual conditionals in the Postclassical stage of the language in comparison with the Classical stage, investigating certain aspects of apodosis and protasis construction. In particular, it addresses the verb morphology and the combination of the verb with the modal particle *án* in the apodosis, the morphology of the verb in the protasis, and the emergence of some new types of conditional clauses, for instance, the type introduced by *ei mḗ hóti* (literally 'if not that').

The present investigation contributes to the general topic of the volume by analyzing the different elements that occur in counterfactual conditional clauses in order to express modal meanings, investigating how they have changed with respect to the previous language stage, and how they interact with further elements found in the conditional structure (e.g., negation and particles). The morphosyntactic analysis is complemented by the pragmatic one, which discusses the functions of *ei mḗ hóti* utterances, with respect to the position of the conditional structure within the discourse. The functions of the coordinator *kaí* 'and', which often precedes the construction under investigation, as well as information structure and clausal relation are also considered.

Keywords: Counterfactual conditionals, event-oriented modality, Postclassical Greek, papyrus private letters, pragmatic and discourse analysis

Acknowledgments: I am very grateful to both editors of this volume, Camille Denizot and Liana Tronci, for their helpful and insightful comments on my paper. For useful comments and remarks, I would also like to thank the anonymous reviewers of this paper, Klaus Maresch, and Anna Bonifazi along with the participants of her colloquium. For providing me with the data from *PapyGreek*, I am grateful to Polina Yordanova.

Giuseppina di Bartolo, University of Cologne, e-mail: g.dibartolo@uni-koeln.de

1 Introduction

The present paper deals with counterfactual conditional clauses in Ancient Greek, focusing on the Postclassical language stage. It addresses constructions found in Greek documentary papyri in order to investigate variation and change with respect to the Classical period. In this regard, it considers protasis and apodosis, respectively, and analyzes the specific construction *ei mḗ hóti* (literally 'if not that') found in the protasis. It aims at contributing to the volume's topic and to more general linguistic research on counterfactuality and *irrealis* markers in different ways: (i) by discussing data from Ancient Greek that are of particular interest for typological research (Timberlake 2007: 323–324); (ii) by explaining how counterfactual conditional clauses are expressed in the language of papyri; (iii) by showing how they changed with respect to Classical Greek; and (iv) by testing the interaction of subordinate structures in the expression of modal content.

Counterfactuals are defined as "conditional judgements about what *would* have happened *if* such-and-such had happened, or more generally, what *would* be the case *if* such-and-such were the case. Thus, they are typically about unrealized possibilities" (Edgington 2021: 30). Every language in the world has lexical or grammatical devices for marking counterfactuals, which are accordingly considered as a semantic primitive and reflect the universal distinction between *realis* and *irrealis* (Wierzbicka 1997: 38; Bartolotta and Kölligan 2020: 421). The term *realis* describes situations "as actualized, as having occurred or actually occurring, knowable through direct perception", while *irrealis* refers to situations "as purely within the realm of thought, knowable only through imagination" (Mithun 1999: 173). If we consider *realis* and *irrealis* as the extremes of a semantic continuum, counterfactuals belong to the side of *irrealis* (Greenberg 1986: 257–258).

Several scholars have considered counterfactuals using the framework of epistemic modality (cf., among others, Elliott 2000: 72). This is based on the fact that epistemic modality defines the event with respect to the actual world and its possible alternatives, which can be actual, possible, or impossible (Chung and Timberlake 1985: 242). It refers to the speaker's evaluation of the actuality of a state of affairs expressed in the clause, involving a scale that runs from absolute certainty via probability to the neutral possibility that the state of affairs is real, and can continue via improbability to absolute certainty that the state of affairs is not real (Nuyts 2014: 38).

Dealing with modality, scholars distinguish further parameters, namely the modal strength and the orientation of the modal expression (Traugott and Dasher 2002: 117–118). This can also be relevant for addressing data from Ancient Greek (cf., for instance, Allan 2013). The scale of modal strength can range from factuality to counterfactuality via necessity and possibility, and the orientation of the modal expression can be defined in terms of speaker-oriented or event-oriented modality. An event-oriented modality implies the existence of internal and external conditions that prevent the agent from completing the action. In the case of a speaker-oriented modality, the internal or external conditions of the agent are irrelevant or non-existent (Allan 2013: 5). Moreover, adverbs or collocations are usually cross-linguistically found together with modals in order to specify or strengthen their meanings (Traugott and Dasher 2002: 117). *Ei mē hóti,* which the second part of this paper focuses on, introduces the protasis of hypothetical structures, for example 'If it had not been for the fact that (= *ei mē hóti*) I have been ill, I would have sent them to you long ago.' Examining the occurrences of *ei mē hóti,* the present analysis shows to what extent it builds a collocation and interacts with other elements in the protasis-apodosis pair in order to express counterfactual, event-oriented modal meaning.

In the literature on conditionals, different approaches are used in order to address conditional structures (cf., among others, Wakker 1994: 21–42). Dealing with synchrony and diachrony in Greek, the present investigation combines a morphosyntactic and a pragmatic approach, addressing questions related to the following issues: (i) the emergence of new modal grammatical devices in Postclassical Greek counterfactual conditionals; (ii) the functional extension of the Greek imperfect; (iii) the interaction of modal devices with other grammatical elements, such as verbal forms, negations, and particles found elsewhere in the conditional structure; (iv) the emergence of *ei mē hóti* in the specific communication setting of private letters for expressing event-oriented counterfactual meaning; and (v) the pragmatic value of this construction.

The data are gathered from documentary papyri, which are the most relevant and copious sources for the study of Ancient Greek low-register varieties. They record the Greek language continuously for more than a millennium (i.e., 4th century BCE – 8th century CE) and they are free from the processes of textual transmission (cf., among others, Dickey 2011: 149–161). Therefore, they allow us to address linguistic usages that arise in every-day contexts without the influence of literary or genre constraints. However, these sources, which all belong to every-day communication settings, are a very heterogeneous corpus in terms of registers (Bentein 2015), spanning from high-formal official documents, which deal with administrative matters, to more or less informal private letters, used as a medium for exchanging information among individuals in their daily lives. This paper addresses data from the communication setting of private letters not only because lower-register texts more clearly show linguistic movements toward later developments (cf., among others, Horrocks 2007), but also because they allow us to operate on large portions of discourse units, which disclose specific pragmatic features regarding the constructions in question. I am referring to the part of the text conventionally called the "body" of the letter, according to the fact that ancient letters were divided into prescript, body, greetings, and closing formula (Palme 2011: 361–364). The body represents the part that is more freely written regarding the topic and the communicational goals. In this respect, the analysis of these types of text highlights the pragmatic dependency of conditional structures on the previous context and specifically shows how the *ei mē hóti* construction contributes to the expression of counterfactual, event-oriented modal meaning at clause and discourse level.

Following this introduction, Section 2 focuses on the apodosis, presenting the main morphosyntactic changes affecting the apodosis of counterfactual conditionals and the imperfect in Postclassical Greek. Section 3 focuses on the protasis and discusses the *ei mē hóti* construction, explaining its distribution (Section 3.1), presenting the instances of this construction from papyrus private letters, and outlining their formal features (Section 3.2). Section 4 provides a general discussion of the data and analyzes them from a pragmatic and discourse perspective. Section 5 draws the conclusions.

2 Focus on the apodosis

This Section addresses the construction of the apodosis in order to sketch the general framework in which specific counterfactual constructions arise and show the new usage of the imperfect in the wake of the loss of the modal particle *án*. It has a more general character in comparison with the next Section, which focuses on the analysis of the protasis and, specifically, on the *ei mē hóti* construction.

Between the Classical and Postclassical periods, we can observe some of the major morphosyntactic changes that crucially affected Greek (Horrocks 2007: 620–621). One of these consists in the reorganization of the Greek modal system, including the construction of counterfactual conditionals.

By counterfactual conditionals, I refer to structures such as 'If X were true, Y would be true (but X isn't true)' or 'If X had happened, Y would have happened (but X didn't happen)'. In Classical Greek (5th – 4th century BCE), these structures are constructed as follows (see example (1)). The protasis is introduced by the hypothetical conjunction *ei* and combined with a secondary tense of the indicative, while the apodosis has a secondary tense of the indicative[1] combined with the modal particle *án* (Schwyzer 1950: 682–684, 686; van Emde Boas *at al.* 2019: 554–555). According to Greek reference grammars, the particle *án*, which marks the modal meaning, is

---

1 Secondary tenses in Ancient Greek include the imperfect, indicative aorist, and pluperfect.

always present in the apodosis. In other words, counterfactuality is marked by a secondary tense with an added modal particle (Palmer 2001: 207–208).

(1) εἰ [...] ὁ Καμβύσης ἐγνωσιμάχεε καὶ ἀπῆγε ὀπίσω τὸν στρατόν, [...] **ἦν ἂν** ἀνὴρ σοφός. (Hdt. 3.25.5)
ei   ho   Kambúsēs   egnōsimákhee   kai   apêge
if   ART.NOM   Cambyses.NOM   relent.3SG.IND.IMPF   and   leave.3SG.IND.IMPF
*opísō   ton   stratón,   **ên**   an   anḕr   sophós*
back   ART.ACC   army.ACC   be.3SG.IND.IMPF   MOD   man.NOM   wise.NOM
'If Cambyses had relented and led his army back he would have been a wise man.' (Translation van Emde Boas *et al.* 2019: 555)

Traditionally, it is argued that the aorist indicative refers to something that would have happened in the past, while the imperfect usually refers to something that would be occurring in the present (van Emde Boas *et al.* 2019: 555). However, data do not always reflect this strict distinction, as recent research has pointed out (la Roi 2022: 248–252).

Since the Hellenistic period (end 4th – end 1st century BCE), low-register works, such as New Testament and documentary papyri, indicate an innovation with respect to texts of the previous period: the particle *án* is not systematically found in combination with the verb in the apodosis. That is to say, apodoses tend to be expressed by secondary indicative forms alone, particularly in the case of imperfect usages (Horrocks 1995: 164–165).

(2) εἰ τὰ ἔργα μὴ ἐποίησα ἐν αὐτοῖς ἃ οὐδεὶς ἄλλος ἐποίησεν, ἁμαρτίαν **οὐκ εἴχοσαν**. (*Ev.Jo.* 15.24)
ei   ta   érga   mē   epoíēsa   en   autoîs   ha
if   ART.ACC work.ACC   NEG   do.1SG.IND.AOR   in   they.DAT   REL.ACC
*oudeis   állos   epoíēsen,   hamartían   **ouk eíkhosan***
no.one.NOM   other.NOM do.3SG.IND.AOR   sin.ACC   NEG have.3PL.IND.IMPF
'If I hadn't done among them the works which no one else did, they wouldn't have had sin.' (Translation American Standard Version 1901)

According to James (1982: 375), there is a general connection between the notions of past tense and the hypothetical situation since they both have the characteristic of being distant or dissociated from the present time reference within the speech act. Ancient Greek imperfect generally conveys two notions that are strongly related to its morphological features. First, there are the notions of imperfectiveness and indefiniteness related to its stem (i.e., the present stem), which expresses imperfective aspect, since the present stem marks the action as incomplete, ongoing, or repeated. In this respect, the present stem radically differs from the aorist stem, which, expressing perfective aspect, characterizes the action as complete, punctual, and as a single whole (Schwyzer 1950: 260–262; van Emde Boas et al. 2019: 406). Second, there is the notion of pastness, which is featured in the indicative forms and is marked by the augment (Schwyzer 1950: 275; van Emde Boas et al. 2019: 415–416). These features make the imperfect particularly eligible for the transfer from indefinite occurrence in the past to the hypothetical past, giving the possibility to express a modal meaning and convey counterfactuality. One must also point out that imperfect forms without *án* with a counterfactual meaning are already found in literary sources of the Classical period in order to express counterfactual statements (van Emde Boas et al. 2019: 443–444). Some examples of counterfactual apodoses without the modal particle *án* are typified by a periphrastic construction, consisting of the imperfect form of the modal verb *méllō* (literally 'be about, be going to') and an infinitive (Basset 1979: 187–189). Instances of this construction with *án* are already found in Classical Greek along with instances without *án* (see, e.g., Lys. 3.2 and Antiph. 2.5 for the construction with and without *án* respectively). This attests to the usage of a modal device that conveys the modal meanings at two different levels: the semantics of the verb itself and its realization in the imperfect form. The construction with *méllō* in the imperfect + infinitive is one of the options found in Postclassical Greek for building counterfactual apodosis, specifically in documentary papyri, as shown by the following example (for further examples, see di Bartolo 2023: 488–489).

(3) εἰ γάρ σοι ἔμελε περὶ ἐμοῦ, **ἔμελλές** μοι γράφιν. (BGU III 845, 2nd century CE)
ei gár   soi   émele   peri   emoû
if PTCL you.DAT.SG care.for.3SG.IND.IMPF about me.GEN
émellés   moi   gráphin
be.about.to.2SG.IND.IMPF me.DAT write.INF.PRS
'Because if you cared about me, you would write to me.'[2]

On the contrary, the bare aorist cannot compensate for the lack of *án* in counterfactual apodoses. Because of the aspectual meaning conveyed by its stem, it does not carry the notion of indefiniteness and the meaning of hypothetical past unless it is specifically marked by means of *án* (Horrocks 1995: 166). This is why, from the Hellenistic period onward, an alternative marker of modality is almost always found within the counterfactual structure when the modal particle *án* is omitted with the aorist, as in the usage of the phrase *ei dunatón* 'if possible' in (4) below (Horrocks 1995: 165).

---

2 Translations are mine if not otherwise noted.

(4) μαρτυρῶ γὰρ ὑμῖν ὅτι **εἰ δυνατὸν** τοὺς ὀφθαλμοὺς ὑμῶν ἐξορύξαντες ἐδώκατέ μοι. (*Ep.Gal.* 4.15)
    marturô   gar   humîn   hóti   **ei**   **dunaton**   tous
    testify.1SG.IND.PRS PTCL you.DAT.PL that if   possibly   ART.ACC
    ophthalmous   humôn   exorúxantes   edókaté   moi
    eyes.ACC   you.GEN.PL   dig.out.PTCP.AOR.NOM   give.2PL.IND.AOR   me.DAT
    'For I testify to you that, if possible, you would have plucked out your eyes and given them to me.' (Translation American Standard Version 1901)

The development of the imperfect in Postclassical Greek provides us with relevant data for typological analysis, and such data contribute to linguistic research in relation to two major issues. The first one is a cross-linguistic feature and concerns the functional value of the imperfect used to mark counterfactual apodoses. Its development in Postclassical Greek shows a general tendency that can be observed in many other languages, for example in Romance languages. In other words, the tendency that non-present tenses, especially past tenses, are particularly eligible for modal use attests to the existence of a semantic link between the notion of past tense and indefiniteness and the notion of remoteness from reality; this makes the imperfect particularly suitable for expressing modal meanings (Coseriu 1976: 139; Lyons 1977: 819). The second issue is a sociolinguistic one and concerns the spread of the Greek imperfect in counterfactual conditionals starting in low-register varieties (Horrocks 1995, 2007; for changes in the categories of tense, aspect and mood and specifically the imperfect in the New Testament, cf. Porter 1989: 198–211). This evidence parallels those of some other languages that, like Ancient Greek, display other markers of counterfactuality in high-register varieties. For example, colloquial Italian counterfactual conditionals show the occurrence of the imperfect in both protasis and apodosis instead of the subjunctive and the conditional, respectively, with the latter two found in high-register varieties (Bertinetto 1986: 378–380; Bazzanella 1990: 442; Dessì Schmid 2010: 46–56).

3 Focus on the protasis

This section deals with the protasis construction of counterfactual conditionals, focusing on the *ei mē hóti* type. I have chosen to focus on this specific type of protasis for different reasons. First, *ei mē hóti* does not straightforwardly typify a negative hypothetical clause, such as 'If X were not true, (Y would be true)' or 'If X had not happened, (Y would have happened)', in which the clause introduced by *ei* constitutes a single unit directly embedded in the matrix clause and dependent on it. Second, *ei mē hóti* builds a collocation with specific pragmatic meanings and functions, as it seems to work as a modal device that marks counterfactual meaning. Third, it can be combined with other particles and illustrates synchronic variation with respect to literary sources.

The collocation *ei mḗ* (lit. 'if not') is already found in Classical Greek as a fixed combination. According to Wakker (1994: 283–284), it typifies an elliptical expression that introduces an exception or a qualification of the preceding negative assertion or question.

(5) καὶ ᾔσθετο οὐδεὶς εἰ μὴ οἱ ἄνδρες οἷς ἐπιμελὲς ἦν εἰδέναι τὴν νύκτα ταύτην. (Th. 4.67.2)
| kai | éistheto | oudeis | ei | mē | hoi | ándres |
| and | perceive.3SG.IND.AOR | nobody.NOM | if | NEG | ART.NOM | men.NOM |

| hoîs | epimeles | ên | | eidénai | tēn |
| REL.DAT | cared.for.NOM | be.3SG.IND.IMPF | | know.INF.PRF | ART.ACC |

núkta   taútēn
night.ACC that.ACC

'And no one perceived it except the men whose business it was that night to know.' (Translation Wakker 1994: 284)

In the case of *ei mē hóti*, we are dealing with a construction constituted by two different syntactic units that are not hierarchically equal. In addition to the *ei mḗ* ('if not/except') unit, we have a further one introduced by the subordinating conjunction *hóti* ('that'), which features a 'that'-clause subordinated to *ei mḗ*. The construction *ei mē hóti*, which literally means 'if not that', elides the verb governed by *ei mḗ* (i.e., 'were') and compresses the meaning of a sentence such as English 'were it not for the fact that'. It presents the alternative unreal scenario with respect to the state of affairs expressed by the *hóti* clause. At the same time, it indicates the reason why what is expressed in the apodosis cannot happen or why someone could not do something (see examples presented in Section 3.2 below). Moreover, by means of this syntactic construction, the counterfactual meaning is placed in foreground, since the *ei mē hóti* protasis always precedes the apodosis.

An analogous collocation treated by Wakker (1994: 284) is *ei mē diá* ('had it not been for') in which the prepositional phrase introduced by *diá* depends on *ei mḗ*. This collocation occurs in counterfactual structures and is already found in Classical period.[3] However, it has to be pointed out that the *ei mē diá* construction always occurs after the main clause.

---

[3] Further occurrences of *ei mē diá* quoted by Wakker (1994: 284) are Ar. *V.* 558; Pl. *Grg.* 516e1–2; D. 19.74.

(6) καὶ ἐδόκουν [...] ἐπελθόντες ἂν διὰ τάχους πάντα ἔτι ἔξω καταλαβεῖν, εἰ μὴ διὰ
τὴν ἐκείνου μέλλησιν. (Th. 2.18.4)
kai	edókoun			epelthóntes		an	dia
and	have.an.opinion.3PL.IND.IMPF			come.upon. PTCP.AOR.NOM		MOD	through
tákhous	pánta	éti	éxō	katalabeîn		ei	mē	dia
speed.GEN	all.ACC	still	out.of	find.on.arrival.INF.AOR		if	NEG	for
tēn	ekeínou	méllēsin						
ART.ACC	DEM.GEN	hesitation.ACC						

'And they believed that with a rapid attack they could have found everything still outside had it not been for his hesitation.' (Translation Wakker 1994: 284)

In what follows, I will describe the distribution of *ei mḗ* and *ei mē hóti* in Classical Greek, the Septuagint, the New Testament, and private letters from documentary papyri (Section 3.1). For the documentary papyri, I will rely on data from secondary literature (cf. Olsson 1925: 36; Tabachovitz 1943: 23–25) as well as data that I manually collected using the search tool of *Papyri.info*.[4] Moreover, I looked for instances in the linguistically annotated corpus *PapyGreek*, which allowed me to make more accurate observations about the number of the instances for this construction in documentary texts.[5] Furthermore, this step has allowed me to compare the *ei mē hóti* construction with an analogous one that does not add the *hóti*-unit. In Section 3.2, I will present the examples and the formal features of these types of protasis constructions. Finally, I will discuss the data in general, including the results of a pragmatic analysis (Section 4).

3.1 Distribution

According to Wakker (1994: 283–284), the collocation *ei mḗ* occurs frequently in all text types of Classical Greek. Searching for the occurrences of *ei mē hóti* in literary and New Testament Greek, one finds that the *ei mḗ* pattern is very frequent; on the contrary, the collocation *ei mē hóti* is not widespread,[6] as it occurs twice in Aristotle

---

4 https://papyri.info (last accessed February 2023).
5 https://papygreek.hum.helsinki.fi/ (last accessed February 2023). For details about the *PapyGreek* linguistically annotated corpus, see Vierros and Henriksson (2021).
6 I have checked the occurrences of *ei mē hóti* on TLG by using the "proximity function" and setting *ei* before *mḗ*. In this way, I could look for the occurrences which indicate *hóti* after *ei mḗ* despite the large number of attestations for the collocation *ei mḗ* in the TLG (i.e., about 30 000 entries for *ei mḗ*). This matches Wakker's analysis (1994: 283), according to which *ei mḗ* frequently occurs in all text types.

(i.e., *Metaph.* 4.1007b3 and *Spir.* 482a2), and once in Xenophon (see example (7)). With respect to the present analysis, these occurrences are not relevant: the two instances in Aristotle do not express counterfactuality; the instance from Xenophon illustrates a counterfactual conditional structure but does not typify the same type of construction discussed here.

(7) ὁ δὲ Εὐθύδημος ὑπέλαβεν οὐκ ἂν ἄλλως ἀνὴρ ἀξιόλογος γενέσθαι, εἰ μὴ **ὅτι μάλιστα** Σωκράτει συνείη. (X. *Mem.* 4.2.40)

ho	de	Euthúdēmos		hupélaben		ouk	an
ART.NOM	PTCL	Euthydemus.NOM		take.up.3SG.IND.AOR		NEG	MOD
állōs	anēr	axiólogos		genésthai	ei	mē	**hóti**
otherwise	man.NOM	remarkable.NOM		be.INF.AOR	if	NEG	that
málista	Sōkrátei	suneíē					
most.of.all	Socrates.DAT	be.with.3SG.OPT.PRS					

'But Euthydemus guessed that he would never be of much account unless he spent **as much time as possible** with Socrates.' (Translation Marchant 1923)

In this case, *hóti* does not build a collocation with *ei mḗ* and does not introduce a further unit dependent on it. Conversely, *hóti* builds an adverbial expression together with *málista*, being equivalent to *hōs málista* 'as much as possible'. Furthermore, the *ei mē hóti* clause is placed after the apodosis.

In the Septuagint (from 3rd century BCE onwards), which represents the earliest Greek translation of the Old Testament from the Hebrew Bible, *ei mē hóti* occurs twice in Psalms for expressing counterfactual meaning. In both cases, the modal particle *án* is still found in the apodosis, as indicated by the following examples:

(8) εἰ μὴ ὅτι ὁ νόμος σου μελέτη μού ἐστιν, τότε ἂν ἀπωλόμην ἐν τῇ ταπεινώσει μου. (*Ps.* 118.92)

ei	mē	hóti	ho	nómos	sou	melétē	moú
if	NEG	that	ART.NOM	law.NOM	you.GEN.SG	meditation.NOM	me.GEN
estin,		tóte	an	apōlómēn		en	têi
be.3SG.IND.PRS		then	MOD	perish.1SG.IND.AOR		in	ART.DAT
tapeinṓsei		mou					
humiliation.DAT		me.GEN					

'If it were not for the fact that your law was my meditation, then I would have perished in my humiliation.' (Translation Pietersma 2000)

(9) εἰ μὴ ὅτι κύριος ἦν ἐν ἡμῖν ἐν τῷ ἐπαναστῆναι ἀνθρώπους ἐφ' ἡμᾶς, ἄρα ζῶντας
ἂν κατέπιον. (*Ps.* 123.2–3)

ei	mē	hóti	kúrios	ên	en	hēmîn	en	tôi
if	NEG	that	Lord.NOM	be.3SG.IND.IMPF	in	us.DAT	in	ART.DAT

epanastênai	anthrṓpous	eph'	hēmâs,	ára
rise.up.against.INF.AOR	men.ACC	against	us.ACC	then

zôntas	an	katépion
alive.PTCP.PRS.ACC	MOD	swallow.up.3SG.IND.AOR

'If it had not been that the Lord was among us, when people rose up against us, then they would have swallowed us up alive.' (Translation Pietersma 2000)

The New Testament attests to this construction as well but in a different usage. In both occurrences from Paul's *Epistles* (*2 Ep.Cor.* 12.13, *Ep.Eph.* 4.9), *ei mē hóti* does not express counterfactuality. Syntactically, it does not function as the protasis of a conditional structure, but rather as an indirect question. Pragmatically, it typifies a rhetorical question, explaining what is expressed at the beginning of the discourse unit (i.e., *to de anébē tí estin*). In addition, the position of the *ei mē hóti* structure differs from the two examples found in the Septuagint and from those from the documentary papyri, since *ei mē hóti* follows the matrix clause (see Section 4 below).

(10) τὸ δὲ Ἀνέβη τί ἐστιν εἰ μὴ ὅτι καὶ κατέβη εἰς τὰ κατώτερα <μέρη> τῆς γῆς; (*Ep. Eph.* 4.9 = *2 Ep.Cor.* 12.13)

to	de	anébē	tí	estin	ei	mē
ART.NOM	PTCL	go.up.3SG.IND.AOR	what.NOM	be.3SG.IND.PRS	if	NEG

hóti	kai	katébē	eis	ta	katṓtera	mérē
that	and	go.down.3SG.IND.AOR	to	ART.ACC	lower.ACC	part.ACC

tês	gês ?
ART.GEN	earth.GEN

'Now this, "He ascended," what is it but that he also first descended into the lower parts of the earth?' (Translation American Standard Version 1901)

Documentary papyri give a different picture. Looking for the occurrences of *ei mē hóti* by using the search tool of *Papyri.info*,[7] I found nine occurrences in all corpus. Out of these, only six occurrences are usable for the present analysis (i.e., they are instances found in private letters of the Roman and Byzantine periods). Three out of the nine are from texts or single passages that are too fragmentary to allow a

---

[7] My search terms were #μη# then #οτι# within two characters, getting twenty occurrences in total. Only nine out of twenty include *ei* before *mē hóti.*

syntactic and pragmatic discussion of the construction. These are from a private letter of the Roman period (P. Strasb. VII 629), an official letter of the Byzantine period (P. Apoll. 39), and a petition from the Byzantine period (P. Flor. III 296). Considering that the *Trismegistos* databank (Depauw and Gheldof 2014)[8] indicates 7157 texts for the category of Greek letters from the Roman and Byzantine periods, we are still dealing with a low total number of instances. However, it is relevant to note that *ei mē hóti* consistently occurs in this communication setting in order to introduce a counterfactual protasis. In addition, none of these instances, except for one, displays the modal particle *án* in the apodosis.

The *PapyGreek* treebank corpus, which allows more accurate linguistic analysis on documentary papyri, confirms that the construction is not frequent: it provides only one instance for the *ei mē hóti* construction out of 493 texts and 46209 words.[9] On the other hand, by performing the query *ei* as a subordinating conjunction and adding *mḗ* as element in the sentence,[10] one could find an instance for the *ei mḗ* collocation that, despite its formal difference, is used for conveying counterfactual meaning as well and shares pragmatic features with the *ei mḗ hóti* construction.

3.2 Instances and their formal features

This section illustrates the instances of *ei mē hóti* presenting them with respect to their formal features. In order to better understand the function of this collocation, I will briefly summarise the general content of the letter and, in particular, the part immediately preceding the example in question. At the end, I will show an instance of *ei mḗ* that can be considered analogous to *ei mē hóti*.

First, two instances indicate that the *ei mē hóti* protasis can combine with an apodosis that shows a further marker of modality. Example (11) is part of a short letter concerning a dispute and an unsuccessful sale. The sender, named Ptolemaios, is in litigation with another Ptolemaios and complains that his return home has been subsequently delayed. The choice of perfect and pluperfect forms in protasis and apodosis, respectively, stresses the effects of the completed action on the current state.

---

[8] https://www.trismegistos.org (last accessed February 2023).
[9] This instance coincides with one of the nine from the Duke Databank of Documentary Papyri (DDbDP) since the *PapyGreek* builds up a corpus of linguistically annotated texts that are taken from the DDbDP. The project is a work in progress. For this reason, the annotated texts are still less than the total number of digitalized documentary texts on DDbDP.
[10] The query was performed by using KTB by Yordanova and Norris (official release is forthcoming).

(11) εἰ μὴ ὅτι συνεζήτηκα τῷ Πτολεμαίῳ πάλαι ἂν ἀπηλλαγμένοι ἦσμεν.[11] (P. Mich. VIII 512 ll. 4–5, 3rd century CE)
ei mē hóti sunezḗtēka   tôi   Ptolemaíōi   pálai
if NEG that dispute.1SG.IND.PRF ART.DAT Ptolemaios.DAT long.ago
an   apēllagménoi   êsmen
MOD leave.PTCP.PRF.NOM   be.1PL.IND.IMPF
'If it hadn't been the case that I have had a dispute with Ptolemaios, we would have left long ago.'

Example (12) deals with the sale of family property. At the beginning of the letter, the sender, a woman, wants to inform the addressee, another woman, that her brother sold his share of the family property. She describes what the family property consists of and relates that her presence prevented him from selling the whole property. At this point comes the following passage, which emphasizes what would have happened if she had not been there. The utterance is found in the middle of the letter's body.

(12) κἂν νινεί,[12] εἰ μὴ ὅτι ἐγενόμην ἐν Ἀλεξανδρίᾳ, ἤμελλεν τὰ σὰ καὶ τὰ ἐμὰ καὶ τὰ τῆς μητρὸς ἡμῶν πάντα πωλῆσαι. (P. Mich. VIII 492 ll. 14–16, 2nd century CE)
kan   nineí, ei mē hóti egenómēn   en Alexandríai
even now   if NEG that be.1SG.IND.AOR in Alexandria.DAT
émellen   ta   sa   kai   ta   ema   kai
would.3SG.IND.IMPF ART.ACC your.ACC and   ART.ACC my.ACC   and
ta   tês   metros   hēmôn   pánta   pōlêsai
ART.ACC ART.GEN mother.GEN us.GEN   all.ACC sell.INF.AOR
'And now, if it hadn't been the case that I was in Alexandria, he would have sold all your property and mine and our mother's.'

Example (11) reflects the Classical usage, indicating the modal particle *án* in the apodosis with a pluperfect form (perfect participle + verb 'be' in the imperfect). In example (12), the modal device *án* is not found, but the apodosis presents an imperfect form of *méllō* with the infinitive. As stated in Section 2, this is one of the strategies used in Postclassical Greek, and specifically in documentary papyri, in order to construct counterfactual apodoses.

Examples (13) and (14) give evidence of the construction *ei mē hóti* preceded by the coordinator *kaí*. Both passages occur in the middle of the letter's body and

---

[11] ἦσμεν corresponds to the Classical form ἦμεν.
[12] κἂν νινεί corresponds to the Attic form κἂν νυνί.

display an imperfect form in the apodosis. Example (13) is part of a letter concerning a failed payment, which is what the anaphoric expression "this thing" refers to. The unit occurring before the *ei mē hóti* clause explains all details related to the situation.

(13) καὶ εἰ μὴ ὅτι ὁ υἱός μου ἀσθενῖ δινῶς τούτου εἵνεκα ἀνηρχόμην.[13] (BGU II 595 ll. 13–15, 75–85 CE)
kai ei mē hóti ho huiós mou asthenî
and if NEG that ART.NOM son.NOM me.GEN be.sick.3SG.IND.PRS
dinôs, toútou heíneka anērkhómēn
permanently this.GEN because.of come.up.1SG.IND.IMPF
'And if it hadn't been for the fact that my son is permanently ill, I would come up for this thing.'

Example (14) is part of a very short letter which, before the *ei mē hóti* clause, contains condolences for the death of a person. The *ei mē hóti* clause expresses the reason that prevents the subject from going upcountry after the death of the person in question.[14]

(14) καὶ εἰ μὴ ὅτι τὰ παιδία μου ἀποδημοῦσι Πτολεμαὶς καὶ Σαραπίων \ἐ/γὼ αὐτὴ ἀνέβενον.[15] (BGU III 801 ll. 7–10, 2nd century CE)
kai ei mē hóti ta paidía mou
and if NEG that ART.NOM children.NOM me.GEN
apodēmoûsi Ptolemaìs kai Sarapíōn,
be.away.from.home.3PL.IND.PRS Ptolemais.NOM and Sarapion.NOM
egō autē anébenon
I.NOM myself.NOM go.up.1SG.IND.IMPF
'And if it hadn't been for the fact that my children are away, Ptolemais and Sarapion, I myself would go upcountry.'

In the following two examples, neither *án*, nor the *méllō*.IMPF + infinitive construction, nor bare imperfect forms are found in the apodosis. Instance (15) shows *ei mē hóti* with a perfect form in the protasis, combined with a pluperfect form in the apodosis (*pepónphēn*). The passage is part of a very concise, private letter that gives

---

[13] The two iotacistic spellings ἀσθενῖ and δινῶς correspond to the Attic forms ἀσθενεῖ and δεινῶς; εἵνεκα corresponds to ἕνεκα (see Gignac 1976: 256).
[14] For the whole letter in translation and further comments, see Bagnall and Cribiore (2006: 180).
[15] The form ἀνέβενον corresponds to ἀνέβαινον (see Gignac 1976: 192–193).

a list of different things. It occurs in the letter's body right after the following piece of information: 'I sent you through Protas 50 dried figs'.

(15) ἰ μὴ ὅτι ἠσθένηκα πάλαι πεπόνφην σοι.[16] (P. Tebt. II 414 l. 9, 2nd century CE)
i mē hóti esthénēka pálai pepónphēn soi
if NEG that be.sick.1SG.IND.PRF long.ago send.1SG.IND.PPRF you.DAT
'If it hadn't been the case that I have been ill, I would have long since sent them to you.'

In example (16), the conditional structure displays two verbal forms in the present tense. The passage is the last sentence of a fragmentary letter. The sender would like to intercede on behalf of a farmer in order to avoid his transfer to another place.

(16) καὶ εἰ μὴ ὅτι ἐγγὺς αὐτοῦ εἰμι, τότε πολλὰ κακὰ γίνονται. (CPR XXX 21 l. 14, 7th century CE)
kai ei mē hóti eggus autoû eimi, tóte
and if NEG that close.to he.GEN be.1SG.IND.PRS then
polla kaka gínontai
many.things.NOM bad.NOM happen.3PL.IND.PRS
'And if it hadn't been the case that I am close to him, then a lot of bad things would happen.'

The last instance presented in this Section belongs to a Greek letter from the bilingual archive of Claudius Teberianus (cf., among others, Adams 2003: 593–597)[17] dealing with private familial matters. It shows an example of the *ei mḗ* collocation (i.e., without *hóti*) used for expressing a counterfactual statement. On the one hand, the formal character of this construction is different with respect to the *ei mē hóti* clause type, since *ei mḗ* does not govern a *hóti*-clause (i.e., any clause is found after the conjunction-negation pattern). On the other hand, the *ei mḗ* in question seems to have a different meaning and function in comparison with the same collocation in the cases presented by Wakker (see the introduction to this Section and example (5)), as it does not express an exception or a qualification of a preceding negative assertion or question. The collocation as used in this passage seems to be more similar to the *ei mē hóti* clause type, especially with regard to its pragmatic meaning. An imperfect form is found in the main clause following *ei mḗ*, as shown in (17).

---

16 Note that ι typifies the iotacistic spelling of *e*, which is very common in documentary texts (see Gignac 1976: 189). For the pluperfect form *pepónphēn* with augment omission, see Gignac (1981: 224).
17 I am leaving aside issues related to language contact since they would exceed the scope of the present analysis.

(17) ἓν δὲ εὐχαριστῶ τοῖς θεοῖς ὅτι πλείον[ας] δέδωκά σο[ι] τῶν ὀκτὼ δραχμῶν, εἰ μή, τὸ αὐτὸ ἦν. (P. Mich VIII 476 l. 25–26, 2nd century CE)

hen	de	eukharistô		toîs	theoîs	hóti
one.thing.ACC	PTCL	thank.1SG.IND.PRS		ART.DAT	gods.DAT	that
pleíonas	dédōká		soi	tôn	oktō	drakhmôn
more.ACC	give.1SG.IND.PRF		you.DAT.SG	ART.GEN	eight	drachmae.GEN
ei	mḗ	to	auto	ên		
if	NEG	ART.NOM	itself.NOM	be.3SG.IND.IMPF		

'For one thing I thank the gods, that I gave you more than eight drachmae. If it had not been the case, the same thing would have happened.'

One other instance of *ei mḗ* is found in the same papyrus letter at line 16. However, it does not typify the elliptical *ei mḗ* collocation for the following reasons: a verbal form is found after *ei mḗ*, which follows the main clause and does not express counterfactual meaning.

Despite the overall low number of instances for the *ei mē hóti* construction, the usage in Greek documentary papyri is worth considering for different reasons. Summing up the general features emerging from the examples, one can observe the following characteristics. First, all instances consistently occur in the same type of text in order to convey counterfactuality. In other words, they all occur in private letters, which can be considered quite similar and homogeneous to one another in terms of topic and relationship between sender and addressee, typifying an horizontal relation between them (for the notion of horizontal and vertical relationships in interaction, cf. Baugh 2011). Second, in all cases except for one, the modal particle *án* does not occur in the apodosis. Third, the *ei mē hóti* construction, which constitutes the protasis of the conditional structure, is always found before the apodosis. Fourth, in the majority of cases the *ei mē hóti* unit is preceded by the particle *kaí* 'and' or a particle combination, e.g. *kan nineí* 'and now'. Fifth, this hypothetical structure occurs in the middle or throughout the end of the letter's body, never as the first utterance. This is relevant in terms of sequence organization and analysis of pragmatic dependency.

4 Data discussion and pragmatic analysis

The data leads to various considerations at the morphosyntactic as well as at the pragmatic and discourse levels.

Considering the morphosyntactic properties of *ei mē hóti*, we have observed so far that it does not typify a simple negative protasis of counterfactual conditions introduced by the subordinator *ei*. This collocation is not found in Classical authors when expressing counterfactual meaning. On the contrary, it is found in low-register sources of Postclassical period. The examples from the Septuagint still indicate the usage of the modal particle *án* in the apodosis, while papyrus letters from the Roman period onwards do not consistently show the usage of *án* in the apodosis. This has to be connected with the general tendencies of Postclassical Greek, which, as a result of the loss of *án*, begins to develop further modal devices for expressing counterfactual meanings. This includes the extension of the functional value of the bare imperfect in apodoses and the periphrastic construction of imperfect forms of *méllō* with the infinitive (Horrocks 2010: 237–238). The specific emergence of *ei mē hóti* in private letters leads to the hypothesis that we are dealing with a collocation that marks counterfactuality either in combination with other modal particles or constructions, such as in the case of examples (11) and (12), or in combination with imperfect forms in the apodosis, such as in examples (13) and (14), or even without any of the previous markers, such as in examples (15) and (16).

The single instance of *án*, shown in example (11), does not contradict the general tendencies mentioned in Section 2. The usage of the modal particle *án* indicates the choice of a construction that reflects the corresponding Classical one. In this respect, the use of *án* in private papyrus letters can be considered as a sociolinguistic marker, featuring a higher register choice. This kind of process is frequent in sources from the Hellenistic period onwards, which illustrate various registers and different degrees of similarity with structures found in Classical authors (cf., among others, Horrocks 2010: 88–90). Moreover, the usage of the particle *án* in P. Mich. 512 (ex. (11)) matches further orthographic, syntactic, and contextual features of the whole letter, which reveal a high educational background of the scribe. Private letters from papyri could reflect different registers with respect to lexical and syntactic choices, non-standard orthography and the situational contexts that they reveal (cf., among others, Bentein 2015; Stolk 2020).

Concerning *ei mē hóti* itself, we can observe that it builds a complex subordinator, consisting of the hypothetical subordinating conjunction *ei*, the subjective negation *mḗ*, and the subordinating declarative conjunction *hóti*. The reason preventing the actuality of the state of affairs expressed by the apodosis is conveyed by the *hóti*-clause. The latter depends, in turn, on *ei mḗ*, which typifies its matrix clause. The negation in *ei mḗ* clearly extends its scope to the *hóti*-clause, opening the possibility of operating on the counterfactual scenario. The collocation *ei mḗ* without *hóti* in example (17) functions similarly. It can be paraphrased by using the *ei mē hóti* collocation in the following way: "I thank the gods that I gave you eight drachmae. If it had not been the case that I gave you eight drachmae, the same thing would have happened." In this case, according to the principle of information recoverability (Cristofaro 2003: 249–250), the proximity to the reference of *ei mḗ* allows one to avoid the repetition of the *hóti*-clause that is found right before and that can be easily inferred by the addressee.

With respect to further pragmatic and discourse issues, we can observe that the collocation *ei mḗ hóti* is found in private letters, which reflect spoken Greek in a more or less authentic way. This type of texts allows us to explore the sequential relation of the different discourse units, address how a specific construction interacts with the other ones in the discourse, and investigate the communication goals covered by specific utterances. With the examples in Section 3.2, I highlighted the position of the *ei mḗ hóti* utterances within the letter. The fact that they either occur in the middle or at the end of the letter's body and never at the beginning, points to a type of utterances that need co-text complementation. These utterances convey the information about the internal or external condition that prevents the agent from completing a specific action. For example, in the letter that contains passage (14), the sender sends her condolences about someone's death and her inability to travel upcountry since her children are away. In other words, an external event prevents her from completing a specific action. Both in this case and in the others, *ei mḗ* forces the addressee to cognitively process not only the state of affairs expressed by the *hóti*-clause, but also its opposite, relating it to previous information in the text. Therefore, it functions as a modal device for expressing event-oriented modality. Moreover, its feature of context-dependency is shown by the fact that it negates the recipient's expectations concerning explicitly or implicitly shared information between sender and addressee. Considering example (14) once more, one could not understand the meaning expressed by the conditional structure without the immediately preceding expression of condolences and the implicit reference to a person's death. For this reason, in any case it does not occur as the first utterance of the letter's body.

As far as the clause order of the conditional structure is concerned, it is worth noting that the hypotactic structure, expressed by *ei mḗ hóti*, always occurs before the main clause, which matches an almost universal feature of conditional structures (Cristofaro 2003: 7). This relation, which contrasts the expectation of nucleus-satellite relation, has to be explained in terms of the broader relational structures of the text (Matthissen and Thompson 1988: 305–307). The *ei mḗ hóti* utterance is found as the first unit of the conditional structure because it conveys new information. In other words, it presents new information that is not recoverable from the preceding discourse context (Halliday 1967: 204). In addition, this is marked by the presence of *kaí* before *ei mḗ hóti* in four instances. In these cases, *kaí* 'and' does not behave as a coordinating conjunction but rather as a discourse particle. Acting at the discourse level rather than at the syntax level, it encompasses a range of functions, such as expanding or linking with a previous discourse unit (Viti 2006; Bonifazi *et al.* 2016 IV: II.4). In the private letters mentioned above, *kaí* connects the unit conveying the information of the *ei mē hóti* structure with the previous one, pointing it out within the information sequence.

Finally, the clausal relation and the occurrence of the particle *kaí* before *ei mē hóti* are crucial in light of the fact that ancient texts did not have punctuation markers in the modern sense. Particles, conjunctions, and clausal order were among the linguistic devices used to segment texts (Bonifazi *et al.* 2016 IV: III.8 for particles) and stress the pragmatic content of specific utterances.

5 Conclusions

This paper has investigated counterfactual conditionals in Ancient Greek, focusing on evidence from low-register varieties. Dealing with the apodosis, it has illustrated some of the morphosyntactic changes occurring in counterfactual conditionals between Classical and Postclassical Greek, including the functional extension of the imperfect. It has been shown that this development of Ancient Greek imperfect, which starts in lower-register varieties, is particularly interesting from a typological perspective. It attests to the general semantic link between the notion of past tense and indefiniteness, on the one hand, and the notion of remoteness from reality, on the other, a link that makes this tense particularly eligible to take a modal meaning and therefore express counterfactuality. In this respect, Ancient Greek imperfect matches the properties of the imperfect in many other languages.

Focusing on the protasis, the paper has investigated the *ei mē hóti* clause type, which emerges in the Septuagint and later on in papyrus private letters in order to express counterfactuality. *Ei mē hóti* has been analysed as a collocation that builds a complex subordinator and introduces the protasis of the conditional structure. In particular, *ei mḗ* typifies an elliptical expression and functions as the matrix clause of a *hóti*-clause. The distribution of *ei mē hóti* shows that it rarely occurs in literary texts of the Classical period, where it either does not convey counterfactual meaning or does not build the same construction as the one found in documentary papyri. On the contrary, private letters on papyrus from the Roman and Byzantine periods attest to this construction. In some cases, *ei mē hóti* occurs with a further modal device in the apodosis. In the majority of cases, it is the only device in the conditional structure that marks counterfactuality. A comparison with analogous examples displaying the collocation *ei mḗ* has been drawn.

Lastly, the paper has discussed the *ei mē hóti* construction from a pragmatic and discourse perspective, considering its position within the letter. In this respect, the paper has demonstrated that *ei mē hóti* needs co-text complementation. One of its main functions is to trigger the counterfactual scenario and deny the recipient's expectation. Moreover, the argument has addressed the protasis-apodosis clausal relation, elucidating that the hypotactic structure *ei mē hóti* is always found before the main clause because it conveys new information. Concerning the occurrences of *kaí* before *ei mē hóti*, it has been argued that they provide an example of *kaí* as a discourse particle, since it contributes to the connection of two discourse units and marks the occurrence of new information within the discourse.

Greek texts and translations

Papyrus editions are cited according to the Checklist:
Oates, John, William Willis, Joshua D. Sosin, Rodney Ast, Roger S. Bagnall, James M.S. Cowey, Mark Depauw, Alain Delattre, Robert L. Maxwell & Paul Heilporn. *Checklist of editions of Greek, Latin, Demotic, and Coptic papyri, ostraca, and tablets*, accessible at www.papyri.info/docs/checklist (last accessed March 2023).
American Standard Version 1901: Rainbow Missions, Inc. World English Bible. Rainbow Missions, Inc.; revision of the American Standard Version of 1901. http://ebible.org/bible/web (last accessed March 2023).
Bagnall, Roger & Raffaella Cribiore. 2006. *Women's letters from Ancient Egypt, 300 BC–AD 800*. Ann Arbor: University of Michigan Press.
Marchant, Edgar C. 1923. *Xenophon*. Cambridge, MA: Harvard University Press.
Pietersma, Albert. 2000. *A new English translation of the Septuagint: The Psalms*. New York: Oxford University Press.

References

Adams, James N. 2003. *Bilingualism and Latin language*. Cambridge: Cambridge University Press.
Allan, Rutger. 2013. Exploring modality's semantic space: Grammaticalization, subjectification and the case of ὀφείλω [*opheílō*]. *Glotta* 89. 1–46.
di Bartolo, Giuseppina. 2023. Some aspects of *irrealis* in Postclassical Greek. In Georgios K. Giannakis, Panagiotis Filos, Emilio Crespo & Jesus de la Villa (eds.), *Classical philology and linguistics: Old themes and new perspectives*, 481–506. Berlin & Boston: De Gruyter.
Bartolotta, Annamaria & Daniel Kölligan. 2020. Modality and injunctive in Homeric Greek: The role of epistemic modality particles and adverbs in counterfactual constructions. In Martti Leiwo, Marja Vierros & Sonja Dahlgren (eds.), *Papers on Ancient Greek linguistics. Proceedings of the ninth international colloquium on Ancient Greek linguistics (ICAGL 9)*, 417–446. Helsinki: Societas Scientiarum Fennica.
Basset, Louis. 1979. *Les emplois périphrastiques du verbe μέλλειν. Étude de linguistique grecque et essai de linguistique générale*. Lyon: Maison de l'Orient.
Baugh, John. 2011. Power, social diversity, and language. In Rajend Mesthrie (ed.), *The Cambridge handbook of sociolinguistics*, 17–27. Cambridge: Cambridge University Press.

Bazzanella, Carla. 1990. 'Modal' uses of the Italian *indicativo imperfetto* in a pragmatic perspective. *Journal of Pragmatics* 14. 439–457.
Bentein, Klaas. 2015. The Greek documentary papyri as a linguistically heterogeneous corpus: The case of the "*Katochoi* of the Sarapeion" archive. *Classical World* 108. 461–484.
Bertinetto, Pier Marco. 1986. *Tempo, aspetto e azione nel verbo italiano*. Firenze: Accademia della Crusca.
Bonifazi, Anna, Annemieke Drummen & Mark de Kreij. 2016. *Particles in Ancient Greek discourse: Exploring particle use across genres*. Washington, DC: Center for Hellenic Studies.
Chung, Sandra & Alan Timberlake. 1985. Tense, aspect and mood. In Timothy Shopen (ed.), *Language typology. Vol. III. Grammatical categories and lexicon*, 202–258. Cambridge: Cambridge University Press.
Coseriu, Eugenio. 1976. *Das romanische Verbalsystem*. Tübingen: Narr.
Cristofaro, Sonia. 2003. *Subordination*. Oxford: Oxford University Press.
Depauw, Mark & Tom Gheldof. 2014. Trismegistos. An interdisciplinary platform for ancient world texts and related information. In: Łukasz Bolikowski, Vittore Casarosa, Paula Goodale, Nikos Houssos, Paolo Manghi & Jochen Schirrwagen (eds.), *Theory and practice of digital libraries - TPDL 2013 Selected Workshops*, 40–52. Cham: Springer.
Dessì Schmid, Sarah. 2010. Modal uses of the Italian *imperfetto* and the Spanish *imperfecto*: a comparison. In Martin G. Becker & Eva-Maria Remberger (eds.), *Modality and mood in Romance*, 39–66. Berlin & Boston: De Gruyter.
Dickey, Eleanor. 2011. The Greek and Latin languages in the papyri. In Roger S. Bagnall (ed.), *The Oxford handbook of papyrology*, 149–169. New York & Oxford: Oxford University Press.
Edgington, Dorothy. 2021. Counterfactual conditionals. In Otávio Bueno & Scott A. Shalkowski (eds.), *The Routledge handbook of modality*, 30–39. New York: Routledge.
Elliott, Jennifer R. 2000. Realis and irrealis: Forms and concepts of the grammaticalisation of reality. *Linguistic Typology* 4(1). 55–90.
van Emde Boas, Evert, Albert Rijksbaron, Luuk Huitink & Mathieu de Bakker. 2019. *The Cambridge grammar of Classical Greek*. Cambridge: Cambridge University Press.
Gignac, Francis Thomas. 1976. *A grammar of the Greek papyri of the Roman and Byzantine periods. Phonology*. Milan: La Goliardica.
Gignac, Francis Thomas. 1981. *A grammar of the Greek papyri of the Roman and Byzantine periods. Morphology*. Milan: La Goliardica.
Greenberg, Joseph H. 1986. The realis-irrealis continuum in the Classical Greek conditionals. In Elisabeth Closs Traugott, Alice Ter Meulen, Judith Snitzer Reilly & Charles A. Ferguson (eds.), *On conditionals*, 247–264. Cambridge: Cambridge University Press.
Halliday, Michael A.K. 1967. Notes on transitivity and theme. *Journal of Linguistics* 3. 199–245.
Horrocks, Geoffrey. 1995. On condition…: Aspect and modality in the history of Greek. *The Cambridge Classical Journal* 41. 153–173.
Horrocks, Geoffrey. 2007. Syntax: From Classical Greek to the Koine. In Antonios F. Christidis (ed.), *A history of Ancient Greek from the beginnings to late antiquity*, 618–631. Cambridge: Cambridge University Press.
Horrocks, Geoffrey. 2010. *Greek. A history of the language and its speakers*. 2nd edn. Chichester: Wiley-Blackwell.
James, Deborah. 1982. Past tense and the hypothetical. A cross-linguistic study. *Studies in Language* 6(3). 375–403.
Lyons, John. 1977. *Semantics*. Vol. 2. Cambridge: Cambridge University Press.

Matthissen, Christian & Sandra A. Thomson. 1998. The structure of discourse and 'subordination'. In John Haiman & Sandra A. Thomson (eds.), *Clause combining in grammar and discourse*, 275–330. Amsterdam & Philadelphia: John Benjamins.
Mithun, Marianne. 1999. *The languages of native North America*. Cambridge: Cambridge University Press.
Nuyts, Jan. 2014. Analyses of the modal meanings. In Jan Nuyts & Johan van der Auwera (eds.), *The Oxford handbook of modality and mood*, 31–49. Oxford: Oxford University Press.
Olsson, Bror. 1925. *Papyrusbriefe aus der frühesten Römerzeit*. Uppsala: Almqvist & Wiksell.
Palme, Bernhard. 2011. The range of documentary texts: Types and categories. In Roger S. Bagnall (ed.), *The Oxford handbook of papyrology*, 358–394. Oxford: Oxford University Press.
Palmer, Frank R. 2001. *Mood and modality*. 2nd edn. Cambridge: Cambridge University Press.
Porter, Stanley. 1989. *Verbal aspect in the Greek of the New Testament, with reference to tense and mood*. New York: Peter Lang.
la Roi, Ezra. 2022. Interlocked life cycles of counterfactual mood forms from Archaic to Classical Greek: Aspect, actionality and changing temporal reference. *Indogermanische Forschungen* 127(1). 235–282.
Schwyzer, Eduard. 1950. *Griechische Grammatik auf der Grundlage Karl Brugmanns griechischer Grammatik* (updated and edited by Albert Debrunner). München: Beck'sche Verlagsbuchhandlung.
Stolk, Joanne Vera. 2020. Orthographic variation and register in the corpus of Greek documentary papyri (300 BCE–800 CE). In Klaas Bentein & Mark Janse (eds.), *Varieties of Post-classical and Byzantine Greek*, 299–326. Berlin & Boston: De Gruyter Mouton.
Tabachovitz, David. 1943. *Études sur le grec de la basse époque*. Uppsala: Almqvist & Wiksell.
Timberlake, Alan. 2007. Aspect, tense and mood. In Timothy Shopen (ed.), *Language typology*, 280–333. Cambridge: Cambridge University Press.
Traugott, Elisabeth C. & Richard B. Dasher. 2002. *Regularity in semantic change*. Cambridge: Cambridge University Press.
Vierros, Marja & Erik Henriksson. 2021. PapyGreek treebanks: A dataset of linguistically annotated Greek documentary papyri. *Journal of Open Humanities Data* 7. 26. DOI: http://doi.org/10.5334/johd.55
Viti, Carlotta. 2006. AND in the early Indo-European languages. *Archivio Glottologico Italiano* 91. 35–64.
Wakker, Gerry. 1994. *Conditions and conditionals: An investigation of Ancient Greek*. Amsterdam: Gieben.
Wierzbicka, Anna. 1997. Conditionals and counterfactuals: Conceptual primitives and linguistic universals. In Angeliki Athanasios & René Dirven (eds.), *On conditionals again*, 15–59. Amsterdam: John Benjamins.

Emilia Ruiz Yamuza
6 Conditional subordinate clauses and verbal moods. A case study

Abstract: In recent times there has been an increasing interest in the analysis of the interactions that occur not only between the different domains of modality but also with other categories unrelated to them. The following work, framed in this line, analyses the interactions that give rise to the different functionalities of a conditional construction with the verb 'to want'. The investigation revolves around three questions: (1) Which verbal moods in the main clause trigger these functions? (2) Which verbal moods in the *if*-clause play a role? (3) Which sentence types are compatible with each function? The results point to the following features: (1) a relatively free relationship with the verbal moods of the main clause; (2) an increase in the use of the indicative in the *if*-clause; (3) compatibility with all sentence types in one of the two functions identified. Other interactions have been detected: the verbal predicate's syntactic structure, the syntactic status of the *if*-clause, and the text's organisation.

Keywords: Verbal moods, sentence types, infinitive, directive acts, reformulation, construction

1 Introduction

In Ancient Greek, as in other languages, there are numerous interactions between the very different elements that express modality. The present work focuses on analysing the interactions that produce the functional differences documented in a subtype of sentences, elliptical conditionals, with a verb meaning 'to want'.

In Ancient Greek, conditional subordinate clauses with the 'want' verbs ἐθέλω (*ethélō*) and βούλομαι (*boúlomai*) have different functions. As is the case with similar expressions in other languages (Kaltenböck 2016: 358 on English; Unceta 2009: 63–64 on Latin, *pace* Dickey 2019: 221), they convey polite orders (Denizot 2011: 442) as in (1):

Acknowledgments: This research was developed within the framework of the project "Grammar of the parenthetical elements of Ancient Greek: Syndetic and asyndetic structures" (GRAPAGA) PGC2018-095147-B-I00.

Emilia Ruiz Yamuza, University of Seville, e-mail: eruiz@us.es

https://doi.org/10.1515/9783110778380-006

(1) [ὅθεν δή μοι δοκοῦσιν αὐτὸ "ψυχὴν" καλέσαι]. εἰ δὲ βούλει – ἔχε ἠρέμα [δοκῶ γάρ μοί τι καθορᾶν πιθανώτερον]. (Pl. Cra. 399e3)
ei de boúlei ékhe eréma
if PTCL want.2SG.PRS keep.2SG.IMP still
'[Therefore, I think they called it *psukhḗ*]. But – please, keep still a moment (lit. if you want, keep still). [I fancy I see something which will carry more conviction].'[1]

Alternatively, they can introduce a new example, as in (2):

(2) εἰ δὲ βούλει, Περικλέα, οὕτως μεγαλοπρεπῶς σοφὸν ἄνδρα, οἶσθ' ὅτι δύο τέκνα ἔθρεψε, Πάραλον καὶ Ξάνθιππον; (Pl. *Men.* 94a7)
ei de boúlei, Perikléa, hoútōs megaloprepôs
if PTCL want.2SG.PRS Pericles.ACC so splendidly
sophon ándra oîsth' hóti dúo tékna
wise.ACC man.ACC be.aware.2SG.PF that two sons.ACC
éthrepse Páralon kai Xánthippon?
bring.up.3SG.AOR Paralus.ACC and Xanthippus.ACC
'Or take another example (if you want) – Pericles, a splendidly accomplished man. Are you aware that he brought up two sons, Paralus and Xanthippus?'

The *if*-clauses can be built with an indicative mood, e.g. βούλει (*boúlei*), or with a subjunctive mood plus modal particle, e.g. ἐ-ὰν βούλῃ (*e-an boúlēi*, if-MOD want.2SG. SBJV), conveying an epistemic modality content, i.e. probability. In the main clause, we find the imperative or subjunctive, in the first type, and the indicative, in the second type.

My research questions are the following:
(1) Are the verbal moods in the main clause of each construction – namely imperative and subjunctive in the first type and indicative in the second type – compulsory or can the contents they convey, i.e. polite orders in the first case and exemplificative contents in the second case, also be conveyed by other moods?
(2) Do the subjunctive and the indicative in the *if*-clauses express differences in the epistemic modality contents, or is the contrast between a *realis* mood and a probability mood faded?
(3) Is there any interaction between functions and sentence types, especially for the second construction?

---

[1] Translations are taken from Loeb Online with minor alterations to make them as literal as possible in the relevant sections.

Answering these questions first requires a detailed analysis of the formal properties of these sentences – following Wakker (1994) – and their pragmatic and discursive functions – following la Roi (2021) and Ruiz Yamuza (2022).

My corpus comprises Homeric poems and the entire works of Sophocles, Euripides, Aristophanes, and Plato. This corpus was selected to study the evolution of the constructions from the 8th century BCE (Homer) to the 4th century BCE (Plato). It includes a wide variety of text types, particularly text structures with a high degree of interaction between speaker and addressee, such as dialogues and monologues in comedy (Aristophanes) and tragedy (Sophocles and Euripides), and dialogues and speeches to present reactive audiences (Plato).

This paper is organised as follows. Section 2 briefly reviews relevant concepts in the field of mood and modality, Construction Grammar, and discourse and pragmatic functions. Section 3 presents the description of my data. Section 4 discusses the results and presents a tentative hypothesis of global interpretation. Finally, Section 5 summarises the conclusions.

2 Theoretical basis

2.1 Mood and modality

Mood and modality can be used in at least two different meanings. In the first one, they are not conceptually different domains. Mood is the grammaticalisation of modal categories, as "modality is the conceptual domain and mood is its inflectional expression" (Bybee, Perkins and Pagliuca 1994: 181; cf. also Palmer 1986: 16). The terms mood and modality can also be used to express different contents. Thus, modality concerns the expression of possibility and necessity (epistemic and deontic modalities). In contrast, the term mood has come to be used to refer to (i) the domain of grammatical coding of modal (and related) meanings on the verb; (ii) the domain of basic sentence types and the illocutionary categories expressed by them; (iii) the domain of indicative vs subjunctive or *realis* vs *irrealis* coding and its semantics (Nuyts 2016: 1–2). There is indeed an enormous polysemy in this use of the term mood, but it also occurs in the first meaning of the term modality. Therefore, I prefer to use the term *mood* for verbal moods, grammaticalised in a language for the expression of modality contents, and use the term *modality* to express all the contents of the domain.

Modality is not a simple category that pairs a form, the verbal mood, with a content, the modality content, in a single way. It is a category whose morphs are not exclusively verbal moods. There are other markers, such as modality adverbs, modal verbs, and lexical items, and there are also some grammatical categories which systematically interact with modality contents, such as tense, aspect, and evidentiality.[2] On the level of content, the issue is even more complicated. At least three different domains must be differentiated: epistemic modality, deontic modality, and speech act modality.[3] Epistemic modality incorporates *realis*, *irrealis*, possibility, and probability. Deontic modality considers obligation and necessity. Sentence-type modality includes the conventionalised connection between types of sentences, verbal moods, and the typical illocutionary force that the sentence type conveys: declarative, directive, interrogative, and expressive (Nikolaeva 2016: 69). Bybee, Perkins and Pagliuca (1994: 176–181) refer to these terms as agent-oriented modality, speaker-oriented modality, epistemic modality, and subordinating modality. Agent-oriented modality includes obligation, necessity, ability and desire. Speaker-oriented modality includes imperative, prohibitive, optative, hortative, admonitive, and permissive constructions.

Consequently, the modality content of a particular instance is produced by the interaction of the content expressed by the verbal mood, additional modality content rendered by sentence adverbs, and elements with modality content, such as tenses, plus the modality content expressed by the type of sentence. Moreover, this shortlist, including moods, modal verbs, adverbs, tenses, and sentence types, does not exhaust the inventory of elements with modality functions or, even better, that of elements interacting in one of the modality domains (Revuelta Puigdollers 2017: 18–22; cf. also Ruiz Yamuza 2014). Furthermore, as stated by Denizot and Tronci (this volume), the way they interact and influence each other to build modal meanings has yet to be explored.

2.2 Construction Grammar

In the cognitive linguistic approach, as described by Croft and Cruse (2004: chapters 9–10), all linguistic elements are seen in terms of constructions, i.e. symbolic pairings of form and meaning. The "form" pole represents the relevant phonological,

---

[2] Not all of them are at the same level: evidentiality is not an inflectional category in Ancient Greek. Evidentiality is related to modality, either as a subpart of epistemic modality (Palmer 1986), or as an independent interacting category (Aikhenvald 2018: 17).
[3] For Dik (1989: 205), there are three sub-areas of modality: inherent, objective, and subjective. Both objective and subjective include two scales of potential differences in epistemic modality (certain-probable-possible-improbable-impossible) and deontic modality (obligatory-acceptable-permissible-unacceptable-prohibited). They operate at different levels: objective modalities work at the extended predication level; subjective modalities work at the proposition level. At the clausal level, illocutionary operators and satellites express the speech act (Dik 1989: 246–262).

morphological, syntactic, and prosodic information. The "meaning" pole can represent semantic as well as discourse-pragmatic information. This type of analysis integrates a complex formal pole with a complex meaning pole and allows explanations to go further than the bare consideration of moods and tenses, introducing other variables as predicate structures and verb persons. The term "construction" has an interesting variety of meanings, including idiomatic structures with meanings that are not deduced from the sum of their members. In this sense, the construction *ei boúlei* 'if you want' is a type of construction that acquires an interactive, pragmatic meaning and ends up expressing an order of its own.

2.3 Exemplification as reformulation

Reformulation is a discursive operation: it is the more or less literal repetition of a previous formulation that the speaker considers insufficient. Roulet (1987) distinguishes between paraphrastic reformulation and non-paraphrastic reformulation. The first links constituents of the same hierarchical level; conversely, the second involves a change of perspective of the utterance. Both reformulations can be identified by the presence of reformulation operators. There is no common opinion on how reformulation is organised: whether it is necessary to maintain the distribution in two different types of paraphrasing and how the semantic class should be described. New functions have been recognised in the field since Roulet (1987), and Gülich and Kotschi (1983): mere identification, correction of a previous element through substitution, definition of a term, denomination, explanation of the general meaning of the term, or even conclusion from the previous segment. Pons Bordería (2013: 162, 167) reduces this multiplicity to four large domains, i.e. paraphrasis, correction, proper reformulation, and conclusion. In short, a reformulation operation can establish: (a) identity between A and B (paraphrasis); (b) distance between A and B (correction); (c) incompatibility between A and B (proper reformulation); (d) B as the consequence of A (conclusion). In this paper, I considered exemplifying one of the functions of the reformulation operation as an "expansion" (Gülich and Kotschi 1983: 328). For this research, I have not established subgroups according to the functions.[4] They are all grouped together as "reformulators".

---

[4] Paraphrase markers, correction markers, and exemplifiers have also been distinguished as subtypes in other languages, e.g. Bazzanella (2006: 457) for Italian. As for Ancient Greek, Verano Liaño (2016: 224) proposed two different types of reformulatory and argumentative exemplifications in Plato and conceived exemplification as a functional continuum in which the coexistence of functions is also possible.

2.4 Politeness

An expression meaning 'if you want' or 'if you please' used in orders tends to be automatically interpreted as polite. It indicates that the order is optional depending on the want of the agent / hearer. It displays negative politeness (Brown and Levinson 1987: 129), a strategy which minimises the potential threat to freedom posed by the order. However, etymology is not sufficient to define the meaning and, as Terkourafi's (2005: 112) work proposes, politeness is the achieved perlocutionary effect ("what we bring about or achieve by saying something" according to Austin 1975: 109) and not the recognition of the speaker's intention. Apparently, polite expressions appear in contexts that contain direct insults, threats, or other indications that the interaction is overtly rude. On these occasions, the expression 'if you please' conveys meaning in conflict with the general interaction of the unit and has to be understood ironically or as an over-politeness mark. On the other hand, conventional and ritualised politeness marks should not be considered automatic politeness markers but markers of normalised behaviour. Two different types of politeness must be considered: politeness, understood as individual volitional action, must be differentiated from politeness as a default, that is, expected behaviour (Terkourafi 2008: 69–70). The Greek expression εἰ βούλει (*ei boúlei*) is not conventionalised. Therefore, it could be assumed that its effectiveness as an expression of politeness is greater than if its use were conventionalised.

3 Data

3.1 Construction conveying polite orders: Moods in the main clause

As for the first question, as to whether it is possible to render a polite order in a construction built with an *if*-clause displaying a 'want' verb, without imperative or subjunctive moods in the apodosis in Ancient Greek, the answer is: it is possible, but occurs only scarcely. In Homeric Greek, it is possible to give polite orders with an *if*-clause + infinitive. In Classical Greek, this possibility is only documented in Plato and Euripides. The most frequent situation is the use of an imperative or subjunctive in the main clause.

Table 1 provides the data of the distribution of moods in the *if*-sentence. Example (3) shows a common combination of the subjunctive in the *if*-clause plus an imperative in the main clause.

Table 1: Distribution of moods in the *if*-sentence.[5]

Moods in the *if*-sentence	Homer	Sophocles	Aristophanes	Euripides	Plato	Total per type
boúlomai + imperative	–	1	3	4	11	19
boúlomai + subjunctive	–	–	–	–	9	9
boúlomai cum infinitivo	–	–	–	2	3	5
(e)thélō + imperative	3	2	–	–	–	5
(e)thélō + subjunctive	–	–	–	–	–	–
(e)thélō cum infinitivo	12	1	–	–	–	13
boúlomai / (e)thélō + future	6	–	–	–	2	8
Total per author	21	4	3	6	25	59

(3) [οὐκ ἂν φθάνοιμι, εἰπεῖν τὸν Ἀλκιβιάδην. καὶ μέντοι οὑτωσὶ ποίησον.] ἐάν τι μὴ ἀληθὲς λέγω, μεταξὺ ἐπιλαβοῦ, ἂν βούλῃ, καὶ εἰπὲ [ὅτι τοῦτο ψεύδομαι]. (Pl. *Smp.* 214e11)

e-án   ti   mē   alēthes   légō   metaxu
if-MOD   something NEG   true   say.1SG.SBJV immediately
epilaboû   an   boúlēi   kai   eipe
take.up.2SG.IMP   if.MOD   want.2SG.SBJV   and   say.2SG.IMP

['You shall hear it this moment,' said Alcibiades, 'but there is something you must do]. If I say anything that is not true, please, interrupt me and say (lit. interrupt me, if you want, and say) [that there I am lying].'

Two *if*-clauses appear in the example: the first one precedes the apodosis ('If I say anything that is not true') and the second one is inserted in it ('if you want'). Obviously, only the first constitutes a truly conditional period. It provides the setting, i.e. the condition for the appropriateness of the speech act conveyed by the imperatives. The second *if*-clause does not convey the condition for the speech act; it only has pragmatic content and contributes to mitigating the order given by the imperatives *epilaboû* and *eipé* by offering options to the addressee.

The construction *ei boúlei* is more frequent with an exhortative subjunctive in the first person plural in the main clause:

---

[5] The label *cum infinitivo* indicates that the infinitive is in the *if*-clause, as an argument of the verb. The + sign indicates that the mood is in the apodosis of the period.

(4) [πρὸς γὰρ τὴν τῆς ἡδονῆς κρίσιν οὐ σμικρὸν μεμνῆσθαι ταύτην ἔσθ' ἡμῖν ἢ μή].
βραχὺ δέ τι περὶ αὐτῆς, εἰ βούλει, διαπεράνωμεν. (Pl. *Phlb.* 33a5)
brakhu   dé   ti   peri   autês,   ei
brief.ACC PTCL something.ACC about it.GEN   if
boúlei,   diaperánōmen
want.2SG.PRS speak.1PL.SBJV
'[Well then, do your best to bear it in mind; for remembering or forgetting it will make a great difference in our judgement of pleasure.] And briefly, if you want, we should speak about it.'

As in other languages (e.g. English and Spanish, cf. Kaltenböck 2016: 357),[6] an elliptical conditional, constructed with an infinitive, expresses a directive:

(5) [οὐκ ἀποδεκτέον κατὰ τὸν σὸν λόγον.] – εἰ σύ, ἔφη, βούλει ἐμὸν τιθέναι· [οὐ γὰρ οὖν δὴ ἀποδεκτέον]. (Pl. *R.* 389b1)
ei sú,   éphē,   boúlei   emon   tithénai
if you.NOM say.3SG.IMPF want.2SG.PRS my.ACC put.INF
'[We must not accept it on your view]. "If it pleases you to call it mine," he said; [at any rate we must not accept it].'

In this group, I included constructions that express offers or advice[7] and a number of examples where the conditional construction[8] conveys the actual content of a request expressed in a very indirect way. In example (6), we must take into consideration that the verb ἱκάνομαι (*hikánomai*) has developed into a performative verb: a movement verb 'go to' shifts to 'approach as suppliant', as in the example, and finally to 'supplicate' or 'beseech' (LSJ *s.u.* ἱκάνομαι 3b).

(6) τοὔνεκα νῦν τὰ σὰ γούναθ' ἱκάνομαι, αἴ κ' ἐθέλησθα / κείνου λυγρὸν ὄλεθρον ἐνισπεῖν, [εἴ που ὄπωπας / ὀφθαλμοῖσι τεοῖσιν, ἢ ἄλλου μῦθον ἄκουσας]. (*Od.* 3.92–94)
toúneka   nûn ta   sa   goúnath'
because.of.this now ART.ACC your.ACC knees.ACC

---

6 Directives have been identified as the main function of insubordinate *if*-clauses in languages other than English (Kaltenböck 2016: 350). For Ancient Greek cf. la Roi (2021: 31–32) and Ruiz Yamuza (2022).
7 In la Roi's words (2021: 33): "[t]o sum up, the illocutionary force of this insubordinate construction is still co-constructed with the pragmatic context to some degree and not as independent as other insubordinate constructions".
8 Wakker (1994: 365–379) includes some of them in the group called "in the hope that".

hikánomai		*aí*[9]	*k'*	*ethélēistha*	*keínou*
approach.as.suppliant.1SG.PRS		if	MOD	want.2SG.SBJV	this.GEN
lugron	*ólethron*	*enispeîn*			
woeful.ACC	death.ACC	tell.INF			

'Therefore, I have now come to your knees if you want to tell me of his woeful death, [whether you saw it, it may be, with your own eyes, or heard the report of some other wanderer].'

In the following example, the coordination between the *if*-sentence and a sentence giving an order, with the subjunctive plus μή (*mḗ*), shows the real pragmatic meaning of the construction:

(7) [τοῖσι δὲ καὶ μετέειπε βοὴν ἀγαθὸς Διομήδης· / ἐγγὺς ἀνήρ οὐ δηθὰ ματεύσομεν·] αἴ κ' ἐθέλητε / πείθεσθαι, καὶ μή τι κότῳ ἀγάσησθε ἕκαστος / [οὕνεκα δὴ γενεῆφι νεώτατός εἰμι μεθ' ὑμῖν]. (*Il.* 14.109–112)

aí	*k'*	*ethélēte*	*peíthesthai*	*kai*	*mḗ ti*
if	MOD	want.2PL.SBJV	give.ear.INF	and	NEG something.ACC
kótōi	*agásēsthe*		*hékastos*		
wroth.DAT	bear.a.grudge.2PL.SBJV		each.NOM		

'[Then among them spoke also Diomedes, good at the war cry: "Nearby is that man; not long shall we seek him,] if you want to give ear, and be in no way indignant with resentment, each one of you, [because I am the youngest among you"].'

In Homer, this construction is not only used in direct but also in indirect supplications. In indirect constructions, the speaker tells a third person his / her intention to ask someone to do something. The origin of the indirect construction should be in the direct construction.

Another group of examples has a different function: the speaker indirectly commits himself / herself to a future action to which he / she invites the listener as a spectator. The following example includes a promise, the expression of the speaker's commitment to a future event. The verb in the apodosis is in the future tense.

---

[9] Αἰ is a dialectal variant for εἰ 'if'.

(8) σοῖσιν δ' ὀφθαλμοῖσιν ἐπόψεαι, αἴ κ' ἐθέλῃσθα, / κτεινομένους μνηστῆρας, [οἳ ἐνθάδε κοιρανέουσι]. (*Od.* 20.233–234)
soîsin   d'   ophthalmoîsin   epópseai,   aí
your.DAT   PTCL   eyes.DAT   see.2SG.FUT   if
k'   ethéleistha   kteinoménous   mnēstêras
MOD   want.2SG.SBJV   slay.PTCP.PASS.ACC suitors.ACC
'And you shall see with your eyes, if you want, the killing of the suitors, [who lord it here].'

3.2 Construction conveying polite orders: Moods in the *if*-clause

As for the second question, whether the moods in the *if*-clause keep their original meaning or whether there is a bleaching of their modality content, the answer should make distinctions between periods. There is an interesting variation in the history of Ancient Greek: the subjunctive mood in the *if*-clause is better represented in Homeric texts, but its frequency tends to decrease in the following centuries. In the Classical period, indicatives appear in the vast majority of examples; subjunctives plus modal particles are limited to a few occurrences. See Table 2 for a summary.

Table 2: Distribution of moods in the *if*-clause.

Moods	Homer	Sophocles	Aristophanes	Euripides	Plato	Total per type
Indicative *boúlomai*	–	1	3	4	20	28
Subjunctive *boúlomai*	–	–	–	–	5	5
Indicative *(e)thélō*	6	2	–	–	–	8
Subjunctive *(e)thélō*	13	–	–	–	–	13
Optative *(e)thélō*	2	–	–	–	–	2
Total per author	21	3	3	4	25	56

In Homeric texts, subjunctives appear in the *if*-clauses accompanied by a modal particle, keeping a future reference. The temporal reference of the host unit is the future, and future tenses appear in the previous sentence. The following example is an instance of an indirect supplication with the verbs μετελεύσομαι (*meteleúsomai*) and καλέσσω (*kaléssō*). The presence of a purpose sentence marked by the purpose conjunction ὄφρα (*óphra*) supports the idea that the conditional sentence does not express a purpose but the content of the plea or request.

(9) [ἀλλὰ σὺ μὲν πρὸς νηὸν Ἀθηναίης ἀγελείης / ἔρχευ,] ἐγὼ δὲ Πάριν μετελεύσομαι ὄφρα καλέσσω / αἴ κ' ἐθέλησ' εἰπόντος ἀκουέμεν [...]. (*Il.* 6. 279–281)
egō   de   Párin   meteleúsomai   óphra   kaléssō
I.NOM PTCL Paris.ACC go.after.1SG.FUT in.order.to summon.1SG.SBJV
aí k'   ethélēis'   eipóntos   akouémen
if MOD want.3SG.SBJV say.PTCP.GEN listen.INF
'[So go to the shrine of Athena, driver of the spoil;] and I will go after Paris, to summon him, if perhaps he will listen to what I say.'

In contrast, the indicative mood in the present tense appears when the situation is contemporaneous with the moment of speech, as in example (10). In this example, no apodosis is expressed. The text continues with a purpose clause introduced by ὄφρα (*óphra*). There are two possibilities: either to understand the infinitive δαήμεναι (*daḗmenai*) as an imperative infinitive or to understand it as an object infinitive of the verb ἐθέλεις (*ethéleis*). In this second case, the entire *if*-clause expresses the modality content.

(10) [φύλλα τὰ μέν τ' ἄνεμος χαμάδις χέει, ἄλλα δέ θ' ὕλη / τηλεθόωσα φύει, ἔαρος δ' ἐπιγίγνεται ὥρη·/ ὣς ἀνδρῶν γενεὴ ἣ μὲν φύει ἣ δ' ἀπολήγει.] / εἰ δ' ἐθέλεις καὶ ταῦτα δαήμεναι [ὄφρ' ἐῢ εἰδῇς / ἡμετέρην γενεήν, πολλοὶ δέ μιν ἄνδρες ἴσασιν]. (*Il.* 6.147–151)
ei d'   ethéleis   kai   taûta   daḗmenai
if PTCL want.2SG.PRS even this.ACC hear.INF
'[As for the leaves, the wind scatters some on the earth, but the luxuriant forest sprouts others when the season of spring has come; so of men one generation springs up and another passes away.] But, if you want, hear this also, [so that you may know well my lineage; and many men know it].'

Promises, *per se*, refer to a state of affairs that has to be fulfilled in the future. It comes as no surprise that the subjunctive plus modal particle appears in them as a rule. As for the occasional use of subjunctives in *if*-clauses in the Classical period, the same idea applies: the subjunctive occurs in the examples with future meaning in the apodosis, as the subjunctive has a meaning of probability with future reference, e.g. (11=3).

(11) [οὐκ ἂν φθάνοιμι, εἰπεῖν τὸν Ἀλκιβιάδην. καὶ μέντοι οὑτωσὶ ποίησον.] ἐάν τι μὴ ἀληθὲς λέγω, μεταξὺ ἐπιλαβοῦ, ἂν βούλῃ, καὶ εἰπὲ [ὅτι τοῦτο ψεύδομαι]. (Pl. *Smp.* 214e11) (=ex.(3))

e-án   ti   mē   alēthes   légō   metaxu
if-MOD something NEG true   say.1SG.SBJV immediately
epilaboû   an   boúlēi   kai   eipe
take.up.2SG.IMP if.MOD want.2SG.SBJV and say.2SG.IMP

'["You shall hear it this moment," said Alcibiades, "but there is something you must do.] If I say anything that is not true, please, interrupt me and say (lit. interrupt me, if you want, and say) [that there I am lying"].'

The global time reference of the conditional period of the construction is the future, as commands, promises, and recommendations *per se* are situated in the future. Consequently, the use of the subjunctive accompanied by the particle is perfectly suitable. This situation is coherently represented in the Homeric texts. One would expect this situation to have been maintained throughout the history of the Greek language, but this is not the case. Present indicative tenses are better documented in the examples outside Homer. Several explanations can be provided. First, the particular situation of verbs meaning 'to want' must be considered. As stative verbs, they tend to have large temporal references. Usually, a state is not momentary but precisely the opposite. Moreover, the temporal reference of stative verbs can be considered inclusive, embracing present and future references.[10] When subjunctives are accompanied by particles, the content, that is the future reference, is blatantly expressed.

To the second question asked in this Section we can now answer that moods keep their meaning. The subjunctive plus particle conveys a probability content, and the present indicative conveys a *realis* content. There is no evidence to support that their contents have been bleached. However, there is only a slight difference in meaning between the use of the indicative and the subjunctive in the construction investigated here.

---

10 The inclusive use of tenses (Martínez Vázquez 2006) is an application of Benveniste' ideas on personal pronouns (1966 [1946]: 233–236) to another deictic category: tenses. It is a way to explain the variety of temporal uses of present tenses. From an aspectual point of view, the present "is the most compatible aspect for use with STATES, since the aspectual sense of 'the situation viewed from within, focusing on the internal make-up, without regard for beginning or end-point' gives a very natural reference to the unchanging condition" (Fanning 1990: 137).

3.3 Construction conveying polite orders: Sentence types

Sentence types may interact with the mood system of a language, and sometimes, the two concepts are equated (Siemund 2018: 65). The concept of sentence type as the formal mark of a speech act needs some specifications. It is not enough to differentiate between direct and indirect speech acts, given that indirect acts are so widely represented. It is more adapted to reality to make a distinction between (a) prototypical sentence types, (b) alternative codifications,[11] including the systematic use of a sentence type to convey a speech act that is different from the speech act usually indicated by the sentence type, and (c) sporadic codifications that include rare uses of a sentence type to convey a content other than its usual content.

In the presence of an imperative or subjunctive in the first person plural, the sentence type is qualified, by default, as a direct directive. Imperatives are by and large restricted to expressing orders, requests, and related illocutionary forces. Imperatives cannot be used for making statements, asking questions (except in echo questions), or exclamations (Siemund 2018: 230–231). However, this illocutionary force includes commands, requests, suggestions, advice, prohibition, pleas, warnings, permission, consent, invitations, want, imprecations, instructions, threats, challenges, conditionals, and grabbing attention (Siemund 2018: 231–235, cf. Denizot 2011: 243–263). The construction εἰ βούλει (*ei boúlei*), because it appeals directly to the will of the listener to whom it refers the decision on the proposal made by the speaker, can be considered a collaborative tool. As such, it contributes to mitigating the imposing force of the illocutionary act.

However, there are other cases when the verbal mood in the sentences does not qualify for a single direct sentence type. There are two verbal moods in question, i.e. infinitive and indicative in future tense. Their situation is not identical (Denizot 2011: 336–339, 423–439). The future produces indirect acts, although it can be considered an alternative encoding because of its frequency and the radical nature of some uses. Nevertheless, in this conditional construction, the sentence type in which the infinitive appears is apparently declarative, and the infinitive is the argument of the verb. It is the construction as a whole which indirectly expresses a directive act. In this construction, the infinitive conveys the content of the order but, syntactically, it is the second argument of the verb βούλομαι (*boúlomai*). The construction alone conveys an indirect directive speech act.

---

[11] In Siemund's (2018: 48) terms "speech act constructions", meaning the association of certain sentential form types with specific illocutionary forces.

To answer the question of whether all sentence types express this function, all of them cannot do that, although it can be conveyed by more than one sentence type since direct and indirect speech acts can be found.

3.4 Construction conveying an example: Moods in the main clause

In the second construction, the distribution of the verbal moods of the unit in which the *if*-clauses are inserted points to the complete predominance of the indicative forms, as represented in Table 3.

Table 3: Distribution of moods in the clause.

Moods in the construction	Sophocles	Aristophanes	Euripides	Plato	Total per type
boúlomai + imperative	1	1	1	1	4
boúlomai + subjunctive	–	–	–	1	1
boúlomai cum infinitivo	–	–	–	2	2
boúlomai + indicative / optative	–	–	–	22 /2	24
ethélō + indicative	–	–	–	1	1
Total per author	1	1	1	29	32

The first example of the second construction helps explain the type's features. It consists of a sequence of imperative + object in the accusative followed by an *if*-sentence and then another object in the accusative. The *if*-clause cannot be understood as a protasis of the imperative sentence. It is not a mitigating device; it is a parenthesis.

(12) [Δι. νὴ τὸν Δί', ὥσπερ γ' εἴ τις εἴποι γείτονι, /] "χρῆσον σὺ μάκτραν, εἰ δὲ βούλει, κάρδοπον." / [Αι. οὐ δῆτα τοῦτό γ', ὦ κατεστωμυλμένε / ἄνθρωπε, ταὖτ' ἔστ', ἀλλ' ἄριστ' ἐπῶν ἔχον]. (Ar. *Ra*. 1158–1161)
khrêson   su   máktran,   ei de boúlei,   kárdopon
lend.2SG.IMP you.NOM kneading.ACC if PTCL want.2SG.PRS mortar.ACC
'[Right! just as if a man said to his neighbour, /] Lend me a kneading trough, or better a mortar. [Aeschylus: That's not so at all, you blabbermouth, / It's not the same, but uses the best choice of words].'

This construction is less represented than the former, and it can be said that it is basically a Platonic one. In the Platonic examples, the *if*-clauses tend to stand alone, e.g. (13), where no element in the text can be related to the conditional construction. It is not even easy to deduce which apodosis has been elided. The *if*-clause εἰ βούλει is constructed with ἀνδρὸς ἀρετήν (*ei boúlei andros aretḗn*). The accusative is the object of *boúlei*. Its function is to introduce a new case, a topic. Structurally, it remains as an extraclausal element:

(13) ἀλλ' οὐ χαλεπόν, ὦ Σώκρατες, εἰπεῖν. πρῶτον μέν, εἰ βούλει ἀνδρὸς ἀρετήν, [ῥᾴδιον, ὅτι αὕτη ἐστὶν ἀνδρὸς ἀρετή, ἱκανὸν εἶναι τὰ τῆς πόλεως πράττειν, καὶ πράττοντα τοὺς μὲν φίλους εὖ ποιεῖν, τοὺς δ' ἐχθροὺς κακῶς, καὶ αὐτὸν εὐλαβεῖσθαι μηδὲν τοιοῦτον παθεῖν]. εἰ δὲ βούλει γυναικὸς ἀρετήν, [οὐ χαλεπὸν διελθεῖν, ὅτι δεῖ αὐτὴν τὴν οἰκίαν εὖ οἰκεῖν, σῴζουσάν τε τὰ ἔνδον καὶ κατήκοον οὖσαν τοῦ ἀνδρός]. (Pl. *Men*. 71e2)

all'	*ou*	*khalepón*	*ô*	*Sṓkrates,*	*eipeîn*	*prôton*	*mén*
but	NEG	difficult.NOM	INTJ	Socrates.VOC	tell.INF	first	PTCL

ei	*boúlei*		*andrós*	*aretḗn* [...]	*ei*	*de*	*boúlei*
if	want.2SG.PRS		man.GEN	virtue.ACC	if	PTCL	want.2SG.PRS

gunaikós	*aretḗn*
woman.GEN	virtue.ACC

'But it is not difficult, Socrates, to tell. First of all, if you want the virtue of a man, [it is easily stated that a man's virtue is this – that he be competent to manage the affairs of his city, and to manage them so as to benefit his friends and harm his enemies, and to take care to avoid suffering harm himself.] Or if you want a woman's virtue: [there is no difficulty in describing it as the duty of ordering the house well, looking after the property indoors, and obeying her husband].'

In the next example, the *if*-clause is located in the left periphery. The unit introduces a new example of Socrates' worthiness, i.e. ἐν ταῖς μάχαις (*en taîs mákhais*) 'in battles', which is a new topic, followed by the particular instance ἡ μάχη (*hē mákhē*) 'the battle'.

(14) [ἔπειτα ᾤχετ' ἀπιὼν προσευξάμενος τῷ ἡλίῳ.] εἰ δὲ βούλεσθε ἐν ταῖς μάχαις [– τοῦτο γὰρ δὴ δίκαιόν γε αὐτῷ ἀποδοῦναι – ὅτε γὰρ ἡ μάχη ἦν ἐξ ἧς ἐμοὶ καὶ τἀριστεῖα ἔδοσαν οἱ στρατηγοί]. (Pl. *Smp*. 220d5)

ei	*de*	*boúlesthe*	*en*	*taîs*	*mákhais*
if	PTCL	want.2PL.PRS	PREP	ART.DAT	battles.DAT

'[Then <he> walked away, after offering a prayer to the Sun.] Or in battles (lit. if you want, in battles) [– for there also he must have his due – on the day of the fight in which I gained my prize for valour from our commanders].'

The *if*-clauses stand alone in all the occurrences except for two instances, i.e. example (15) and Pl. *Smp.* 177b1. These two exceptions are examples with infinitives. They seem to be transitional examples in which the *if*-clauses play two roles: they work at the speech act domain level, expressing a suggestion, and at the text organisation level, introducing an example, a new element. In both meanings, they can be understood as conveying a suggestion and introducing an example. These occurrences provide the bridging context for the change from the speech act domain level to the discourse level. The presence of οἷον (*hoîon*) in the *if*-clause, a marker of exemplification, plays a role in the development.

(15) οἷον εἰ βούλει ἰδεῖν τοὺς ζωγράφους, τοὺς οἰκοδόμους, [τοὺς ναυπηγούς, τοὺς ἄλλους πάντας δημιουργούς, ὅντινα βούλει αὐτῶν, ὡς εἰς τάξιν τινὰ ἕκαστος ἕκαστον τίθησιν ὃ ἂν τιθῇ]. (Pl. *Grg.* 503e4)

hoîon	*ei*	*boúlei*	*ideîn*	*tous*	*zōgráphous*
as	if	want.2SG.PRS	look.INF	ART.ACC	painters.ACC

tous *oikodómous*
ART.ACC builders.ACC

'If you want to look at the painters, the builders, [the shipwrights, or any of the other craftsmen, whichever you like, to see how each of them arranges everything according to a certain order].'

3.5 Construction conveying an example: Moods in the subordinate clause

Concerning the second question, whether the subjunctive and the indicative in the *if*-clauses express differences in the content of epistemic modality or whether the contrast between a mode of reality and a mode of probability has faded, the distribution of verbal moods in the *if*-construction is shown in Table 4. The indicative is the most prevalent mood.

Table 4: Distribution of moods in the *if*-clause.

Moods	Sophocles	Aristophanes	Euripides	Plato
Indicative *boúlomai*	1	1	1	24
Subjunctive *boúlomai*	–	–	–	3
Indicative *(e)thélō*	–	–	–	1
Subjunctive *(e)thélō*	–	–	–	–
Other *ethélō* (optative)	–	–	–	–

There are only three occurrences of the subjunctive, all of which come from the same passage in Plato's *Gorgias* 472a4. The text in question is preceded by a complete conditional period: the protasis with the subjunctive accompanied by the modal particle ἄν (*án*), which expresses probability, and the apodosis with a verb in the future tense:

(16) a. [καὶ νῦν περὶ ὧν σὺ λέγεις ὀλίγου σοι πάντες συμφήσουσιν ταὐτὰ Ἀθηναῖοι καὶ οἱ ξένοι,] ἐὰν βούλῃ κατ' ἐμοῦ μάρτυρας παρασχέσθαι [ὡς οὐκ ἀληθῆ λέγω] μαρτυρήσουσί σοι [...]. (Pl. *Grg.* 472a4)
e-an   boúlēi   kat' emoû   márturas
if-MOD want.2SG.SBJV PREP me.GEN witnesses.ACC
paraskhésthai   marturḗsousi   soi
bring.forward.INF give.evidence.3PL.FUT you.DAT
'[And so now you will find almost everybody, Athenians and foreigners, in agreement with you on the points you state], if you want to bring forward witnesses [against the truth of what I say], they will give evidence on your behalf [...].'

It is followed by three parenthetical *if*-clauses introducing alternatives:

(16) b. ἐὰν μὲν βούλῃ, Νικίας ὁ Νικηράτου καὶ οἱ ἀδελφοὶ μετ' αὐτοῦ, [ὧν οἱ τρίποδες οἱ ἐφεξῆς ἑστῶτές εἰσιν ἐν τῷ Διονυσίῳ]. (Pl. *Grg.* 472a5)
e-an   men boúlēi   Nikías   ho   Nikērátou
if-MOD PTCL want.2SG.SBJV Nicias.NOM ART.NOM Niceratus.GEN
kai   hoi   adelphoí   met' autoû
and ART.NOM brothers.NOM PREP he.GEN
'If you want, there is Nicias, son of Niceratus, with his brothers, [whose tripods are standing in a row in the Dionysium].'

(16) c. ἐὰν δὲ βούλῃ, Ἀριστοκράτης ὁ Σκελλίου, [οὗ αὖ ἐστιν ἐν Πυθίου τοῦτο τὸ καλὸν ἀνάθημα]. (Pl. *Grg.* 472a7)
e-an   de   boúlēi   Aristokrátēs   ho   Skellíou
if-MOD PTCL want.2SG.SBJV Aristocrates.NOM ART.NOM Scellias.GEN
'Or if you want, Aristocrates, son of Scellias, [whose goodly offering again is well known at Delphi].'

(16) d. ἐὰν δὲ βούλῃ, ἡ Περικλέους ὅλη οἰκία [ἢ ἄλλη συγγένεια ἥντινα ἂν βούλῃ τῶν ἐνθάδε ἐκλέξασθαι]. (Pl. *Grg.* 472b2)

e-an	de	boúlēi	hē	Perikléous	hólē
if-MOD	PTCL	want.2SG.SBJV	ART.NOM	Pericles.GEN	whole.NOM

oikía
house.NOM

'Or if you want, there is the whole house of Pericles [or any other family you may like to select in this place].'

These subjunctives could be explained by the first conditional period built with the same verb, i.e. *eán boúlēi* (*kat' emoû márturas parakhésthai [...] marturḗsousi*). The conditional period has an apodosis in the future and a protasis in the subjunctive plus modal particle. It is possible to think of automatic repetition of the construction. It is a phenomenon similar to the cases of modal attraction.[12] Therefore, the answer to the second question is that only the indicative appears in the *if*-sentence.

3.6 Construction conveying an example: Sentence types

The *if*-clause is loosely integrated into a unit conveying various speech acts. The speech act expressed in the host unit can be a directive, expressive, or interrogative speech act, as shown in Table 5.

Table 5: Distribution of sentence types.

	Sophocles	Euripides	Aristophanes	Plato
Directive	1	1	1	4
Interrogative	–	–	–	5
Expressive	–	–	–	1
Declarative	–	–	–	19

In what follows, I will give one example for each type.

(A) Directive: the directive sentence in (17) is preceded by a declarative sentence, which is, in fact, an indirect request. The *if*-clause is isolated from the host unit and introduces an alternative to the first proposal.

---

[12] Attraction implies the repetition of an element, mood or case, which has already appeared (Napoli 2014). Attractions or assimilations to the subjunctive occur precisely in conditional sentences of this type and in relative and temporal ones (Smyth 1956: 2183–2188, 2189–2190).

(17) ἄξιον οὖν πυθέσθαι αὐτοῦ ἃ αὐτῷ συνέβη ἀπὸ ταύτης τῆς ἀσκήσεως. εἰ δὲ βούλεσθε, τὸν Τιμάρχου ἀδελφὸν Κλειτόμαχον ἔρεσθε [τί εἶπεν αὐτῷ Τίμαρχος ἡνίκα ἀποθανούμενος ᾔει †εὐθὺ τοῦ δαιμονίου†, ἐκεῖνός τε καὶ Εὔαθλος ὁ σταδιοδρομῶν ὃς Τίμαρχον ὑπεδέξατο φεύγοντα]. (Pl. *Thg.* 129a1)

áxion	oûn	puthésthai	autoû	ha	autôi
worthwhile.NOM	PTCL	inquire.INF	he.GEN	REL.ACC	he.DAT

sunébē	apo	taútēs	tês	askḗseōs	ei	de
happen.3SG.AOR	PREP	this.GEN	ART.GEN	training.GEN	if	PTCL

boúlesthe	ton	Timárkhou	adelphon	Kleitómakhon
want.2PL.PRS	ART.ACC	Timarchus.GEN	brother.ACC	Cleitomachus.ACC

éresthe
ask.2PL.IMP

'And so it is worthwhile to inquire of him as to the results he got from his training. Or, if you like, ask Cleitomachus, brother of Timarchus, [what Timarchus said to him when he was going straight to the prison to meet his death, he and Euathlus the racing runner, who had harboured Timarchus as a fugitive].'

(B) Expressive

(18) εἰ δ' αὖ βούλει, τὸ εὔπνουν τοῦ τόπου ὡς ἀγαπητὸν καὶ σφόδρα ἡδύ. (Pl. *Phdr.* 230c1)

ei	d'	aû	boúlei	to	eúpnoun	toû
if	PTCL	PTCL	want.2SG.PRS	ART.ACC	breeziness.ACC	ART.GEN

tópou	hōs	agapēton	kai	sphódra	hēdú
place.GEN	how	charming.NOM	and	perfectly	lovely.NOM

'Then again, if you please, how lovely and perfectly charming the breeziness of the place is!'

(C) Interrogative

(19) [τί οὖν δή; οὐκ οἴει τοῦτο σεμνόν τι εἶναι γνῶναι, ὅπῃ ποτὲ ὀρθῶς ἔχει ἐκεῖνον τὸν ποταμὸν Ξάνθον καλεῖν μᾶλλον ἢ Σκάμανδρον;] εἰ δὲ βούλει, περὶ τῆς ὄρνιθος [ἣν λέγει ὅτι – "χαλκίδα κικλήσκουσι θεοί, ἄνδρες δὲ κύμινδιν", φαῦλον ἡγῇ τὸ μάθημα ὅσῳ ὀρθότερόν ἐστι καλεῖσθαι χαλκὶς κυμίνδιδος τῷ αὐτῷ ὀρνέῳ;] (Pl. Cra.392a3)

ei de boúlei peri tês órnithos
if PTCL want.2SG.PRS PREP ART.GEN bird.GEN

'[Well, do you not think this is a grand thing to know, that the name of that river is rightly Xanthus, rather than Scamander?] Or, if you want, [do you think it is a slight thing to learn] about the bird [which he says "gods call chalcis, but men call cymindis", that it is much more correct for the same bird to be called chalcis than cymindis?]'

(D) Declarative

(20) ὡς περὶ ἄλλου ὁτουοῦν. οἷον, εἰ βούλει, στρογγυλότητος πέρι [εἴποιμ' ἂν ἔγωγε ὅτι σχῆμά τί ἐστιν, οὐχ οὕτως ἁπλῶς ὅτι σχῆμα. διὰ ταῦτα δὲ οὕτως ἂν εἴποιμι, ὅτι καὶ ἄλλα ἔστι σχήματα]. (Pl. Men. 73e3)

hōs peri állou hotouoûn. hoîon, ei boúlei,
as about other.GEN any.GEN like if want.2SG.PRS
stroggulótētos péri
roundness.GEN about

'In this way in any other case. If you want to take roundness, for instance, [I should call it a figure, and not figure pure and simple. And I should name it so because there are other figures as well].'

4 Discussion and tentative hypothesis of global interpretation

Each of the two constructions functions differently. Even in the former, two cases can be distinguished: a sub-type expressing an indirect directive speech act and a subtype inserted into a direct directive act, which modifies it by mitigating it. Both sub-types have a clear modal dimension. In the former, the construction as a whole expresses the modality of the speech act;[13] in the latter, it is the verbal mood, the imperative, which is the marker, and the construction is similar to an illocutionary level satellite. From a syntactic point of view, in both cases, the subordinate status of the conditional clause is called into question. The elliptical or truncated conditional is an exempt form; therefore, it is logically impossible to consider it subordinate to anything. In the case of the illocutionary conditional, its function is established in the last layer of the layered sentence structure. The relation of both constructions to the expression of modalities and their interaction with verbal moods is evident. The genetic relationship between the two can be described as a parent construction and a daughter construction, from a conditional period – protasis + apodosis with an imperative verb – to an elliptical conditional with an infinitive working as an indirect directive.

The second construction does not express modality content in itself. It is compatible with the major sentence types described, i.e. directive, declarative, interrogative, and even expressive. Moreover, this indicates that it does not provide its own force, which would be compatible only with some sentence types. It functions at another, purely text construction level. It is reformulatory in the sense of reformulation as an operation which includes exemplification. It introduces new examples, new topics or subtopics of a subject being addressed. As an exemplification, it is often used to introduce interesting argumentative turns of phrase and goes beyond the simple addition of one more case. As an exemplifier, it acts like a discourse marker would, as a linking element. The purely reformulatory characteristics of the construction are its isolated nature and its close relationship to an element to which it introduces an alternative. These two features, i.e. the reduced domain and lack of syntactic linkage, are features of the prototypical case of corrections.

The second construction's function has been duly identified but not explained. Denniston (1959: 171) points out that "[w]e may notice here (in the use of δέ (*dé*) for ἤ (*ḗ*)) the common εἰ βούλει (*ei boúlei*): suggesting an alternative 'or, if you like', where the English 'or' is perhaps more logical". Although the meaning of the construction is clearly noticed as "suggesting an alternative", the explanation is a different issue. *Pace* Denniston, it is not the case that the additive particle δέ (*dé*) can express alternatives by itself. If it were, if the particle alone were responsible for the meaning, this would be its value every time the particle appears in the construction εἰ δὲ βούλει (*ei de boúlei*), and that is not the case. The particle δέ (*dé*) is not the reason for the meaning; the meaning is conveyed by the entire construction, not by

---

13 "An *if*-clause can occur on its own, as a polite directive, usually a request. This is a feature of numerous varieties of Modern English. An isolated *if*-clause in its directive function "allows the speaker to express that he / she is not assuming the performance of the act requested of the hearer; the hearer has an option" [Stirling 1998: 71]" (Aikhenvald 2016: 161).

the particle alone. Bonifazi *et al.* (2016: 44) recently reconsidered the meaning of the particle: "[t]he particle has a relatively neutral function, signalling that a new step in the discourse has begun. The step can correspond to anything: a new event in a narrative, an argumentative point, a vocative, a contrastive noun phrase, an apposition, and so on". The construction can also be considered as derived from the previous ones, namely from the directive with an imperative.

5 Conclusions

As for the first question, whether the verbal moods in the main clauses of each type, namely the imperative, subjunctive, and indicative, are compulsory to convey these contents or whether the directive contents (polite orders) can be expressed without the imperative or the subjunctive and the discourse contents (exemplificative) conveyed without indicative moods – the answer is: not always. A sub-type, *if*-clause *cum infinitivo*, constitutes a specific case. Although the infinitive on its own is able to render an order, in this particular case, the form of this content is the construction formed by *if* + 'want' verb in the second person singular + infinitive. On the other hand, occurrences with discourse function do not require a particular verbal mood in their host, as they are extraclausal components and constitute a unit.

As for the second question, the distribution of moods in the *if*-clauses changes in the history of Ancient Greek. The indicative mood supersedes the subjunctive in both constructions. In the first construction, the opposition between indicative and subjunctive has faded. The character of the verb – a stative verb – and the inclusive use of present tenses contribute to reducing the difference. On the contrary, in the second construction, the indicative is the rule, with minor exceptions.

As for the third question, the first construction is incompatible with marked speech acts, namely interrogative ones. It is limited to appearing with directive acts that deliver different contents. However, the cases of construction with the infinitive cannot be considered direct acts but indirect acts. The speech act is an indirect directive, apparently declarative or expressive. Occurrences with a discourse function appear in host units with different speech act contents. Since they act as extra clausal components, they do not interact with the speech act expressed in the host; therefore, they are highly compatible with different speech acts, lacking sensitivity to modality.

References

Aikhenvald, Alexandra. 2016. Sentence types. In Jan Nuyts & Johan van der Auwera (eds.), *The Oxford handbook of modality and mood*, 141–165. Oxford: Oxford University Press.
Aikhenvald, Alexandra. 2018. Evidentiality: The framework. In Alexandra Aikhenvald (ed.), *The Oxford handbook of evidentiality*, 2–44. Oxford: Oxford University Press.
Austin, John L. 1975. *How to do things with words*. New revised edition. Edited by Marina Sbisà & James O. Urmson. Oxford: Clarendon Press.
Bazzanella, Carla. 2006. Discourse markers in Italian: Towards a "compositional" meaning. In Kerstin Fischer (ed.), *Approaches to discourse particles*, 449–465. Amsterdam: Brill.
Benveniste, Émile. 1966 [1946]. Structure des relations de personne dans le verbe. *Problèmes de linguistique générale 1*, 225–236. Paris: Gallimard.
Bonifazi, Anna, Annemieke Drummen & Mark De Kreij. 2016. *Particles in Ancient Greek discourse. Exploring particles use across genres*. Washington DC: Center for Hellenic Studies.
Brown, Penelope & Stephen C. Levinson. 1987. *Politeness. Some universals in language usage*. Cambridge: Cambridge University Press.
Bybee, Joan, Revere Perkins & William Pagliuca. 1994. *The evolution of grammar*. Chicago & London: The University of Chicago Press.
Croft, William & Alan D. Cruse. 2004. *Cognitive linguistics*. Cambridge: Cambridge University Press.
Denniston, John D. 1959 [1934]. *Greek particles*. 2nd edn. Oxford: Oxford University Press.
Denizot, Camille. 2011. *Donner des ordres en grec ancien. Étude linguistique des formes de l'injonction*. Rouen: Publications des Universités de Rouen et du Havre.
Denizot, Camille & Liana Tronci. 2023. For a syntactic approach to modality and its application to Ancient Greek. (this volume)
Dickey, Eleanor. 2019. When "please" ceases to be polite: The use of *sis* in early Latin. *Journal of Historical Pragmatics* 20(2). 204–224.
Dik, Simon. 1989. *The theory of Functional Grammar. Part One*. Dordrecht: Foris.
Fanning, Buist. M. 1990. *Verbal aspect in New Testament Greek*. Oxford: Oxford University Press.
Gülich, Elisabeth & Thomas Kotschi. 1983. Les marqueurs de la reformulation paraphrastique. *Cahiers de linguistique française* 5. 305–346.
Kaltenböck, Gunther. 2016. On the grammatical status of insubordinate *if*-clauses. In Gunther Kaltenböck, Evelien Keizer & Arne Lohmann (eds.), *Outside the clause*, 341–379. Amsterdam: John Benjamins.
Martínez Vázquez, Rafael. 2006. Tiempo verbal en griego antiguo. Valores inclusivos y exclusivos. In Miguel Rodríguez Pantoja (ed.). *Las raíces clásicas de Andalucía I*, 48–54. Córdoba: Caja de Ahorros.
Napoli, Maria. 2014. Attraction. In Georgios K. Giannakis (ed.), *Encyclopedia of Ancient Greek language and linguistics*, Vol. 1, 208–215. Leiden: Brill.
Nikolaeva, Irina. 2016. Analysis of the semantics of moods. In Jan Nuyts & Johan van der Auwera (eds.). *The Oxford handbook of modality and mood*, 68–85. Oxford: Oxford University Press.
Nuyts, Jan. 2016. Surveying modality and mood. An introduction. In Jan Nuyts & Johan van der Auwera (eds.), *The Oxford handbook of modality and mood*, 1–8. Oxford: Oxford University Press.
Palmer, Frank R. 1986. *Mood and modality*. Cambridge: Cambridge University Press.
Pons Bordería, Salvador. 2013. Un solo tipo de reformulación. *Cuadernos de la Asociación de Hispanistas Italianos (AISPI)* 2. 151–170.

Revuelta Puigdollers, Antonio R. 2017. Illocutionary force and modality. In Camille Denizot & Olga Spevak (eds.), *Pragmatic approaches to Latin and Ancient Greek*, 17–43. Amsterdam: John Benjamins.

la Roi, Ezra. 2021. The insubordination of *if-* and *that-*clauses from Archaic to Post-Classical Greek: A diachronic constructional typology. *Symbolae Osloenses* 95. 1–63.

Roulet, Eddy. 1987. Complétude interactive et connecteurs reformulatifs. *Cahiers de linguistique française* 8. 111–140.

Ruiz Yamuza, Emilia. 2014. Mood and modality. In Georgios K. Giannakis (ed.), *Encyclopedia of Ancient Greek language and linguistics*, Vol. 2, 452–459. Leiden: Brill.

Ruiz Yamuza, Emilia. 2022. Parenthetical conditionals and insubordinate clauses in Ancient Greek. *Journal of Greek Linguistics* 22(2). 232–259.

Siemund, Peter. 2018. *Speech acts and clause types.* Oxford: Oxford University Press.

Smyth, Herbert W. 1956. *Greek grammar.* Revised by G.M. Messing. Cambridge, Mass.: Harvard University Press.

Terkourafi, Maria. 2005. An argument for a frame-based approach to politeness. Evidence from the use of the imperative in Cypriot-Greek. In Robin T. Lakoff & Sachiko Ide (eds.), *Broadening the horizon of linguistic politeness*, 99–116. Amsterdam: John Benjamins.

Terkourafi, Maria. 2008. Towards a unified theory of politeness, impoliteness, and rudeness. In Derek Bousfield & Miriam A. Locher (eds.), *Impoliteness in language: Studies on its interplay with power in theory and practice*, 45–77. Berlin & New York: Mouton de Gruyter.

Unceta Gómez, Luis. 2009. *La petición verbal en latín. Estudio léxico, semántico y pragmático.* Madrid: Ediciones clásicas.

Verano Liaño, Rodrigo. 2016. Ejemplificación reformulativa y ejemplificación argumentativa en griego antiguo. Un estudio de corpus basado en *La República* de Platón. *Habis* 47. 123–145.

Wakker, Gerry. 1994. *Conditions and conditionals.* Amsterdam: J.C. Gieben.

Rodrigo Verano & Alberto Pardal Padín

7 (Inter)subjectivity, modality, and syntax in Classical Greek: *Dokéō* and *phaínomai* in addressee-oriented assertions in the dialogues of Plato

Abstract: Asserting information about the addressee can be a challenging communicative activity. In this paper we explore how two similar perception verbs, δοκέω (*dokéō*) and φαίνομαι (*phaínomai*), are deployed in Ancient Greek in order to hedge the propositional content of the utterances in which speakers comment on their addressees. The analysis, based on a pragmatically built corpus of second person instances in Plato's dialogues, classifies the different contexts and constructions used in order to mitigate such assertions. It is argued that subjectivity is key to understanding the distribution of the data, with a clear preference for non-subjectivised modality patterns in negative assertions, as opposed to a higher occurrence of subjectivization strategies in positive ones. Finally, the constructions where these two verbs are found are explained according to their frequency of use and their apparition in politeness- and interaction-related formulas.

Keywords: Subjectivity, epistemic modality, dialogue, hedging strategies, evidentiality

1 Introduction

(Inter)subjectivity and modality are highly related linguistic domains. The former refers to how the speaker's beliefs and attitudes (subjectivity) and the addressee's presence and face (intersubjectivity) are linguistically embodied in discourse

---

Acknowledgments: This work has been supported by a Logos Research Grant funded by Fundación BBVA (PRAGDICAM – *Pragmaticalización de verbos de dicción y actividad mental en griego antiguo y latín*), and by the Spanish Government, within the State Plan for Scientific and Technical Research and Innovation (PGC2018-093779-BI00). We thank the editors of the volume and the anonymous readers for their valuable suggestions and contributions to our paper.

Rodrigo Verano, Complutense University of Madrid, e-mail: rverano@ucm.es
Alberto Pardal Padín, University of Salamanca, e-mail: pardal@usal.es

https://doi.org/10.1515/9783110778380-007

(Traugott 2010).¹ The latter is concerned with the status of the proposition expressed in an utterance; in particular, it applies to how that proposition is presented in terms of factuality – as a certain, probable, or impossible event – or how it relates to a given code of values and principles (Narrog 2012: 6–8).² Since factuality often rests on the speaker's knowledge of the predicated state of affairs, and the deontic framework to which utterances are subjected is prototypically shared by speaker and addressee, it is not surprising that there is a significant overlap between these phenomena that can be approached from (inter)subjectivity- and modality-oriented perspectives in language.

The nature of such phenomena is varied. (Inter)subjectivity and modality can be linguistically encoded with the help of diverse formal strategies, including lexical items (such as the contribution of certain adverbs and particles) and grammatical categories (such as the use of certain verbal moods). From a broad perspective, the mere allusion to the speaker or the addressee in a sentence – for instance, by using first- or second-person forms – can be considered (inter)subjectivity traits, and the choice of specific words can result in utterances loaded with modality values. Indeed, as in other linguistic areas, there is no biunivocal coupling between form and function in this case either.

Among the lexically-based strategies that can contribute to the expression of modality in ancient Greek are some verbs whose semantics favour their use in such contexts. In particular, the verbs δοκέω (*dokéō*) 'seem' and φαίνομαι (*phaínomai*) 'appear' include, among their possible meanings in Classical Greek, 'appear to be' (LSJ s.u. φαίνω [*phaínō*]), 'seem', and 'seem likely' (LSJ s.u. δοκέω [*dokéō*]), either combined with infinitives that introduce secondary events (ex. (1a), (2a)) or used in parenthetical clauses (ex. (1b), (2b)).³ Through these syntactic patterns, the modality of the state of affairs presented by the infinitive or main clause is altered as its truth-conditional proposition is attenuated. The following passages illustrate these uses:

---

1 In particular, the acquisition and conventionalization of values associated with this domain by certain forms through grammaticalization processes has aroused great interest in linguistic studies (Traugott 2010: 29–30).
2 There are different approaches to modality in language, from those that only distinguish the domains of epistemic and deontic modality (cf. Lyons 1977) to broader ones that include other subtypes – Narrog (2012: 8–12), for instance, lists nine subcategories. Recent approaches to modality in Ancient Greek are those by Ruiz Yamuza (2014) and Revuelta Puigdollers (2020). For an overview of the typology of modality, see Denizot and Tronci (this volume).
3 All the parenthetical clauses included in our corpus are introduced by ὡς (*hōs*). Although they are formally comparative sentences, they function as extra-clausal constituents.

(1) a. δοκεῖ μοι νῦν οὐδὲν διαφέρειν πᾶν τε καὶ ὅλον. (Pl. *Tht.* 205a7)[4]
   dokeî   moi   nûn   ouden   diaphérein
   seem.3SG.PRS I.DAT now nothing differ.INF
   pân   te kai   hólon
   all.NOM and complete.NOM
   'To me there seems to be no difference between "all" and "complete".'
   b. σοφὸς οὖν οὗτος, ὥς μοι δοκεῖ, ἀλλ' οὐχ ὁ κακὸς γίγνεται. (Pl. *R.* 409e1)
   sophos   oûn   hoûtos   hṓs   moi   dokeî
   wise.NOM PTCL DEM.NOM COMP I.DAT seem.3SG.PRS
   all' oukh   ho   kakos   gígnetai
   but NEG ART.NOM bad.NOM become.3SG.PRS
   'So this will be the wise one, as I see it, and not the wicked one.'

(2) a. καὶ φαίνεταί μοι τῶν πολιτικῶν μόνος ἄρχεσθαι ὀρθῶς. (Pl. *Euthphr.* 2c8)
   kai   phaínetaí   moi   tôn   politikôn
   and appear.3SG.PRS I.DAT ART.GEN politicians.GEN
   mónos   árkhesthai orthôs
   only.NOM start.INF correctly
   'He seems to me to be the only one among the politicians to start correctly.'
   b. ἔστι δὴ δύο ταῦτα, ὡς φαίνεται, κακῶν ἐν αὐτῇ γένη. (Pl. *Soph.* 228d6)
   ésti   dè   dúo   taûta,   hōs   phaínetai,
   be.3SG.PRS PTCL two.NOM DEM.NOM COMP appear.3SG.PRS
   kakôn   en   autêi   génē
   evil.GEN in it.DAT types.NOM
   'There are, apparently, these two types of evil in it.'

The events expressed in the above examples are presented as possible, but not necessarily true, showing instances of so-called epistemic modality.[5] In (1a) and (2a) the semantics of the verb together with the presence of the subordinate construction result in an attenuation of the propositional content of the assertions stated in the infinitive clauses. In (1b) and (2b), the extraclausal constructions – ὥς μοι δοκεῖ (*hṓs moi dokeî*) / ὡς φαίνεται (*hōs phaínetai*) – affect the truth-conditional value of the sentences in which they are embedded by tempering the degree of certainty of

---

[4] Plato's text is from Burnet (1900–1907). All translations are our own, unless otherwise stated.
[5] According to the traditional, broad definition of epistemic modality, covering all cases of factual assessment. Some of these passages will be analysed also as instances of non-prototypical evidential modality later in this paper (cf. Section 4).

the events expressed in their main clauses. In all cases, a certain syntactic-semantic encoding is necessary for the verbs to function as modality modifiers, besides their lexical contribution.

At the same time, three of the cited examples, i.e. (1a), (1b) and (2a), host explicit references to the speaker (*moi*), against one, i.e. (2b). The linguistic indexing of the speaker in discourse results in the subjectivization of the utterance and, consequently, involves a greater commitment to the (un)certainty of the expressed proposition. In other words, in (1a), (1b) and (2a) the speakers classify the predicated events as possible according to their knowledge and / or opinion, whereas in (2b), the source of information on which the modality of the utterance is based remains unknown. As the analysis presented in this paper will show, this difference may be relevant for the pragmatic interpretation of these utterances.

Finally, the modification of a sentence's modality can serve different purposes. Speakers do not always resolve to mitigate the assertiveness of what they say because they are uncertain of its factuality. Sometimes they do so to avoid undesired consequences in communication, to shape their identity in interaction, or to protect their social faces, as in the following passage:

(3) καὶ νῦν μοι δοκεῖς οὐ μανθάνειν ὅτι [...]. (Pl. *Prt.* 341a5)
kai nûn moi dokeîs ou manthánein hóti
and now I.DAT seem.2SG.PRS NEG understand.INF COMP
'And now it seems to me that you don't understand that [...].'

Socrates may not be entirely sure whether or not his interlocutor has understood what was previously said, but the choice to attenuate the propositional content may be due to other reasons, to prevent the utterance from being interpreted as offensive. In fact, it is a well-known fact that (inter)subjectivity and modality play a role in linguistic politeness.[6]

This paper will explore the different varieties of modality conveyed by δοκέω (*dokéō*) and φαίνομαι (*phaínomai*) through their syntactic-semantic configurations, and their pragmatic performance in connection to (inter)subjectivity in Classical Greek discourse through their analysis in a restricted set of utterances, namely

---

[6] It is not possible to summarise all the literature on linguistic politeness in Ancient Greek. On the pragmatic rendering of modality in terms of politeness, see Denizot (2011), Drummen (2013), Revuelta Puigdollers (2017), and more recently, Conti (2020), among others. For an up-to-date overview of research in this field, see the recently published collective volumes by Denizot and Spevak (2017), Redondo (2022), and Unceta and Berger (2022), which contain substantial contributions concerning politeness, intersubjectivity, and modality in the context of Ancient Greek literature.

those containing assertions that refer to the interlocutors in the dialogues of Plato. This specifically designed corpus possesses certain features relevant to our study. Firstly, as speech acts strongly linked to interpersonal communication, assertions are fertile ground for the emergence of (inter)subjectivity mechanisms. Secondly, as utterances that refer to the addressee, they may compromise and threaten the face of both participants in conversation in different ways. Finally, the corpus of this study is based on the philosophical dialogues of Plato, a literary genre that allows us to examine urbane and polite conversation in Ancient Greek, which has been proven to be particularly rich in this type of practice (cf. Fedriani and Verano 2021).

2 Addressee-oriented assertions in conversation

Assertions (Stalnaker 1978) appear to be quite neutral speech acts from a pragmatic perspective. However, when they occur in a conversation with specific participants and agendas, they become impregnated with illocutionary force and communicative intentions. Therefore, the information they convey goes far beyond the literal content they express. Their relevance is also measured by what they reveal about the speaker's presuppositions about the addressee, finding common ground and identity in interaction issues (Clark and Brennan 1991; Bucholtz and Hall 2005).

Among all possible types of assertions, those which make reference to the addressee are particularly delicate, as they involve a number of different factors of social communication, including politeness issues (Brown and Levinson 1987: 145–172; Culpeper and Kádár 2010) and the rules of preference in conversational interaction (Pomerantz 1984; Pomerantz and Heritage 2013). Cooperative speakers, who do not desire to threaten the positive face of their co-participants in communication through utterances that can be taken as criticism or reproach, must be very careful when designing their turns-at-talk – that is, unless they are willingly insulting (ex. (4)), in which case harming the interlocutor's face is the speaker's main purpose (cf. Verano 2021):

(4) συκοφάντης γὰρ εἶ, ἔφη, ὦ Σώκρατες, ἐν τοῖς λόγοις. (Pl. *R.* 340d2)
    sukophántēs   gar   eî,   éphē,   ô   Sṓkrates,
    sycophant.NOM PTCL   be.2SG.PRS he.said   INTJ   Socrates.VOC
    en   toîs   lógois
    PREP   ART.DAT   arguments.DAT
    'You are a sycophant, Socrates, in your arguments.'

Most utterances in Platonic conversation, however, subscribe to the principle of communicative cooperation and tend to account for possible face-threatening acts with the help of linguistic politeness, especially when expressing negative comments to the interlocutor. However, utterly offensive assertions are not the only ones that need to be handled with care. Praising statements about the addressee, such as compliments, can also be (and have been proven to be, cf. Pomerantz 1978) problematic and difficult to accommodate in the dynamics of conversational interaction. Even the most apparently neutral statements can be a source of all sorts of awkwardness in conversation because they are based on the speaker's presuppositions about the addressee that reveal the latter's social image; or because they can be considered an invasion of the interlocutor's sphere of privacy; or they may simply not be true, leading the addressee to the usually unwanted task – also contrary to the rules of interactional preference (Schegloff, Jefferson and Sacks 1977) – of correcting the speaker, as in (5).

(5) [ΕΥΘ. Τί νεώτερον, ὦ Σώκρατες, γέγονεν, ὅτι σὺ τὰς ἐν Λυκείῳ καταλιπὼν διατριβὰς ἐνθάδε νῦν διατρίβεις περὶ τὴν τοῦ βασιλέως στοάν;] οὐ γάρ που καὶ σοί γε δίκη τις οὖσα τυγχάνει πρὸς τὸν βασιλέα ὥσπερ ἐμοί.
ΣΩ. Οὔτοι δὴ [Ἀθηναῖοί γε, ὦ Εὐθύφρων, δίκην αὐτὴν καλοῦσιν ἀλλὰ γραφήν].
(Pl. *Euthphr.* 2a1–6)

ou	gár	pou		kai	soí	ge	díkē
NEG	PTCL	somehow		and	you.DAT	PTCL	action.NOM
tis		oûsa		tugkhánei		pros	ton	basiléa
INDF.NOM		be.PTCP.NOM		happen.3SG.PRS		PREP	ART.ACC	king.ACC
hṓsper	emoí.	oútoi	dḕ				
like	I.DAT	NEG	PTCL				

'[EUTHYPHRO. What unusual thing happened, Socrates, that you have stopped socializing in the Lyceum and are now socializing in the *stoa*, where the king sits?] It cannot be that you have an action before the king, as I have.
SOCRATES. No. Actually, [Euthyphro, the Athenians do not call it an action, but an indictment].'

The potential threat to the faces of the speaker and addressee attached to these types of speech acts are countered through different strategies, including the use of the interrogative, instead of declarative sentence types in the design of the utterance, and the modulation of modality, often resorting to subjectivization formulas to downgrade the assertive force of the utterance.[7]

The next section analyses the role of the verbs φαίνομαι (*phaínomai*) and δοκέω (*dokéō*) in different syntactic configurations within these strategies and the pragmatic values associated with their uses. Attention will be paid to the nature of the assertion, differentiating those that display positive (ex. (6)), negative (ex. (7)), and neutral (ex. (8)) comments about the interlocutor and identifying the different strategies associated with each of them:

(6) τοτὲ μέν μοι δοκεῖς μανθάνειν ὅτι λέγω. (Pl. *Grg.* 518a6)
tote   mén   moi   dokeîs   manthánein   hóti   légō
then   PTCL I.DAT seem.2SG.PRS understand.INF REL.ACC.N.SG say.1SG.PRS
'It seems to me then that you understand what I'm saying.'

(7) καὶ νῦν μοι δοκεῖς οὐ μανθάνειν ὅτι […]. (Pl. *Prt.* 341a5) (=ex. (3))
kai   nûn   moi   dokeîs   ou   manthánein   hóti
and   now   I.DAT seem.2SG.PRS NEG   understand.INF COMP
'And now it seems to me that you don't understand that […].'

(8) ἀριθμητικὴν φαίνῃ μοι λέγειν καὶ ὅσας μετὰ ταύτης τέχνας ἐφθέγξω νυνδή. (Pl. *Phlb.* 56c10)
arithmētikēn   phaínēi   moi   légein   kai   hósas
arithmetics.ACC   appear.2SG.PRS   I.DAT say.INF   and   REL.ACC
meta   taútēs   tékhnas   ephthégxō   nundé
with   DEM.GEN   arts.ACC   speak.2SG.AOR   now
'I think you are referring to arithmetics and those arts with it you just mentioned.' (lit. 'you appear to me to […]')

Despite the fact that these categories are apparently loose and possibly overlapping, the analysis of the corpus hardly yields any problematic examples in terms of their classification. In general, positive assertions praise the addressee's ideas and his choice of words, neutral ones introduce reformulations or propose interpretations of the interlocutor's previous statements (see example (8)), and negative comments usually point at possible misunderstandings.

---

[7] See Fedriani and Verano (2021) for a contrastive overview of those strategies in the philosophical dialogues of Plato and Cicero.

3 An overview of the data: *dokéō* and *phaínomai* in addressee-oriented assertions

In this study we analysed the entire *corpus platonicum* for all instances of *dokéō* and *phaínomai* referring to the addressee, as well as their use in parenthetical expressions, in the prototypes shown in Tables 1 and 2 below, including any dialogues considered doubtful or spurious. Since our field of study focuses more on the language of the dialogue itself than on Plato's authorial stylistics, it seemed appropriate to use the entire corpus. However, the works normally excluded from the corpus have not provided any particularly significant data for this research.

3.1 An analysis of δοκέω (*dokéō*)

The two verbs studied in this chapter are partially homonyms: both can mean 'to seem'; their frequency of use, however, is completely different: *dokéō* is used in the context selected for this study about five times as much as *phaínomai*. The corpus yields a total of 154 examples where *dokéō* introduces or accompanies an assertion made to the addressee.

The distribution of the examples across the different possible constructions can be observed in Table 1.[8] As can be seen in the table, the uses of *dokéō* in addressee-oriented assertions show variations according to three parameters: the choice of the second- versus third-person forms, the integration of the verb in the surrounding syntax (it may appear within the main clause or as an extraclausal constituent, ECC), and the presence or absence of a first-person pronoun dative as a complementiser.

First, there is an opposition between δοκεῖς (*dokeîs* [second-person]) and δοκεῖ (*dokeî* [third-person]), as seen in examples (9a) and (9b). In (9a) the addressee is taken as the subject for δοκέω (*dokéō*), whereas in (9b), it is the situation itself that plays that role.[9]

---

[8] Examples where the dative pronoun is a first-person plural ἡμῖν (*hēmîn*) have been grouped along with the first-person singular μοι (*moi*). It is understood that the speaker is modalising an assertion about the addressee regardless of whether they use a singular 'me' or a plural 'us', which includes the speaker (who acts as spokesperson of the group).

[9] Note that it is not the impersonal construction of *dokéō* ('it seems good / fine to me'), but the personal construction taking the whole situation as its subject ('this seems to be [...]'). The impersonal construction is not taken into account for this study, since it has a different meaning unparalleled in *phaínomai*.

Table 1: Instances of *dokéō* in addressee-oriented assertions in Plato.

	Syntactic integration		Dative (*moi*)	Type of evaluation in the assertion			TOTAL
	Main clause	ECC		Positive	Neutral	Negative	
dokeîs	+	−				4	4
dokeîs moi	+		+	73	52	19	144
hōs dokeîs moi		+	−	2		2	4
hōs dokeî moi		+	+		1	1	2
TOTAL				75	53	26	154

(9) a. νῦν, ὥς γέ μοι δοκεῖς, γοητεύεις με. (Pl. *Men.* 80a2)
    nûn, hṓs gé moi dokeîs, goēteúeis me
    now COMP PTCL I.DAT seem.2SG.PRS beguile.2SG.PRS I.ACC
    'Now, at least as it seems to me [lit. as you seem to me], you fool me.'

b. ᾠήθης δέ, ὡς ἐμοὶ δοκεῖ τεκμαιρομένῃ [ἐξ ὧν σὺ λέγεις, τὸ ἐρώμενον ἔρωτα εἶναι]. (Pl. *Smp.* 204c2)
    ōiḗthēs dé, hōs emoi dokeî tekmairoménēi
    think.2SG.AOR PTCL COMP I.DAT seem.3SG.PRS judge.PTCP.DAT
    'And you thought, as it seems to me judging [from what you say, that the beloved was love].'

There do not seem to be significant differences in the choice of one form or another from the corpus data. However, it is interesting to note that the first construction is more intersubjective than the second one, since it places the addressee in a preeminent position within the syntactic and semantic structure of the utterance by promoting it to the subject function.

Similarly, second-person forms also show variability in their usage as main verbs governing infinitive constructions (ex. (10a)) or in parenthetical clauses (ex. (10b)). It is worth noting that these two parameters do not fully coincide (second-person / integrated vs. third-person / parenthetical), since there are documented cases of parenthetical sentences displaying the verb in the second person (10b).

(10) a. ἀληθῆ μοι δοκεῖς λέγειν. (Pl. *Cra.* 393e9)
    alēthê moi dokeîs légein
    true.ACC.N.PL I.DAT seem.2SG.PRS say.INF
    'It seems to me that you say the truth.'

b. οὐ σύ γε, ὥς ἐμοὶ δοκεῖς. (Pl. *Cra.* 393b5)
   ou   sú   ge,   hōs   emoi   dokeîs
   not you.NOM PTCL COMP I.DAT seem.2SG.PRS
   'Definitely not you, in my opinion.' (lit. 'as you seem to me')

Finally, it is possible to find a few examples where the first-person dative is absent, as in (11); however, most of the examples (150/154) host an explicit EXPERIENCER (usually the first-person pronoun). There are no instances without the dative in parenthetical clauses, regardless of whether they are ὡς δοκεῖς (*hōs dokeîs*) or ὡς δοκεῖ (*hōs dokeî*).

(11) ἴσως γὰρ σὺ μὲν δοκεῖς σπάνιον σεαυτὸν παρέχειν. (Pl. *Euthphr.* 3d5)
     ísōs   gar   su   men   dokeîs   spánion
     maybe   PTCL you.NOM PTCL seem.2SG.PRS scarce.ACC.M.SG
     seauton   parékhein
     yourself.ACC.M.SG   offer.INF
     'For, perhaps, you seem to show yourself scarcely.'

All in all, examples like those in (9a), (9b), (10b), and (11) are infrequent: the vast majority of uses of δοκέω (*dokéō*) in combination with an assertion relative to the addressee (144/154 = 93.5%) presents some form of the sequence δοκεῖς μοι (*dokeîs moi*) when introducing the comment in a subordinate clause, as in (10a). All 154 examples are instances of the single predicate frame shown in Figure 1, where the *nominativus cum infinitivo* (or NcI) construction functions as the STIMULUS of the predicate.[10]

| *dokéō*$_v$ | [[/X/] + [/Event/]]$_{STIMULUS}$ | [/Human/]$_{EXPERIENCER}$ |

Figure 1: Predicate frame of *dokéō*.

---

[10] The NcI construction is an overlap of two situations with a common theme: the commented event and that expressed by *dokéō* (Pardal Padín 2021). This explains why the STIMULUS role is applied to the combination of two elements: a subject with no lexical restrictions (hence, /X/) and the commented event (/Event/ in the figure). As one of the referees of this paper pointed out, this construction is similar to a "raising" phenomenon; however, raising implies a movement that requires a transformational approach to grammar (which is not the one applied here) and / or a basic construction from which the raised structure is formed. There is no actual basic construction in Ancient Greek to serve as a departing point and the most similar (the impersonal construction) has a different meaning and is, most probably, secondary (Pardal Padín 2021). For an overview of the raising phenomena and the problems of movement, see Langacker (1995); for its application within a functional framework, see Dik (1997: 344–351).

As has been established in previous studies (Jiménez López 1990; Pardal Padín 2021), *dokéō* has three possible predicate frames. Apart from the personal construction schematized in Figure 1, *dokéō* can appear in an impersonal construction meaning 'to seem fine, to approve' (ex. (12a)) and in a transitive construction with an object complement clause meaning 'to think' (ex. (12b)).[11] Both of these constructions are secondary and will not be discussed here since the former relates to directive modality[12] (Jiménez López 1990) and the latter is far less frequent and has no parallel with *phaínomai*.

(12) a. τοῖς μὲν Λακεδαιμονίοις καὶ τοῖς ξυμμάχοις ταῦτα δοκεῖ. (Th. 4.118.10)
   toîs   men Lakedaimoníois   kai   toîs
   ART.DAT.PL PTCL Lacedaemonians.DAT   and   ART.DAT
   xummákhois   taûta   dokeî
   allies.DAT   this.NOM.PL.N   seem.fine.3SG.PRS
   'This seems fine to the Lacedaemonians and their allies.'
   b. δοκεῖς ἂν αὐτὸν ἐπιθυμητικῶς αὐτῶν ἔχειν; (Pl. *R.* 516d2)
   dokeîs   an   autón   epithumētikôs   autôn   ékhein
   think.2SG.PRS MOD him.ACC   desiring.ADV   them.GEN   have.INF
   'Do you think he would be desiring them?'

Therefore, the examples of *dokéō* included in our corpus, while being highly frequent, shows little variability. The opposite is the case of *phaínomai*, which shows a great deal of variability in its limited number of instances.

3.2 An analysis of *phaínomai*

Assertions referring to the second person in the Platonic corpus and hosting constructions with the verb *phaínomai* display different syntactic configurations. In all of them, the verb means 'to appear' or 'to seem'. The analysis of the data yields a total of 31 relevant occurrences, as shown in the following table:[13]

---

11 Note that the EXPERIENCER subject σύ (*sú*) in (12b) does not match the subject of the infinitive ἔχειν (*ékhein*).
12 According to Jiménez López (1990: 237), the infinitive in the impersonal construction is equivalent to an imperative or some other "jussive" form (hence its meaning similar to Latin *placet*), while the infinitive in the personal construction is equivalent to a declarative sentence.
13 As in the case of *dokéō*, examples where the dative pronoun is a first-person plural ἡμῖν (*hēmîn*) have been grouped along with the first-person singular μοι (*moi*).

Table 2: Data for *phaínomai* in addressee-oriented assertions.

	Syntactic integration		Dative (*moi*)	Type of assertion			TOTAL
	Main clause	ECC		Positive	Neutral	Negative	
phaínēi	+		–			4	4
phaínēi moi	+		+	12	7		19
hōs phaínēi		+	–		2	1	3
hōs phaínetai		+	–		2		2
hōs phaínetai moi		+	+	2	1		3
TOTAL				14	12	5	31

As the table shows, the use of *phaínomai* in this type of assertion reveals several prototypes arising from the combination of the three parameters already applied to the data for *dokéō*, i.e. choice of second / third-person, syntactic integration, and presence / absence of the first-person dative. The first of these parameters points at the opposition of the second-person – φαίνῃ (*phaínēi*) (ex. (13a)) – versus the third person – φαίνεται (*phaínetai*) (ex. (13b)).

(13) a. οὐχ ἕσπου τοῖς λεχθεῖσιν, ὡς φαίνῃ. (Pl. *Pol.* 280b5)
    oukh   héspou   toîs   lekhtheîsin,   hōs   phaínēi
    NEG   follow.2SG.AOR ART.DAT   said.PTCP.DAT.PL COMP   appear.2SG.PRS
    'You did not follow the arguments, *apparently*.' (lit. 'as you appear')

b. τὸν πολύτροπον ψευδῆ λέγεις, ὥς γε φαίνεται. (Pl. *Hp.Mi.* 365b8)
    ton   polútropon pseudê   légeis,   hṓs   ge   phaínetai
    ART.ACC wily.ACC   liar.ACC say.2SG.PRS COMP PTCL   appear.3SG.PRS
    'You call the wily a liar, *apparently*.' (lit. 'as it appears')

The second parameter refers to the use of the verb in the main clause of the sentence that expresses the assertion (ex. (14a)), as opposed to its appearance in parenthetical clauses introduced by the conjunction ὡς (*hōs*) (ex. (14b)). There is a tendency for the third-person type to appear in parenthetical sentences, in line with the higher frequency of use of the expression ὡς φαίνεται (*hōs phaínetai*). Finally, the verb may or may not be complemented ((14a), (14b) vs. (13a), (13b)) by the dative of the first-person pronoun μοι (*moi*), both in integrated and extraclausal constructions and with second- or third-person forms. Parenthetical constructions with a second-person verb and dative –*ὡς φαίνῃ μοι (*hōs phaínēi moi*) –, however, have not been documented, unlike in the case of *dokéō*.

(14) a. [οὔκ, ἀλλ' οὕτω.] φαίνῃ γάρ μοι ὀρθῶς λέγειν. (Pl. *Euthphr.* 12d4)
   phaínēi   gár   moi   orthôs   légein
   appear.2SG.PRS PTCL I.DAT correctly   say.INF
   '[No, but rather that way,] since you appear to me to speak correctly.'

b. [καὶ μάλα ἀληθὲς τοῦτό γε λέγεις·] κελεύεις γὰρ δή με, ὡς ἐμοὶ φαίνεται, τῆς αὐτῆς ὁδοῦ ἐχθοδοποῦ γεγονυίας πολλοῖς. (Pl. *Prt.* 324c8)
   keleúeis   gar   dế   me,   hōs   emoi phaínetai,
   command.2SG.PRS PTCL PTCL I.ACC COMP   I.DAT appear.3SG.PRS
   tês   autês   hodoû   ekhthodopoû   gegonuías   polloîs
   ART.GEN same.GEN   road.GEN hasteful.GEN   become.PTCP.GEN   many.DAT
   '[And it is completely true what you say.] For you are commanding me – it appears to me – the same path that has become hasteful to so many.'

As can be seen in Table 2, personal constructions of *phaínomai* as the main verb of the sentence displaying the assertion (ex. (14a)) are the most frequent. These are always constructions with the infinitive, in which the subject of *phaínēi* (second person) corefers with the (understood) subject of the infinitive.[14] This predicate frame (Figure 2), which is identical to that described for *dokéō* (cf. Section 3.1), can be found in full (as in ex. (14a)) or in the highly elliptical version that characterizes its parenthetical use (as in ex. (13a)).

| phaínēi$_v$ | [[/X/] + [/Event/]]$_{STIMULUS}$ | [/Human/]$_{EXPERIENCER}$ |

Figure 2: Predicate frame of *phaínomai*.

One of the most relevant aspects of the syntactic-semantic configuration of the *phaínomai*-sentence is the presence – or lack thereof – of the EXPERIENCER, which allows us to distinguish two types of constructions that show different degrees of subjectivity. The first is an experiential construction, whose subject holds the STIMULUS as a semantic function – in the specific case of the assertions studied here, it would always be the addressee (or an event in which they play the lead) – and a third argument featuring the EXPERIENCER in the dative – which, likewise, would always be the speaker in our corpus. The second construction consists of a reduction of the previous one, in which there is no explicit reference to the EXPERIENCER. These different syntactic-semantic configurations bring with them nuances in the

---

14 It is known that *phaínomai* can also form periphrases with participles with the meaning 'to be evident that'. These constructions, which set another type of modality in motion, are not part of the object of this study. On these constructions, see Rijksbaron (2006: 117) and Bentein (2012: 24).

meaning of the verb that affect the type of modality expressed in the utterance: epistemic modality or evidential modality.

4 The pronoun is the key: Epistemic modality and subjectivity

The presence (or absence) of a dative first-person pronoun in sentences with *phaínomai* determines the semantics and pragmatics of the whole construction. In the case of utterances hosting an EXPERIENCER in the dative (μοι [*moi*]) – either within the main clause or as an extra-clausal constituent – the assertion's truth-conditional content is presented as possible according to the speaker's assessment and knowledge. Following Narrog (2012), such cases are typical instances of epistemic modality modification.[15] Utterances without the dative, on the other hand, present the event as something apparent from some unidentified source of information. However, they indicate a reduced commitment of the speaker in the factual assessment of the proposition since they avoid an explicit reference to the first person. Besides epistemic modality, these can be also considered instances of a sort of evidential modality, since they may (even vaguely) imply the existence of a source of information for the state of affairs other than the speaker.[16]

In our corpus, such epistemic and so-called evidential modality values would differ in terms of subjectivity, the former being [+ subjective] and the latter [- subjective]. This difference is also seen in extraclausal constructions in which the interlocutor-related event is expressed in an independent sentence in which the paren-

---

[15] "Epistemic modality refers to someone's world knowledge, typically that of the speaker. If the proposition is entailed by this person's knowledge of the world it is necessarily true; if it is compatible his or her knowledge it is possibly true" (Narrog 2012: 8).

[16] We use the opposition between epistemic and evidential in a loose sense, building on Narrog (2012: 11): "The difference is that while with epistemic modality the proposition is undetermined with respect to its factuality relative to the world of knowledge and beliefs of the speaker, with evidentiality it is undetermined relative to sources of information other than the speaker". We are aware that the instances analysed in this paper are not prototypical cases of evidentiality as "grammatical marking of information source" (Aikhenvald 2018: 1), since the constructions of *phaínomai* without dative are not used to specify whether the specific source of information is either perception or hearsay or inference, and the resulting effect in the proposition is a lowered degree of certainty, which falls within the range of epistemic modality. However, we find the distinction helpful to approach the different nuances associated to the explicit designation (or not) of the speaker as the point of view from which the expressed state of affairs is assessed in terms of factuality.

thetical clause is embedded. In these cases, the presence or absence of the dative implements identical processes in terms of modality.

The difference between the use of *phaínomai* as an epistemic and evidential modal auxiliary has a pragmatic correlation in the data analyzed in the corpus. If we compare the presence of the EXPERIENCER in the dative with the type of assertion introduced in the utterance, we find that there is a general tendency to avoid the subjective construction in negatively evaluated assertions and, at the same time, avoid the so-called evidential one in positive assertions. In other words, positive assertions about the interlocutor (ex. (15), also (14a) above) are prototypically attributed to the speaker, and negative assertions remain unassigned to a specific source (ex. (16)). In neutral assertions, either one or the other may be the case, e.g. (17a) and (17b).

(15) καὶ καλῶς γέ μοι, ὦ Εὐθύφρων, φαίνῃ λέγειν. (Pl. *Euthphr.* 12e9)
kai   kalôs   gé   moi,   ô   Euthúphrōn,   phaínēi   légein
and   well   PTCL   I.DAT   INTJ   Euthyphro.VOC   appear.2SG.PRS   say.INF
'And I think, Euthyphro, you are speaking well.'

(16) σὺ δὲ ἄλλων πολλῶν ἔμπειρος ὢν ταύτης ἄπειρος εἶναι φαίνῃ. (Pl. *Prt.* 341a3)
su   de   állōn   pollôn   émpeiros   ōn
you.NOM   PTCL   other.GEN   many.GEN   well.versed.NOM   be.PTCP.NOM
taútēs   ápeiros   eînai   phaínēi
DEM.GEN   unused.NOM   be.INF   appear.2SG.PRS
'You, who are so well-versed in many other things, appear to be unacquainted with this.'

(17) a. ἐκ τυραννίδος ἀρίστην φῂς γενέσθαι πόλιν ἄν, ὡς φαίνῃ. (Pl. *Lg.* 710d7)
ek   turannídos   arístēn   phēis   genésthai   pólin   án,
PREP   tyranny.GEN   better.ACC   say.2SG.PRS   become.INF   city.ACC   MOD
hōs   phaínēi
COMP   appear.2SG.PRS
'Apparently, you say that a city may become better after a tyranny.'

b. τὰ Πρωταγόρειά μοι φαίνῃ περί τε πάλης καὶ τῶν ἄλλων τεχνῶν εἰρηκέναι. (Pl. *Sph.* 232d9)
ta   Prōtagóreiá   moi   phaínēi   perí=te   pálēs
ART.ACC   of.Protagoras.ACC   I.DAT   appear.2SG.PRS   PREP=and   fight.GEN
kai   tôn   állōn   tekhnôn   eirēkénai
and   ART.GEN   other.GEN   techniques.GEN   speak.INF
'I think you refer to Protagoras' works on fighting and other techniques.'
(lit. 'You seem to me to refer...').

It is possible to provide a pragmatic explanation for this distribution. If one takes into account that the difference between both constructions is the degree of subjectivity and engagement by the speaker, explicitly present in discourse through the pronoun μοι (*moi*), it is not surprising that positive comments about the interlocutor appear as the result of the speaker's own evaluation. These comments reinforce the positive image of the interlocutor but, as mentioned in the introduction, they carry a certain risk of invading the addressee's personal space and, therefore, usually contain negative politeness strategies. By attenuating the propositional content of the utterance, the speaker solves this possible face-threatening act. At the same time, by aligning the presented event with his own point of view, he strengthens the cooperative spirit of the conversational exchange and reinforces his relationship with the interlocutor.

In the case of negative comments, presented only as a deducible or apparent possibility based on certain external indicators and without personally committing to their veracity, the speaker distances him- / herself from potentially face-threatening assertive content. In this way, the propositional mitigation strategy is dissociated from the speaker, as the event is presented as something apparent, but not judged with respect to the speaker's knowledge, beliefs, and attitudes.

As previously stated, *dokéō* shows far less variability than *phaínomai* in this regard and there are no traces of such a pragmatic rendering of subjective / non-subjective opposition, with the dative being compulsory in positive assertions and banned from negative ones as seen in examples (15), (17a), and (17b). On the contrary, *dokeîs moi* ('you seem to me') is used indifferently with positive (ex. (18) and (9a) above), neutral (ex. (19)), and negative (ex. (20a), (20b), also (8a) and (10) above) assertions.

(18) καὶ ὀρθῶς γέ μοι δοκεῖς ποιεῖν. (Pl. *Grg.* 454c6)
      kai   orthôs   gé   moi   dokeîs   poieîn
      and   right.ADV PTCL I.DAT seem.2SG.PRS do.INF
      'And I think you are acting right.' (lit. 'you seem to me to act right')

(19) δοκεῖς γάρ μοι λέγειν τὴν πολιτικὴν τέχνην. (Pl. *Prt.* 319a3)
      dokeîs   gár   moi   légein   tēn   politikēn   tékhnēn
      seem.2SG.PRS   PTCL   I.DAT say.INF ART.ACC political.ACC technique.ACC
      'It seems to me that you mean the political art.'

(20) a. δοκεῖς γάρ μοι καὶ μάλα σφόδρα δεῖσθαι μαθεῖν. (Pl. *La.* 200b7–200c1)
        dokeîs   gár   moi   kai   mála   sphódra   deîsthai   matheîn
        seem.2SG.PRS   PTCL   I.DAT and   very   very.much need.INF   learn.INF
        'For it seems to me that you need to learn a great deal.'

b. ἀπορρᾳθυμεῖν ἡμῖν δοκεῖς. (Pl. *R.* 449c2)
   aporraithumeîn hēmîn   dokeîs
   slack.off.INF   we.DAT seem.2SG.PRS
   'It seems to us that you are slacking off.'

However, even if the distribution is not as clear-cut as with *phaínomai*, the instances where the dative is absent are all related to negative assertions, in the same way as *phaínomai* in (15). This can be seen in the following examples, where the addressee is said to act wantonly (21a) or to be lacking virtue (21b).

(21) a. δοκεῖς νεανιεύεσθαι ἐν τοῖς λόγοις. (Pl. *Grg.* 482c4)
     dokeîs   neanieúesthai   en   toîs   lógois
     seem.2SG.PRS act.wantonly.INF in   ART.DAT words.DAT
     'You seem to be acting recklessly in your words.'
   b. εἰ δ' ἔτι τούτων ἐπιδεὴς εἶναι δοκεῖς [...]. (Pl. *Chrm.* 158c1)
     ei   d'   éti   toútōn   epideḗs   eînai   dokeîs
     if   PTCL still this.GEN.PL in.need.NOM be.INF seem.2SG.PRS
     'If you still seem to be lacking these [...].'

In conclusion, in the case of *phaínomai*, the recourse to the two syntactic schemes of the verb, which translate into two different forms of modality, has a pragmatic motivation, at least from the data examined here. In Plato's dialogues, there is a tendency to mitigate assertions referring to the interlocutor by using this verb as a subjectivised modal auxiliary (+ epistemic) in the case of positive (and part of the neutral) comments and reserves its use as a non-subjectivised modal auxiliary (+ evidential) for negative (and part of the neutral) remarks. This tendency is observed both in cases in which the verb appears fully integrated into the syntax of the sentence expressing the assertion and in those cases in which it appears as a parenthetical constituent. The situation is not as clear for *dokéō*, where the subjectivised epistemic modality appears with any kind of assertion, whereas the so-called evidential one is also reserved for negative comments. In this way, the interaction between lexicon and syntax enables the expression of different modal forms that have, in turn, a specific pragmatic performance, serving different communicative purposes in the conversations represented in Plato's dialogues.

5 Modal constructions and frequency of use

Finally, the difference that we found between these two apparently interchangeable verbs can be approached from a different perspective: their frequency of use. The *dokéō* construction is far more usual than the *phaínomai* one, and frequency of use has been shown to have a connection with language change: more frequently used predicates are prone to develop new meanings or conventionalize inferences more easily (Bybee 2006). This is the case of *dokéō* and its dative EXPERIENCER: it is almost always present and almost exclusively refers to the speaker (*moi* or *hēmîn*) in statements about the addressee. The sequence *dokeîs moi* is highly entrenched and easily accessible when a modalising strategy is needed, almost as a formulaic schema, as represented in Figure 3, exemplified above in (10a).[17]

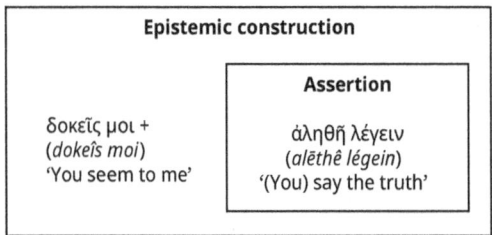

Figure 3: Constructional schema of δοκεῖς μοι (*dokeîs moi*) + assertion.

Since frequency of use leads to semantic bleaching and conventionalization of modal values, it is not surprising that *phaínomai* preserves a more complete palette of uses, including those which keep its fully lexical meaning in an active voice. *Dokéō*, on the other hand, almost always conveys a modal meaning, this being the most frequently used personal construction (Pardal Padín 2021). A corollary to these arguments would be the development of the transitive construction of *dokéō*, with a syntactic change whereby the EXPERIENCER becomes the subject of a verb that expresses epistemic modality.

Therefore, *dokéō* shows less variability because its construction with a dative EXPERIENCER and, specifically, with the subjective μοι (*moi*), is both more common

---

17 Similar expressions (i.e. verbs of cognition functioning as epistemic modalisers) have been considered formulaic in nature (Scheibman 2001). Thompson and Hopper (2001: 31), following Thompson and Mulac (1991), go as far as to consider sequences such as 'I think', 'I know', etc. "as markers of epistemicity and evidentiality [...] and not as main clauses with complement-taking predicates and object complements".

and more entrenched. Thus, it is probably retrieved as a whole chunk[18] when the speaker needs to express epistemic modality through a syntactic construction. On the contrary, the speaker can more easily choose whether to include the EXPERIENCER in the *phaínomai* construction, which triggers two different modal meanings: the subjectivized epistemic modality used with positive assertions and the so-called evidential one used for negative assertions. This latter option is also observed with *dokéō*, although only seldomly.

All these differences are, ultimately, related to the highly formulaic nature of the constructions under study.

6 Formulaic expressions

In the exposition of the data in the previous sections, it is possible to observe that most of the positive assertions are instances in which the speaker reaffirms the addressee: "I think you are right", "I think you are telling the truth", "I think you have a point there", etc. (ex. (22a), (22b)). Most of the neutral assertions are, once again, reformulations ("I think you mean this") or explanations of the addressee's actions ("I think you are doing this") (ex. (23a), (23b)).

(22) a. δοκεῖς μοι, ὦ Σώκρατες, εὖ εἰρηκέναι. (Pl. *R.* 541b1)
    dokeîs   moi,   ô   Sṓkrates   eû   eirēkénai
    seem.2SG.PRS I.DAT   INTJ   Socrates.VOC well   say.INF
    'I think you have spoken well, Socrates.'
 b. φαίνῃ τί μοι λέγειν, ὦ Σώκρατες. (Pl. *Cra.* 402c4)
    phaínēi   tí   moi   légein,   ô   Sṓkrates
    appear.2SG.PRS INDF.ACC   I.DAT   say.INF   INTJ   Socrates.VOC
    'I think you are saying something (important), Socrates.'

---

18 'Chunking' is a cognitive process by which a sequence is stored and retrieved as a single unit (Bybee 2010: 34–37).

(23) a. τὰ δέ γε κινούμενα ἐν πολλοῖς φαίνῃ μοι λέγειν ὅσα φορᾷ κινεῖται. (Pl. *Lg.* 893d7)
    ta   dé   ge   kinoúmena   en   polloîs   phaínēi
    ART.ACC PTCL PTCL move.PTCP.ACC in many.DAT appear.2SG.PRS
    moi   légein   hósa   phorâi   kineîtai
    I.DAT say.INF   REL.NOM locomotion.DAT move.3SG.PRS
    'And by objects moving in many places, you seem to me to mean all that moves by locomotion.'
  b. μουσικήν μοι δοκεῖς λέγειν. (Pl. *Alc.1.* 108d3)
    mousikḗn   moi   dokeîs   légein
    music.ACC   I.DAT seem.2SG.PRS say.INF
    'I think you mean music.'

Both contexts are highly formulaic, with several instances of similar expressions within Plato's corpus, as can be seen in Table 3.

Table 3: Formulaic expressions.

Type of assertion	Formula	Frequency		Example
		dokéō	*phaínomai*	
Positive	καλῶς λέγειν (*kalôs légein*) 'speak well'	12	4	(15)
	ἀληθῆ λέγειν (*alēthê légein*) 'speak the truth'	10	1	(9a)
	εὖ λέγειν (*eû légein*) 'speak well'	8	0	(20a)
	ὀρθῶς λέγειν (*orthôs légein*) 'speak correctly'	8	1	(14a)
	λέγειν τι (*légein ti*) 'say something'	2	1	(20b)
Neutral	X λέγειν (X *légein*) 'X say / mean' (reformulation)	25	11	(17a), (17b), (19)

The *formularisation* of such expressions could help explain the ratio found in the corpus. Both *dokéō* and *phaínomai* are found introducing mainly positive and neutral assertions. They roughly represent half of the positive (36/73 = 49.3%) and neutral (25/52 = 48.1%) comments for *dokéō* and half of the examples of positive assertions (7/14 = 50%) and almost all the neutral ones (11/12 = 91.6%) for *phaínomai*. By contrast, it is impossible to establish a formula for the cases where *dokéō* modalises a negative assertion; these latter contexts seem to be free combinations.

Furthermore, since the formulas can show some variability,[19] despite usually having preferred elements to fill in the gaps, all the instances can be subsumed into two different formulas: one for positive comments (agreement formula in Figure 4) and one for neutral comments (reformulation formula in Figure 5).

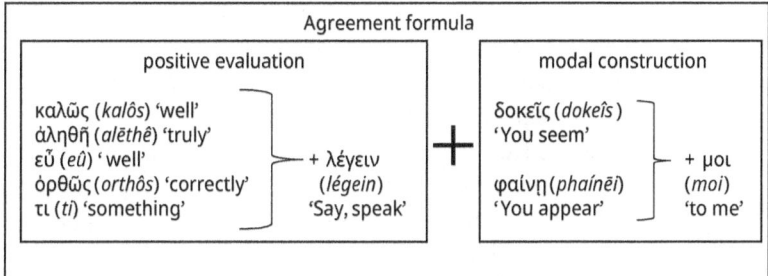

Figure 4: Agreement formula.

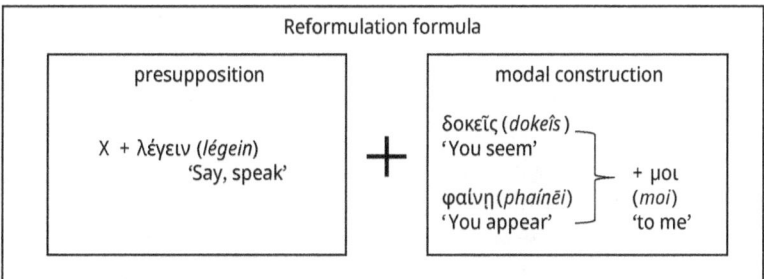

Figure 5: Reformulation formula.

Agreement formulas typically involve modal construction with *légein*-clauses hosting adverbials as main complementizers. Reformulation formulas, on the other hand, combine the modal construction with *légein*-clauses complemented by a direct object, which results in a semantic change of the verb from 'to say' to 'to mean'. The flexible nature of the formulas could also explain some other examples that show little variation from these patterns, such as ὀρθῶς ποιεῖν (*orthôs poieîn* 'act

---

19 All the formulas discussed in this chapter are actually instances of prefabs: "a combination of at least two words favoured by native speakers in preference to an alternative combination which could have been equivalent had there been no conventionalization" (Erman and Warren 2000), that is, they are not completely fixed as idioms would be. They are, in any case, constructions as defined by Croft (2001) or Goldberg (2006): a form-meaning pair.

correctly') in (18), where the speech verb λέγειν (*légein* 'say') is simply substituted by ποιεῖν (*poieîn* 'do'), or εὖ εἰρηκέναι (*eû eirēkénai* 'speak well') in (22a), with a different *verbum dicendi*.

This formulaic nature is ultimately linked to the conventionalization of the structure and its own development as a politeness strategy. As some research shows (Terkourafi 2002, 2015), politeness has in part to do with learning and using conventionalized formulas in interaction.[20] From this perspective, politeness is linked to resorting to the socially appropriate formulas in a given context, not as much to the indirectness of the expression: the speaker does not necessarily need to mitigate an assertion such as "you are right", but a formula such as "I think you are right" – ἀληθῆ μοι δοκεῖς λέγειν (*alēthê moi dokeîs légein*) – is socially expected (and favoured). Therefore, a construction that formally expresses an epistemic modality becomes a politeness marker through the conventionalization of a formula thanks to its frequent use.

7 Conclusions

Plato's dialogues show a great number of utterances containing allusions to the interlocutor. These allusions entail a certain risk in interaction since they can be seen as threatening to the positive or negative faces of the speaker and the addressee, either due to their content or to the presuppositions on which they are built.

Among the linguistic mechanisms that exist in Ancient Greek to control the assertive force of these utterances are the verbs *dokéō* and *phaínomai* in different syntactic-semantic configurations. These configurations show some variation according to certain parameters that occur in both verbs: they may use second- or third-person forms; they may constitute the main predication of the utterance or be part of an extraclausal constituent; they may or may not host an explicit reference to the speaker as the EXPERIENCER of the construction.

In the case of *phaínomai*, the most interesting parameter analysed is the presence of the EXPERIENCER in the dative, always referring to the first person in our data, which allows us to distinguish the implementation of two types of modalities: the epistemic construction, in which the factuality of the proposition relies on the speaker's knowledge, and, therefore, has a greater load of subjectivity; and the so-called evidential construction, which attenuates the content of the utterance,

---

[20] For the use of agreement formulas in turn-initial position for politeness-related purposes in the dialogues of Plato, see Verano (2022). For an overview of reformulation in discourse in Ancient Greek, including a complete account of its instances in Plato's *Republic*, see Verano (2015).

but without explicitly engaging the speaker, resulting in less subjectivity. This difference has an important pragmatic performance: while the first one is used as a mitigation strategy in positive and neutral utterances about the interlocutor, the second is reserved for negative utterances, thus it avoids linking the speaker's opinion to an observation about the addressee that may be considered a threat to his / her social face.

As for *dokéō*, the data are both more frequent and more homogeneous. The sequence with the personal pronoun μοι (*moi*) is generalised to all the possible contexts, rendering the distinction based on subjectivity almost irrelevant, apart from a few examples where the dative is absent. This points to the conventionalization of the formula δοκεῖς μοι (*dokeîs moi*), that seems to have undergone a chunking process whereby it is stored and retrieved from the memory as a single unit, regardless of the type of assertion it introduces.

In both cases, the analysis of the data shows how lexicon and syntax interfaces involving modality and intersubjectivity are relevant resources, used in conversation to deal with communicative challenges that may involve face-threatening acts to the speaker and the addressee. As we have seen, the modal values of the verbs are linked to specific syntactic-semantic configurations and, in some cases, it is possible to identify patterns with a high frequency of use, which points to a possible conventionalization. Particularly, the uses of these verbs to introduce agreements and reformulations are recurrent, to the point that one can speak of formulas associated with certain functions in discourse. In this way, the study of the use of these verbs in such a particular context can shed light on their semantic evolution pathways.

From a pragmatic point of view, the conclusions of this study are partial since the analysis has been limited to a small portion of utterances referring to the second person, namely those that include forms of the selected verbs. To properly understand the contribution of these constructions, it would be necessary to analyse all references to the interlocutor and compare them with each other, an undertaking that exceeds the limits of this paper. However, the results obtained, although preliminary, are interesting and invite us to continue exploring this field in search of the parameters of variation that might explain the use of different mitigation strategies in Ancient Greek conversation.

Greek texts

Burnet, John. 1900–1907. *Platonis Opera*. Oxford: Oxford University Press.

References

Aikhenvald, Alexandra Y. 2018. *The Oxford handbook of evidentiality*. Oxford: Oxford University Press.
Bentein, Klaas. 2012. Verbal periphrasis in Ancient Greek: A state of the art. *Revue Belge de philologie et d'histoire* 90. 5–56.
Brown, Penelope & Stephen C. Levinson. 1987. *Politeness: Some universals in language usage*. Cambridge: Cambridge University Press.
Bucholtz, Mary & Kira Hall. 2005. Identity and interaction: A sociocultural linguistic approach. *Discourse Studies* 7(4–5). 585–614.
Bybee, Joan. 2006. From usage to grammar: The mind's response to repetition. *Language* 82(4). 711–733.
Bybee, Joan. 2010. *Language, usage and cognition*. Cambridge: Cambridge University Press.
Clark, Herbert H. & Susan E. Brennan. 1991. Grounding in communication. In Lauren B. Resnick, John M. Levine & Stephanie D. Teasley (eds.), *Perspectives on socially shared cognition*, 127–149. Washington DC: American Psychological Association.
Conti, Luz. 2020. La cortesía verbal en Sófocles: Análisis del optativo potencial en actos de habla directivos. *Emerita* 88(2). 229–250.
Croft, William. 2001. *Radical construction grammar. Syntactic theory in typological perspective*. Oxford & New York: Oxford University Press.
Culpeper, Jonathan & Dániel Kádár. 2010. *Historical (im)politeness*. Bern: Peter Lang.
Denizot, Camille. 2011. *Donner des ordres en grec ancien. Étude linguistique des formes de l'injonction*. Rouen: Publications des universités de Rouen et du Havre.
Denizot, Camille & Olga Spevak (eds.). 2017. *Pragmatic approaches to Latin and Ancient Greek*. Amsterdam & Philadelphia: John Benjamins.
Denizot, Camille & Liana Tronci. 2023. For a syntactic approach to modality and its application to Ancient Greek. (this volume)
Dik, Simon C. 1997. *The theory of functional grammar. Part 2: Complex and derived constructions*. Edited by Kees Hengeveld. Berlin & New York: Mouton de Gruyter.
Drummen, Annemieke. 2013. A constructionist approach to the potential optative in Classical Greek drama. *Glotta* 89. 68–108.
Erman, Britt & Beatrice Warren. 2000. The idiom principle and the open choice principle. *Text* 20(1). 29–62.
Fedriani, Chiara & Rodrigo Verano 2021. Common ground and politeness in Latin and Greek philosophical dialogue. In Antonio M. Martín Rodríguez (ed.), Linguisticae Dissertationes. *Current perspectives on Latin grammar, lexicon and pragmatics. Selected papers from the 20th international colloquium on Latin linguistics (Las Palmas de Gran Canaria, Spain, June 17–21, 2019)*, 651–664. Madrid: Ediciones Clásicas.
Goldberg, Adele E. 2006. *Constructions at work. The nature of generalization in language*. Oxford & New York: Oxford University Press.

Jiménez López, María Dolores. 1990. Δοκεῖν [*dokeîn*] + infinitivo: construcción personal e impersonal. *Cuadernos de filología clásica* 24. 235–243.
Langacker, Ronald W. 1995. Raising and transparency. *Language* 71(1). 1–62.
Lyons, John. 1977. *Semantics*. Cambridge: Cambridge University Press.
Narrog, Heiko. 2012. *Modality, subjectivity, and semantic change. A cross-linguistic perspective*. Oxford: Oxford University Press.
Pardal Padín, Alberto. 2021. Marcos predicativos y cambio sintáctico-semántico en δοκέω. In Juan Antonio González Iglesias, Julián V. Méndez Dosuna & Blanca M. Prósper Pérez (eds.), *Curiositas nihil recusat (Homenaje a Isabel Moreno)*, 395–408. Salamanca: Ediciones Universidad de Salamanca.
Pomerantz, Anita. 1978. Compliment responses. Notes on the co-operation of multiple constraints. In Jim Schenkein (ed.), *Studies in the organization of conversational interaction*, 79–112. New York: Academic Press.
Pomerantz, Anita. 1984. Agreeing and disagreeing with assessments: Some features of preferred / dispreferred turn shapes. In J. Maxwell Atkinson & John Heritage (eds.), *Structures of social action: Studies in conversation analysis*, 57–101. Cambridge: Cambridge University Press.
Pomerantz, Anita & John Heritage. 2013. Preference. In Jack Sidnell & Tanya Stivers (eds.), *The handbook of conversation analysis*, 210–228. Oxford: Wiley-Blackwell.
Redondo, Elena (ed.). 2022. New insights into politeness and impoliteness in Ancient Greek literary dialogue. [Special issue]. *Veleia. Revista de prehistoria, historia antigua, arqueología y filología clásica* 39.
Revuelta Puigdollers, Antonio R. 2017. Illocutionary force and modality. How to tackle the issue in Ancient Greek. In Camille Denizot & Olga Spevak (eds.), *Pragmatic approaches to Latin and Ancient Greek*, 17–43. Amsterdam & Philadelphia: John Benjamins.
Revuelta Puigdollers, Antonio R. 2020. Modo y modalidad. In María Dolores Jiménez López (ed.), *Sintaxis del griego antiguo*, 637–378. Madrid: Consejo Superior de Investigaciones Científicas.
Rijksbaron, Albert. 2006 [1984]. *The syntax and semantics of the verb in Classical Greek*. 3rd edn. Chicago & London: The University of Chicago Press.
Ruiz Yamuza, Emilia. 2014. Mood and modality. In Georgios K. Giannakis (ed.), *Encyclopedia of Ancient Greek language and linguistics*, 452–459. Leiden & Boston: Brill.
Schegloff, Emmanuel A., Gail Jefferson & Harvey Sacks. 1977. The preference for self-correction in the organization of repair in conversation. *Language* 53(2). 361–382.
Scheibman, Joanne. 2001. Local patterns of subjectivity in person and verb type in American English conversation. In Joan Bybee & Paul Hopper (eds.), *Frequency and the emergence of linguistic structure*, 61–90. Amsterdam & Philadelphia: John Benjamins.
Stalnaker, Robert C. 1978. Assertion. In Peter Cole (ed.), *Syntax and semantics 9: Pragmatics*, 315–332. New York: Academic Press.
Terkourafi, Marina. 2002. Politeness and formulaicity. Evidence from Cypriot Greek. *Journal of Greek Linguistics* 3(1). 179–201.
Terkourafi, Marina. 2015. Conventionalization: A new agenda for im/politeness research. *Journal of Pragmatics* 86. 11–18.
Thompson, Sandra A. & Paul Hopper. 2001. Transitivity, clause structure, and argument structure: Evidence from conversation. In Joan Bybee & Paul Hopper (eds.), *Frequency and the emergence of linguistic structure*, 27–60. Amsterdam & Philadelphia: John Benjamins.
Thompson, Sandra A. & Anthony Mulac. 1991. The discourse conditions for the use of the complementizer *that* in conversational English. *Journal of Pragmatics* 15. 237–251.

Traugott, Elizabeth Closs. 2010. (Inter)subjectivity and (inter)subjectification: A reassessment. In Kristin Davidse, Lieven Vandelanotte & Hubert Cuyckens (eds.), *Subjectification, intersubjectification and grammaticalization*, 29–74. Berlin & New York: Mouton de Gruyter.

Unceta, Luis & Łukasz Berger (eds.). 2022. *(Im)politeness in Greek and Roman literature*. Cambridge: Cambridge University Press.

Verano, Rodrigo. 2015. *La reformulación del discurso en griego antiguo. Un estudio sobre la* República de Platón. Sevilla: University of Sevilla dissertation.

Verano, Rodrigo. 2021. El insulto (y otras formas de descortesía) en el diálogo platónico. In Jesús de la Villa, Antonio López Fonseca, Emma Falque Rey, María Paz de Hoz García-Bellido, María José Muñoz Jiménez, Irene Villarroel Fernández, Victoria Recio Muñoz (eds.), *El foro de los clásicos*, vol. I, 359–366. Madrid: Sociedad Española de Estudios Clásicos.

Verano, Rodrigo. 2022. Politeness and interaction in Ancient Greek: Preventing and avoiding dispreferred reactions in the Dialogues of Plato. *Veleia. Revista de prehistoria, historia antigua, arqueología y filología clásica* 39. 209–223.

Ezra la Roi
8 A pragmatic syntax of counterfactual mood attraction and mood (a)symmetry from Archaic to Classical Greek

Abstract: Ancient Greek has been said to have a form of morphosyntactic symmetry called mood attraction or mood assimilation where a subordinate clause was formally assimilated to the same mood as the matrix clause (i.e. an optative, indicative or subjunctive with certain temporal reference limitations). As counterproposal, this article uses a corpus study of Archaic (8th–5th century BCE) and Classical Greek (6th–4th century BCE) to demonstrate that this aspect of modal syntax is in fact pragmatically conditioned. Subordinate clauses in counterfactual mood attraction do not need the expected modal particle (*án / ke(n)*) because they obtain their counterfactuality via transfer of counterfactual implicature from the matrix clause. This transfer resembles how counterfactual matrix clauses receive counterfactual implicature from preceding counterfactual conditionals, because (i) transfer only takes place with temporally iconic subordinate clauses with a causal connection, (ii) the negative or positive polarity of the matrix clause is also transferred, and (iii) both the counterfactual optative (in Archaic) and indicative (in Archaic and Classical Greek) can be found in the matrix and subordinate clause, even asymmetrically in Archaic Greek. Furthermore, non-counterfactual mood symmetry with the optative or subjunctive is also pragmatically conditioned, as choosing a symmetrical mood in the subordinate clause has both a pragmatic and semantic motivation, just as when it is asymmetrically marked by mood in the so-called oblique optative.

Keywords: Counterfactuality, mood attraction, implicature, iconicity, mood, polarity, temporal reference, modal particle

1 The syntax of mood attraction in Ancient Greek

In Ancient Greek the mood of a subordinate clause can be "assimilated" or "attracted" to the mood of the main clause (to an optative, indicative or, rarely, a subjunctive mood), a phenomenon called mood attraction or mood assimilation (Napoli 2014). Napoli defines it as follows:

Ezra la Roi, Ghent University, e-mail: Ezra.LaRoi@UGent.be

https://doi.org/10.1515/9783110778380-008

Mood attraction (or 'modal assimilation', as it is also called) takes place when the mood of a verb occurring in a subordinate clause, which may be dependent or sub-dependent, is *assimilated to the mood of the matrix clause*. In other words, one does not find *the expected mood* in a given subordinate clause, but *the same mood* as in the corresponding matrix clause. (Napoli 2014: 213, my italics).

Mood attraction occurs with three different moods (in order of decreasing frequency): (i) attraction to the optative, (ii) attraction to the counterfactual[1] indicative, and, most rarely, (iii) attraction to the subjunctive. Since the mood in the subordinate clause is, as it were, unexpectedly matched with the mood in the matrix clause, this phenomenon can be called a symmetrical mood phenomenon. As such, it contrasts with the asymmetrical phenomenon of the so-called oblique optative (Duhoux 1992: 43), where researchers at least agree that the optative is found in a subordinate clause after a past indicative for a pragmatic reason (e.g. as reportative evidential, indirect speech, perspectival effect).[2]

An aspect of mood attraction that has not received much attention is how the counterfactual types of mood attraction fit into the phenomenon of mood attraction in Ancient Greek more generally. After all, both the optative and the indicative were used counterfactually in Archaic Greek (la Roi 2022a with references), which opens up the theoretical possibility that they were both used in mood attraction after a counterfactual matrix clause (whether in the counterfactual optative or counterfactual indicative). However, such cases are not admitted into standard definitions of mood attraction, since mood attraction to the optative is only said to happen when the matrix clause with the optative refers to the non-counterfactual future, in potential or wish use (e.g. Smyth and Messing 1968: 489; Napoli 2014). In other words, the notion of "expected mood" is also problematically based on temporal reference grounds, excluding counterfactual uses of the optative that refer to the past or present, or non-counterfactual potential optatives that refer to the present[3] from mood attraction. Since the most frequent uses of mood attraction occur with the optative and the indicative, and they are also used for counterfactuality in different clause types in Ancient Greek, a diachronic study of the use of counterfactual mood attraction with the optative and the indicative could yield insights relevant to

---

1 A sentence or clause is generally called counterfactual (or contrary-to-fact) when it is implied or assumed that what is said does not hold in the actual world (cf. Declerck and Reed 2001: 7; Dancygier 2006: 25).
2 I am aware that the origins and pragmatic value of the oblique optative construction are debated within Ancient Greek linguistics. The effects mentioned here are based on some of the analyses given of the construction, cf. Méndez Dosuna (1999); Faure (2014); Lillo (2017).
3 Some grammars falsely suggest that the potential optative always refers to the future (*pace* van Emde Boas *et al.* 2019: 436), but see Wakker (1994: 211).

the diachronic syntax of counterfactuality, mood attraction and the syntactic and pragmatic conditions of mood usage in both Archaic and Classical Greek.

Furthermore, the distribution of mood attraction with the optative and indicative is allegedly limited to certain subordinate clause types (e.g. the optative is allegedly limited to temporal clauses, conditional relative clauses if the antecedent has an indefinite, final clauses, interrogative indirect clauses as equivalent of dubitative subjunctive, and relative clauses of purpose), but the reasons for that are unaddressed thus far. By contrast, counterfactual mood attraction with the counterfactual indicative (i.e. when the indicative is used counterfactually in non-conditional[4] subordinate clauses without its expected modal particle (*án / ke(n)*), Kühner and Gerth 1898: 259) is said to occur with conditional relative clauses, temporal clauses and final clauses (Napoli 2014). Yet, it can actually be found with other subordinate clause types as well, as in the comparative subordinate clause type of example (1). In this example, the comparative clause refers to the counterfactual past in which Aminias would have knowingly sought to catch Artemisia in that ship. Rather than marking the counterfactuality of the indicatives in the non-conditional subordinate clause using an expected modal particle, it is "assimilated" to the same counterfactual function as the indicative mood in the matrix clause. Note how the matrix clause does have the expected modal particle, following morphosyntactic rules of the mood system of Ancient Greek (see discussion below in Table 1).

(1) [εἰ μέν νυν ἔμαθε ὅτι ἐν ταύτῃ πλέοι Ἀρτεμισίη,] οὐκ **ἂν ἐπαύσατο** πρότερον ἢ **εἷλέ** μιν ἢ καὶ αὐτὸς **ἥλω**. (Hdt. 8.93.5–6)
ouk **an** *epaúsato* *próteron ē* **heîlé**
NEG MOD stop.3SG.IND.AOR sooner than capture.3SG.IND.AOR
min ē kai autos **hḗlō**
he.ACC or also self.NOM be.caught.3SG.IND.AOR
'[If he had known that Artemisia was in that ship,] **he would not have stopped** earlier than that **he captured** it or **was captured** himself.'[5]

In addition to such undiscovered distributional aspects, existing hypotheses about mood attraction cannot fully explain counterfactual mood attraction yet (i) as a mechanical formal phenomenon because a symmetrically marked sentence can have a counterfactual matrix clause but a non-counterfactual subordinate clause (ex. (3)), nor (ii) semantically as caused by the main clause verb as a variety of coun-

---

[4] In Archaic and Classical Greek conditional clauses and some Archaic Greek comparative clauses formed like conditionals with *hōs ei* 'as if', the modal particle is not necessary, see la Roi (2022a).
[5] The translations in this article are based on the most recent Loeb translations available via https://www.loebclassics.com/ (last accessed February 2023).

terfactual verb forms occur in cases of counterfactual mood attraction (see Sections 2 and 3), nor (iii) through a combination of the above and stylistic factors[6] since the attracted subordinate clauses have a variety of values per mood.

Therefore, I argue, we should try and separate the different aspects of mood attraction in order to distinguish between factors that contribute to mood attraction and factors that determine mood attraction, both morphosyntactic and pragmatic. Accordingly, I propose to distinguish between formal optative mood attraction (FOMA), formal indicative mood attraction (FIMA) and pragmatic counterfactuality transfer. Formal mood attraction (FOMA and FIMA) refers to the traditional conception of mood attraction, i.e. the attraction to the same mood as the matrix clause instead of the "expected mood". For the counterfactual indicative and optative this means that, as shown in the lowest row of Table 1 below, a modal particle is not necessary to mark counterfactuality in non-conditional subordinate clauses when we have a case of counterfactual mood attraction; conversely, when there is no counterfactual mood attraction from the matrix clause, i.e. "attracting" a counterfactual mood use without the modal particle, a modal particle is needed to mark a mood as counterfactual in non-conditional subordinate clauses (for explanations see Sections 2 and 3). The absence of the modal particle in such clauses, I suggest, indicates that their counterfactuality is obtained from their matrix clause (see below in Sections 2 and 3). Pragmatic counterfactuality transfer thus refers to those subordinate clauses which have a counterfactual meaning without the modal particle because they gained their counterfactual meaning from the matrix clause. As shown by the overview in Table 1, the modal particles (*án / ke(n)*) play a crucial part in the mood system in Ancient Greek in signalling the modal value of a clause. They have obligatory usages, as in the counterfactual mood usages in Table 1,[7] and optional usages, as with the potential optative in main clauses (la Roi 2023).

Note that the overview focuses on mood forms and leaves out the many counterfactual modal verbs such as (*e*)*khrên* 'it should', *édei* 'it ought', *eboulómēn* 'I wished' (see Revuelta Puigdollers 2017 for a recent overview) which do not, strictly speaking, need a modal particle to be used counterfactually. Space also prevents me from discussing many of the diachronic changes shown by counterfactual markers from Archaic Greek to Classical Greek, e.g. changes in temporal reference from past to present by all aspects, clause type extensions (see la Roi 2022a) or the creation of insubordinate counterfactual alternatives to counterfactual wish illocutions

---

[6] E.g. Amigues (1977: 205–224) or Napoli (2014) who states "often, it rather represents only a matter of stylistic choice".

[7] An exception is the infrequent construction of an adverb meaning 'almost' (e.g. *olígou*) with a past indicative which together yield a counterfactual implicature (*he almost won=he did not win*), for which see la Roi (2023).

Table 1: Counterfactual mood strategies in Ancient Greek.

Illocution	Archaic Greek		Classical Greek
	Counterfactual optative	Counterfactual indicative	Counterfactual indicative
Wish	– wish optative – insubordinate wishes with the optative (*aíthe, ai gár, ei gár, eíthe* or *ei*)	– insubordinate *aíthe, hōs* with *óphel(l)on* – *óphel(l)on*	– insubordinate *ei gár, eíthe, hōs* with *óphel(l)on* – *óphel(l)on* – insubordinate *ei gár, eíthe* with past indicative
Declarative	– optative with modal particles *án / ke(n)*	– past indicative with modal particles *án / ke(n)*	– past indicative with modal particle *án*
Interrogative	– optative with modal particle *ken* (1x)		
De-activated (conditional)	– optative	– past indicative	– past indicative
De-activated (non-conditional)	– optative with modal particles *án / ke(n)* – [*optative in attraction*]	– past indicative with modal particles *án / ke(n)* – [*indicative in attraction*]	– past indicative with modal particle *án* – [*indicative in attraction*]

based on mood only (la Roi 2021). Still, the present study can investigate whether the cases of counterfactual mood attraction play any role for the development of counterfactual strategies more generally (see Section 3). The de-activated label (in the last two rows) refers to the use of counterfactual mood forms in subordinate clauses, as they prototypically take part in the illocutionary force of their matrix clause, e.g. declarative 'I walked to the shop so that I could buy bread' or interrogative 'Can I go the shop if it's a Sunday?' (see la Roi 2021).

This paper is divided into five sections. Sections 2 and 3 discuss counterfactual mood attraction from a pragmatic perspective, respectively in Archaic and Classical Greek. Subsequently, Section 4 seeks to move beyond traditional explanations of mood attraction and suggest that we can do without this formal and temporal reference based notion. Section 5 offers some concluding remarks. This study is based on a corpus-based analysis of counterfactual mood attraction in Ancient Greek, comparing Archaic Greek (Homer, Hesiod and the Homeric Hymns) and Classical Greek texts (the three tragedians, Aristophanes, the histories of Thucydides, Herodotus and Xenophon, the authentic Platonic dialogues and the orators Lysias, Isocrates, Isaeus and Demosthenes). Using the Thesaurus Linguae Graecae, I collected those cases in which a non-conditional subordinate clause in the optative or indicative without the modal particle followed a counterfactual matrix clause (126 examples). These I subsequently analysed for counterfactual mood attraction. To maximize coverage, I also checked the examples given in the standard grammars listed at the end of this paper.

2 Counterfactual mood attraction in Archaic Greek

In Archaic Greek, the counterfactual optative is used especially to refer to the present (and sometimes the future), but there are also still some archaic past-referring uses in Homer which are being replaced by the counterfactual indicative diachronically, e.g. in relative clauses and in declarative or interrogative main clauses (la Roi 2022a). In example (2) below from the *Iliad*, a past-referring counterfactual optative in the matrix clause (*onósaito*) is followed by past-referring counterfactual optatives in its subordinate relative clause which express what no such man would have done (as he could not have). Traditional grammars have called such past counterfactual uses a past potential usage but Wakker (1994: 156–166) has convincingly shown that these uses have a counterfactual implicature in context. To illustrate, in example (2) the Homeric narrator wants to suggest to the reader that it was impossible that any man would have made light of it and moved through there, because the fighting was that intense back then. Oddly enough, Wakker (1994: 161) does admit the existence of the past potential construction from a diachronic perspective to understand the creation of the past habitual construction with the modal particle *án*. Therefore, la Roi (2022b) has now suggested that the past habitual developed directly from the past counterfactual through an invited inference of epistemic certainty (what certainly would have happened in the past > must have happened regularly in the past) as also revealed by the existence of counterfactual habitual examples (see the preceding context of example (4)) and the use of both the imperfect and aorist aspect in the past habitual construction in Classical Greek, as past counterfactual indicatives did in Archaic Greek (la Roi 2022a).

(2) ἔνθά **κεν** οὐκέτι ἔργον ἀνὴρ **ὀνόσαιτο μετελθών**, / **ὅς τις** ἔτ' ἄβλητος καὶ ἀνούτατος ὀξέϊ χαλκῷ / **δινεύοι** κατὰ μέσσον, **ἄγοι** δέ ἑ Παλλὰς Ἀθήνη / χειρὸς ἑλοῦσ', αὐτὰρ βελέων **ἀπερύκοι** ἐρωήν. (*Il.* 4. 539–542)

enthá **ken** oukéti érgon anēr **onósaito**
then MOD not.anymore battle.ACC man.NOM underrate.3SG.OPT
metelthṓn hós tis ét' áblētos kai anoútatos
enter.PTCP.NOM REL.NOM INDF.NOM still unhit.NOM and unhurt.NOM

oxéï	*khalkôi*	***dineúoi***	*kata*	*mésson,*	***ágoi***	
sharp.DAT	bronze.DAT	move.3SG.OPT	through	midst.ACC	lead.3SG.OPT	
dé	*he*	*Pallas Athḗnē*	*kheiros*	*heloûs',*	*autar*	
PTCL	he.ACC	Athene.NOM	hand.GEN	take.PTCP.NOM	PTCL	
beléōn	***aperúkoi***	*erōḗn*				
missiles.GEN	guard.3SG.OPT	onrush.ACC				

'Then a man **could** not any more **have entered** into the battle and **made light of it**, **one who** still unwounded by missile or by thrust of sharp bronze **would have moved** through their midst, Pallas Athene would lead by the hand, and **would have guarded him** from the onrush of missiles.'

Despite the symmetry of optatives in this example, they would not fall under FOMA in the traditional definition due to their past-temporal reference. However, they do fall under the more inclusive notion of pragmatic counterfactuality transfer, since both the matrix and the subordinate clause that lacks a modal particle refer to the counterfactual past that the narrator is talking about.[8] The use of different aspectual forms with the past-referring counterfactual optatives in the matrix and subordinate clause serve to provide the fitting aspectual construal (see la Roi 2022a): a bounded construal of making light of something (*onósaito*) and an unbounded construal of moving and being guarded during the battle (*dineúoi* & *aperúkoi*). In fact, the counterfactuality of the matrix clause optative is transferred pragmatically to the subordinate clause optatives via a counterfactual implicature, because the statement that *a man* could *not* have entered this intense battle and made light of it *implicates* that *nobody would have* easily moved through it unwounded and protected by Athena. In other words, the state of affairs expressed by the optative in the matrix clause (M) as well as those in the subordinate relative clause (S) belong to the same counterfactual world by (scalar) counterfactual implicature:[9] (M) not a man could have > nobody could have M and therefore not have S.

By contrast, in the next example which is symmetrical in mood, we find a past-referring counterfactual indicative in the matrix clause from which the counterfactual implicature does not transfer to the subordinate clause. So even though the subordinate clause with a past indicative is governed by a matrix clause with a counterfactual past-referring indicative and there is formal symmetry of moods, no pragmatic counterfactuality transfer takes place, because the reality status of the

---

8 For another example of pragmatic counterfactuality transfer with counterfactual optatives in matrix and subordinate relative clause, see *Il.* 13.344. A variant with counterfactual indicatives is *Od.* 1.217.

9 One can compare the scalar implicature of an indefinite with negation such as "she didn't give a red cent" = "she gave nothing at all" (Haspelmath 1997: 115).

subordinate clause is not affected by the counterfactuality of the matrix clause:[10] *Aeneas would have struck* does not change the fact that the shield had guarded him before.

(3) ἔνθά **κεν** Αἰνείας μὲν ἐπεσσύμενον **βάλε** πέτρῳ / ἢ κόρυθ' ἠὲ σάκος, **τό** οἱ **ἤρκεσε** λυγρὸν ὄλεθρον. (*Il.* 20.288–289)
    enthá **ken** Aineías   men   epessúmenon   **bále**   pétrōi
    there MOD   Aeneas.NOM PTCL rush.PTCP.ACC hit.3SG.IND.AOR rock.DAT
    ē   kóruth'   ēe   sákos   tó   hoi   **érkese**
    or helmet.ACC or shield.ACC REL.NOM he.DAT ward.3SG.IND.AOR
    lugron   ólethron
    woeful.ACC ruin.ACC
    'Then **would** Aeneas **have struck** him with the stone as he rushed on him, either on the helmet or on the shield **that had defended** him from woeful destruction.'

La Roi (forthc.) discusses predictive counterfactual conditionals, which he argues is one of the major types of counterfactual clause types in Ancient Greek (e.g. *If I had eaten more at breakfast, I would not be starving now*). The striking similarity between cases of pragmatic counterfactuality transfer and predictive counterfactual conditionals is that the sequentiality of their events facilitates the pragmatic transfer of the counterfactual implicature. In example (3), on the contrary, there is no sequentiality between the events in the matrix and subordinate clause (Dancygier 2006: 73), meaning that the temporal relationship between the matrix clause and the subordinate clause is not iconic of the temporal order of events. By contrast, in example (4), the counterfactual implicature of the matrix clause (i.e. in that counterfactual scenario nothing would have parted them) transfers to the temporally sequential event of death enfolding them together (expressed by the attracted indicative without modal particle). The past indicative in the clause attracted through pragmatic counterfactuality transfer ('[would have] enfolded us') thus refers to the counterfactual past which is, from a temporal and causal viewpoint, the outcome of the counterfactual scenario of the matrix clause.[11]

---

[10] Compare the existence of combinations of the counterfactual optative with non-counterfactual indicatives such as *Od.* 9.459 or 11.613.
[11] Contrast the use of a post-posed temporal clause to refer to something that temporally precedes the action in the matrix clause as in *Il.* 12.465 'nobody could have stopped him except the gods, when he jumped in the gates'.

(4) καί **κε** θάμ' ἐνθάδ' ἐόντες **ἐμισγόμεθ**', οὐδέ **κεν** ἥμεας / ἄλλο **διέκρινεν** [...], / πρίν γ' **ὅτε** δὴ θανάτοιο μέλαν νέφος **ἀμφεκάλυψεν**. (*Od.* 4.178–180)
kaí   ke   thám'   enthád'   eóntes   emisgómeth'   oudé   ken
and   MOD   often   there   be.PTCP.NOM   mix.1PL.IMPF   nor   MOD
hḗmeas   állo   diékrinen   prín   g'   hóte   dē
we.ACC   something.NOM   part.3SG.IND.AOR   before PTCL when   PTCL
thanátoio   mélan   néphos   amphekálupsen
death.GEN   black.NOM   cloud.NOM   enfold.3SG.IND.AOR
'Then, living here, should we often have met together, nor **would** anything **have parted** us, [...], **until** the black cloud of death **enfolded us**.'

Still, even when the events are sequential the counterfactual implicature may not transfer due to a speaker's presupposition about the events, as we see in example (5) from the *Odyssey* where, in contrast to example (2), a modal particle is added to a counterfactual subordinate clause which follows a counterfactual matrix clause. These lines are spoken by Odysseus when he wakes up on Ithaca but, crucially, thinks he is somewhere else and that the Phaeacians have not brought him back home but elsewhere. Here the counterfactuality of the matrix clause (i.e. I did not stay there and find another king to bring me home) does not transfer to the relative clause due to Odysseus' wrong supposition about where he is, even though he actually has been entertained by them and sent on his homeward way (*épempe [...] néesthai*). In other words, the addition of the modal particle *ken* is crucial here, since it reveals the contrast between Odysseus' supposition and his reality, or in linguistic terms between pragmatic counterfactuality transfer and independent counterfactuality marking with the modal particle.

(5) [πλάζομαι; αἴθ' ὄφελον μεῖναι παρὰ Φαιήκεσσιν / αὐτοῦ·] ἐγώ δέ **κεν** ἄλλον ὑπερμενέων βασιλήων / ἐξικόμην, ὅς **κέν** μ' **ἐφίλει** καί **ἔπεμπε** νέεσθαι. (*Od.* 13.204–206)
egṓ   dé   ken   állon   hupermenéōn   basilḗōn   exikómēn
I.NOM   PTCL   MOD   other.ACC   mighty.GEN   kings.GEN   reach.3SG.IND.AOR
hós   kén   m'   ephílei   kai   épempe   néesthai
REL.NOM   MOD   me.ACC   love.3SG.IMPF   and   send.3SG.IMPF   return.INF
'I wander? Would that I had remained there among the Phaeacians, and had then come to some other of the mighty kings, who **would have entertained** me and **sent** me on my homeward way.'

Furthermore, in the following example (6), the counterfactuality of Odysseus' present-referring wish can transfer to the temporally sequential event for the present, because there is an implicature from not having a contest (i.e. the counterfactual insubordinate wish) to not therefore being able to test (*peirēsaímetha*) their work now. The subordinate purpose clause facilitates counterfactual implicature transfer, because purpose clauses prototypically have a "determined time reference" (Noonan 1985: 92; Schmidtke-Bode 2009: 43) in relation to the matrix clause situation (see more extensively Section 3 for the relevance of this feature for the distribution of pragmatic counterfactuality transfer across clause types).

(6) Εὐρύμαχ', **εἰ γὰρ** νῶϊν ἔρις ἔργοιο **γένοιτο** / ὥρῃ ἐν εἰαρινῇ, [...] / [...] **ἵνα πειρησαίμεθα** ἔργου. (*Od.* 18.366–369)
Eurúmakh',   **ei gar**   nôïn   éris   érgoio   **génoito**
Eurymachus.VOC if.only we.DU.DAT strife.NOM work.GEN be.3SG.OPT
hṓrēi   en   eiarinêi   **hína**   **peirēsaímetha** érgou
season.DAT in   spring.DAT so.that   test.1PL.OPT   work.GEN
'Eurymachus, **if only we had** a contest in working in the season of spring [...] **so that we tested** our work.'

Now, in the next symmetrical mood example (7), the optative is found in a subordinate dependent question and refers to the past but is not used counterfactually. This example is part of an exceptional group of uses of the optative that refers to the past but is not counterfactual and thus resembles the uses of the optative after past forms of doubt in the indicative in Homer (Monro 1891: 278; Méndez Dosuna 1999: 345–346).

(7) Τυδεΐδην δ' οὐκ **ἂν γνοίης** ποτέροισι **μετείη** / ἠὲ μετὰ Τρώεσσιν **ὁμιλέοι** ἦ μετ' Ἀχαιοῖς. (*Il.* 5.85–86)
Tudeḯdēn   d'   ouk   **an**   **gnoíēs**   potéroisi   **meteíē**
Tydeus'son.ACC PTCL NEG MOD know.2SG.OPT REL.DAT   be.with.3SG.OPT
ēe   meta   Trṓessin   **homiléoi**   ê   met'   Akhaioîs
or   with   Trojans.DAT   side.3SG.OPT   or   with   Achaeans.DAT
'But of Tydeus' son you could not **have known** which army he **was with**, whether he **sided with** the Trojans or with the Achaeans.'

Méndez Dosuna has argued that such uses of the optative, to express doubt from the speaker as to the validity of the information, are the historical source for the reportative evidential usage of the so-called oblique optative,[12] with the optative

---

[12] He also suggests that the oblique optative cannot be found replacing a counterfactual indicative, because it only replaces moods that present something with certainty, with which he refers to the subjunctive or past indicative (Méndez Dosuna 1999: 343–344).

in this early use expressing a form of epistemic distance with regards to the validity of the event expressed by the optative. An example such as (7) would fit this view, since the past-referring counterfactual ('you would not have known' i.e. if you had been there on the battlefield at that time) stresses the very fact of not being able to know. Also, the counterfactual implicature cannot transfer to the subordinate clause, because there is no causality between the matrix and subordinate clause. The subordinate clause has an oblique optative like non-counterfactual meaning which resembles the meaning of the oblique optative and here is temporally simultaneous with the past-referring counterfactual optative (Méndez Dosuna 1999).

Finally, I would like to discuss an asymmetrical example of counterfactual optative and indicative which displays pragmatic counterfactuality transfer but would also fall outside the scope of traditional mood attraction (FOMA / FIMA). It is found in an answer by Proteus who tells Menelaos how he could have gotten home the quickest, something which he evidently has not, since it is his delay which brings him to try to find out from Proteus how to appease the gods and finally come home. As explained by Allan (2013) the counterfactual verb *óphelles* is used as a counterfactual deontic modal verb 'you ought to have'. The optative in the subordinate clause is explained by Allan (2013: 17) as triggered by the past form ("The optative ἵκοιο [*híkoio*] in the final subordinate clause confirms that the main clause refers to a past"). That would in fact imply that the optative presents a type of oblique optative, but the optative does not express a pragmatic effect associated with the oblique optative (e.g. epistemic uncertainty, reportative evidential, indirect speech). Rather, the optative in the purpose clause expresses an event that is sequential to that expressed by the past counterfactual in the matrix clause and therefore, I argue, the counterfactual implicature can transfer to the subordinate clause: [matrix clause] you ought to have made offerings but you did not means that [subordinate clause] you would not have reached your country *the quickest*. In other words, the counterfactuality of making offerings implicates the counterfactuality of reaching his homeland the quickest, as that has delayed him. Thus, contrary to what is said in the literature (see above in Section 1), the optative in a subordinate clause dependent on a counterfactual matrix clause in a different mood can still display pragmatic counterfactuality transfer. After all, the past-referring counterfactual optative is actually one of the expected mood options together with the counterfactual past indicative, because both still referred to the counterfactual past in Homeric Greek. Such a case then strongly calls into question traditional definitions of counterfactual mood attraction which are limited to the counterfactual indicative, based on formal symmetry and limited temporal grounds. It also underlines that pragmatic counterfactuality transfer is a sign that the counterfactuality of the matrix verb *óphelles* is conventionalized.

(8) ἀλλὰ μάλ' **ὤφελλες** Διί τ' ἄλλοισίν τε θεοῖσι / ῥέξας ἱερὰ κάλ' ἀναβαινέμεν, **ὄφρα** τάχιστα / σὴν ἐς πατρίδ' **ἵκοιο** [...]. (*Od.* 4.472–474)

alla mál' **óphelles** Dií t' álloisín te
but surely ought.2SG.IND.IMPF Zeus.DAT PTCL others.DAT PTCL
theoîsi rhéxas hiera kál' anabainémen,
gods.DAT do.PTCP.NOM offerings.ACC good.ACC embark.INF
óphra tákhista sēn es patríd' **híkoio**
so.that soonest your.ACC to country.ACC reach.2SG.OPT

'But surely **you ought to have** made choice offerings to Zeus and the other gods before embarking, so that **you would have come** to your country the quickest.'

To sum up, we have found that traditional explanations of mood attraction based on only formal and temporal grounds (FOMA and FIMA) do not have sufficient explanatory power to explain counterfactual mood attraction in Archaic Greek. For example, we may find formal mood symmetry which is not mood attraction (ex. (3)) or cases of formal mood symmetry but with different temporal reference (ex. (6)) that fall outside the traditional temporal reference conditioned idea of mood attraction. Therefore I argue that counterfactual mood attraction actually depends on the pragmatic relationship between the matrix and subordinate clause, that is, whether the counterfactual implicature can transfer to the subordinate clause, as in example (6) or (8), or cannot as in example (3) or (7) where there is formal mood symmetry but no counterfactual mood attraction. If the event expressed in the subordinate clause is temporally sequential to that expressed by the counterfactual mood in the matrix clause, whether in the counterfactual optative or indicative, the counterfactual implicature transfers unless the event in the matrix clause is presented as an independent proposition with its own reality status.

Moreover, the pragmatic reinterpretation of traditional mood attraction notions that I proposed above can actually explain why certain clause types are favoured for pragmatic counterfactuality transfer: (i) relative clauses with an indefinite antecedent (e.g. anyone who) in the counterfactual matrix clause are by default implication counterfactual, through the scalar implication (anyone who=all those) that all persons are affected by what is said about them in the matrix clause; (ii) post-posed temporal clauses in cases of FIMA / FOMA are of the posterior type (until / before) in Archaic Greek; they express events that are sequential to the event expressed in the matrix clause and therefore open themselves up to pragmatic counterfactuality transfer; (iii) post-posed[13] purpose clauses have a temporal reference which is predetermined by their matrix clause; the events expressed by such post-posed purpose clause are therefore not only naturally iconic from a temporal perspective (i.e. sequential) but also can easily be (although need not be, Section 3) also causally iconic. As such, the notion of pragmatic counterfactuality transfer has more explanatory power than traditional conceptions of mood attraction. Moreover, it is similar to how counterfactual implicature transfer is explained in predictive counterfactual conditionals (e.g. *If I had eaten more at breakfast, I would not be starving now*). In those cases, the counterfactual implicature from the conditional clause (e.g. I did *not* eat enough at breakfast) pragmatically implicates[14] the counterfactuality of the matrix clause (i.e. I am saying that I am starving). Moreover, as with pragmatic counterfactuality transfer, we find both asymmetrical (counterfactual indicative + optative) and symmetrical (counterfactual optative + optative) examples in Archaic Greek, because predictive counterfactual conditionals similarly can be marked asymmetrically in Archaic Greek: *Il.* 22.20 counterfactual optative and counterfactual optative, *Il.* 16.618 counterfactual indicative and counterfactual indicative, and *Il.* 2.80 counterfactual indicative and counterfactual optative.[15]

3 Counterfactual mood attraction in Classical Greek

In Classical Greek, there is less formal variation in the marking of counterfactual mood attraction, since the optative cannot be used counterfactually anymore (la Roi 2022a). However, pragmatic counterfactuality transfer occurs with more clause types than in Archaic Greek and more than mentioned in the literature (e.g. *pace* Kühner and Gerth 1898: 257–258, cf. the italicized): relative, temporal, purpose, *result, and comparative clauses*. Crucially, when such subordinate clauses are counterfactual after a preceding non-counterfactual matrix clause, they need the modal particle as a rule, e.g. in a relative clause Ar. *Lys.* 109 or D. 45.13 (*pace* Goodwin 1889: 214–215), a dependent question Isoc. 11.8, a purpose clause Pl. *Lg.* 967b3, a

---

[13] By contrast, pre-posed subordinate clauses are often used in an illocutionary way e.g. '(just) so you know' *hína eidês / eidête*, see la Roi (2021).
[14] Cf. Wakker (1994: 301); Declerck and Reed (2001: 107–108).
[15] Note that predictive counterfactual conditionals of a counterfactual optative in the conditional clause followed by a counterfactual optative in the matrix clause are not found, because the counterfactual indicative has already replaced the counterfactual optative in past-referring instances in conditional subordinate clauses (la Roi 2022a).

causal clause E. *Alc.* 555, or a result clause Lys. 14.27 or Isoc. 16.7). The first example below is a present-referring counterfactual wish with an indefinite subject that is elaborated on by a relative clause.[16] As in example (2), the counterfactual implicature transfers due to the denial of the indefinite subject in the matrix clause: there is no kinsman or relative for me here now, so there is nobody to give me such criticism (i.e. a scalar implicature). Note that the events in the matrix clause (expressed by the counterfactual insubordinate wish in the indicative, *eíth' óphelen eînai* 'if only would be') and the subordinate clause both refer to the present but have a presuppositional bound, because being present necessarily precedes giving criticism.

(9) εἴθ' ὤφελέν μοι κηδεμὼν ἢ ξυγγενὴς εἶναί τις **ὅστις** τοιαῦτ' **ἐνουθέτει**. (Ar. *V.* 731)
 eíth' óphelén moi kēdemṓn ḗ xuggenḗs
 if.only ought.3SG.IND.AOR me.DAT kinsman.NOM or relative.NOM
 eînaí tis **hóstis** toiaût' **enouthétei**
 be.INF someone.NOM REL.NOM such.ACC rebuke.3SG.IND.IMPF
 '**If only there would be some** kinsman or relative **who would give** me such criticism.'

In the following example, we find confirmation of the similarity between counterfactual implicature transfer from the conditional to the matrix clause in predictive counterfactuals and from the matrix to the subordinate clause in pragmatic counterfactuality transfer: the counterfactual implicature transfers from the counterfactual condition to the matrix clause and subsequently to the attracted subordinate clause. Since Socrates has no money (the counterfactual conditional in the indicative), he could not have proposed a fine (the counterfactual matrix clause) nor have paid a sum that large (the attracted subordinate clause). Thus, counterfactual mood attraction is actually pragmatically conditioned, a pragmatic counterfactuality transfer.

(10) εἰ μὲν γὰρ **ἦν** μοι χρήματα, **ἐτιμησάμην ἄν** χρημάτων ὅσα **ἔμελλον** ἐκτείσειν. (Pl. *Ap.* 38b1)
 ei men gar **ên** *moi khrḗmata,* **etimēsámēn**
 if PTCL PTCL be.3SG.IMPF me.DAT money.NOM estimate.1SG.IND.AOR
 an khrēmátōn **hósa** **émellon** *ekteísein*
 MOD money.GEN which.ACC be.to.1SG.IND.IMPF pay.INF
 '**If I had** money, **I would have proposed** a fine, as large as **I were** to pay.'

---

16 Other examples are Pl. *Ap.* 20a7, 38b1, *Men.* 94c7, *Phlb.* 22b4, and Is. 2.25.

In fact, we can have pragmatic counterfactuality transfer from a subordinate conditional clause to a relative clause which is dependent on it,[17] underlining that counterfactual implicature transfer from the matrix clause is the motor behind pragmatic counterfactuality transfer. In example (11) the counterfactual premise of there not being a stronger authority in the city than the Thirty tyrants (matrix clause) implicates that such a non-existing authority could also not have ordered him (attracted relative clause). The counterfactuality from the conditional clause therefore transfers to the relative clause dependent on it through pragmatic counterfactuality transfer.[18]

(11) εἰ μὲν γάρ **τις ἦν** ἐν τῇ πόλει ἀρχὴ ἰσχυροτέρα ὑφ' **ἧς** αὐτῷ **προσετάττετο** παρὰ τὸ δίκαιον ἀνθρώπους ἀπολλύναι [ἴσως ἂν εἰκότως αὐτῷ συγγνώμην εἴχετε]. (Lys. 12.29)
*ei   men   gár   **tis**   **ên**   en   têi   pólei*
if   PTCL   PTCL   INDF.NOM   be.3SG.IND.IMPF   in   ART.DAT   city.DAT
*arkhē   iskhurotéra   **huph' hês**   autôi   **prosetátteto***
power.NOM   stronger.NOM   under.which   he.DAT order.3SG.PASS.IND.IMPF
para   to   díkaion   anthrṓpous   apollúnai
against   ART.ACC   justice.ACC   people.ACC   destroy.INF
'For **had there been some** stronger authority in the city, **whose orders were given** him to destroy people in defiance of justice, [you might perhaps have some reason for pardoning him].'

At the same time, as discussed above in relation to example (3), formal symmetry between a counterfactual past indicative in the matrix clause and a past indicative in the subordinate clause is not necessarily pragmatic counterfactuality transfer, as shown by the following example where the relative clause expresses something which temporally precedes the present-referring counterfactual wish. Standard grammars explain such examples as not displaying FIMA because the subordinate clause is not "intimately connected with the thought of the clause on which it depends" (Smyth and Messing 1968: 489).[19] From a pragmatic perspective, however, we can clarify such intuitive qualifications by pointing to the lack of sequentiality and causal impossibility of counterfactual implicature transfer from the matrix to the subordinate clause.

---

17 See also Isoc. 13.1, E. *IA* 1213, Pl. *Prt.* 327a5, and *Chrm.* 171d3.
18 The same phenomenon is found with a result clause which is dependent on a counterfactual condition preceding the counterfactual matrix clause, see D. 39.26.
19 Similarly, Kühner and Gerth (1898: 258–259) who speak about the same mental conception in the matrix and subordinate clause of FOMA and FIMA.

(12) ἠβουλόμην δ' ἂν ὑμῖν οἷός τ' εἶναι ποιῆσαι φανερὸν **οἷος** περὶ αὐτὸν ἐγενόμην. (Isoc. 19.28)
ēboulómēn d' **an** humîn hoîós t' eînai
wish.1SG.IMPF PTCL MOD you.DAT able.NOM PTCL be.INF
poiêsai phaneron **hoîos** *peri auton* **egenómēn**
make.INF clear.ACC REL.NOM around he.ACC be.1SG.AOR
'I wish I could make clearly apparent to you **the nature of which I was around him.**'

This brings us to the role of clause types for FIMA and pragmatic counterfactuality transfer, since some clauses have been said to lack mood attraction due to their relationship with the matrix clause, e.g. dependent statements, dependent fear clauses and dependent questions for being "innerlich abhängig", i.e. internally dependent (Kühner and Gerth 1898: 259). Indeed, as observed above in relation to examples (6) and (8)–(11), with counterfactual mood attraction in relative clauses and purpose clauses, there is an inherent relation (e.g. scalar implicature or temporal-causal connection) which facilitates the transfer of the counterfactual implicature to the attracted clause. This explains why relative clauses and purpose clauses represent the majority of examples of pragmatic counterfactuality transfer in my corpus for Classical Greek. Yet, note that these clauses can also have a modal particle and counterfactual indicative, for example when following a non-counterfactual matrix clause (see la Roi 2022a who records 46 of such relative clauses, e.g. Th. 8.66.5, but only 1 such purpose clause). For similar semantic-pragmatic reasons, we find pragmatic counterfactuality transfer with a temporal clause when the temporal clause specifies a time frame (esp. *prín* 'before' or *héōs* 'until') within the same counterfactual world as the matrix clause (e.g. 'the senate would have carried on the torture until (*mékhri hoû*) they saw fit' D. 53.25),[20] or with a purpose clause when the counterfactuality of the purpose is created by the matrix clause (e.g. 'sureties ought to have been taken then so that (*hṓs*)' X. *An*. 7.6.23). However, in example (13) we find neither FIMA nor pragmatic counterfactuality transfer, but a present in the dependent statement. This illustrates that both the speaker sceptically accepts that the Persian is only heading towards the Scythians, and this proposition is not altered by the counterfactuality of the Persian being able to show that he is (see the matrix clause and preceding context).

---

20 See also Lys. 12.1, D. 20.96, Pl. *Men.* 84c5, 86d5, *Grg.* 506b5.

(13) [εἰ γὰρ ἐπ' ἡμέας μούνους ἐστρατηλάτεε ὁ Πέρσης [...] χρῆν αὐτὸν πάντων τῶν ἄλλων ἀπεχόμενον ἰέναι οὕτω ἐπὶ τὴν ἡμετέρην,] καὶ **ἂν ἐδήλου** πᾶσι **ὡς** ἐπὶ Σκύθας **ἐλαύνει** καὶ οὐκ ἐπὶ τοὺς ἄλλους. (Hdt. 4.118.15–20)
kai **an edḗlou** pâsi **hōs** epi Skúthas **elaúnei**
and MOD show.2SG.IMPF all.DAT that to Scythians.ACC march.3SG.PRS
kai ouk epi tous állous
and NEG to ART.ACC other.ACC
'[if indeed the Persian were marching against us alone [...], he ought to leave others alone and make straight for us,] and **would show** everyone that Scythia and no other country **is his goal**.'

By contrast, in example (1) the counterfactuality of the matrix clause (he would not have stopped earlier) transfers to the attracted comparative clause even though it is internally dependent on the matrix clause (viz. *próteron ḗ* 'earlier than').

Furthermore, the marking of polarity in cases of pragmatic counterfactuality transfer also reveals the similarity to counterfactual implicature transfer in predictive counterfactual conditionals. The negation in the attracted purpose clause in (14) targets the reversed polarity of the matrix clause. We thus could paraphrase the causal relation between the matrix and attracted clause as: It does not have a mind and a voice according to the rule of a messenger, so that it does not waver between two minds. The negator in the attracted clause targets the counterfactuality of the matrix clause, that is, its reversed polarity.[21]

(14) **εἴθ' εἶχε** φωνὴν ἔμφρον' ἀγγέλου δίκην, **ὅπως** δίφροντις οὖσα **μὴ 'κινυσσόμην**. (A. *Ch.* 195–196)
eíth' eîkhe phōnḗn émphron' aggélou díkēn,
if.only have.3SG.IMPF voice.ACC wise.ACC messenger.GEN rule.ACC
hópōs díphrontis oûsa mē 'kinussómēn
in.order.that doubting.NOM be.PTCP.NOM NEG waver.1SG.IMPF
'**If only it had** a wise voice according to the rule of a messenger, **in order that I wouldn't waver** between two minds.'

Furthermore, in example (15), the negator *ouk* targets the counterfactuality of the preceding condition, a causal relationship that we could paraphrase as: I cannot block my hearing (conditional) and therefore cannot refrain from shutting off my wretched self (matrix clause, with double negation interpreted as single negation)

---

[21] For a comparable example with negation markers in both the counterfactual markers in the matrix and attracted clause, see Pl. *Smp.* 181d7.

in order that I am blind and deaf (attracted purpose clause).²² Thus, the counterfactual implicature transfer is revealed by the negation in the matrix clause which targets the reversed polarity of the conditional and matrix clause.²³ This transfer is after all also why Oedipus cannot be deaf as well as blind.

(15) [ἀλλ' εἰ τῆς ἀκουούσης ἔτ' ἦν / πηγῆς δι' ὤτων φραγμός], **οὐκ ἂν ἐσχόμην** / τὸ μὴ ἀποκλῇσαι τοὐμὸν ἄθλιον δέμας, / **ἵν' ἦ** τυφλός τε καὶ κλύων **μηδέν**. (S. *OT.* 1386–1389)
ouk   an   eskhómēn   to   **mē   apoklêisai** toumon   áthlion
NEG   MOD   can.1SG.AOR   ART.ACC   NEG   shut.off.INF   mine.ACC   sad.ACC
démas,   **hín'**   ê   tuphlós   te kai   klúōn
body.ACC   so.that   be.3SG.IMPF   blind.NOM   and   hear.PTCP.NOM
mēdén
nothing.ACC
'[Why, if there had been a means of blocking the stream of hearing through my ears], I **could not refrain from shutting off** my wretched self, **in order that I were blind and deaf**.'

These findings raise the question how to account for other alleged cases of counterfactual mood attraction which do not have a counterfactual in the matrix clause (Goodwin 1889: 120–121; Kühner and Gerth 1898: 285; Revuelta Puigdollers 2017: 28–30), viz. *tí ou(k)* 'why not' + past indicative questions which are followed by a final clause with a past indicative. Using example (16), Revuelta Puigdollers concludes that the presence of the final clause with a past tense in this construction is the same as the final clause with a past tense depending on a matrix clause with a counterfactual verb:

> The counterfactuality (conversational and conventionalized implicatures) of these constructions (*tí ou* + past in interrogatives and *eboulómēn* (*an*) 'I would have wanted') is proved by the behavior of final clauses depending on them, since they take the past tense as they usually do when they are under the scope of explicit counterfactual expressions (past + *án*). (Revuelta Puigdollers 2017: 29–30)

I would argue that his interpretation conflates the semantics of the construction (why not past event) with the pragmatic implicature that the speaker wants the addressee to infer. After all, 'why not' combined with a past tense does not express

---

22 For more examples of pragmatic counterfactuality transfer with purpose clauses, see, for example, S. *El.* 1132, A. *Pr.* 154, Ar. *Ec.* 151, Isoc. 15.51, Lys. 3.21, 3.44.
23 See la Roi (2023) for the role of polarity reversal in counterfactuals and similar constructions.

a counterfactual past in itself (i.e. considered false by the speaker), but only something unrealized which is negated. For obvious rhetorical effect (see *euthús* 'at once'), Oedipus presents it as a possible past that Cithaeron had killed him instead of receiving him and therefore that he never revealed his origin in the past. Note the sequentiality between the matrix and purpose clause. Now, the pragmatic interpretation of the question is a directive reproach:[24] you should have killed me at once so that I could never have revealed to mortals what was my origin. It is only in the pragmatic analysis that a counterfactual interpretation of the whole sentence is implicated.

(16) [ἰὼ Κιθαιρών, τί μ' ἐδέχου;] **τί μ' οὐ** λαβών / **ἔκτεινας** εὐθύς, **ὡς ἔδειξα μήποτε** / ἐμαυτὸν ἀνθρώποισιν ἔνθεν ἦ γεγώς; (S. *OT* 1391–1393)
tí   m'   ou   labōn   ékteinas   euthús   hōs
why   me.ACC NEG   take.PTCP.NOM   kill.2SG.AOR at.once   so.that
édeixa   mḗpote   emauton   anthrṓpoisin   énthen
show.1SG.AOR   never   myself.ACC   humans.DAT   where.from
ê   *gegṓs* ?
be.1SG.IMPF   be.PTCP.NOM
'[Ah, Cithaeron, why did you receive me?] **Why did you** not take me and **kill me** at once, **so that** I **had never revealed** to mortals what was my origin?'

Thus, such constructions should not be put on the same level as cases of pragmatic counterfactuality transfer (*pace* Goodwin 1889: 120–121; Kühner and Gerth 1898: 285 who cite counterfactual examples next to only two of these instances; Revuelta Puigdollers 2017: 28–30).

In sum, pragmatic counterfactuality transfer provides a pragmatic basis for comprehensively explaining cases previously explained as FIMA. As discussed in this section, pragmatic counterfactuality transfer occurs across different clause types (e.g. relative, temporal, purpose, result, and comparative clauses). In cases of pragmatic counterfactuality transfer, the absence of the modal particle is the result of the trans-

---

24 Cf. also Kühner and Gerth (1898: 258). Nijk (2021: 4–5) in a recent discussion of the behavior of tense and aspect in these *tí ou(k)* 'why not' questions calls this use the indignant interpretation and suggests that a hortative interpretation of (16) is out of the question "as the opportunity for carrying out the designated event has expired". This would seem too strict of an interpretation of hortative, since directives can concern the past and still exhort someone at present. For example, if a parent sees that his son has not finished his homework before today's deadline, he could say "why did you not finish it yesterday?" or "you should have finished it yesterday" in order to get him to finish it now. Cf. the directive values of past-referring counterfactual modal verbs in Ancient Greek, Ruiz Yamuza (2021).

fer of the pragmatic implicature from the matrix clause to the subordinate clause. In fact, the striking similarities between the counterfactual implicature transfer from conditionals to the main clause in predictive counterfactual conditionals and cases of pragmatic counterfactuality transfer, as well as the similarities in how the counterfactual implicature cancels negated propositions (i.e. the polarity reversal from negative to positive) confirm that the formal side of counterfactual mood attraction has a pragmatic basis. Therefore, the next section will assess whether the formal phenomena collated by non-counterfactual mood attraction (FOMA and FSMA, i.e. with the optative and subjunctive), might also be pragmatically conditioned.

4 Moving beyond mood attraction

An example such as (17), where Trygaeus explains what the Moon and the Sun hope to gain by betraying the gods and plotting with the barbarians, receives the traditional explanation of FOMA stating that a subjunctive or future is 'expected' in the purpose clause but here the "mood attracts to that of the potential βούλοιντ' ἄν" [*boúloint' an* 'they would want'] (van Emde Boas *et al.* 2019: 501).[25]

(17) [ὁτιὴ νὴ Δία / ἡμεῖς μὲν ὑμῖν θύομεν, τούτοισι δὲ / οἱ βάρβαροι θύουσι.] διὰ τοῦτ' εἰκότως / **βούλοιντ' ἄν** ἡμᾶς πάντας ἐξολωλέναι,/ **ἵνα** τὰς τελετὰς **λάβοιεν** αὐτοὶ τῶν θεῶν. (Ar. *Pax* 409–413)
dia toût' eikótōs **boúloint'** **an** hēmâs pántas
through DEM naturally want.3PL.OPT MOD us.ACC all.ACC
exolōlénai **hína** tas teletas **láboien** autoi
destroy.INF so.that ART.ACC rites.ACC take.3PL.OPT self.NOM
tôn theôn
ART.GEN gods.GEN
'[Simple: we sacrifice to you and the barbarians sacrifice to them;] so naturally **they'd want** us all annihilated, **in order that** they **could take** over the rites of the gods themselves.'

I would argue, however, that we could do without such an artificial explanation, because it seems to be based on preconceived expectations of mood symmetry and

---

[25] The same explanation is found in commentaries, e.g. on this example Olson (1998: 158) citing Goodwin (1889: 60–61).

a strict temporal reference understanding of mood usage.[26] Rather, the optative appears to be used here in its standard way of expressing non-subjective epistemic modality (la Roi 2019) of a potential event in the present (as here) or the future, i.e. something may take place but the speaker does not take epistemic responsibility for that. In other words, Trygaeus purposely presents it as a possibility that the Moon and Sun could successfully complete their plot to overturn all the gods and receive their rites, i.e. the purpose of their present wish.[27] After all, this lower degree of likelihood corresponds to reality[28] as one may want to do such thing to the gods now, but *given* that they are the gods it is unlikely that they would succeed in taking the rites from the gods (*láboien*). Assuming an "original" or "replaced" subjunctive in the matrix clause is unnecessary because the temporal reference and epistemic likelihood is pragmatically conditioned by the potential optative in the matrix clause.

Thus, an alternative interpretation of such traditional cases of FOMA that I would like to propose in part actually traces back to a discrepancy found in the literature on how to interpret mood attraction/assimilation. Whereas most grammarians view mood attraction as a true form of replacement and thereby imply that, for example, the optative mood is used as to replace the expected subjunctive (Smyth and Messing 1968: 489; e.g. Crespo, Conti and Maquieira 2003: 297; van Emde Boas *et al.* 2019: 501), some had already stated that the mood in cases of mood attraction retains its own force (esp. Kühner and Gerth 1898: 254–258). In fact, Kühner and Gerth have observed some of the problems that have troubled accounts of mood attraction more generally. Their definition of mood attraction reflects this, as they do not use a temporal reference criterion for mood attraction but rather state that the mood in both the matrix and subordinate clause share the same mental conception by the speaker.[29] With regards to the idea of replacement of the subjunctive by the optative, they stated emphatically that an optative has its own force when found in a place where one might have expected a subjunctive.[30] Since they suggest that the

---

26 This issue probably connects to the understanding of moods in terms of tenses by earlier grammars as reflected by their discussions of "the tenses of the moods" (Goodwin 1889: 22). See la Roi (forthc.) who shows that the classifications of conditionals by grammars have similarly been guided by temporal reference and chance of fulfillment (i.e. mood choice) as main criteria, although pragmatic functions cover functional variation in temporal reference and mood asymmetries.
27 Note that the present-referring potential optative would not even qualify as FOMA in stricter definitions of FOMA based on future reference such as Smyth and Messing (1968: 489).
28 See, however, Wakker (1994: 113) who astutely observes that the choice of mood need not always correspond to reality but may depend on the speaker's goal, e.g. to present something unlikely as possible with a potential optative.
29 Kühner and Gerth (1898: 254).
30 Kühner and Gerth (1898: 252).

mood in the "attracted" subordinate clause retains its own meaning, it would actually follow that there is no genuine 'attraction' or 'assimilation' and that the phenomena of FSMA (which Kühner and Gerth do not even acknowledge), FOMA and FIMA as conceived by most grammarians nowadays do not have enough explanatory power (as I argue in this paper). In my view, they already are hinting to this hypothesis (see the translated quote of Kühner and Gerth 1898: 258), a hypothesis that this paper substantiates:

> For the modal symmetry of subordinate clauses with the main clause discussed above (*which are most clearly revealed in the optatival and unreal conditional clauses* § 576 and 574), the term modal assimilation has become usual, *which of course should not tempt to the opinion that the subordinate clause due to the predominant influence of the main clause were imposed with a mood which did not belong to it*. Much more the agreement is almost everywhere based on that the subordinate clause arises from the same mental opinion of attitude of the speaker as the main clause, that is, likewise either constitutes a purely subjective conception, for which the optative is the corresponding utterance form (cf. also no. 3), or the conception of an unrealized action, which in Greek usage is accordingly expressed in the past (cf. §391, 5). *When the subordinate clause is not part of the same mental conception as the main clause, then it will not receive the same mood.* (Kühner and Gerth 1898: 258, my italics)

They signal three points which require further qualification. Firstly, mood attraction should not be interpreted as the main clause mood causing a change to a mood in the subordinate clause although this is how mood attraction has mostly been interpreted. Secondly, there are asymmetrical mood examples, where the mood in the subordinate clause is not attracted because the event in the subordinate clause is not conceived in the same mental way by the speaker (see more precise pragmatic analysis above in Section 3). This evidence in fact supports the idea that the mood in cases of FOMA has its own value. Thirdly and finally, they compare the phenomenon of mood attraction to the mood symmetry found in conditional clauses. I think that the fact that they put these two phenomena on the same level illustrates that they see these mood symmetries as a merely formal phenomenon, especially since the moods retain their own force in their view.[31] After all, it is common knowledge that the moods in conditional sentences need not be symmetrical (Goodwin 1889: 188–195; la Roi forthc.), because that is a didactic simplification of the complex conditional system of Ancient Greek. To sum up, not only can mood attraction be interpreted without the notions of FOMA, FIMA and FSMA, there is existing evidence suggesting that FOMA is only relevant from a didactic formal perspective. This can

---

[31] This would also explain why instances of a preposed conditional with optative and a main clause with optative are cited as instances of FOMA in some grammars (e.g. Kühner and Gerth 1898: 256).

be illustrated further by a contrastive example of a wish optative followed by an allegedly attracted optative (example (18)) and followed by a subjunctive (example (19)). In example (18) Orestes is addressing an absent goddess to come to his aid using a wish optative. Since the wish refers to a possibility for which Orestes would have to be very lucky to actually happen, it follows that the sequential possibility dependent on it in the purpose clause is also merely potential, viz. that she would also liberate him from his troubles.

(18) ἔλθοι [...] **ὅπως γένοιτο** τῶνδ' ἐμοὶ λυτήριος. (A. *Eu.* 297–298)
élthoi   hópōs   génoito   tônd'   emoi   lutḗrios
come.3SG.OPT in.order.that be.3SG.OPT   DEM.GEN.PL   me.DAT   liberator.NOM
'**May she come here** [...] **in order that she may be** my liberator from these troubles.'

By contrast, the wish for immediate death (*tethnaíēn* die.1SG.OPT) in (19) presupposes that the speaker would not remain here, since he would be dead, and therefore warrants the use of the more certain subjunctive. In sum, the mood in both examples have their own force in representing a possibility as potential (17, 18) or likely (19), while the pragmatic relation between the two events clarifies why a speaker would use the optative or subjunctive in the subordinate clause.

(19) [αὐτίκα, φησί, τεθναίην, δίκην ἐπιθεὶς τῷ ἀδικοῦντι,] **ἵνα μὴ** ἐνθάδε **μένω** καταγέλαστος παρὰ νηυσὶ κορωνίσιν. (Pl. *Ap.* 28d2)
hína   **mē**   entháde   **ménō**   katagélastos   para
so.that   NEG   here   stay.1SG.SBJV   laughed.at.NOM   at
nēusí   korōnísin
ships.DAT   curved.DAT
'[May I die right now,' he says, 'when I have made the unjust man pay the penalty,] **in order not to remain here** a laughing stock beside the crooked-beaked ships.'

In fact, the same explanation holds in other subordinate clause types, for example relative clauses in such FOMA contexts. Example (20), presented as FOMA by van Emde Boas *et al.* (2019: 501), actually has a contextual motivation for the optative in the relative clause. A man from Sybaris had fallen out of a chariot and seriously injured his head. He was an inexperienced driver. A friend of his stood over him and then reproaches him in the following way:

(20) "ἔρδοι τις ἦν ἕκαστος εἰδείη τέχνην." / [οὕτω δὲ καὶ σὺ παράτρεχ' εἰς τὰ Πιττάλου]. (Ar. V. 1431–1432)
érdoi   tis   hēn   hékastos   eideíē   tékhnēn
do.3SG.OPT INDF.NOM   REL.ACC each.NOM   know.3SG.OPT craft.ACC
'**Let** each **practice** the craft **he knows**.' [So why don't you do the same and run off to Pittalus' clinic!]'

As explained in the commentary by Biles and Olson (2015: 492–493), the wish is meant as a witty reproach to his friend that it was stupid to try a trade that is not one's own and therefore he should go to Pittalus, a proverbially sarcastic turn of phrase. The choice for the optatives is ideally suited to this context, as, on the one hand, the generalized wish (*érdoi tis*) is clearly to be interpreted personally by the hearer,[32] and, on the other hand, to present what one would know (*eideíē*) in the optative as a mere possibility is obviously instructed by the fact that his friend clearly does not know this trade, that is, a form of negative scalar implicature from possibility: anyone would know what he does but you clearly do not. Thus, an explanation in terms of FOMA is unnecessary.[33] At the same time, the optative in the subordinate clause is pragmatically conditioned by the generalized wish optative in the matrix clause.

5 Concluding remarks

It has been argued in this paper that what has been called counterfactual mood attraction is a pragmatically conditioned morphosyntactic phenomenon. The morphosyntactic rule whereby a modal particle is not needed in a counterfactual non-conditional subordinate clause has a pragmatic basis: it is determined by whether the counterfactual implicature from the matrix clause (i.e. main or subordinate clause) transfers to the subordinate clause, called pragmatic counterfactuality transfer. For pragmatic counterfactuality transfer to occur, the events in both clauses are at least sequential (i.e. temporally iconic) but, more importantly, causally dependent on each other in the same way as a counterfactual implicature in a predictive counterfactual conditional transfers to the apodosis (*If I had eaten more at breakfast, [then it follows that] I would not be starving now*). Pragmatic counterfactuality transfer

---

[32] For the indirect directive effects of the wish optative and its different interactive functions, see la Roi (2020: 224–229).
[33] Cf. also the usage of "the optative properly used" in purpose clauses when dependent on a present indicative (Goodwin 1889: 115).

may take place in asymmetrical counterfactual mood contexts in Archaic Greek due to the fact that the counterfactual optative was still around but is being filtered out (la Roi 2022a). The transfer of counterfactual implicature is confirmed by the scope of negation in such sentences as it targets the polarity reversal brought about by counterfactuality. Pragmatic counterfactuality transfer also sets itself apart from constructions likened to them in the past (e.g. *tí ou(k)* 'why not' + past interrogative), as in that construction the counterfactual implicature is merely implied pragmatically whereas the counterfactuality of markers in the matrix clauses of pragmatic counterfactuality transfer is conventionalized. Similarly, non-counterfactual "mood attraction" cannot sufficiently explain the distribution of moods in symmetrical and asymmetrical contexts because mood usage in subordinate clauses is both semantically conditioned (i.e. mood meaning in context) and pragmatically conditioned by the meaning of the matrix clause. Finally, from the perspective of the language system of Ancient Greek, this pragmatic re-evaluation of non-counterfactual mood attraction makes more sense, because the so-called oblique optative is also not obligatory and has its own distinct force in asymmetrical morphosyntactic contexts.

Greek texts

Biles, Zachary P. & S. Douglas Olson. 2015. *Aristophanes: Wasps*. Oxford: Oxford University Press.
Olson, S. Douglas. 1998. *Peace*. Oxford: Clarendon Press.

References

Allan, Rutger J. 2013. Exploring modality's semantic space: Grammaticalization, subjectification and the case of ὀφείλω [*opheílō*]. *Glotta* 89. 1–46.
Amigues, Suzanne 1977. *Les subordonnées finales par ὅπως [hópōs] en attique classique*. Paris: Klincksieck.
Crespo, Emilio, Luz Conti & Helena Maquieira. 2003. *Sintaxis del griego clásico*. Madrid: Gredos.
Dancygier, Barbara. 2006. *Conditionals and prediction: Time, knowledge, and causation in conditional constructions*. Cambridge: Cambridge University Press.
Declerck, Renaat & Susan Reed. 2001. *Conditionals: A comprehensive empirical analysis*. Berlin & New York: Mouton de Gruyter.
Duhoux, Yves. 1992. *Le verbe grec ancien: Éléments de morphologie et de syntaxe historiques*. Louvain-la-Neuve: Peeters.
van Emde Boas, Evert, Albert Rijksbaron, Luuk Huitink & Mathieu De Bakker. 2019. *Cambridge grammar of Classical Greek*. Cambridge: Cambridge University Press.
Faure, Richard. 2014. The oblique optative, a case of narrative tense. The example of the future optative. In Annamaria Bartolotta (ed.), *The Greek verb. Morphology, syntax, semantics. Proceedings*

of the 8th International Meeting of Greek Linguistics (Agrigento, October 1–2, 2009), 131–148. Louvain-la-Neuve: Peeters.

Goodwin, William W. 1889. *Syntax of the moods and tenses of the Greek verb*. New York: Macmillan & Co.

Haspelmath, Martin. 1997. *Indefinite pronouns*. Oxford: Clarendon Press.

Kühner, Raphael & Bernard Gerth. 1898. *Ausführliche Grammatik der griechischen Sprache. Zweiter Teil: Satzlehre. Erster Band*. Hannover: Hahnsche Buchhandlung.

Lillo, Antonio. 2017. Subjunctive and optative in Herodotus' purpose clauses as relative tense markers. In Klaas Bentein, Mark Janse & Jorie Soltic (eds.), *Variation and change in Ancient Greek tense, aspect and modality*, 9–21. Leiden & Boston: Brill.

Méndez Dosuna, Julián V. 1999. La valeur de l'optatif oblique grec: Un regard fonctionnel-typologique. In Bernard Jacquinod (ed.), *Les complétives en grec ancien. Actes du colloque international de Saint-Étienne (3–5 septembre 1998)*, 331–352. Saint-Étienne: Publication de l'Université de Saint-Étienne.

Monro, David B. 1891. *A grammar of the Homeric dialect*. Oxford: Clarendon Press.

Napoli, Maria. 2014. Attraction (Mood, Case etc.). In Georgios Giannakis, Vit Bubenik, Emilio Crespo, Chris Golston, Alexandra Lianeri, Silvia Luraghi & Stephanos Matthaios (eds.), *Encyclopedia of Ancient Greek Language and Linguistics*, vol. 1, 208–215. Leiden & Boston: Brill.

Nijk, Arjan A. 2021. The 'polite' aorist: Tense or aspect? *The Classical Quarterly* 71(2). 1–18.

Noonan, Michael. 1985. Complementation. In Timothy Shopen (ed.), *Language typology and syntactic description 2*, 42–140. Cambridge: Cambridge University Press.

Revuelta Puigdollers, Antonio R. 2017. Ὤφελ(λ)ον [*óphel(l)on*] in Ancient Greek counterfactual desiderative sentences: From verb to modal particle. In Klaas Bentein, Mark Janse & Jorie Soltic (eds.), *Variation and change in Ancient Greek tense, aspect and modality*, 158–188. Leiden & Boston: Brill.

la Roi, Ezra. 2019. Epistemic modality, particles and the potential optative in Classical Greek. *Journal of Greek Linguistics* 19(1). 58–89.

la Roi, Ezra. 2020. The variation of Classical Greek wishes: A Functional Discourse Grammar and Common Ground approach. *Glotta* 96(1). 213–245.

la Roi, Ezra. 2021. The insubordination of *if*- and *that*-clauses from Archaic to Post-Classical Greek: A diachronic constructional typology. *Symbolae Osloenses* 95. 2–64. https://doi.org/10.1080/00397679.2021.1951005

la Roi, Ezra. 2022a. Interlocked life-cycles of counterfactual mood from Archaic to Classical Greek: Between aspect and changing temporal reference. *Indogermanische Forschungen* 127. 235–282.

la Roi, Ezra. 2022b. Down the paths to the past habitual: Its historical connections with counterfactual pasts, future in the pasts, iteratives and lexical sources in Ancient Greek. *Folia Linguistica Historica*. Published online 24.10.2022: https://doi.org/10.1515/flin-2022-2042

la Roi, Ezra. 2022c. Towards a chronology of the modal particles: The diachronic spread in the Ancient Greek mood system. *Graeco-Latina Brunensia* 27(2). 113–135.

la Roi, Ezra. 2023. Polarity reversal constructions and counterfactuals in Ancient Greek: Between implicature and conventionalization. *Journal of Historical Linguistics*. Published online 30.03.2023: https://doi.org/10.1075/jhl.22048.lar

la Roi, Ezra. forthc. The pragmatics of the past: A novel typology of conditionals with past tenses in Ancient Greek. *Listy Filologické* 145(3/4).

Ruiz Yamuza, Emilia. 2021. Past tenses of modal verbs: ἔδει [*édei*] and (ἐ)χρῆν [*(e)khrên*] in Attic tragedy and comedy. In Georgios K. Giannakis, Luz Conti, Jesús de la Villa & Raquel Fornieles (eds.), *Synchrony and diachrony of Ancient Greek*, 279–290. Berlin & Boston: De Gruyter.
Schmidtke-Bode, Karsten. 2009. *A typology of purpose clauses*. Amsterdam: Benjamins.
Smyth, Herbert W. & Gordon M. Messing. 1968. *A Greek grammar*. Cambridge, Mass.: Harvard University Press.
Wakker, Gerry C. 1994. *Conditions and conditionals: An investigation of Ancient Greek*. Amsterdam: Gieben.

Antonio R. Revuelta Puigdollers

9 Mood, modality and speech acts in clause combination. The case of conditionals

Abstract: This article discusses (i) mood, modality and speech acts formulated by conditional periods, (ii) how their features differ from those of their constituent clauses (main and subordinate) and (iii) the differences between the indirect speech acts they formulate and those conveyed by direct sentence types.

Keywords: Conditionals, mood, modality, speech act, oath, directive, assertion, wish, commissive

1 Contents

The study of mood, modality and speech acts in Ancient Greek is generally confined to the study of these categories in main and subordinate clauses. This paper focuses on indirect speech acts formulated by conditional periods and investigates how their properties deviate from those of their constituents (main and subordinate clause). In the following example, the main clause (1a) is an epistemic (modality) assertion (speech act) formulated by a declarative (sentence type)[1] in indicative (mood), whereas the whole conditional period (1b) formulates a directive speech act (deontic):

(1)   a. If you don't obey, I will kill you.
        b. > Obey me.

Acknowledgments: This paper has been written within research projects "Preverbiación en griego antiguo y moderno" (FFI2015-69749-P) and "Corpora y preverbiación en griego" (PGC2018-096171-B-C22) funded by the Spanish Ministry of Economy and Competitiveness and the Ministry of Science, Innovation and Universities.

---

[1] I am referring to declarative, imperative, interrogative and exclamative sentences, that is, simple sentences with a certain grammatical form that convey a prototypical illocutionary force (Aikhenvald 2016; Panther and Köpcke 2008).

Antonio R. Revuelta Puigdollers, Autonomous University of Madrid, e-mail: antonio.revuelta@uam.es

https://doi.org/10.1515/9783110778380-009

Some of these special 'meanings' of conditionals are mentioned in grammars and monographs (e.g. Wakker 1994: 193–195; Revuelta 2020a, b), but there is no comprehensive study on the subject. In this paper, I discuss several aspects of this phenomenon:
a) Section 2 is devoted to establishing a classification and description of conditional periods formulating oaths and directives (speech acts).
b) Section 3 describes the features of the main and subordinate clause playing a relevant role in that typology.
c) Section 4 provides some linguistic clues supporting the classification.
d) The final Section discusses the differences between these conditional periods (1a) and more prototypical direct speech acts (1b).

Although additional material has been added from the TLG and Sommerstein's project on Greek oaths,[2] the corpus consists of the following authors (complete works): Aeschylus, Aristophanes, Demosthenes, Euripides, Herodotus, Lysias, Plato, Sophocles, and Xenophon.

2 Classification of conditional periods

Although there are other possible meanings, this paper presents a description of conditional periods used for formulating oaths and directives.

2.1 Oaths

Oaths are speech acts by which the speaker commits themselves to the truth either of their own words (oaths that something is true in the past, present, or future) or of their future course of action (oaths to do something).[3] The following two Sections discuss both possibilities and their formulation through conditional periods.[4]

---

[2] https://www.nottingham.ac.uk/~brzoaths/index.php (last accessed February 2023).
[3] See Searle & Vanderveken (1985: 188).
[4] See Wakker's (1994: 189–190) 'Pseudo-self-damnation'.

2.1.1 Assertive oaths: Oaths that something is true

Despite some apparent differences, the two following conditional periods are both used to vehemently deny the truth of the proposition conveyed by the subordinate clause:[5]

(2) ἐπεὶ ἄθεος ἄφιλος ὅ τι πύματον / **ὀλοίμαν**, <u>φρόνησιν εἰ τάνδ' ἔχω</u>. (S. *OT* 661–662)
    *epei   átheos   áphilos   hóti   púmaton   **oloíman**,*
    when   unblest.NOM   unbefriended.NOM   what   worst   die.1SG.OPT
    phrónēsin   ei   tánd'   ékhō
    thought.ACC if   this.ACC have.1SG.IND.PRS
    'Unblest, unbefriended, **may I die** the worst possible death if I have this thought!'
    a. May I die the worst possible death **if I have this thought**.
    b. > **I don't have this thought**, I swear.

(3) [ΟΙ. ξύμφημι· δρῶντα γάρ νιν, ὦ γύναι, κακῶς / εἴληφα τοὐμὸν σῶμα σὺν τέχνῃ κακῇ. / ΚΡ. Μὴ νῦν ὀναίμην, ἀλλ'] ἀραῖος, <u>εἴ σέ τι / δέδρακ'</u>, **ὀλοίμην**, ὧν ἐπαιτιᾷ με δρᾶν. / [ΙΟ. ὦ πρὸς θεῶν πίστευσον, Οἰδίπους, τάδε, / μάλιστα μὲν τόνδ' ὅρκον αἰδεσθεὶς θεῶν]. (S. *OT* 642–647)
    araîos,   ei   sé   ti   dédrak',
    accursed.NOM.SG if   you.ACC.SG anything.ACC.SG do.1SG.PRF
    ***oloímēn**   hôn   epaitiâi   me   drân*
    die.1SG.OPT   REL.GEN.PL   accuse.2SG.PRS me.ACC.SG do.INF
    '[OEDIPUS. Yes indeed, for I have caught him, lady, working evil against my person with his wicked craft. CREON. **May I** derive no benefit, but] **perish** accursed, if I have done any of the things of which you charge me. [IOCASTA. In the name of the gods, believe it, Oedipus, first for the sake of this awful oath to the gods].'
    a. May I perish accursed **if I have done** any of the things you charge me.
    b. > **I have not done** any of the things you charge me, I swear.

Despite some differences the two conditional periods share some common features:

---

5 Translations have been taken from the Perseus Project (http://www.perseus.tufts.edu/hopper/) with some changes.

(i) The whole conditional period formulates an oath about the truth of the propositional content[6] of the subordinate clause, which is denied in a strong way (polarity inversion):

(4) a. May I die **if A is true / false**.
 b. > **A is not true / false**, I swear.

(ii) The subordinate clause refers to the present (present indicative, example (2)) or past (example (3)).[7]
(iii) In all cases the main clause is formally a potential or realizable (modality) wish (speech act) in optative (morphological mood) referring to the future (temporal reference). However, these features are not inherited by the resultant speech act formulated by the whole conditional period, which expresses a present (deixis of utterance) negative assertive oath (speech act) about a present, past, or future fact (temporal reference).
(iv) The State of Affairs (SoA) depicted by the main clause could be evaluated as negative for the speaker (self-curse), since it refers to the speaker's death (which is not truly desired by the speaker here). The speaker utters this as a guarantee of the truthfulness of their words.

There are also cases where the main clause formulates a self-blessing (ex. (5)) and then the whole conditional period is used to strongly assert the content of the subordinate clause (no polarity inversion):[8]

(5) [ταῦτ' ἐγὼ καὶ τότ' ἠθέλησ' ὀμόσαι, καὶ νῦν ὀμνύω τοὺς θεοὺς καὶ τὰς θεὰς ἅπαντας καὶ πάσας ὑμῶν ἕνεκ', ὦ ἄνδρες δικασταί, καὶ τῶν περιεστηκότων, ἦ μὴν παθὼν ὑπὸ Κόνωνος ταῦθ' ὧν δικάζομαι, καὶ λαβὼν πληγάς, καὶ τὸ χεῖλος διακοπεὶς οὕτως ὥστε καὶ ῥαφῆναι, καὶ ὑβρισθεὶς τὴν δίκην διώκειν.] καὶ εἰ μὲν εὐορκῶ, **πολλά μοι ἀγαθὰ γένοιτο** καὶ μηδέποτ' αὖθις **τοιοῦτο μηδὲν πάθοιμι**, εἰ δ' ἐπιορκῶ, ἐξώλης **ἀπολοίμην** αὐτὸς [καὶ εἴ τί μοι ἔστιν ἢ μέλλει ἔσεσθαι. ἀλλ' οὐκ ἐπιορκῶ]. (D. 54.41–42)
  kai   ei   men   euorkô,   pollá   moi   agatha
  and   if   PTCL swear.truly.1SG.PRS   many.NOM.PL   me.DAT   good.NOM.PL

---

6 For the sense of 'propositional content' see Searle and Vanderveken (1985: 1–8).
7 No examples with imperfect, indicative aorist or pluperfect have been found, but those with perfect refer to the present result of a past action. The future should be possible, but all future examples found are in first person and express commissive oaths.
8 For blessings see Faraone (2005).

9 Mood, modality and speech acts in clause combination. The case of conditionals

génoito kai mēdépot' aûthis toioûto mēden
happen.3SG.OPT and never again such.ACC.N nothing.ACC.N
páthoimi, ei d' epiorkô, exólēs *apoloímēn*
suffer.1SG.OPT if but forswear.1SG.PRS ruined.NOM.SG die.1SG.OPT
autos
self.NOM.SG

'[This oath I was at that time ready to take, and now, to convince you and those who stand gathered about, I swear by all the gods and goddesses that I have in very truth suffered at the hands of Conon this wrong for which I am suing him; that I was beaten by him, and that my lip was cut open so that it had to be sewn up, and that it is because of gross maltreatment that I am prosecuting him.] If I swear truly, **may** many blessings **be** mine, and **may** I never again **suffer** such an outrage; but, if I am forsworn, **may I perish** utterly, I [and all I possess or ever may possess. But I am not forsworn].'

a. **If I swear truly**, may many **blessings** be mine, and may I never again suffer such an outrage.
a'. > **I am telling the truth**, I swear.
b. But, **if I am forsworn**, may I **perish** utterly, I and all I possess or ever may possess.
b'. > **I am not forsworn**, I swear.

As the example also shows, blessings (paraphrases a–a') and curses (paraphrases b–b') may appear together encompassing all possibilities: 'If I swear truly, may many blessings be mine [...] But, if I am forsworn, may I perish utterly'.

2.1.2 Commissive oaths: Oaths to do something

The indirect interpretation of the conditional period is slightly different if the conditional refers to a future action (*if* + future / *if*-MOD + subjunctive) carried out by the speaker, as in the following example:[9]

(6) ΔΙ. **Κάκιστ' ἀπολοίμην**, <u>Ξανθίαν εἰ μὴ φιλῶ</u>. / [...] Ἀλλ' <u>ἤν σε τοῦ λοιποῦ ποτ' ἀφέλωμαι χρόνου</u>, / πρόρριζος αὐτός, ἡ γυνή, τὰ παιδία, / **κάκιστ' ἀπολοίμην** [...]. / [ΞΑ. Δέχομαι τὸν ὅρκον κἀπὶ τούτοις λαμβάνω]. (Ar. *Ra.* 579–589)
Kákist' apoloímēn, Xanthían ei mē philô [...] All' én
worst die.1SG.OPT Xanthias.ACC if NEG love.1SG.PRS but if.MOD

---
9 See Searle and Vanderveken's (1985: 194) *swear₂*.

se	*toû*	*loipoû*		*pot'*	*aphélōmai*	*khrónou,*
you.ACC	ART.GEN	remaining.GEN		ever	deprive.1SG.MED.SBJV	time.GEN
prórrizos	*autós,*	*hē*	*guné,*	*ta*		*paidía,*
complete.NOM	self.NOM	ART.NOM	wife.NOM	ART.NOM		children.NOM
kákist'	***apoloímēn***					
worst.ACC	die.1SG.OPT					

'DIONYSUS. **May I die**, Xanthias, if I do not love you. [...] But if I ever take anything from you in time to come, may I be cut off root and branch! **May I myself, my wife, my children perish,** [...], all together! [XANTHIAS. I accept the oath, and on these terms I'll take them].'

a. **If I ever take** anything from you, may I myself, my wife, my children perish.
b. > **I won't ever take** anything from you, I swear.

In example (6), Dionysus utters two different oaths. In the first one (assertive oath) he strongly states that he loves Xanthias ('May I die, Xanthias, if I do not love you'), but in the second one (commissive oath) he swears not to do something in the future ('If I ever take anything from you in time to come, may I myself, my wife, my children perish, [...], all together!'). The only difference between these two oaths is that in the latter case, the conditional clause refers to a future state of affairs whose agent is the speaker and not to a past, present of future possible fact.

Up to this point, I have discussed full conditional periods. However, it is worth noting that in many cases the conditional clause may be elliptic, but can be elicited from the context, as in this passage from Aristophanes' *Lysistrata*:[10]

(7) [ΚΙ. Τὰ τῆς Ἀφροδίτης ἱέρ' ἀνοργίαστά σοι / χρόνον τοσοῦτόν ἐστιν. Οὐ βαδιεῖ πάλιν; / ΜΥ. Μὰ Δί' οὐκ ἔγωγ', ἢν μὴ διαλλαχθῆτέ γε / καὶ τοῦ πολέμου παύσησθε. ΚΙ. Τοιγάρ, ἢν δοκῇ, / ποήσομεν καὶ ταῦτα. ΜΥ. Τοιγάρ, ἢν δοκῇ, / κἄγωγ' ἄπειμ' ἐκεῖσε· νῦν δ' ἀπομώμοκα. / [...] ΜΥ. Τὸ στρόφιον ἤδη λύομαι. Μέμνησό νυν·] / μή μ' ἐξαπατήσῃς τὰ περὶ τῶν διαλλαγῶν. / ΚΙ. **Νὴ Δί' ἀπολοίμην**. (Ar. *Lys.* 898–903, 931–935)

mḗ	*m'*	*exapatḗseis*	*ta*	*peri*	*tôn*	*diallagôn*
NEG	me.ACC	deceive.2SG.SBJV	ART.ACC	about	ART.GEN	treaty.GEN.PL

---

10 The "condition" may be elliptic (example 7) or expressed by participles (example 26) or temporal clauses (see la Roi 2020: 223 fn. 25, 26).

Nē   Dí'   apoloímēn
yes.by   Zeus.ACC die.1SG.OPT
'[CINESIAS. The sacred rites of wedded love have been so long neglected. Won't you come? MYRRHINE. Not unless you make a treaty and stop the war. CINESIAS. If you must have it, then we'll get it done. MYRRHINE. Do it and I'll come home. Till then I am bound. [...] MYRRHINE. I'm loosening my girdle now. Remember:] don't deceive me about the Treaty. CINESIAS. No, by Zeus, **may I die**.' (i.e. if I deceive you)

Myrrhine and the other Greek women have stopped any sexual contact with their husbands until they put an end to the war by signing a treaty. Cinesias promises Myrrhine to do so ('We'll get it done'), but she does not believe him ('Don't deceive me about the treaty') and he dispels her doubts with a commissive oath ('By Zeus, may I die, [if I deceive you / I don't do so]').

In other cases, the conditional period reinforces a threat (see the hearer's reaction 'he diverts me with his threats'). A threat consists of a statement by which the speaker commits himself to harm the hearer in the future ('I'm going to destroy you'). Its inclusion in this conditional period turns it into an oath, thus increasing the degree of strength of its illocutionary force ('May my name be lost, if I am not going to destroy you' > 'I am going to destroy you, I swear'):

(8) ΠΑ. Εἰ μή σ' ἀπολέσαιμ', εἴ τι τῶν αὐτῶν ἐμοὶ / ψευδῶν ἐνείη, **διαπέσοιμι** πανταχῇ. [ΑΛ. Ἥσθην ἀπειλαῖς]. (Ar. *Eq.* 694–695)
ei   mḗ   s'   apolésaim',   ei   ti   tôn   autôn
if   NEG   you.ACC kill.1SG.OPT if   something.NOM   ART.GEN   same.GEN
emoi   pseudôn   eneíē,   **diapésoimi**   pantakhêi
me.DAT   lie.GEN.PL   be.in.3SG.OPT crumble.in.pieces.1SG.OPT   everywhere
'CLEON. If I don't destroy you, if some of my own lies are in me, **may I perish**. [SAUSAGE-SELLER. Oh! how he diverts me with his threats!]'

a. May I perish **if I am not going to destroy you**.
b. > **I am going to destroy you**, I swear.

There is an additional possibility: a self-blessing ('May I live a long life') could be used by the speaker to show their commitment about a future course of action (either positive or negative). This construction exhibits no polarity inversion, as the English and Greek examples show:[11]

---

[11] This example was pointed out to me by Ezra la Roi.

(9) a. May I live a long life **if I do A**.
    b. > **I will do A**, I swear.

(10) a. May I live a long life **if I don't do A**.
     b. > **I won't do A**, I swear.

(11) [ὡς ἓν γ' ἀκούσασ' ἴσθι, μὴ ψευδῶς μ' ἐρεῖν· / ψευδῆ λέγων δὲ καὶ μάτην ἐγκερτομῶν, / θάνοιμι·] **μὴ θάνοιμι** δ', ἢν σώσω κόρην. (E. *IA* 1005–1007)
    mḗ **thánoimi** d'   ēn   sṓisō   kórēn
    NEG die.1SG.OPT PTCL if.MOD save.1SG.SBJV girl.ACC.SG
    '[Be assured that you have heard this: I shall never speak falsely. If I ever lie or deceive anyone, may I die!] But may I live if I save your daughter!'

    a. May I live (= not die) **if I save your daughter**.
    b. > **I will save your daughter**, I swear.

Summarizing this section, we can say that conditional periods ('May I [...], if A') containing self-curses ('May I die') and self-blessings ('May I live a long life') are used by the speaker to formulate oaths about the truth or falseness of the content conveyed by the conditional clause. If the conditional clause refers to a possible fact located in the past, present or future ('If A is true'), the whole conditional period formulates a strong denial (self-curses) or assertion (self-blessings) of that proposition (assertive oaths). However, when the conditional clause refers to a future action carried out by the speaker themselves ('If I do A'), the conditional period formulates the speaker's strong refusal (self-curse) or commitment (self-blessing) to do something (commisive oaths).[12] The following flowchart (see Figure 1) represents the four main possibilities and the properties of both the main and subordinate clauses and the whole conditional period:[13]

---

12 In this second case ('If I do A'), if the SoA depicted by the subordinate is negative for the hearer's interest and the agent is the speaker, the oath refers to a threat ('May I die if I don't kill you' > 'I kill you, I swear'). I do not include this and other subtypes in the flowchart so as to keep things as simple as possible.

13 For the use of such algorithms and flowcharts, see López-Rousseau and Ketelaar (2004, 2006) and López-Rousseau, Diesendruck and Benozio (2011).

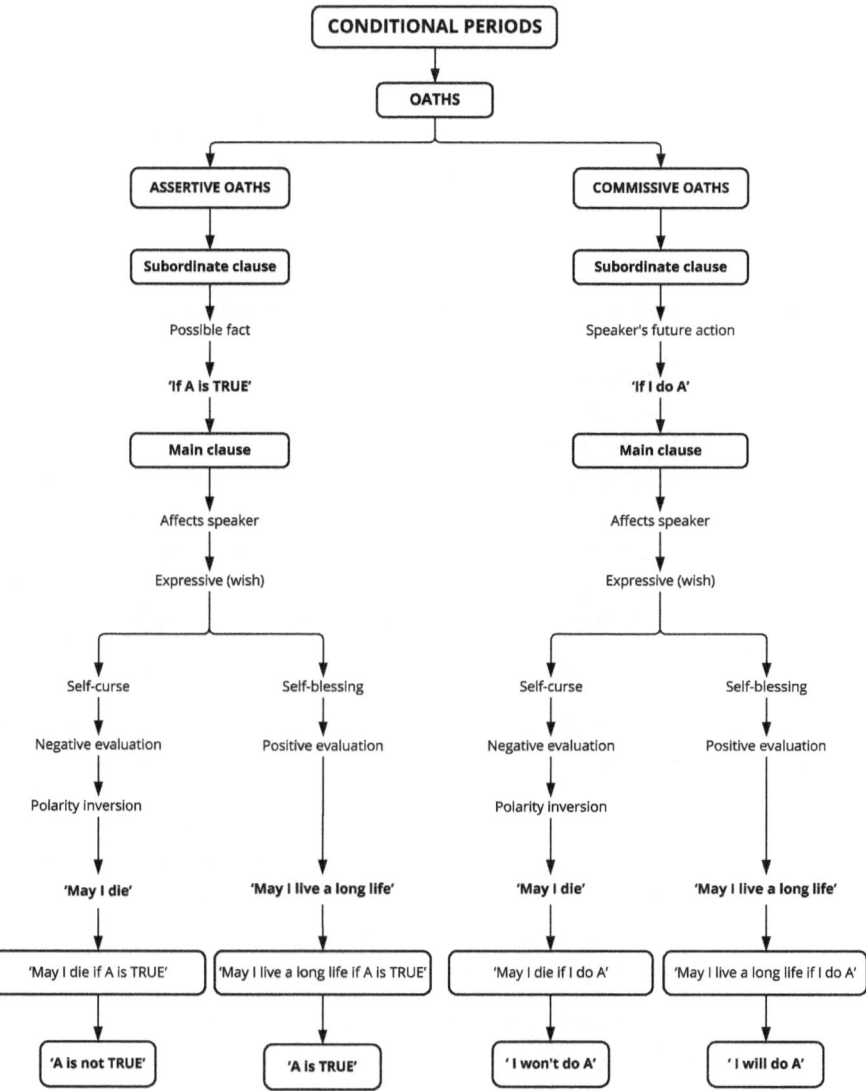

Figure 1: Conditional periods formulating oaths.

2.2 Directives

A second group of conditional periods is used to formulate directives (e.g. 'If you don't stop speaking, I will kill you' > 'Stop speaking').[14] The following subsections classify the whole conditional periods according to the typology of their main clauses.

2.2.1 Desiderative clauses: Speaker's curses or blessings (expressives)

The following example depicts a conditional period that is almost identical from a purely morphosyntactic point of view to those of the second group in Section 2.1.2 (commissive oaths to do something): the main clause constitutes a wish (speech act) in optative (morphological mood) expressing a possible fact (modality) and the subordinate refers to a future (time reference) event in the optative (morphological mood) expressing a possible (modality) future (time reference) fact. However, the whole conditional period formulates a different speech act: a directive and not a strong assertion (oath). In this passage Hierocles is speaking about Bacis, and Trygaeus tries to stop him.

(12) [ΙΕ. Εἰ γὰρ μὴ νύμφαι γε θεαὶ Βάκιν ἐξαπάτασκον, / μηδὲ Βάκις θνητούς, μηδ' αὖ νύμφαι Βάκιν αὐτὸν] / ΤΡ. Ἐξώλης **ἀπόλοι'**, <u>εἰ μὴ παύσαιο βακίζων</u>. (Ar. *Pax* 1070–1072)
exṓlēs   **apóloi'**,   ei   mē   paúsaio   bakízōn
ruined.NOM.SG die.2SG.OPT if NEG stop.2SG.OPT say.Bacis.PTCP.NOM.SG
'[HIEROCLES. Nay, nay! if only the Nymphs had not fooled Bacis, and Bacis mortal men; and if the Nymphs had not tricked Bacis a second time] TRYGAEUS. May the plague seize you, if you don't stop Bacizing!'

    a. May you die **if you don't stop Bacizing**. (≈ mentioning Bacis)
    b. > **Stop Bacizing**. (*directive curse*)

However, despite this formal parallelism, there are some differences in both the main and subordinate clause in comparison with the previous sections ('May I die, if I don't do A') that trigger a different interpretation:
(i) The main clause depicts a curse that does not affect the speaker ('May I die'), but rather the hearer ('May you die').

---

[14] This section partially draws on Fillenbaum (1975, 1976, 1977) and Wakker (1994: 193–195).

(ii) The SoA referred to by the subordinate does not refer to a future SoA carried out by the speaker ('If I (don't) do A') or to a possible fact referring to the past, present or future ('If A has happened / happens / is going to happen'), but rather to an SoA carried out by the hearer that is detrimental to the speaker ('If you (don't) do A'). In the above example, the hearer will not stop talking about Bacis and this seems to annoy the speaker.

As a result, the whole conditional period is used by the speaker as a kind of directive curse (illocutionary point of the main clause) meant to stop the hearer's behavior (content conveyed by the subordinate clause). The speech act formulated by the whole period is equivalent to a directive with the propositional content of the subordinate clause, but with polarity inversion, as in the previous sections.

(13) a. May you die **if you don't stop talking**.
     b. > **Stop talking**! *(directive curse)*

(14) a. May you die **if you stop talking**.
     b. > **Don't stop talking**! *(directive curse)*

Theoretically, it is also possible to use blessings instead of curses to formulate a directive, but such cases have not been found in the corpus or references. The difference between curses and blessings is that main clauses containing blessings refer to SoAs that are positive to the hearer and encourage them to act in the way proposed by the subordinate. Therefore, there is no polarity inversion, as the following English examples show:

(15) a. May you have a long life **if you do A**.
     b. > **Do A**! *(directive blessing)*

(16) a. May you have a long life **if you don't do A**.
     b. > **Don't do A**! *(directive blessing)*

2.2.2 Declarative clauses: Directive threats or promises (commissives)

The class of conditional periods discussed in this section differs from the ones presented in the three previous sections from a purely syntactic point of view, since the main clause does not express a wish ('May I', 'May you'), but an assertion about the future (indicative 'I will do X'):

(17) [ΠΑ. Βλέψον εἴς μ' ἀσκαρδάμυκτος. / ΑΛ. Ἐν ἀγορᾷ κἀγὼ τέθραμμαι.] / ΠΑ. **Διαφορήσω σ'**, εἴ τι γρύξεις. / ΑΛ. **Κοπροφορήσω σ'**, εἰ λαλήσεις. / [ΠΑ. Ὁμολογῶ κλέπτειν· σὺ δ' οὐχί]. (Ar. *Eq.* 292–296)

diaphorḗsō   s',   eí   ti   grúxeis.
tear.in.pieces.1SG.FUT you.ACC if something.ACC.SG murmur.2SG.FUT
koprophorḗsō   s',   ei   laléseis
cover.with.dung.1SG.FUT you.ACC if speak.2SG.FUT

'[CLEON. Dare to look me in the face! SAUSAGE-SELLER. I too was brought up in the market-place.] CLEON. **I will cut** you to shreds if you whisper a word. SAUSAGE-SELLER. If you open your mouth, **I'll shut** it with shit. [CLEON. I admit I'm a thief; that's more than you do].'

a. **If you open your mouth**, I'll shut it with shit.
a'. > **Don't open your mouth.** *(directive threat)*
b. I will cut you to shreds, **if you whisper a word**.
b'. > **Don't whisper a word.** *(directive threat)*

However, despite the formal differences this period resembles the one discussed in the previous subsection since it also formulates a kind of directive. The common features between both structures are the following:

(i) Like the structure in the previous section, the possible SoA referred to by the main clause ('I'll shut it [i.e. your mouth] with shit') is detrimental to the hearer, who is supposed to be eager to avoid it.
(ii) The subordinate clause ('If you open your mouth') refers to (a) a future SoA whose agent or controller is the hearer and (b) which is supposed to be undesirable to the speaker (the speaker wants the hearer to stop talking).

However, unlike directives in the previous section, in this case the speaker does not use a curse ('May you die if you do A'), but a threat ('I'll shut it with shit if you do A') in order to stop the hearer's course of action. As in the previous sections, the directive formulated by the whole conditional period is equivalent to the propositional content of the subordinate clause with negative polarity inversion.

(18) a. I will kill you **if you do A**.
b. > **Don't do A.** *(directive threat)*

(19) a. I will kill you **if you don't do A**.[15]
b. > **Do A.** *(directive threat)*

---

[15] See Ar. *Pl.* 65 in Wakker (1994: 193, example 107).

9 Mood, modality and speech acts in clause combination. The case of conditionals — 233

As in the previous section (Section 2.2.1), if the main clause refers to a SoA that benefits the hearer ('I will reward you'), there is no polarity inversion, and the whole conditional period formulates a directive promise, as the following English and Greek examples show:[16]

(20) a. I will reward you **if you do A**.
b. > **Do A** *(directive promise)*

(21) a. I will reward you **if you don't do A**.
b. > **Don't do A**. *(directive promise)*

(22) οἶκον δέ κ' ἐγὼ καὶ κτήματα **δοίην**, / εἴ κ' ἐθέλων γε μένοις. (*Od.* 7.314–315)[17]
oîkon   dé   k'   egṓ   kai   ktḗmata   **doíēn**,
house.ACC.SG and MOD I.NOM and   property.ACC.PL give.1SG.OPT
eí   k'   ethélōn   ge   ménois
if   MOD   want.PTCP.NOM.SG   PTCL   remain.2SG.OPT
'A house and possessions **would I give** thee, if thou shouldst choose to remain.'

a. I would give you house and possessions **if you chose to remain**.
b. > **Do choose to remain**. *(directive promise)*

2.2.3 Declarative clauses: Directive predictions (assertions): warnings and advice

The same sentence type (declarative) discussed in the previous section can be used to formulate a partially different kind of directives as the one exemplified in the following passage:

(23) ["καὶ πᾶς ὁ ναυτικὸς τῷ πεζῷ ἀρήξει καὶ ὁ πεζὸς τῷ ναυτικῷ ὁμοῦ πορευόμενος·] εἰ δὲ διασπάσεις, οὔτε σὺ **ἔσεαι** ἐκείνοισι χρήσιμος οὔτε ἐκεῖνοι σοί. [...]" ["Ἀχαίμενες, εὖ τε μοι δοκέεις λέγειν καὶ ποιήσω ταῦτα"].
(Hdt. 7.236.8–16)
ei   de   diaspáseis,   oúte   su   **éseai**   ekeínoisi
if   PTCL   separate.2SG.FUT   nor   you.NOM.SG be.2SG.FUT   they.DAT.PL

---

16 See *Od.* 7.314–315 in Wakker (1994: 194, example 111).
17 The optative mood combined with the modal particle ἄν / *án* conveys a possibility meaning in declarative clauses.

	khrḗsimos	*oúte*	*ekeînoi*	*soí*
	useful.NOM.SG	nor	they.NOM.PL	you.DAT.SG

'["All your navy will be a help to your army and your army to your navy, both moving together.] If you separate some of your fleet from yourself, **you will be** of no use to them, nor they to you". ["Achaemenes, I think that you speak well, and I will do so"].'

   a. **If you separate** some of your fleet from yourself, you will be of no use to them, nor they to you.
   b. > **Don't separate** any of your fleet from yourself. (*warning*)

The conditional period exhibits a declarative (as in Section 2.2.2) and not a desiderative main clause (as in Section 2.2.1), but differs from the two previous directive types in two ways:

(i) The speaker does not control either indirectly (curse, 'May you die, if you do A' > 'Don't do A') or directly (threat, 'I will kill you, if you do A' > 'Don't do A') the SoA depicted in the main clause. Rather, the SoA is simply a possible negative consequence of the hearer's own actions depicted by the subordinate ('Something bad will happen to you, if you do A' > 'Don't do A'). The declarative sentence formulates a prediction (assertive speech act).[18]

(ii) The speaker does not seem to have any personal interest[19] in the hearer's choice and does not intend to influence them in any sense: the speaker just states the consequences of the hearer's own actions.

The whole conditional period formulates a warning. As in previous sections, there is polarity inversion, since the SoA depicted by the subordinate has negative consequences for the hearer:

(24) a. Something bad will happen to you **if you do A**.
     b. > **Don't do A**. (*warning*)

(25) a. Something bad will happen to you **if you don't do A**.
     b. > **Do A**. (*warning*)

---

[18] Searle and Vanderveken (1985: 186).
[19] For this distinction see Risselada (1993: 34, 47–48) and Haverkate (1979: 31–34).

However, the same combination of features in main and subordinate clause can be used to achieve the opposite effect if the main clause expresses a SoA that is positive for the hearer: a piece of advice encouraging them to act in a certain way.[20]

(26) [οἱ Θηβαῖοι κατελάμβανον τὸν Μαρδόνιον καὶ συνεβούλευον αὐτῷ λέγοντες ὡς [...] (*advices for Mardonios*) [...] "εἰ δὲ ποιήσεις τὰ ἡμεῖς παραινέομεν," ἔφασαν λέγοντες, "**ἕξεις** ἀπόνως πάντα τὰ ἐκείνων ἰσχυρὰ βουλεύματα. [πέμπε χρήματα ἐς τοὺς δυναστεύοντας ἄνδρας ἐν τῇσι πόλισι, πέμπων δὲ τὴν Ἑλλάδα διαστήσεις· ἐνθεῦτεν δὲ τοὺς μὴ τὰ σὰ φρονέοντας ῥηιδίως μετὰ τῶν στασιωτέων καταστρέψεαι." οἱ μὲν ταῦτα συνεβούλευον, ὁ δὲ οὐκ ἐπείθετο]. (Hdt. 9.2.2–3.3)

ei   de   poiḗseis   ta   hēmeîs   parainéomen,
if   PTCL do.2SG.FUT what.REL.ACC.PL we.NOM advise.1PL.PRS
*éphasan   légontes,   **héxeis**   apónōs   pánta*
say.3PL.IMPF say.PTCP.NOM.PL have.2SG.FUT easily   all.ACC.PL
ta   ekeínōn   iskhura   bouleúmata
ART.ACC.PL   DEM.GEN.PL strong.ACC.PL plan.ACC.PL

'[The Thebans attempted to stay Mardonius, advising him that [...] (*advices for Mardonios*) [...] "But if you do as we advise," said the Thebans, "you will without trouble be master of all their battle plans. [Send money to the men who have power in their cities, and thereby you will divide Hellas against itself; after that, with your partisans to aid you, you will easily subdue those who are your adversaries." Such was their advice, but he would not follow it].'

a. **If you do as we advise**, you will without trouble be master of all their battle plans.
b. > **Do as we advise.** *(advice)*

The following examples provide some prototypical cases:

(27) a. Something good will happen to you **if you do A**.
b. > **Do A.** *(advice)*

(28) a. Something good will happen to you **if you don't do A**.
b. > **Don't do A.** *(advice)*

---

[20] See example (109) in Wakker (1994: 194).

2.2.4 Declarative clauses: Directive pleas

Conditional periods with declarative main clauses in indicative can be used to formulate a fourth type of directives that could be labeled as pleas,[21] as this passage exemplifies:

(29) TP. Οὐ σιωπήσεσθ', [ὅπως μὴ περιχαρεῖς τῷ πράγματι / τὸν Πόλεμον ἐκζωπυρήσετ' ἔνδοθεν κεκραγότες; / [...] XO. Οὔτι καὶ νῦν ἔστιν αὐτὴν ὅστις ἐξαιρήσεται, / ἢν ἅπαξ εἰς χεῖρας ἔλθῃ τὰς ἐμάς. Ἰοῦ ἰοῦ.] / TP. **Ἐξολεῖτέ μ'**, ὦνδρες, <u>εἰ μὴ τῆς βοῆς ἀνήσετε</u>· [ἐκδραμὼν γὰρ πάντα ταυτὶ συνταράξει τοῖν ποδοῖν]. (Ar. *Pax.* 309–319)

ou	siōpḗsesth' [...] ?	exoleîté	m'	ôndres	ei	mḕ
NEG	keep.quiet.2PL.FUT	kill.2PL.FUT	me.ACC.SG	INTJ:men.VOC	if	NEG
tês	boês	anḗsete				
ART.GEN.SG	shout.GEN.SG	subdue.2PL.FUT				

'TRYGAEUS. Won't you keep quiet? [If War should hear your shouts of joy, he would bound forth from his retreat in fury. [...] CHORUS-LEADER. Once we have hold of her, none in the world will be able to take her from us. Hurrah! hurrah!] TRYGAEUS. **You will work my death** if you don't subdue your shouts. [War will come running out and trample everything beneath his feet].'

  a. Won't you keep quiet [...] You will work my death **if you don't subdue your shouts**. (= keep quiet)
  b. > **Subdue your shouts**. (= keep quiet) *(plea)*

Once more the whole period formulates a directive whose propositional content is the one expressed by the subordinate clause ('If you don't subdue your shouts') with negative polarity inversion ('Subdue your shouts'). The main clause provides the reason for the hearer to obey the speaker, but it does not refer to a curse affecting the hearer ('May you die, if you do A'), a threat issued by the speaker ('If you do A, I will kill you'), nor a negative consequence of the hearer's own actions ('If you do A, you will suffer a disgrace'). What it does refer to is a possible damage inflicted on the speaker by the hearer ('If you do A, you will kill me / I will die' > 'Don't do A, I beg you'). The speaker is requesting that the hearer reverses a course of action which is damaging to them, the speaker. Therefore, the differences between this directive speech act and all those discussed in the previous sections is (i) that in the main clause the speaker is the person suffering the negative consequences of the

---

21 See Risselada (1993: 3–10).

hearer's actions (and not the other way round) and (ii) that the hearer is therefore the agent ('You will kill me' / 'I will die because of you'). This is exactly the opposite situation to the one referred to in the previous sections, where the hearer was the person affected. The speaker has no power over the hearer to change their course of action. Instead, the speaker counts on the hearer's good will, compassion, or pity, or just complains and protests. The following English examples illustrate the pattern:

(30) a. You will kill me **if you do A**.
 b. > **Don't do A**, please / I beg.

(31) a. You will kill me **if you don't do A**.
 b. > **Do A**, please / I beg.

Theoretically a situation where the hearer benefits the speaker with their actions could be possible, but no examples have been found. In this case there would be no polarity inversion:

(32) a. You will save me **if you do A**.
 b. > **Do A**, please / I beg.

(33) a. You will save me **if you don't do A**.
 b. > **Don't do A**, please / I beg.

2.3 Directive clauses: Directive prohibitions or permissions

A third group of conditional periods presents a main clause in the imperative, as exemplified in the following passage:

(34) [ΔΙ. οὗτος, σὲ λέγω μέντοι, σὲ τὸν τεθνηκότα· / ἄνθρωπε βούλει σκευάρι' εἰς Ἅιδου φέρειν; / ΝΕ. πόσ' ἄττα; ΔΙ. ταυτί. ΝΕ. Δύο δραχμὰς μισθὸν τελεῖς; / ΔΙ. Μὰ Δί', ἀλλ' ἔλαττον. ΝΕ. Ὕπαγεθ' ὑμεῖς τῆς ὁδοῦ. / ΔΙ. Ἀνάμεινον, ὦ δαιμόνι', ἐὰν ξυμβῶ τί σοι.] / ΝΕ. Εἰ μὴ καταθήσεις δύο δραχμάς, **μὴ διαλέγου**. / [ΔΙ. Λάβ' ἐννέ' ὀβολούς. ΝΕ. Ἀναβιοίην νυν πάλιν]. (Ar. *Ra.* 173–177)
 ei mē katathḗseis dúo drakhmás, **mē dialégou**
 if NEG put.down.2SG.FUT two drachma.ACC.PL NEG talk.to.2SG.IMP

'[DIONYSUS. Hallo you there! —you, the dead man, I mean. Will you take this baggage down to Hell? CORPSE. How much is there? DIONYSUS. This here. CORPSE. Will you pay two drachmas? DIONYSUS. God no, less than that. CORPSE. Get out of the way, you! DIONYSUS. Wait, my good man, maybe we can strike a bargain.] CORPSE. If you don't put down two drachmas, **don't even talk to me**. [DIONYSUS. Come, take nine obols. CORPSE. I'd rather be alive again].'

a. **If you don't put down two drachmas**, don't even talk to me.
b. > **Put down two drachmas**. *(directive prohibition)*

In example (34) Dionysus wants to talk to the dead man, but the latter will only let him if he pays two drachmas ('If you don't put down two drachmas, don't speak to me'). The dead man's aim is not to prevent Dionysus from speaking to him: he wants the money ('Do put down two drachmas'). In fact, Dionysus understands the dead man's indirect request and pays (perlocutionary effect), although he only gives nine obols instead of two drachmas ('Take nine obols').

As in previous cases, the conditional clause ('If you don't put down two drachmas') provides the propositional content of the resultant speech act ('Do put down two drachmas'). The main clause triggers the interpretation too, but in this case it does not depict a negative or positive consequence of the hearer's own acts ('If you do A, you will win / be defeated' > 'Do / don't do A') or a threat or promise by the speaker ('If you do A, I will kill you' > 'Don't do A') nor a bad consequence for the speaker themselves ('You'll kill me, if you don't stop speaking' > 'Stop speaking'), but it has the form of an imperative sentence referring to a SoA that the hearer wants to accomplish and the speaker prohibits if their conditions are not satisfied ('If you don't put down two drachmas, don't speak to me' > 'Put down two drachmas').

The following English examples show the possibilities (the hearer is supposed to want to eat the sweets and this possibility depends on the speaker):

(35) a. Don't eat the sweets *(prohibition)* **if you do A**.
b. > **Don't do A**. *(directive prohibition)*

(36) a. Don't eat the sweets *(prohibition)* **if you don't do A**.
b. > **Do A**. *(directive prohibition)*

This type of conditional is used in contexts where the hearer wants something from the speaker (in 35–36 the hearer wants the speaker's permission to eat the sweets) and the speaker connects this to something they want to obtain from the hearer (the speaker wants the hearer to (not) do A): it is a kind of bargaining that is frequent between parents and children. Example (35) could be paraphrased this way: 'You want to eat the sweets (this possibility depends on me) and I want you to tidy up your room (this possibility depends on you). Don't eat the sweets unless (= if not) you tidy up your room'.

As in previous cases, if the main clause formulates a positive result for the hearer (e.g., if supposedly the hearer wants the speaker's permission to eat the sweets), there is no polarity inversion:

(37) a. Eat the sweets *(permission)* **if you do A.**
 b. > **Do A.** *(directive permission)*

(38) a. Eat the sweets *(permission)* **if you don't do A.**
 b. > **Don't do A.** *(directive permission)*

The diagram in Figure 2 below represents all the possibilities of the directive conditional periods.

3 Factors contributing to the resultant illocutionary force

In this section, I will discuss the properties of both the main and subordinate clause and how they contribute to the indirect speech act formulated by the whole conditional period. The minimal English pairs used in the discussion are parallel to the Greek examples presented in previous sections.

3.1 Subordinate clause: Propositional content and type of speech act

One common feature of the conditional periods under study is that the subordinate clause provides the propositional content of the indirect speech act formulated by the conditional period (with or without polarity inversion, Section 3.4) in all cases: assertive (39) and commissive (40) oaths and directives (41).

(39) a. May I die the worst possible death **if I have this thought.**
 b. > **I don't have this thought**, I swear. *(assertive oath)*

(40) a. May I die the worst possible death **if I don't help you.**
 b. > **I will help you**, I swear. *(commissive oath)*

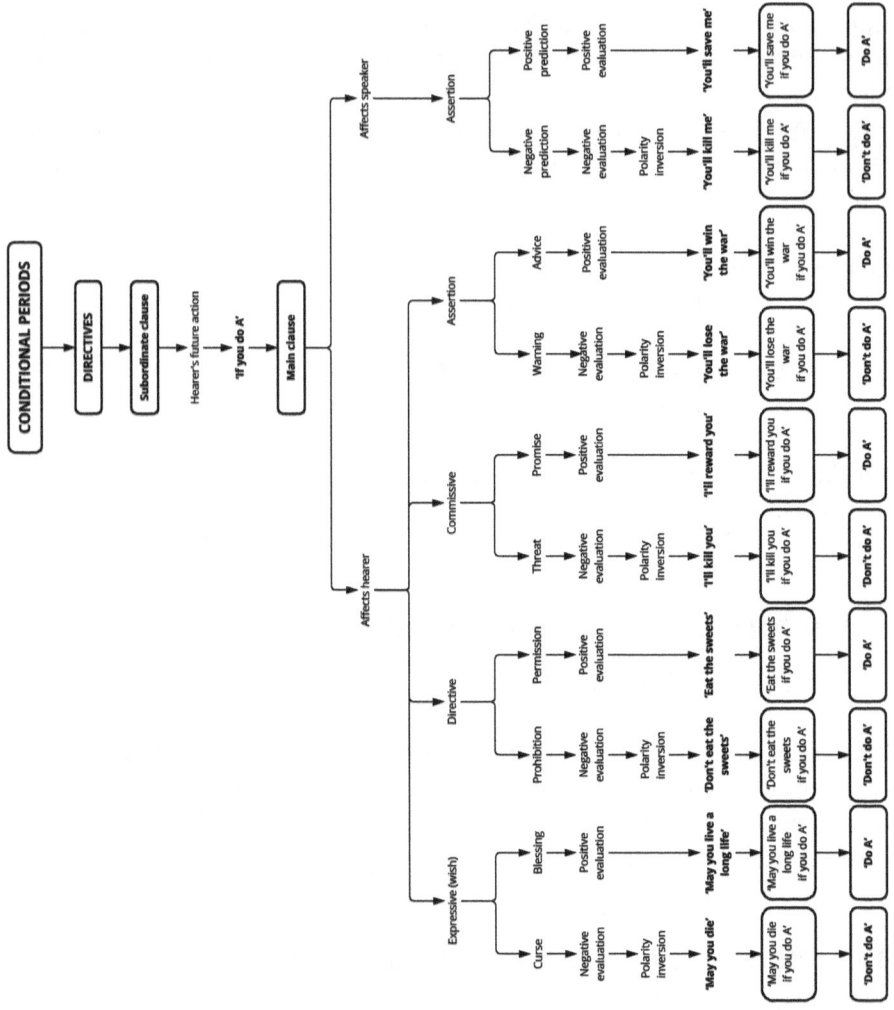

Figure 2: Conditional periods formulating directives.

(41) a. May you die **if you don't stop talking**.
b. > **Stop talking**. *(directive)*

Apart from providing the propositional content, the conditional subordinate is one of the main factors for interpreting the final speech act formulated by the whole conditional period: (i) when the subordinate refers to a possible fact in the past, present or future, conditional periods formulate assertive oaths (ex. (39)), (ii) when the subordinate describes a future action of the speaker, they formulate commissive oaths (ex. (40)) and (iii) when they describe a future action of the hearer, they formulate a directive (ex. (41)).

3.2 Mood, modality, sentence type, and speech act of the main clause

The second feature is that the illocutionary force of the whole conditional period (oath, directive and subtypes) does not exclusively depend on the mood, modality, and sentence type of the main clause, as the previous examples show. In all of them (39–41) the main clauses ('May I die', 'May you die') constitute desiderative clauses (sentence type) expressing curses or negative wishes (expressive speech acts) referring to a future possible SoA (modality) in optative mood in the Greek examples (morphological mood). However, the resultant illocutionary force of the whole conditional periods is different: the first two examples formulate an oath (speech act), whereas the third one formulates a directive (speech act).

On the other hand, conditional periods with main clauses exhibiting differences in mood, modality, sentence type and speech act, may formulate similar speech acts (directives), as in the following examples:

(42) a. **May you** die if you don't stop talking. *(main clause: desiderative wish)*
b. > **Stop** talking. *(directive curse)*

(43) a. If you open your mouth, **I'll shut** it with shit. *(main clause: assertive declarative)*
b. > **Don't open** your mouth. *(directive threat)*

(44) a. If you don't put down two drachmas, **don't speak** to me. *(main clause: directive imperative)*
b. > **Do put down** two drachmas. *(directive prohibition)*

Therefore, we cannot attribute the illocutionary force of the conditional period (oath or directive) to the modal features of the main clause: the mood, modality, sentence type and speech act of the main clause is just one of the many features contributing to the illocutionary force of the whole conditional period.

3.3 Evaluation of the main clause

The evaluation of the SoA depicted by the main clause considers if this SoA serves or harms the interests of any entity[22] and if this entity is the speaker or the addressee.

In both assertive (ex. (39)) and commissive (ex. (40)) oaths, the main clause always refers to a SoA that affects the speaker in a negative (self-curses) or positive (self-blessings) way, as in examples (45)–(46) (assertive oaths).

(45) a. May the gods **punish** me *(self-curse)* if I **helped** him.
 b. > I have **not helped** him, I swear. *(assertive oath)*

(46) a. May the gods **love** me *(self-blessing)* if I **helped** him.
 b. > I **helped** him, I swear. *(assertive oath)*

When the main clause describes a situation that negatively affects the speaker ('May the gods punish me'), it formulates a self-curse, and the speaker uses that self-curse as evidence that they are truthful when asserting that the possible fact described by the subordinate ('If I helped him') is false ('I have not helped him'). However, when the situation is positive for the speaker ('May the gods love me'), the main clause formulates a blessing, and that blessing is used as a guarantee of the truth of the propositional content of the subordinate clause ('I helped him').

By contrast, conditional periods with directive illocutionary force describe a different and more complex situation. In general, the main clause refers to a SoA that affects not the speaker, but the hearer in a negative (versions a) or positive (versions b) way (see the main clauses).

(47) a. May the gods **punish you** if you **don't** help him. > Help him. *(directive curse)*
 b. May the gods **reward you** if you help him. > Help him. *(directive blessing)*

---

22 See Wakker (1994: 195).

(48) a. I'll **kill you** if you **don't** help him. > Help him. *(directive threat)*
b. I'll **reward you** if you help him. > Help him. *(directive promise)*

(49) a. You'll **lose the war** if you **don't** help him. > Help him. *(directive warning)*
b. You'll **win the war** if you help him. > Help him. *(directive advice)*

(50) a. **Don't talk to me** ever again if you **don't** help him. > Help him. *(directive prohibition)*
b. **Talk to me** whenever you want if you help him. > Help him. *(directive permission)*

As the examples in (47–50) show, the main clause depicts situations that are detrimental (versions a) or favourable (versions b) to the hearer's interests in some way: the hearer wants to be benefitted and not punished by the gods (47), they want to be treated well by the speaker (48), they want to prevent any undesirable consequences of their own acts (49) and they want to obtain permission to fulfil their wishes (50). These negative and positive consequences of the subordinate clauses are used by the speaker to impel the hearer to, respectively, avoid (versions a) or carry out (versions b) the course of action formulated by the subordinate clauses and therefore the whole period functions as a directive speech act.

Therefore, in general conditional periods formulating oaths and directives differ in the entity affected by the SoA described by the main clause, either the speaker ('May **I** die, if A is true' > 'A is false', oath) or the hearer ('May **you** die, if you do A' > 'Don't do A', directive). However, in one case of directive conditionals, the main clause refers to the speaker's interests (either damaged or benefitted):

(51) a. You will **kill me** if you **don't** help him. *(plea)*
b. > Do help him, I beg you.

(52) a. You will **save me** if you help him. *(plea)*
b. > Do help him.

Unlike the previous directive conditional periods (47–50), in the examples (51–52) the speaker is using the effects of the hearer's behavior (main clauses) on themselves (the speaker) in order to influence the hearer. In this case the speaker is trying to provoke the hearer's compassion or is protesting against the hearer's actions in order to manipulate their behavior.

In the case of both oaths and directives, this evaluation is not an intrinsic feature of the SoA itself depicted by the main clause and can change from hearer to hearer according to the circumstances:

(53) The boat is going to sink **if you do** that again!
    a. > **Do** that again. *(the hearer wants to sink the boat)*
    b. > **Don't** do that again. *(the hearer doesn't want to sink the boat)*

The SoA 'The boat is going to sink' is not itself positive or negative: its interpretation completely depends on what the hearer considers beneficial or damaging for their own interests at a certain point of time.

3.4 Polarity inversion

As discussed before, the indirect interpretation of the conditional period is equivalent to the propositional content of the subordinate clause. However, its polarity depends on the evaluation of the main clause: if this evaluation is positive, the content is the same as in the conditional clause (either positive or negative), but if it is negative, the content undergoes polarity inversion. This feature applies both to oaths (see examples 39–40, 45–46) and directives (see examples 47–52).

3.5 Evaluation of the conditional period

Another important factor for internally distinguishing between different types of directives is the evaluation of the indirect speech act formulated by the conditional period as a whole. In both warnings and pieces of advice, the speaker has no interest in the execution of the action by the hearer (see ex. (49)): the speaker provides their opinion (frequently an expert's opinion) about the consequences of the hearer's action, but they are not personally interested in any particular course of action. In the rest of the directives, the speaker is interested in the execution of a particular SoA (see examples 47–48, 50–52).[23]

3.6 Agency

The identity of the agent in both the subordinate and the main clause is an important factor too. All the conditional periods formulating directive speech acts contain subordinate clauses whose SoA is directly or indirectly controlled by the hearer:

---

[23] See the distinction between impositive and non-impositive in Haverkate (1979: 31–34) and Risselada (1993: 4, 7, 47–49 mainly).

(54) If **you do A**, I will reward you / something good will happen to you / may the gods love you / do what you want > **Do A!**

(55) If **you do A**, I will punish you / something bad will happen to you / may the gods punish you / don't do what you want > **Don't do A!**

This is logical if we consider that the conditional clause provides the propositional content of the speech act formulated by the conditional period and that directives prototypically have as agents second persons.

If the agent of the subordinate is not the hearer, but a third person, the whole period can be understood in the same way, if that third person is supposed to be controlled by the hearer:

(56) a. **If Peter does A**, I will reward you / something good will happen to you / may the gods love you / do what you want.
    b. > **Try to influence** Peter into doing A!

(57) a. **If Peter does A**, I will punish you / something bad will happen to you / may the gods punish you / don't do what you want.
    b. > **Try to prevent** Peter from doing A!

When the second person is not the direct or indirect agent controlling the action or cannot be understood as such, but the only real agent is the third person, the directive interpretation of the conditional period is excluded.

In the case of all conditional periods formulating commissive oaths, the agent of the conditional clause is not the hearer, but the speaker. This is logical too, since the resultant commissives have as agents first persons by definition:

(58) a. May I die **if** I don't help him > I will help him.
    b. May the gods reward me **if** I help him > I will help him.

The agency of the main clause is also important to distinguish conditional periods based on threats or promises (e.g. 48) from the other directive periods (e.g. 47, 49–52). Threats and promises (see 48) happen when the speaker is able to control the SoA. Of course, the line between threats / promises and the other types of directives (for example, warnings / advice, see 49) is extremely fine and depends on context. The following examples can be understood differently depending on the person uttering it: if uttered by a mafioso, they are clearly understood as a directive threat and promise (here the subtype bribe), since the mafioso has the power to make things happen; otherwise, they are a warning and a piece of advice, respectively.

(59) a. **Something bad** will happen to you if you **don't** help me. (*directive threat / warning*)
   b. **Something good** will happen to you if you help me. (*directive promise / advice*)

All the features of the main and subordinate clauses as well as the illocutionary force of the whole conditional period appear represented in the flowchart below (see Figure 3). The resultant illocutionary force of each conditional period should be considered as the product of those features.

The dotted area reflects the algorithm for interpreting conditional periods when their main clauses are desiderative clauses (sentence type) formulating potential (modality) wishes (expressive speech act) in optative (morphological mood). As the speech acts formulated by the whole conditional period show (see the bottom of the chart), the main factor to distinguish between oaths and directives in this specific context, when the main clause expresses a wish, is the person affected by the SoA referred to by the main clause: either the speaker (oaths) or the hearer (directives). The type of subordinate allows to further distinguish between assertive oaths (conditionals referring to possible facts) and commissive oaths (conditionals referring to the speaker's future actions). If we consider all the speech acts represented in the flowchart, the main factor distinguishing between assertive oaths, commissive oaths and directives is the entity referred to by the type of subordinate clause: respectively, possible facts, speaker's future actions and hearer's future actions.

Therefore, the illocutionary force of conditional periods should be considered the result of the interaction of many formal and pragmatic features of both their main and subordinate clause. The sentence type, modality and morphological mood of the main clause are just part of these.

9 Mood, modality and speech acts in clause combination. The case of conditionals — 247

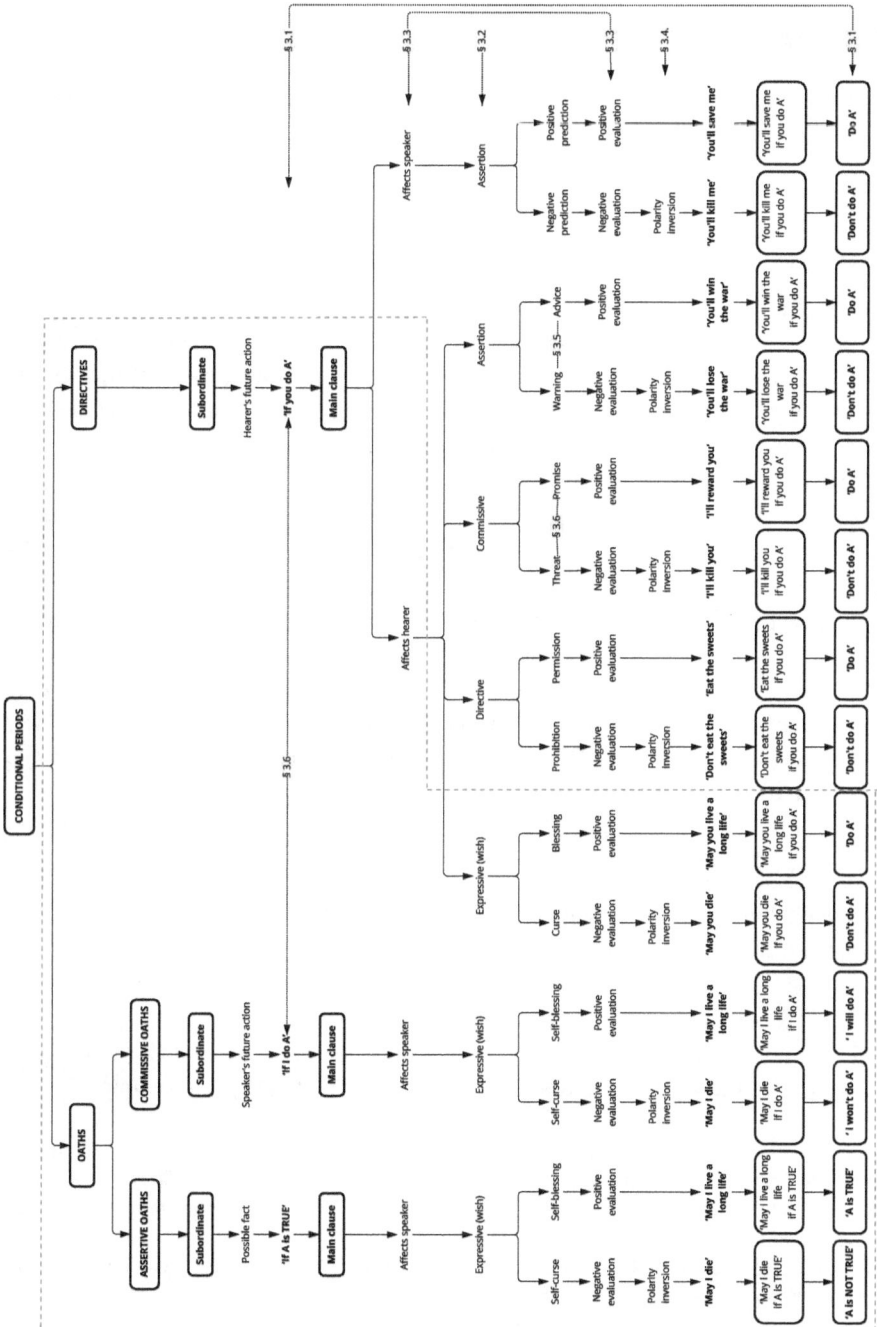

Figure 3: Relevant features in conditional periods formulating oaths and directives.

4 Linguistic clues

This section is devoted to the features of the conditional periods that can support the interpretation discussed in the previous sections.

4.1 Oaths

(i) Conditionals as penalties.
Oaths are complex speech acts[24] whereby the speaker (a) commits themselves to the truth of a proposition, (b) call upon God, another supernatural agent, a sacred person or object or revered institution, and (c) establish penalties in case of perjury. From a linguistic point of view, each of these elements can be formulated in different ways in Greek:[25]

(a) The speaker's assertion or commitment can be conveyed by a direct speech act ('A is true', 'I will do A') or it can be expressed through performatives like *ómnumi* / ὄμνυμι 'I swear' ('I swear that A is true / to do A'). In both cases, the direct speech act or the complement clause of the perfomative can be additionally preceded by the particles *ê* / ἦ or *mēn ê* / μὴν ἦ in Ancient Greek.[26]

(b) The gods or the entities the speaker takes as guarantees of the oath may optionally appear in accusative with the performative verb (*ómnumi Día* / ὄμνυμι Δία, lit. 'I swear (by) Zeus') or preceded by particles (*ma* / *nē Día*, μὰ / νὴ Δία 'by Zeus'). Those guarantors are not always explicitly mentioned.

(c) In all cases, the penalties for the speaker if they are not truthful are formulated through conditionals.

Although there are many possible combinations of these elements, the two discussed in this article are the most frequent:[27]

(60) (I swear) by the gods (that) A is true / I will do A [...]
    a. [...] And if I commit **perjury** (= if A is **not** true / if I **don't** do A), may I die.
    b. [...] And if I swear **truly** (= if A is true / if I do A), may I live a long life.

---

[24] See Searle and Vanderveken 1985 (188, 194); Sommerstein and Fletcher (2007: 2–3); Sommerstein and Bayliss (2012: 1–5); Sommerstein and Torrance (2014: 3–4). Sommerstein describes the non-linguistic rituals.
[25] Sommerstein (2014: 76–85) presents three formulas, but there are other possibilities he does not contemplate.
[26] See Denniston (1954: 350–351); Wakker (1997).
[27] According to Sommerstein (2014) the second one (61), which makes up the bulk of my examples, is statistically the most frequent.

(61) a. If A is **not** true / if I **don't** do A, may I die.
b. If A is true / if I do A, may I live a long life.

Therefore, the conditional periods discussed in this paper are an essential part of oaths: they formulate the penalties included in oaths or constitute themselves oaths.

(ii) Performatives, particles, invocations and explicit descriptions.
The conditional periods can appear side by side with performative oaths, as in the following passage from Euripides:

(62) [νῦν δ' **ὁρκιόν** σοι **Ζῆνα** καὶ **πέδον χθονὸς** / **ὄμνυμι** τῶν σῶν μήποθ' ἅψασθαι γάμων / μηδ' ἂν θελῆσαι μηδ' ἂν ἔννοιαν λαβεῖν.] / **ἦ** τἄρ' **ὀλοίμην** ἀκλεὴς [ἀνώνυμος / ἄπολις ἄοικος, φυγὰς ἀλητεύων χθόνα,] / καὶ μήτε πόντος μήτε γῆ **δέξαιτό** μου / σάρκας θανόντος, εἰ κακὸς πέφυκ' ἀνήρ. (E. *Hipp.* 1025–1031)

ê   tár'   **oloímēn**   akleḗs   kai   méte   póntos
PTCL PTCL   die.1SG.OPT   inglorious.NOM.SG   and   nor   sea.NOM
méte gê   **déxaitó**   mou   sárkas   thanóntos
nor   earth.NOM receive.3SG.OPT me.GEN   flesh.ACC.PL   die.PTCP.GEN
ei   kakos   péphuk'   anḗr
if   bad.NOM.SG be.born.1SG.PRF man.NOM.SG

'[As things stand, I swear by Zeus, god of oaths, and by the earth beneath me that I never put my hand to your wife, never wished to, never had the thought.] **May I perish** with no name [or reputation, citiless, homeless, wandering the earth an exile] and **may** neither sea nor earth **receive** my body when I am dead if I am guilty!'

a. May I perish [...] **if I am guilty**!
b. > **I am not guilty**, I swear.

The speaker formulates an oath using the performative verb *ómnumi* / ὄμνυμι ('I swear'), invoking as witness the god Zeus 'who guards oaths' (*hórkion Zêna* / ὅρκιον Ζῆνα) and stating the content of the oath ('I never put my hand to your wife, never wished to, never had the thought'). The conditional period appears immediately afterwards reiterating the oath and formulating the penalties the speaker is incurring if they commit perjury ('May I die, if [...]'). What makes this passage particularly relevant is that the conditional period is introduced by the particle *ê* / ἦ, which proves that it is understood as an oath itself.[28]

---

[28] La Roi (2020: 223–224) interprets this combination in a different way.

A similar case is example (5), where an oath is formulated through performative verbs with invocations to the gods (*omnúō tous theoús* / ὀμνύω τοὺς θεούς 'I swear by the gods') and the presence of the combination *ê mēn* / ἦ μήν heads the content of the oath. The conditional period adds an oath that expresses the positive and negative consequences in case the speaker takes a true oath (*euorkéō* / εὐορκέω) or commits perjury (*epiorkéō* / ἐπιορκέω).

Conditional periods with no previous explicit performative oath may include the invocation of gods like Zeus (see ex. (7)) and they may be explicitly referred to as oaths with the word *hórkos* / ὅρκος by the interlocutors (see ex. (3) and (6)).

(iii) Illocutionary force: the truth.
Since the purpose of oaths is to ensure that the speaker is really telling the truth, it is no wonder that the passages discussed contain numerous explicit references to this concept and to its opposite, the lie (*pseúdomai* / ψεύδομαι 'lie', *pseudḗs* / ψευδής 'false', examples (11) and (63)) and deceit (*exapatáō* / ἐξαπατάω 'to deceive', example (7), commissive oath), as in the following passage, where the chorus-leader makes an assertion and swears that he is not lying ('If I am lying, then damnation take my father'):[29]

(63) [ΧΟ. Αὐτὸς ἔχ'. ἔγωγε τοῖς ξένοις τὰ χρήματα / περνάντα σ' εἶδον·] **εἰ δ' ἐγὼ ψευδῆ λέγω,** / **ἀπόλοιθ'** ὁ πατήρ μου· [τοὺς ξένους δὲ μὴ ἀδίκει.] / ΚΥ. **Ψεύδεσθ'** [ἔγωγε τῷδε τοῦ Ῥαδαμάνθυος / μᾶλλον πέποιθα]. (E. *Cyc.* 270–274)
ei d'   egō   **pseudê**   légō   apóloith'   ho
if PTCL I.NOM false.ACC.PL.N say.1SG.IND.PRS die.3SG.OPT ART.NOM
patḗr   mou [...] **pseúdesth'**
father.NOM me.GEN   lie.2PL.IND.PRS
'[CHORUS-LEADER. On your head, rather! I saw you selling the goods to these strangers.] If I am **lying**, then **damnation take** my father! [But do no wrong to the strangers.] CYCLOPS. You **lie**. [For my part, I put more trust in this man than in Rhadamanthys].'

(iv) Perlocutionary effect.
By uttering an oath, the speaker aims to convince the hearer that they are telling the truth. However, the hearer can react in two different ways: (i) accepting the speaker's words as the truth, as in example (6), where Xanthias explicitly accepts Dionysus' oaths (*dékhomai ton hórkon* / δέχομαι τὸν ὅρκον 'I accept the oath'); (ii) or rejecting them, as in (63), where the Cyclops decides not to believe the chorus

---

[29] See la Roi (2020: 229) for a discussion of similar examples with the condition expressed by a participle.

(*pseúdesthe* / ψεύδεσθε 'you're lying'). In example (3), we know that Oedipus will not believe Creon's oath, but Iocasta encourages him to do so (*písteuson* / πίστευσον 'do believe [him]').

4.2 Directives

The directive nature of the second group of conditional periods can also be indicated in other ways.

(i) Description of the speech act.
As in oaths, the narrator or the speaker may explicitly state the nature of the illocutionary speech acts they are involved in by referring to them with the terms συμβουλεύω (*sumbouleúō* 'advise, counsel', ex. (26)), παραινέω (*parainéō* 'exhort, recommend, advise', ex. (26)) or νουθετέω (*nouthetéō* 'put in mind' > 'admonish, warn, rebuke', ex. (64)), among others:

(64) [Κᾆτ' αὐτὸν εἰσιδών τις ἐμφερὴς ἐμοὶ / ὀργήν θ' ὅμοιος εἶπε τοιοῦτον λόγον·] / "Ὤνθρωπε, **μὴ δρᾶ** τοὺς τεθνηκότας κακῶς· / <u>εἰ γὰρ ποιήσεις</u>, **ἴσθι πημανούμενος**". / Τοιαῦτ' ἄνολβον ἄνδρ' **ἐνουθέτει** παρών. (S. *Aj.* 1152–1156)
ṓnthrōpe   mē   drâ   tous   tethnēkótas   kakôs :
INTJ:man.VOC NEG do.2SG.IMP ART.ACC.PL.M dead.ACC.PL.M badly
ei   gar   poiḗseis,   isthi   pēmanoúmenos.   toiaût'
if   PTCL do.2SG.FUT   know.2SG.IMP damage.PTCP.NOM.SG such.ACC.PL.N
*ánolbon   ándr'   **enouthétei**   parṓn*
luckless.ACC.SG.M man.ACC.SG.M warn.3SG.IMPF be.near.PTCP.NOM.SG
'[It turned out that a man like me and of similar temperament stared at him and said,] "Man, do not wrong the dead; for, if you do, rest assured that you will come to harm." So he **warned** the misguided man before him.'

(ii) Perlocutionary effect.
As happens with other directives, these conditional periods can face two main prototypical reactions by the addressees: they can be obeyed or not. In example (23) Xerxes accepts to follow (*poiḗsō taûta* / ποιήσω ταῦτα 'I'll do so') Achaemenes' advice formulated by a conditional period, and in example (34) Dionysus follows the dead man's directive and offers him nine obols (*láb' enné' oboloús* / λάβ' ἐννέ' ὀβολούς 'Take nine obols'). By contrast, in example (26) the conditional directives are disobeyed by the hearer (*ho de ouk epeítheto* / ὁ δὲ οὐκ ἐπείθετο 'He did not follow (the advice)').

5 Direct and indirect speech acts (conditional periods): Differences

This section discusses the differences between the – let's say – indirect[30] uses of conditional periods studied in this paper (see versions b–f in examples (65)–(67)) and similar speech acts formulated by more direct prototypical sentence types (versions a).

(65) a. **Help him.** *(directive)*
 b. I'll kill you if **you don't help him.** *(directive threat)*
 b'. I'll reward you if **you help him.** *(directive promise)*
 c. May the gods punish you if **you don't help him.** *(directive curse)*
 c'. May the gods reward you if **you help him.** *(directive blessing)*
 d. You will lose the war if **you don't help him.** *(directive warning)*
 d'. You will win the war if **you help him.** *(directive advice)*
 e. Don't talk to me ever again if **you don't help him.** *(directive prohibition)*
 e'. Talk to me whenever you want if **you help him.** *(directive permission)*
 f. I'll die if **you don't help him.** *(plea)*
 f'. I'll live a long life if **you help him.** *(plea)*

(66) a. I **will help him.** *(commissive)*
 b. May I die if **I don't help him.** *(commissive oath)*
 b'. May the gods reward me if **I help him.** *(commissive oath)*

(67) a. Yesterday I **helped him.** *(assertion)*
 b. May I die if yesterday I **didn't help him.** *(assertive oath)*
 b'. May the gods reward me if yesterday I **helped him.** *(assertive oath)*

5.1 Qualitative differences: Argumentation

Unlike direct prototypical sentence types ('Help him', 'I will help him', 'I helped him'), conditional periods additionally provide the (un)wanted consequences for either the hearer or speaker if the hearer does (not) obey the speaker's directives ('If you (don't) help him […], A will happen to you / me' > 'Do help him') or for the speaker if they do (not) tell the truth or do (not) comply with their own com-

---

[30] See Risselada (1993: 66–95) and Siemund (2018: 45–48) for a discussion of "direct" and "indirect" speech acts.

mitment ('May I die / I live a long life, if I don't / do help him' > 'I will help him, I swear'). These consequences act for the hearer (i) as inducements or deterrents to follow the speaker's directives and (ii) as a guarantee to believe the speaker's oath: humans tend to do what benefits them and to avoid what harms them; humans are more likely to believe someone who will face penalties (curses) if they lie.

5.2 Specialization

In the case of both assertive and commissive oaths, these arguments are just self-curses or self-blessings. In the case of directives, however, the speaker presents different (un)wanted consequences for the hearer or for themselves: (i) the speaker's own possible reactions (threats and promises, 65b–b'), (ii) the reactions of superior entities (e.g. the gods) invoked by the speaker (curses and blessings, 65c–c'), (iii) the material consequences of the hearer's own actions (warnings and advice, 65d–d'), (iv) the speaker's permission or prohibition of the hearer's actions (65e–e'), (v) the negative consequences for the speaker and not for the hearer (pleas, 65f–f').

5.3 Discursive differences

From a discursive point of view, conditional periods cannot be used out of the blue without context. In this section I will discuss three kinds of context.

(i) Repetition within the same discursive move.
In many cases, the conditional period just appears within the same discursive move immediately after a direct speech act as a way to prevent the hearer from disobeying the speaker's directive (68) or from distrusting the speaker's assertion (69) or commitment (70):

(68) Help him. If **you don't do so** (= you don't help him), something **bad** will happen to you / me.

(69) I helped him. If **that is not true** (= I didn't help him), may something **bad** happen to me.

(70) I will help him. If **I don't do that** (= I don't help him), may something **bad** happen to me.

In the following passage, Bdelycleon instructs the slaves (directive speech act) to help him seize his father using an imperative sentence ('Come and help. Seize this man [...]'). In order to urge the slaves to do so or fearing they are not complying (at least fast enough), he repeats his command adding a threat in case they do not follow his order ('if you don't [follow my orders] you shall starve to death in chains').

(71) [ὦ Μίδα καὶ Φρύξ, **βοήθει** δεῦρο, καὶ Μασυντία, / καὶ **λάβεσθε** τουτουὶ καὶ μὴ **μεθῆσθε** μηδενί·] / <u>εἰ δὲ μή</u>, 'ν πέδαις παχείαις οὐδὲν **ἀριστήσετε**. (Ar. *V.* 433–435)

ei de mḗ, 'n pédais pakheíais ouden
if PTCL NEG in chain.DAT.PL thick.DAT.PL nothing.ACC
aristḗsete
breakfast.2PL.FUT

'[Midas, Phryx, Masyntias, here! Come and help. Seize this man and hand him over to no one,] otherwise you shall starve to death in chains.'

a. Help [...] seize and do hand him over to no one. *(first order)*
b. **If not** *(otherwise = if you don't follow my commands)*, you shall starve to death. *(reinforced reiteration of the order)*

In example (63), the chorus tells the Cyclops (assertive speech act) that the Silenus gave Odysseus and his men some of the Cyclops' belongings and that therefore they did not steal them and are innocent. Immediately after this assertion, the chorus utters an assertive oath describing the penalties for lying.

(ii) Repetition in a different exchange.
In other cases, the speaker issues a directive, assertive or commissive speech act, but their interlocutor does not react as they have intended and in a second exchange they repeat the same type of speech act, but this time through a conditional period. This applies both to oaths and directives.

(a) Oaths. In example (72), Dicaeopolis asks the chorus leader to listen to him ('You will not hear me?' > 'Listen to me') and the chorus answers negatively (commissive, 'No, I will not hear you'). Dicaeopolis complains in order to make him change his course of action ('This is a hateful injustice' > 'Hear me'), and the chorus leader repeats his refusal in a reinforced way through a conditional period formulating a commissive oath ('May I die, if I listen [to you]' > I am not going to listen, I swear).

(72) [ΔΙ. Οὐκ ἀκούσεσθ', οὐκ ἀκούσεσθ' ἐτεόν, ὠχαρνηΐδαι; / ΧΟ. Οὐκ ἀκουσόμεσθα δῆτα. / ΔΙ. Δεινὰ τἄρα πείσομαι.] / ΧΟ. **Ἐξολοίμην**, ἢν ἀκούσω. (Ar. *Ach.* 322–325)
Exoloímēn ēn akoúsō
die.1SG.OPT if.MOD listen.1SG.SBJV
'[DICAEOPOLIS. Won't you listen to me? Won't you really listen to me, Acharnians? CHORUS. No, I will not listen to you. DICAEOPOLIS. I'm going to suffer terrible things.] CHORUS. May I die if I listen.'

Figure 4 represents the structure of the dialogue (Kroon 1995: 89–95):

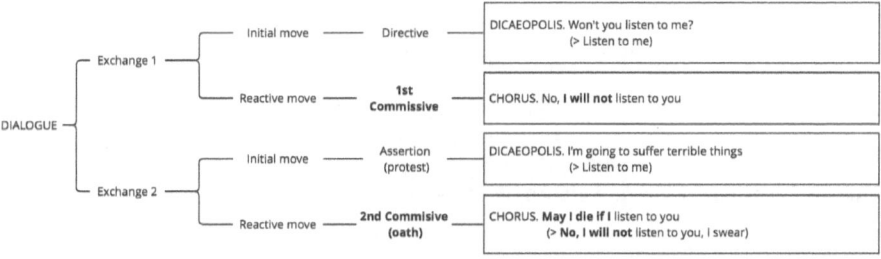

Figure 4: Conditional repeating a previous commissive (example 72).

The same type of situation takes place in example (7). Myrrhine refuses Cinesias' request to go back to him and have sex if the men do not end the war through a treaty. Cinesias accepts and expresses his commitment to her plea invoking Zeus (first commissive speech act), but she does not quite believe him. Then Cinesias uses a truncated conditional period to repeat what he has said. In this way, he aims to remove any doubt in her mind about his commitment, as represented in Figure 5.

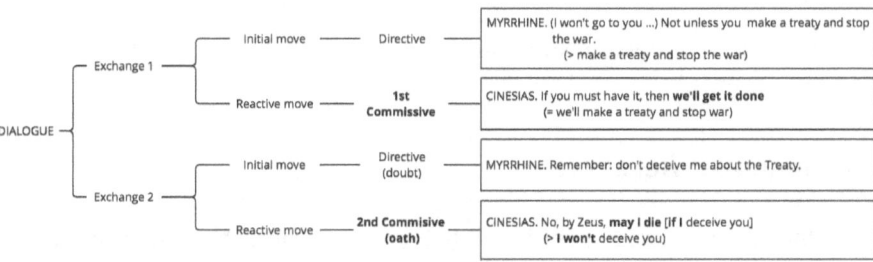

Figure 5: Conditional repeating a previous commissive (example 7).

(b) Directives. Directive conditional periods are often used to reformulate a previous directive that the hearer seems to resist to comply with. In example (29), Trygaeus orders the chorus leader to keep quiet lest War leave his retreat in fury (first directive). The chorus leader disobeys and Trygaeus issues again his order in a more urgent way through a conditional period (second directive), but the chorus disobeys again (see Figure 6):

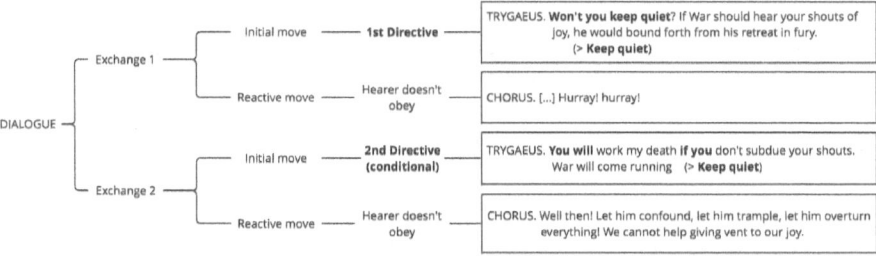

Figure 6: Conditional repeating a previous directive (example 29).

(iii) Reaction to an accusation within an exchange

In this article only, three oaths are used by the speaker to deny a previous accusation by their interlocutor: the chorus (ex. (2)) and Creon (ex. (3)) deny Oedipus' accusations that they are plotting against him; Hippolytos (62) refutes Theseus' accusation against him that he has raped Phaedra. Figure 7 describes the discursive context of example (3):

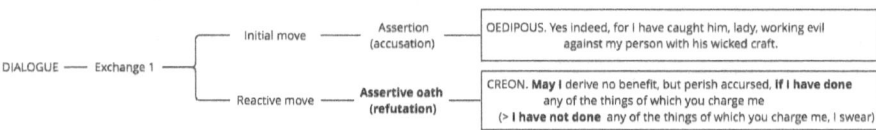

Figure 7: Conditional refuting a previous accusation (example 3).

5.4 General differences

From the data discussed in Sections 5.1–5.3, we can conclude that, in contrast to direct speech acts formulated by prototypical sentence types, conditional periods exhibit a greater degree of strength of the illocutionary point and are more specialized constructions. This reinforced degree derives from the fact that conditional periods detail the consequences for speaker and hearer if the hearer does not follow the directive the speaker issues and for the speaker if they are not truthful; these consequences operate on the hearer as arguments for obeying the directives and believing the truth of the assertives and commissive those conditional periods formulate. On the other hand, this reinforced degree is reflected in the discursive position of these conditional periods: (i) they appear in contexts where the speaker wants to reiterate (a) a previous direct speech act (within the same discursive move) which they fear will face some opposition from the hearer or (b) a previous similar speech act (within a previous exchange) which has not been attended by their interlocutor; (ii) assertive oaths appear after serious accusations. Apart from exhibiting a greater degree of strength the conditional periods fit into more specialized pragmatic contexts and reveal – particularly in the case of directives – the power relations between interlocutors. The fact that conditional periods constitute reiterations or reinforcements of previous directives and oaths is another contextual clue of their true illocutionary force (see Section 4).

This interpretation of Greek conditionals coincides with Haverkate's (1979: 80–83, 1984: 41) conclusions about the use of conditionals as reinforcing devices in Spanish directives: this paper extends the conclusion to oaths.

6 Summary and conclusions

The following points summarize the main conclusions of this paper.

1) Some conditional periods constitute very idiomatic and specialized indirect speech acts. This paper discusses their use as oaths (assertive and commisive) and directives. A full classification and description of both speech acts has been provided (Section 2). Although not all possibilities have been attested in the Greek corpus, they are indeed available in other languages (see the English examples) and more thorough research could show that they existed in Greek.

2) The indirect speech act they convey is the result of the different features exhibited by both the main and subordinate clause:
a) The subordinate clause (Section 3.1) provides the propositional content of the resultant indirect speech act and allows the distinction between assertive oaths (conditionals referring to possible facts), commissive oaths (speaker's future actions) and directives (hearer's future actions).
b) The mood, modality, sentence type and speech act of the main clause (Section 3.2) are important, but not the only and most relevant factors influencing the resultant illocutionary force of the conditional periods.

c) The evaluation of the SoAs (Section 3.3) depicted by the main clause allows us to distinguish between oaths (the speaker is always affected) and directives (the hearer is mainly affected, except in pleas, where it is the speaker).
d) When the SoA depicted by the main clause is detrimental, there is polarity inversion and the propositional content of both the oath and the directive contrast the one provided by the subordinate clause, whereas it remains the same if it is beneficial (Section 3.4).
e) The evaluation of the conditional period as a whole (Section 3.5) allows us to distinguish warnings and advice from the other directives.
f) The agency (Section 3.6) of the SoA depicted by the subordinate clause is an additional factor in the distinction between commissive oaths (the speaker is the agent) and directives (the hearer is the agent). Additionally, the agency of the main clause distinguishes threats and promises (the speaker is the agent) from the other directives.

3) The description of the speech acts formulated by the conditional clauses as oaths or directives are supported by different factors (Section 4): (i) the kind of speech acts formulated are made explicit in their context by performative verbs expressing either directives ('I advise, warn') or oaths ('I swear') or by particles, or invocations of the gods as guarantees of the oath (νὴ Δία / *nē Día* 'by Zeus'); (ii) the same applies to the perlocutionary effects intended by the speaker in directives ('I obey / follow your advice') and oaths ('I accept / believe your oath').

4) Differences between 'direct' speech acts and conditional 'indirect' speech acts seem to lie in the degree of strength of the illocutionary point and their specialization. The conditional periods seem to be reinforced versions of similar direct speech acts formulated by prototypical sentence types. This is probably so because conditional periods provide the consequences for the speaker when uttering such assertions or commissives (oaths), and for the hearer or speaker if the hearer obeys or not the directives. This difference in the degree of strength of the illocutionary force is reflected in the discursive position of the conditionals: they appear after previous utterances by the speaker of a similar speech act (oaths and directives) or to rebut a previous accusation (assertive oaths).

References

Aikhenvald, Alexandra Y. 2016. Sentence types. In Jan Nuyts & Johan van der Auwera (eds.), *The Oxford handbook of modality and mood*, 141–165. Oxford: Oxford University Press.
Denniston, John Dewar 1954. *The Greek particles*. 2nd edn. Revised by Kenneth J. Dover. Oxford: Clarendon Press.
Faraone, Christopher A. 2005. Curses and blessings in Ancient Greek oaths. *Journal of Ancient Near Eastern Religions* 5(1). 139–156.
Fillenbaum, Samuel. 1975. *If*: Some uses. *Psychological Research* 37(3). 245–260.
Fillenbaum, Samuel. 1976. Inducements: On the phrasing and logic of conditional promises, threats, and warnings. *Psychological Research* 38(3). 231–250.
Fillenbaum, Samuel. 1977. A condition on plausible inducements. *Language and Speech* 20(2). 136–141.
Haverkate Henk. 1979. *Impositive sentences in Spanish: Theory and description in linguistic pragmatics*. Amsterdam: North Holland Publishing Company.
Kroon, Caroline. 1995. *Discourse particles in Latin: A study of* nam, enim, autem, vero, *and* at. Amsterdam: J. C. Gieben.
López-Rousseau, Alejandro & Timothy Ketelaar. 2004. "If ...": Satisficing algorithms for mapping conditional statements onto social domains. *European Journal of Cognitive Psychology* 16(6). 807–823.
López-Rousseau, Alejandro & Timothy Ketelaar. 2006. Juliet: If they do see thee, they will murder thee. A satisficing algorithm for pragmatic conditionals. *Mind & Society* 5(1). 71–77.
López-Rousseau, Alejandro, Gil Diesendruck & Avi Benozio. 2011. My kingdom for a horse: On incredible promises and unpersuasive warnings. *Pragmatics & Cognition*, 19(3). 399–421.
Panther, Klaus-Uwe & Klaus-Michael Köpcke. 2008. A prototype approach to sentences and sentence types. *Annual Review of Cognitive Linguistics* 6. 83–112.
Revuelta Puigdollers, Antonio R. 2020a. 18. El verbo (III). Modo y modalidad. In María Dolores Jiménez López (ed.), *Sintaxis del griego antiguo*, 637–678. Madrid: CSIC.
Revuelta Puigdollers, Antonio R. 2020b. 21. Coordinación, subordinación, asíndeton. In María Dolores Jiménez López (ed.), *Sintaxis del griego antiguo*, 765–812. Madrid: CSIC.
Risselada, Rodie. 1993. *Imperatives and other directive expressions in Latin: A study in the pragmatics of a dead language*. Amsterdam: J. C. Gieben.
la Roi, Ezra. 2020. The variation of Classical Greek wishes: A Functional Discourse Grammar and Common Ground approach. *Glotta* 96(1). 213–245.
Searle, John R. & Daniel Vanderveken. 1985. *Foundations of illocutionary logic*. Cambridge: Cambridge University Press.
Siemund, Peter. 2018. *Speech acts and clause types: English in a cross-linguistic context*. Oxford: Oxford University Press.
Sommerstein, Alan H. 2004. The oath in Archaic and Classical Greece. https://www.nottingham. ac.uk/~brzoaths/index.php (last accessed February 2023).
Sommerstein, Alan H. 2014. The language of oaths. In Alan H. Sommerstein & Isabelle C. Torrance (eds.), *Oaths and swearing in Ancient Greece*, 76–85. Berlin & Boston: De Gruyter.
Sommerstein, Alan H. & Andrew J. Bayliss. 2012. *Oath and state in Ancient Greece*. Berlin & Boston: De Gruyter.

Sommerstein, Alan H. & Judith Fletcher (eds.). 2007. *Horkos: The oath in Greek society*. Exeter: Bristol Phoenix Press.
Sommerstein, Alan H. & Isabelle C. Torrance (eds.). 2014. *Oaths and swearing in Ancient Greece*. Berlin & Boston: De Gruyter.
Wakker, Gerry C. 1994. *Conditions and conditionals. An investigation of Ancient Greek*. Amsterdam: Gieben.
Wakker, Gerry 1997. *Emphasis and affirmation: Some aspects of μήν [mḗn] in Tragedy*. In Albert Rijksbaron (ed.), *New approaches to Greek particles*, 209–231. Amsterdam: Gieben.

List of contributors

Giuseppina di Bartolo is currently a research assistant to the chair of "Comparative Discourse Analysis" in the Department of Linguistics of the University of Cologne. Her PhD thesis, conducted in the Classics Department of the University of Cologne, was published in 2021 (*Studien zur griechischen Syntax dokumentarischer Papyri der römischen Zeit*). Together with Daniel Kölligan (University of Würzburg), she is the co-founder and co-organizer of the "Postclassical Greek Network" funded by the German Research Foundation (DFG). Her main research interests include historical morphosyntax, historical pragmatics, language change, diachrony of Ancient Greek, clause linkage strategies, coordination, subordination and insubordination phenomena.

Marina Benedetti is professor of Historical and General Linguistics at the University for Foreigners of Siena and is President of the *Società Italiana di Glottologia*. Her interests are mainly focused on the morphology and syntax of Ancient Greek and on the history of grammatical thought. Her most recent publications concern voice oppositions, complementation patterns, and resultative constructions in Ancient Greek and the developments of grammatical terminology and of grammatical categories in the Greek-Roman tradition.

Camille Denizot is associate professor of Greek Linguistics at the University of Paris Nanterre. She is the author of *Donner des ordres en grec ancien* (Presses Universitaires de Rouen et du Havre 2011) and has co-authored with Michèle Biraud and Richard Faure *L'exclamation en grec ancien* (Peeters 2021). Her research focuses mainly on syntax, semantics and pragmatics, with a special interest in the interaction between modality, indefinites, negatives and speech acts.

Chiara Gianollo is associate professor of Linguistics at the University of Bologna. She is a historical linguist, with expertise in the diachrony of Greek, Latin, and Old Romance and has a particular interest in formal approaches to historical syntax and semantics. She is the author of *Indefinites between Latin and Romance* (Oxford University Press 2018). She co-edited, with Agnes Jäger and Doris Penka, *Language Change at the Syntax-Semantics Interface* (de Gruyter 2015) and, with Maria Napoli and Klaus von Heusinger, *Determiners and Quantifiers. Functions, Variation, and Change* (Brill 2022).

Martin Masliš is a PhD student at Charles University in Prague. The aim of his dissertation project is to research evidential strategies in classical Greek prose, with special emphasis on the domain of inferential reasoning. His research interests also include functional grammar, grammaticalization, and discourse analysis.

Alberto Pardal is associate professor of Greek Philology at the University of Salamanca. His research focuses on Greek linguistics, especially on the interaction of syntax with semantics, phonology and pragmatics from a usage-based perspective within Construction Grammar. Thus, he has worked on crasis, clisis, argument structure and prosody. He has coordinated a project on the pragmaticalization of verbs of thought and speech in Ancient Greek and Latin and is currently editing a volume on these phenomena in the languages of the world. His research has delved particularly into dialogic texts, both drama and platonic dialogues.

Antonio R. Revuelta Puigdollers is professor of Greek Philology at the Autonomous University of Madrid and a sworn translator of Modern Greek. His main research areas are the semantics, syntax and pragmatics of Greek, but his work includes incursions into other languages such as Latin. He is the co-author of a new syntax of Ancient Greek (2020) and has authored several entries in Brill's *Encyclopaedia of Ancient Greek Language and Linguistics* (2014).

Ezra la Roi is currently a PhD student in the Linguistics department at Ghent University. In his PhD project (2019–2023) funded by the Flemish Fund for Scientific Research, he investigated the variation and change of counterfactual constructions in Ancient Greek. In his research, he applies recent insights from the fields of pragmatics, historical linguistics and typology to a corpus-based analysis of ancient languages. His main research interests are mood and modality, tense-aspect, morphosyntax and pragmatics. Most recently, he has published on the morphosyntax and pragmatics of counterfactuals, insubordination, habituals and (fossilized) mood forms in Ancient Greek.

Emilia Ruiz Yamuza is professor of Greek Philology at the University of Seville. Her field of interest is the syntax, semantics and pragmatics of Ancient Greek. She has mainly focused on the study of modality, devoting special attention to modal verbs, on which she published the book *Tres verbos que significan deber en Griego Antiguo* (2008), to semi-modals and to adverbs of modality. In recent years she has focused on the study of the structures, evolutions and functions of extra-clausal elements, including insubordinate and parenthetical sentences. In this field, she has published *The right periphery in Ancient Greek* (2017), *Insubordination in Ancient Greek: the case of ὥστε sentences* (2020) and *Parenthetical conditionals and insubordinate clauses in Ancient Greek* (2022).

Liana Tronci is associate professor of General and Historical Linguistics at the University for Foreigners of Siena. Her research focuses on the morphosyntax of Ancient Greek and Latin and its interactions with the lexicon, information structure, and pragmatics. She published a book on passive aorists in Ancient Greek (2005) and has devoted many recent publications to Biblical translations from Greek to Latin, with special attention to participial constructions and pseudo-coordination.

Sophie Vassilaki is professor of Modern Greek language and linguistics at the University of Languages and Civilizations – INALCO Paris. She teaches Modern Greek grammar and linguistics. Her research interests include the mediopassive voice in Modern Greek, complex sentences and the subordination system with special focus on aspect and modality marking and discourse particles. Her most recent publications concern a comparison of coordinating conjunctions / discourse markers in Modern Greek *KE* and Russian *I* (in collaboration with Christine Bonnot, 2017, 2021, 2023); she co-edited the volume *Approches linguistiques comparatives grec moderne-français* (2022).

Rodrigo Verano is assistant professor in Greek Philology at the Complutense University of Madrid. His research lines in Greek linguistics include syntax, pragmatics and discourse studies, with a focus on the interplay of patterns and elements from spoken speech in classical prose. He has worked extensively on the language of Plato's dialogues, with publications on topics such as reformulation, discourse markers, oral syntax, and politeness. He was principal investigator of the project "Conversation in Antiquity: Analysis of Verbal Interactions in Ancient Greek and Latin" and is currently editing the volume *Conversation Analysis and Classics: Talk in Interaction in Greek and Latin Literature*, which explores the application of the methodology of ethnomethodological conversation analysis to classical literary texts.

Index locorum

Aeschines (Aeschin.)
1.47	70
2.81	68
3.157	62
3.174	64

Aeschylus (A.)
Eumenides (Eu.)
86	36
276–278	35
297–298	215

Libation-bearers (Ch.)
195–196	209
234	31

Andocides (And.)
1.122	64

Antiphon (Antiph.)
3.4	57

Aristophanes (Ar.)
Acharnians (Ach.)
322–324	255

Frogs (Ra.)
173–177	237–238
579–589	225–226
1158–1161	156

Knights (Eq.)
292–296	232
694–696	227

Lysistrata (Lys.)
898–903	226–227
931–933	226–227

Peace (Pax)
309–319	236
409–413	212
1070–1072	230

Wasps (V.)
433–435	254
731	206
1431–1432	216

Demosthenes (D.)
1.18	72
7.21	104
9.49	58
10.72	75
14.38	108
18.137	69
19.157	78–79
19.292	107
21.72	104
21.93	72
54.41–42	224–225

Euripides (E.)
Fragments (Fr.) ed. Nauck
909.3	30, 36
1067.1	30

Cyclops (Cyc.)
270–274	250

Hecuba (Hec.)
397	31

Hippolytus (Hipp.)
1025–1031	249

Iphigenia in Aulis (IA)
1005–1007	228

Herodotus (Hdt.)
1.96.8	29
3.25.5	125
3.71.13	29
3.139.16	32
4.118.15–20	209
6.107.17	41
7.236.8–16	233–234

264 — Index locorum

8.93.5–6	195	**Hyperides (Hyp.)**	
9.2.2–3.3	235	6.col.7	59
Homeric hymns		**Isaeus (Is.)**	
Hymn to Dionysus (h. Bacch.)		2.10	70
18	44	6.35	60
		6.50	76
Homeric poems		9.4	63
Iliad (Il.)		9.10	65
1.80	100	10.8	76
1.519	98	11.37	71
1.565–567	99		
2.720	35	**Isocrates (Isoc.)**	
3.236	44	4.156	69
4.257–260	98–99	9.59	65
4.539–542	198–199	19.28	208
5.11	35	21.5	78
5.85–86	202		
5.89–91	100	**Lycurgus (Lycurg.)**	
6.147–151	153	1.20	78
6.279–281	153	1.95	67
7.238	30		
8.180	98	**Lysias (Lys.)**	
8.338–341	100	7.7	68
8.475–476	95	10.1	103
12.278–280	96	12.29	207
13.238	42	34.5	107
14.109–112	151		
16.141–142	39	**New Testament (NT)**	
19.162–163	42	*Acts of the Apostles (Act.Ap.)*	
19.388–389	39	27.39	114
20. 288–289	200		
21.320–321	42	*2nd Epistle to the Corinthians (2 Ep.Cor.)*	
22.359–360	95	12.13	131
22.471–472	95		
		Epistle to the Ephesians (Ep.Eph.)	
Odyssey (Od.)		4.9	131
3.92–94	150–151		
4.178–180	201	*Epistle to the Galatians (Ep.Gal.)*	
4.472–474	204	4.15	127
7.314–315	233		
13.204–206	201	*Gospel according to John (Ev.Jo.)*	
15.532	31	4.23	114
18.366–369	202	14.29	109
20.233–234	152	15.24	125

19.23	115
21.18	110

Gospel according to Luke (Ev.Luc.)
6.22	110
11.34	111
23.33	87

Gospel according to Mark (Ev.Marc.)
3.11	112

Gospel according to Matthew (Ev.Matt.)
6.22	111
24.32	113
25.31	87

Pindar (Pi.)
Pythian Odes (P.)
3.81–82	44

Plato (Pl.)
Alcibiades 1 (Alc.1)
108d3	186

Apology (Ap.)
28d2	215
38b1	206

Charmides (Chrm.)
158c1	183

Cratylus (Cra.)
392a3	162
393b5	176
393e9	175
399e3	144
402c4	185

Euthyphro (Euthphr.)
2a1–6	172
2c8	169
3d5	176
12d4	179
12e9	181

Gorgias (Grg.)
454c6	182
472a4–b2	159–160
482c4	183
503e4	158
518a6	173

Hippias Minor (Hp.mi.)
365b8	178

Laches (La.)
200b7–200c1	182

Laws (Lg.)
710d7	181
893d7	186

Meno (Men.)
71e2	157
73e3	162
80a2	175
94a7	144

Phaedrus (Phdr.)
230c1	161

Philebus (Phlb.)
33a5	150
56c10	173

Protagoras (Prt.)
319a3	182
324c8	179
341a3	181
341a5	170, 173

Republic (R.)
340d2	171
383c1	105
389b1	150
409e1	169
449c2	183
516d2	177
541b1	185
583e1	106

Sophist (Sph.)
228d6	169
232d9	181

Statesman (Plt.)
280b5 — 178

Symposium (Smp.)
204c2 — 175
214e11 — 149, 154
220d5 — 157

Theaetetus (Tht.)
205a7 — 169

Theages (Thg.)
129a1 — 161

Septuagint
Exodus (Ex.)
17.11 — 112

Psalms (Ps.)
118.92 — 130
123.2–3 — 131

Tobit (To.)
8.1 — 114, 115

Sophocles (S.)
Ajax (Aj.)
807 — 31
1152–1156 — 251

Antigone (Ant.)
1089 — 31

Oedipus at Colonus (OC)
733 — 30

Oedipus Tyrannus (OT)
642–647 — 223
661–662 — 223
1386–1389 — 210
1391–1393 — 211

Thucydides (Th.)
2.18.4 — 129
4.67.2 — 128
4.118.10 — 177
7.50.3 — 106

Xenophon (X.)
Memorabilia (Mem.)
4.2.40 — 130

Documentary papyri
BGU II 595.13–15 — 134
BGU III 801.7–10 — 134
BGU III 845 — 126
CPR XXX 21.14 — 135
P.Mich. VIII 476.25–26 — 136
P.Mich. VIII 492.14–16 — 133
P.Mich. VIII 512.4–5 — 133
P.Tebt. II 414.9 — 135

Index verborum

án (ἄν)
- (absence in counterfactuals) 195–197
- (contrast with and without) 85–116
- (loss in Postclassical Greek) 124–127

boúlomai (βούλομαι) 143–164, 196, 210

dúnamai (δύναμαι) 41–46

ê mḗn (ἦ μήν) 248–250
ei boúlei (εἰ βούλει) 144–162
ei mḗ (εἰ μή) 128–129
ei mē hóti (εἰ μὴ ὅτι) 127–139
eîdon (εἶδον) 53–54, 63–64
ḗmati tôi hót- (ἤματι τῷ ὅτ-) 94–96
epán (ἐπάν) 111
ethélō (ἐθέλω) 39, 143–164

horáō (ὁράω) 53–54, 60, 63
hōs / hóti (ὡς / ὅτι) 52–56, 74–81

kaí (καί) 110, 133–136, 139
ke (κε) 90–101, 195–197

manthánō (μανθάνω) 54, 76
méllō (μέλλω) 39, 125–126, 137
mḗn (μήν) 248–250

oîda (οἶδα) 25–41, 53–56, 75
oloímēn (ὀλοίμην) 223–227, 249, 255
óphel(l)on (ὤφελ(λ)ον) 197, 203–206

tí ou (τί οὐ) 210–211

Index notionum

aspect
- aoristic aspect 31, 63–64, 96, 109–115
- aspectual differences 37, 112–113, 125–126, 198–199

assertion 74, 228, 230, 233, 253

commitment (speaker's) 5, 10, 151, 170, 222, 227–228, 253–255
- low speaker commitment 55, 74–78, 180

complementation
- see finite / non finite complementation
- see infinitive complementation
- see participial complementation

deixis 5, 96, 98
- see also person

directive (illocutionary act) 150, 155, 162–163, 230–239, 251–259

dynamic modality 3–4, 16, 25–45

epistemic modality 25–45, 77, 122, 169–170, 180–185, 188, 221

evidentiality 5, 52–81, 180–183, 189, 202–203

experiencer 61, 69, 176, 179–185, 188

finite / non finite complementation 29–33, 74–81

future
- future forms 75, 151–152
- futurity (meaning) 89, 97, 104–108, 151–154, 194, 222–232, 241

genericity 89, 105–108

grammaticalization 16, 40–46, 52

iconicity 200–205

imperative (uses of) 144, 148, 155–156, 237

imperfect (uses of) 107, 112, 125–127, 137, 198

implicature 60–61, 198–212

indefinite 89, 103–104, 204–206

infinitive complementation 30–46, 54, 75, 148–150, 155, 158, 175–176

information source
- see source

(inter)subjectivity 4–5, 53, 74–80, 167–170, 179–182, 188–189

negation
- negative markers 42, 63, 75, 127–128, 209–212
- negative polarity 232–236, 239–244

optative mood
- oblique optative 194, 202–204
- uses of the optative mood 194–217, 223–233, 246–250

parenthetical clauses 156, 174–176, 178–179

participial complementation 30–33, 57–74

past
- past tenses 101, 125–127, 210
- past habitual 198

person (as regards modality) 97–98, 168, 174–183, 188–189

politeness 143–144, 148–156, 170–172, 188

presupposition 54–58, 73–79, 172, 187, 201, 206

referentiality
- see indefinite

register (low) 123, 125, 127, 137

sentence types 98, 146, 155–156, 160–162, 241–242, 257

source
- information source 52–55, 59, 66, 74, 77, 170, 180–181
- visual source 59–61, 66–67, 71–73, 80

subjectivity
- see (inter)subjectivity

subjunctive mood (uses of) 86–115, 144, 148–160, 214–215

temporal reference 33, 37, 89, 152–154, 194, 196–205, 213

www.ingramcontent.com/pod-product-compliance
Lightning Source LLC
Chambersburg PA
CBHW020225170426
43201CB00007B/317